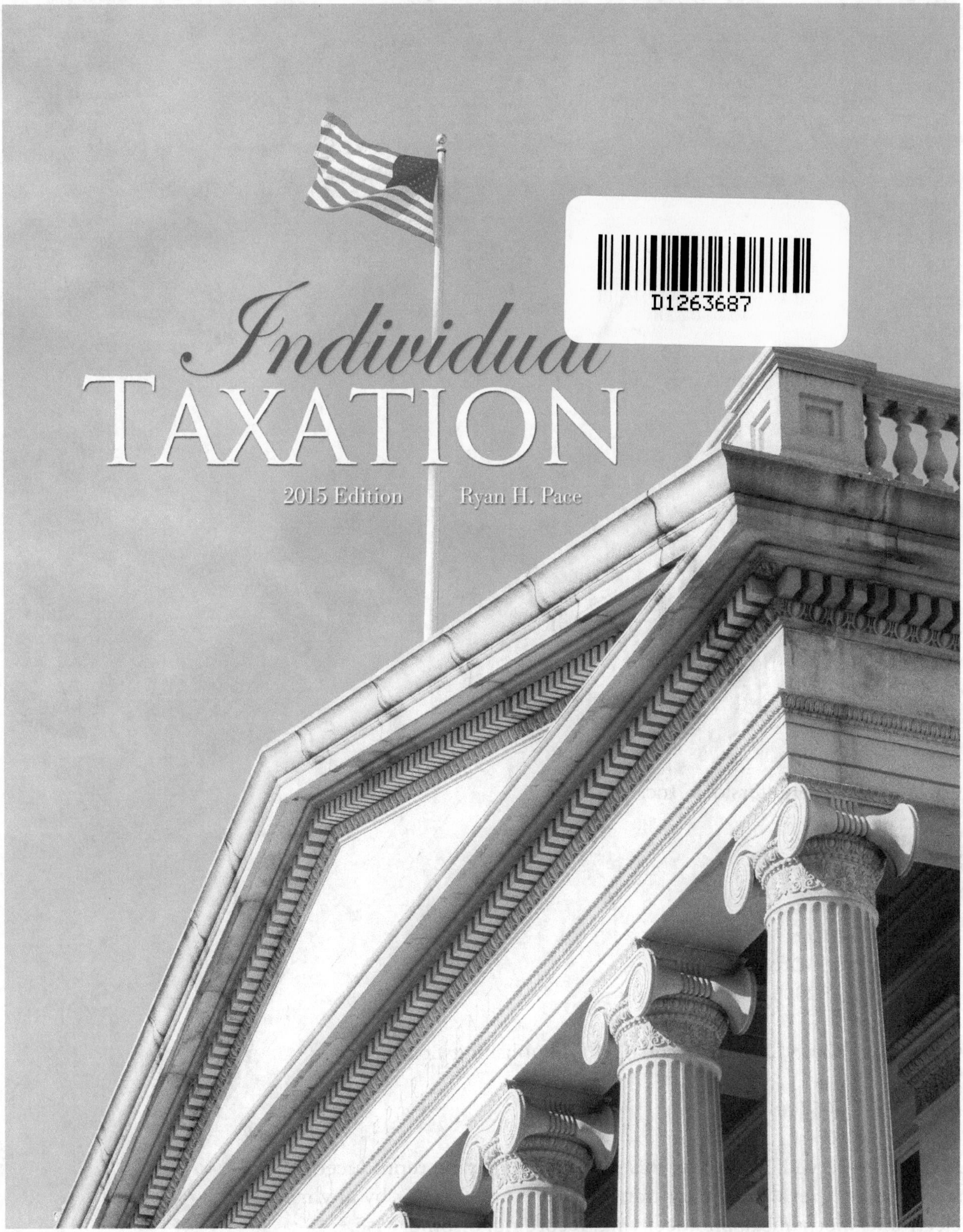

Kendall Hunt
publishing company

Kendall Hunt
publishing company

www.kendallhunt.com
Send all inquiries to:
4050 Westmark Drive
Dubuque, IA 52004-1840

ISBN 978-1-4652-4814-5

Printed in the United States of America
10 9 8 7 6 5 4 3 2 1

Dedication

To my wife, Janet, and my children, Madeline, Matthew, and Nathan, whose love, support and patience allowed me to write this textbook.

Contents

Preface

This text is unique in its conceptual approach to studying the taxation of individuals.

Tax law is complex and dynamic. Students can be overwhelmed by the extraordinary detail in most tax textbooks. Indeed, a student's frustration quickly builds as a new semester begins and the student tackles large reading assignments containing enormously technical, complicated material. As a result, students can lose motivation and interest early on.

This text rejects the traditional textbook method of providing the student with an onslaught of detail and complication. Rather, the focus is on a strong presentation of the fundamentals. To use a basketball analogy, a player must first develop a strong ability to pass, dribble and shoot. Once those skills are mastered, the student can readily adapt his or her skills to execute more advanced plays and sophisticated strategies presented by the coach. Similarly, when studying individual taxation, a student must first learn the tax fundamentals. Details and complexities on the periphery can then be given proper attention in more advanced courses.

The following features highlight the approach of this text:

- Reader-friendly language
- Simple math so the student can focus on the concept, not the math
- Shorter chapters to enhance retention and minimize reader fatigue
- Direct quotations from the Internal Revenue Code so the student becomes familiar with it
- Practical questions and problems
- Straightforward tax return problems
- Affordable text that provides enough material to cover a semester of study, but not so much that the instructor cannot effectively cover it all

Acknowledgments

I would like to acknowledge the contributions of Kimberly Elliott, Beth Trowbridge, Charmayne McMurray, and many others at Kendall Hunt Publishing. Also, thank you to my colleagues Eric Smith and Bill Bailey at Weber State University for their constructive comments and to the many students who have provided feedback on the presentation of the material in this textbook.

About the Author

Ryan H. Pace, M.Tax, J.D., LL.M., is currently an associate professor of taxation at Weber State University. He teaches graduate and undergraduate courses in taxation and business law, including:

- Advanced Corporate Taxation
- Advanced Partnership Taxation
- Mergers, Acquisitions & Consolidations
- Advanced Individual Taxation
- International Taxation
- Tax Research & Communication
- Business Entity Taxation
- Legal Environment of Business

Mr. Pace also serves as the Director of both the Master of Accounting program and the Master of Taxation program at Weber State. Prior to his teaching career, Mr. Pace was a full-time tax attorney at large law firms in Arizona and Utah. Mr. Pace graduated from New York University with a Master of Laws degree in taxation after receiving his Juris Doctor with honors from Washburn University School of Law. He also received a Master of Taxation degree from Arizona State University and his Bachelor of Science degree from the University of Utah. He is admitted to practice law before the United States Supreme Court, The United States Tax Court, and is a member of the Utah State Bar and State Bar of Arizona (inactive).

Mr. Pace has written several articles in the area of taxation including in the following journals:

- *Journal of Legal Tax Research*
- *Tax Notes*
- *The Tax Adviser*
- *Business Entities*
- *The CPA Journal*

In addition to this textbook, Mr. Pace has authored two other textbooks—*Business Entity Taxation and Legal Environment of Business*, both published by Kendall Hunt Publishing. Mr. Pace has also participated in many continuing education programs and academic conferences. He currently lives in Morgan, Utah, with his wife and three children and enjoys reading and playing basketball.

PART 1

Introduction to Individual Taxation

Chapter 1

Tax Law in General

Although accountants can develop expertise in a variety of subject areas related to accounting (*e.g.*, financial accounting, managerial accounting, auditing, accounting information systems, etc.), most people perceive accountants as knowing a lot about taxes. Before we engage in studying the particulars about the tax law applicable to individuals, however, we should spend a little time discussing the fundamental structure of the tax law. We will do that in this chapter.

A. Constitutional Authority of Congress to Impose a Tax

The United States Constitution gives Congress the power to impose a tax.

> **U.S. CONSTITUTION**
>
> ARTICLE 1, SECTION 8
> The Congress shall have power to lay and collect taxes, duties, imposts and excises, to pay the debts and provide for the common defense and general welfare of the United States; . . .

Congress has utilized this constitutional power to impose a variety of different types of taxes. Nevertheless, certain court decisions in the late 1800's held that Congress did not have the constitutional authority to impose an *income* tax on individuals. After considerable debate, this issue was clarified in 1913 by the adoption of the Sixteenth Amendment, which states as follows:

> **U.S. CONSTITUTION**
>
> SIXTEENTH AMENDMENT
> The Congress shall have power to lay and collect taxes on incomes, from whatever source derived, without apportionment among the several states, and without regard to any census or enumeration.

We should remember that states also have taxing powers. The focus of this textbook, however, will be on *federal* income taxes.

Occasionally, a taxpayer contends that the income tax is unconstitutional. You should be aware that these taxpayers have repeatedly lost their arguments in court and have faced significant civil and/or criminal penalties as a result.

B. Organization of the Internal Revenue Code

Federal statutory law governing taxes is contained in the Internal Revenue Code (IRC). The IRC is Title 26 of the United States Code (which has 51 titles). Each title of the United States Code is broken down into subtitles. Subtitles are broken down into chapters. Chapters are broken down into subchapters. Subchapters are broken down into parts. Parts are broken down into subparts. Subparts are broken down into sections. Sections are broken down into subsections. Subsections are broken down into paragraphs. Paragraphs are broken down into subparagraphs. Subparagraphs are broken down into clauses. Clauses are broken down into subclauses. Presented another way:

Title

→ Subtitles

→ Chapters

→ Subchapters

→ Parts

→ Subparts

→ Sections

→ Subsections

→ Paragraphs

→ Subparagraphs

→ Clauses

→ Subclauses

EXAMPLE 1.1. Assume you come across a reference to Code Section 401(k)(2)(B) (i). What terminology would you use to explain where that provision is?

Answer: Section 401
Subsection (k)
Paragraph (2)
Subparagraph (B)
Clause (i)

When reading particular provisions of the Code, which we will do throughout this text, it is good to know how the Code is organized because one provision of the Code may reference other provisions of the Code.

C. Other Sources of Tax Law

In addition to the Internal Revenue Code, tax law and other authoritative rulings that impact taxpayers can arise from court decisions, Treasury regulations, and Internal Revenue Service (IRS) rulings. Many court cases involving federal taxes are heard by the United States Tax Court. Some cases can also be decided by United States District Courts and the United States Court of Federal Claims. Appeals from these courts go to the particular United States Circuit Court of Appeals that has jurisdiction over the taxpayer. Appeals from the circuit courts of appeal go to the United States Supreme Court if the Supreme Court agrees to hear the case.

The Treasury Department, as part of its administrative law function, has the authority to issue regulations to interpret the Code and provide further guidance on how taxpayers can comply with the Code. The IRS also issues other documents to assist taxpayers and tax professionals in understanding the law. Such documents include revenue rulings, revenue procedures, private letter rulings, publications, and many others. A further explanation of these documents and tax research in general is in Chapter 28 (Overview of Tax Research).

D. Types of Taxes

As mentioned, Congress has imposed several types of taxes including, for example, income, estate, gift, and excise taxes. States have also imposed various taxes including, for example, income, sales, use, property, and excise taxes. This textbook, however, will focus solely on *federal income* taxes on *individuals*. For a discussion of tax laws applicable to corporations, partnerships, exempt organizations, trusts and estates, etc., please refer to the *Business Entity Taxation* text by this author.

E. THE IRS

One of the challenges the federal government and state governments has is collecting the tax that is legally owed. The IRS, an agency within the Treasury Department, is charged with that task at the federal level. The Commissioner of the IRS is appointed by the president and oversees IRS operations and policy. The IRS employs thousands of employees across the United States to interpret the law, help taxpayers comply with the law, and enforce the law when taxpayers have tax delinquencies. The IRS is organized into four main specialized areas with regard to tax services and enforcement: (1) Wage and Investment Division; (2) Large Business and International Division; (3) Small Business/Self Employed Division; and (4) Tax Exempt and Government Entities Division. Of course, there are other IRS units beyond just these four, such as the Office of Professional Responsibility, Whistleblower Office, and Criminal Investigation, to name a few. Please see the Appendix for a more detailed IRS organizational chart.

CHAPTER 1: QUESTIONS

1. *Authority of Congress to tax.* What provision in the United States Constitution gives Congress the power to impose an *income* tax?

2. *Organization of federal statutory law.* How many "titles" are in the United States Code?

3. *Organization of the Internal Revenue Code.* What title of the United States Code is the Internal Revenue Code?

4. *Organization of the Internal Revenue Code.* In the following reference to Section 1031, how would you refer to the "(C)" using the proper terminology?

   1031(a)(2)(C)

5. *Organization of the Internal Revenue Service.* The IRS is part of what federal department?

6. *Organization of the Internal Revenue Service.* What is the title of the person who is the chief executive of the IRS?

7. *Organization of the Internal Revenue Service.* What are the four main divisions within the IRS regarding tax services and enforcement?

8. *Sources of tax law.* Name three sources from where tax laws, rules, and regulations originate.

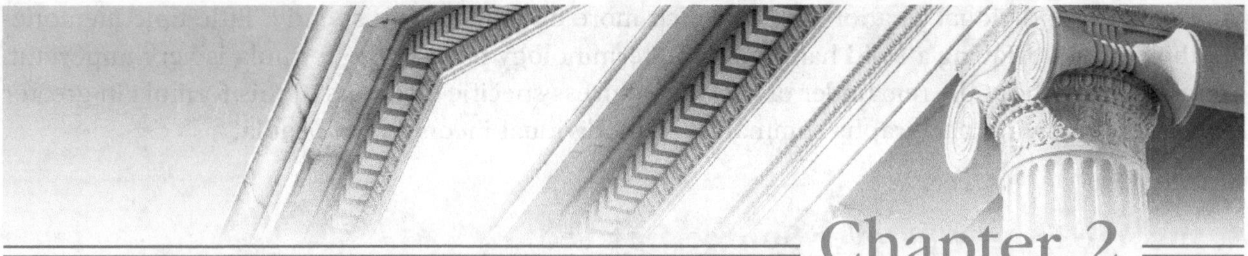

Chapter 2

Individual Income Tax Formula and Tax Rates

While the Internal Revenue Code has a reputation of being very complicated, the fundamentals of individual income taxation are quite straightforward. The Code sets forth a formula for the calculation of an individual's tax liability. This chapter will focus on that formula as well as the various tax rates that apply to individuals.

A. Individual Income Tax Formula

By piecing together various sections of the Code we are able to ascertain the following income tax formula applicable to individuals.

INDIVIDUAL INCOME TAX FORMULA

Income from whatever source dervied
− Exclusions
= Gross income
− Deductions "for" adjusted gross income
= Adjusted gross income
− Deductions "from" adjusted gross income
- Standard deduction or itemized deductions
- Personal exemptions
- Dependency exemptions

= Taxable income
× Applicable tax rate
= Gross tax liability
− Tax credits and prepaid taxes
= Net tax liability or refund

Your study of individual taxation will be much more effective if you spend a little time memorizing this formula. Having a solid handle on the terminology used in the formula is very important. Chapters throughout the remainder of this text address specific elements of this formula in greater detail. The following paragraphs summarize the individual income tax formula.

1. Income from Whatever Source Derived

Notice that the starting point in calculating an individual's income tax liability is to determine the individual's "income from whatever source derived." This language comes directly from the Sixteenth Amendment to the United States Constitution (see Chapter 1). Obviously, the concept of "income from whatever source derived" is extraordinarily broad. As a practical matter, you can usually assume that all income that a taxpayer receives is included in the taxpayer's "gross income" unless the Code specifically excludes the income. Note that **unrealized** income is not included in income until there is a **realization event**. Once a realization event has occurred, an analysis of the tax consequences is required.

EXAMPLE 2.1. On Date 1, Sam purchases some stock in MNO Corporation for $40 per share. On Date 2, the value of MNO Corporation's stock has increased to $50 per share. Does Sam have income to report for tax purposes on Date 2?

Answer: No. The $10 of appreciation in the value of the stock is not yet included in Sam's income for tax purposes. Sam will include the appreciation in his income, for example, when he sells the stock. Selling the stock is an example of a realization event.

2. Exclusions

For economic, social, or political reasons, Congress has elected to **exclude** certain types of income from a taxpayer's gross income. Examples of common exclusions are the receipt of life insurance proceeds, the receipt of a gift, certain fringe benefits employers provide to employees, and qualified scholarships, just to name a few.

3. Gross Income

The Code frequently uses the term **gross income**. As discussed, if income is not specifically *excluded* from gross income it is presumed to be *included* in gross income. From gross income, various deductions, exemptions and credits usually come into play before a taxpayer's ultimate tax liability is determined.

4. Deductions "for" Adjusted Gross Income

Deductions are either "for" **adjusted gross income (AGI)** or "from" AGI. Deductions "for" AGI reduce gross income to arrive at a taxpayer's AGI. To a certain extent, these deductions receive more favorable treatment than deductions "from" AGI because, as you will see, some deductions that are "from" AGI may be limited or not at all beneficial to the taxpayer if the taxpayer's total itemized deductions do not exceed the taxpayer's standard deduction. Examples of "for" AGI deductions include moving expenses, contributions to individual retirement accounts, and alimony payments, among others.

5. Adjusted Gross Income

A taxpayer's AGI is an important number. As we will see throughout this text, many other calculations in determining a taxpayer's ultimate tax liability are based upon a taxpayer's AGI. In order to arrive at a taxpayer's taxable income, deductions "from" AGI are allowed.

6. Deductions "from" Adjusted Gross Income

At this point, the taxpayer calculates the total of his or her **itemized deductions**. Itemized deductions consist of charitable contributions, medical expenses, property taxes, state income taxes, interest paid on a loan to acquire a principal residence, among other items. If the total of the taxpayer's itemized deductions is greater than the taxpayer's standard deduction, then the taxpayer benefits by itemizing. If the **standard deduction** is greater than the itemized deductions, then the taxpayer just takes the standard deduction and the itemized deductions do not help the taxpayer in lowering the taxpayer's tax liability. The standard deduction is a set amount established by the IRS each year. For 2014, for example, the standard deduction is $6,200 for single taxpayers and $12,400 for married taxpayers filing jointly.

Taxpayers are also allowed to deduct *personal* and *dependency* **exemptions** in addition to itemized deductions or the standard deduction. The personal and dependency exemption amount is established by the IRS each year. For 2014, for example, it is $3,950 for the taxpayer and $3,950 for each dependent. The definition of "dependent" is discussed in more detail in Chapter 4.

7. Taxable Income

After taking into account deductions "from" AGI, the taxpayer's taxable income is established. The applicable tax rate is then ascertained in order to calculate the taxpayer's gross tax liability.

8. Tax Rate

The United States has adopted a graduated income tax rate system. This means that the higher the taxable income a taxpayer has, the higher the tax rate that applies. The tax rates that apply are discussed later in this chapter.

9. Gross Tax Liability

Once taxable income is multiplied by the applicable tax rate, the result is a taxpayer's gross tax liability for the year.

10. Tax Credits and Prepaid Taxes

The tax law requires that an employer withhold income taxes from an employee's paycheck throughout the year. This, in effect, prepays a portion of a taxpayer's ultimate tax liability for the year. If an individual is self-employed, the individual must estimate his or her ultimate tax liability and submit quarterly self-employment tax payments to the IRS. Congress has also established certain tax **credits** for which a taxpayer may qualify. A popular and oft-claimed credit is the earned income credit. Other credits include the child tax credit, adoption credit, certain business-related credits, and more. A credit is a dollar-for-dollar reduction in a taxpayer's tax liability whereas a deduction just lowers the taxpayer's taxable income, which in turn only lowers the taxpayer's ultimate tax liability by an amount equal to the deduction multiplied by the applicable tax rate.

11. Net Tax Liability or Refund

An individual will have a **net tax liability** if the individual's tax credits and prepaid taxes are less than the individual's gross tax liability. An individual will be entitled to a **refund** if the individual's tax credits and prepaid taxes are in excess of the individual's gross tax liability.

B. Income Tax Rates for Individuals

As discussed previously, once an individual has determined his or her taxable income, the individual must apply the applicable tax rate. For 2014, the following tax rates (*i.e.*, tax "brackets") apply to a taxpayer's **ordinary income**: 10%, 15%, 25%, 28%, 33%, 35% and 39.6%. Lower tax rates apply to a taxpayer's net **long-term capital gain** and **qualified dividend** income. Long-term capital gain and qualified dividend rates are 0%, 15% and 20% depending upon a taxpayer's ordinary income bracket. In short, the net long-term capital gain rates apply to gains generated from the sale or exchange of a capital asset that the taxpayer has held for more than one year. Other tax rates may apply on other, unique transactions such as the sale of collectibles. More on the distinction relating to ordinary income, capital gain income, qualified dividend income, and the applicable tax rates will be discussed in subsequent chapters.

C. IRS Form 1040

As you are now familiar with the individual income tax formula, please look at the blank IRS Form 1040 in the Appendix. Look at how it is organized relating to income and deductions and our discussion in this chapter. You may notice that the IRS Form 1040 is organized similar to the individual income tax formula, but not exactly the same. The differences are primarily for administrative convenience and do not alter the ultimate determination of the taxpayer's net tax liability or refund due.

CHAPTER 2: QUESTIONS

1. *Individual income tax formula—terminology*. "Income from whatever source derived" is reduced by exclusions, deductions, exemptions, and credits. Discuss the meanings of these terms.

2. *Realization event*. What is the significance of a realization event?

3. *Realization event*. Provide an example of a realization event.

4. *Adjusted Gross Income*. Why is a taxpayer's AGI an important number?

5. *Deductions*. Why would a taxpayer generally prefer a deduction "for" AGI over a deduction "from" AGI?

6. *Deductions vs. credits*. Why would a taxpayer generally prefer a $1,000 credit instead of a $1,000 deduction?

7. *Exemptions*. What is the personal exemption amount for the year 2014?

8. *Standard deduction*. What is the standard deduction amount for single taxpayers for the year 2014?

9. *Tax rates*. What are the ordinary income tax brackets for the year 2014?

10. *Tax rates*. What are the long-term capital gain and qualified dividend tax rates for the year 2014?

11. *Getting to know IRS Form 1040*. Please refer to the IRS Form 1040 at the end of the text.
    a. On what line does the taxpayer indicate how many total exemptions (personal and dependency) the taxpayer is claiming?
    b. On what line does the taxpayer report any alimony received?
    c. On what line does the taxpayer deduct any moving expenses?
    d. The adjusted gross income figure is calculated on what line?
    e. On what line does the taxpayer report the total of his or her itemized deductions or the standard deduction?
    f. On what line does the taxpayer calculate his or her taxable income?
    g. On what line does the taxpayer claim the child tax credit?

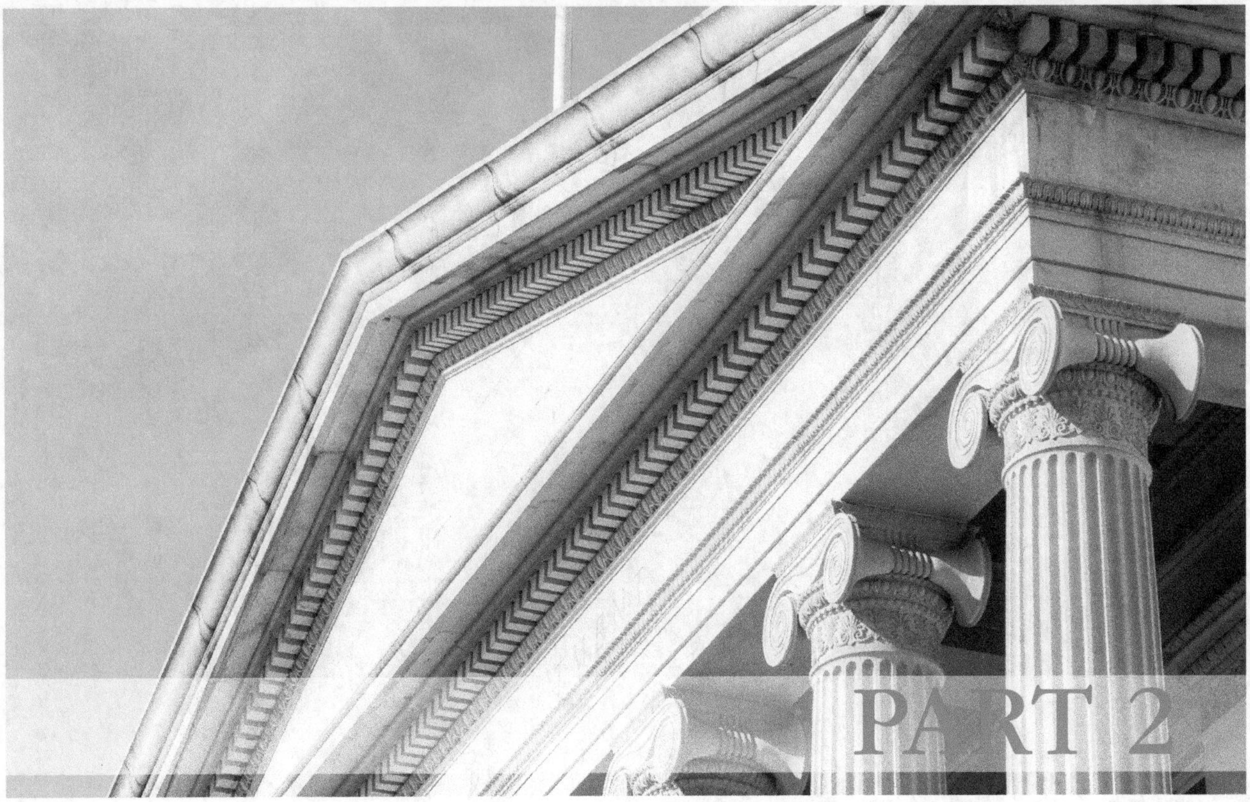

PART 2

Filing Status, Personal and Dependency Exemptions Standard Deduction, and Filing Requirements

Chapter 3

Filing Status

One of the first issues an individual must address on his or her income tax return is the taxpayer's **filing status**. The taxpayer identifies one of five categories: single, head of household, married filing jointly, married filing separately, or surviving spouse (sometimes called "qualifying widow(er) with dependent child"). This chapter provides further detail on each of these different categories of filing status.

A. Single

An individual will file as **single** if the individual is not married and does not qualify for **head of household** or **surviving spouse** status.

B. Head of Household

The Code provides a definition of "head of household" as follows.

INTERNAL REVENUE CODE

SECTION 2. DEFINITIONS AND SPECIAL RULES

. . .

(b) **Definition of head of household.**

(1) **In general.**—For purposes of this subtitle, an individual shall be considered a head of a household if, and only if, such individual is not married at the close of his taxable year, is not a surviving spouse ..., and either

(A) maintains as his home a household which constitutes for more than one-half of such taxable year the principal place of abode, as a member of such household, of—
  (i) a qualifying child of the individual ..., but not if such child—
    (I) is married at the close of the taxpayer's taxable year, and
    (II) is not a dependent of such individual ..., or
  (ii) any other person who is a dependent of the taxpayer ..., or

(B) maintains a household which constitutes for such taxable year the principal place of abode of the father or mother of the taxpayer, if the taxpayer is entitled to a deduction for the taxable year for such father or mother ....

For purposes of this paragraph, an individual shall be considered as maintaining a household only if over half of the cost of maintaining the household during the taxable year is furnished by such individual.

. . .

Thus, to qualify for "head of household" filing status a taxpayer cannot be married or a surviving spouse, must have at least one individual as a dependent, and must provide the principal place of abode for such dependent in addition to providing more than half the cost of maintaining the household for the dependent. Code Section 2 also provides clarification regarding situations involving divorce, separation, abandoned spouses, nonresident alien spouses and certain married individuals living apart.

C. Married Filing Jointly and Married Filing Separately

Married individuals have a choice to file jointly or separately. Most married taxpayers choose to file jointly because their ultimate combined tax liability is lower (see rate schedules later in the chapter). In some situations, one spouse may have significant itemized deductions and the other spouse may not. In such a case, filing separately may be beneficial. For example, since deductions for medical expenses are limited to an amount above a certain percentage of adjusted gross income (AGI), a couple's overall tax liability could be lower by filing separately because each spouse's separate AGI would be lower than the couple's combined AGI.

One significant consideration relating to the decision to file jointly or separately is the potential liability of each spouse for any underpayment of tax. Can the IRS seek to collect from either spouse the entire amount of tax due? The answer is generally 'no' if the spouses file a separate return and 'yes' if they file a joint return.

INTERNAL REVENUE CODE

SECTION 6013. JOINT RETURNS OF INCOME TAX BY HUSBAND AND WIFE

. . .

(d) **Special rules.**—For purposes of this section—

(3) if a joint return is made, the tax shall be computed on the aggregate income and the liability with respect to the tax shall be joint and several.

. . .

What happens in a situation where the spouses file a joint return but one spouse is unaware that the other spouse significantly understated his or her income? Is the "innocent" spouse still liable for the unpaid taxes attributable to the other spouse's understated income? The Code provides some relief for innocent spouses as follows.

INTERNAL REVENUE CODE

SECTION 6015. RELIEF FROM JOINT AND SEVERAL LIABILITY ON JOINT RETURN

. . .

(b) **Procedures for relief from liability applicable to all joint filers.—**

(1) **In general.**—Under procedures prescribed by the Secretary, if—

(A) a joint return has been made for a taxable year,

(B) on such return there is an understatement of tax attributable to erroneous items of 1 individual filing the joint return,

(C) the other individual filing the joint return establishes that in signing the return he or she did not know, and had no reason to know, that there was such understatement,

(D) taking into account all the facts and circumstances, it is inequitable to hold the other individual liable for the deficiency in tax for such taxable year attributable to such understatement, and

(E) the other individual elects ... the benefits of this subsection not later than the date which is 2 years after the date the Secretary has begun collection activities with respect to the individual making the election, then the other individual shall be relieved of liability for tax (including interest, penalties, and other amounts) for such taxable year to the extent such liability is attributable to such understatement.

While qualifying for the innocent spouse provisions can be quite difficult, at least the Code recognizes that in some situations fairness dictates that one spouse not be liable for the other spouse's understatement of tax on a joint return.

D. Surviving Spouse

The Code provides the following definition of "surviving spouse."

SECTION 2. DEFINITIONS AND SPECIAL RULES

(a) **Definition of surviving spouse.—**

(1) **In general.**—For purposes of section 1, the term "surviving spouse" means a taxpayer—

(A) whose spouse died during either of his two taxable years immediately preceding the taxable year, and

(B) who maintains as his home a household which constitutes for the taxable year the principal place of abode ... of a dependent (i) who ... is a son, stepson, daughter, or stepdaughter of the taxpayer, and (ii) with respect to whom the taxpayer is entitled to a deduction for the taxable year under section 151.

For purposes of this paragraph, an individual shall be considered as maintaining a household only if over half of the cost of maintaining the household during the taxable year is furnished by such individual.

. . .

A common misconception is that an individual qualifies as a "surviving spouse" for filing purposes if his or her spouse died during the current taxable year. Rather, the surviving spouse filing status applies to the widow or widower for the two years following the death of his or her spouse if the widow(er) has a qualifying dependent child. In the year of a spouse's death, the surviving spouse may in most cases still file a joint return.

E. Tax Rate Schedules Based on Filing Status

The Code provides for four tax rate schedules based on filing status. The married filing jointly status and surviving spouse (qualifying widow(er) with dependent child) status use the same schedule. The following rate schedules are for the year 2014.

1. Single

If taxable income is:	The tax would be:
Not over $9,075	10% of taxable income
Over $9,075 but not over $36,900	$907.50 + 15% of the excess over $9,075
Over $36,900 but not over $89,350	$5,081.25 + 25% of the excess over $36,900
Over $89,350 but not over $186,350	$18,193.75 + 28% of the excess over $89,350
Over $186,350 but not over $405,100	$45,353.75 + 33% of the excess over $186,350
Over $405,100 but not over $406,750	$117,541.25 + 35% of the excess over $405,100
Over $406,750	$118,118.75 + 39.6% of the excess over $406,750

2. Head of Household

If taxable income is:	The tax would be:
Not over $12,950	10% of taxable income
Over $12,950 but not over $49,400	$1,295.00 + 15% of the excess over $12,950
Over $49,400 but not over $127,550	$6,762.50 + 25% of the excess over $49,400
Over $127,550 but not over $206,600	$26,300.00 + 28% of the excess over $127,550
Over $206,600 but not over $405,100	$48,434.00 + 33% of the excess over $206,600
Over $405,100 but not over $432,200	$113,939.00 + 35% of the excess over $405,100
Over $432,200	$123,424.50 + 39.6% of the excess over $432,200

3. Married Filing Jointly and Surviving Spouses (Qualifying Widow(er))

If taxable income is:	The tax would be:
Not over $18,150	10% of taxable income
Over $18,150 but not over $73,800	$1,815.00 + 15% of the excess over $18,150
Over $73,800 but not over $148,850	$10,162.50 + 25% of the excess over $73,800
Over $148,850 but not over $226,850	$28,925.00 + 28% of the excess over $148,850
Over $226,850 but not over $405,100	$50,765.00 + 33% of the excess over $226,850
Over $405,100 but not over $457,600	$109,587.50 + 35% of the excess over $405,100
Over $457,600	$127,962.50 + 39.6% of the excess over $457,600

4. Married Filing Separately

If taxable income is:	The tax would be:
Not over $9,075	10% of taxable income
Over $9,075 but not over $36,900	$907.50 + 15% of the excess over $9,075
Over $36,900 but not over $74,425	$5,081.25 + 25% of the excess over $36,900
Over $74,425 but not over $113,425	$14,462.50 + 28% of the excess over $74,425
Over $113,425 but not over $202,550	$25,382.50 + 33% of the excess over $113,425
Over $202,550 but not over $228,800	$54,793.75 + 35% of the excess over $202,550
Over $228,800	$63,981.25 + 39.6% of the excess over $228,800

While there is no need to memorize the considerable detail in these schedules, it is beneficial to have a rough idea about how much taxable income causes a taxpayer to move to the next-higher bracket.

F. "KIDDIE" TAX

As taxpayers earn more money and enter into higher income tax brackets, there may be an incentive to shift some investment income to their children who are likely in a lower tax bracket.

> **EXAMPLE 3.1.** Assume that over a period of years Michael and Sharla give their daughter, Jessica, a total of $60,000. Jessica has placed this money in an interest-bearing account. This year the account generates $1,200 of interest income for Jessica, who is 16 years old. Is the $1,200 taxed at Jessica's tax rate or her parents' rate?
>
> **Answer:** Her parents' rate if the "kiddie" tax applies.

Congress thought that at some level this type of "income shifting" should be discouraged because it would result in the loss of revenue to the government. The kiddie tax applies when a child under age 18 has *unearned* income in excess of $2,000 (in 2014). In some cases if the child is a full-time student, the kiddie tax could apply until the child reaches age 24. IRS Form 8615 is provided in the Appendix for your reference. "Unearned" income consists of taxable interest, dividends, capital gains, rents, royalties, etc. If the child's unearned income is less than $2,000, then the income is taxed at the child's rate. The child is taxed at his or her own rate on all *earned* income. "Earned" income includes wages received for services rendered in a part-time job, for example.

CHAPTER 3: QUESTIONS

1. *Filing status in general.* Name the five different categories of filing status.

2. *Head of household filing status.* What are the requirements for someone to qualify for the head of household filing status?

3. *Head of household filing status.* Elizabeth is not married. She lives on her own and supports herself. She has no children or other dependents. May Elizabeth file as head of household this year?

4. *Head of household filing status.* Elizabeth is not married. She and her five-year-old son live together in an apartment for the entire year, and Elizabeth provides all the support for both of them. May Elizabeth file as head of household this year?

5. *Surviving spouse filing status.* What are the requirements for someone to qualify for the surviving spouse (qualifying widow(er) with dependent child) filing status?

6. *Surviving spouse.* Mario's spouse died this year. He has three grown children who have moved away and support themselves. May Mario file as a surviving spouse (qualifying widow(er) with dependent child) this year? Next year?

7. *Surviving spouse.* Mario's spouse died this year. He has a daughter that lives with him and he provides all of her support. May Mario file as a surviving spouse (qualifying widow(er) with dependent child) this year? Next year?

8. *Married filing jointly.* If spouses file jointly, are both spouses liable for any unpaid taxes? Explain the "innocent spouse" exception.

9. "*Kiddie*" *tax.* In general, when does the "kiddie" tax apply?

10. *Getting to know IRS Form 1040.* Refer to the IRS Form 1040 in the Appendix. On what line(s) of the form does a taxpayer identify his or her filing status?

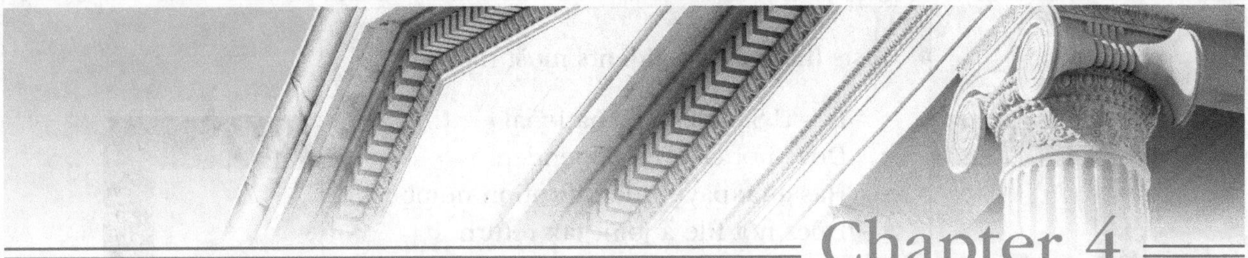

Chapter 4

Exemptions and the Standard Deduction

Recall the individual income tax formula presented in Chapter 2. From the AGI amount an individual can further reduce his or her taxable income by itemizing deductions or by taking the standard deduction (discussed later in this chapter). In addition to itemized deductions or the standard deduction, a taxpayer subtracts from AGI personal and dependency **exemptions**.

A. Personal Exemption

Each taxpayer is entitled to a **personal exemption**, which is a specific amount determined by the IRS each year. For 2014, the personal exemption amount is $3,950. For 2013, the personal exemption amount was $3,900. A taxpayer cannot use his or her personal exemption deduction if another person claims the taxpayer as a **dependent** (see the following discussion relating to dependency exemptions).

B. Dependency Exemption

In addition to a personal exemption deduction, a taxpayer may be entitled to a **dependency exemption** deduction for each person that qualifies as the taxpayer's dependent. The Code has very detailed requirements relating to who can qualify as a dependent. Basically, there are two different categories of dependents: (1) a **qualifying child**, and (2) a **qualifying relative**. The following chart sets forth the required tests a person must meet in order to be a qualifying child or qualifying relative.

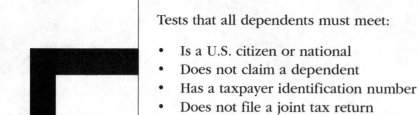

Tests that all dependents must meet:

- Is a U.S. citizen or national
- Does not claim a dependent
- Has a taxpayer identification number
- Does not file a joint tax return

Qualifying child tests:

- Relationship test
- Principal place of abode test
- Age test
- Support test

Qualifying relative tests:

- Relationship test
- Gross income test
- Support test

A taxpayer may claim a dependency exemption deduction for a person that qualifies as a dependent under the qualifying child test <u>or</u> the qualifying relative test. Let us first address in a little more detail the tests applicable to a qualifying child.

1. Qualifying Child

i. Relationship Test

To meet the relationship test, the child must be the taxpayer's child or a child of the taxpayer's siblings. A descendent of a taxpayer's child or a taxpayer's sibling's child also qualifies. Step-children, adopted children, and foster children also meet the definition.

ii. Principal Place of Abode Test

For more than one-half the year, the child must have the same principal place of abode as the taxpayer seeking to claim the child as a dependent. Some exceptions may apply when the child's parents are divorced, legally separated, etc. (*e.g.*, the custodial parent may allow the non-custodial parent to claim the dependency exemption even though the non-custodial parent did not meet the principal place of abode test).

iii. Age Test

A "qualifying child" must be under age 19. A child under age 24 can also meet the age test if the child is a full-time student for at least five months of the calendar year. Totally disabled children may also meet the test without regard to age.

iv. Support Test

Under the support test, the child cannot have provided for more than one-half of his or her own support for the year. The term "support" generally means food, shelter, clothing, medical bills, etc.

2. Qualifying Relative

i. Relationship Test

The Code provides an expansive definition of "relative" for purposes of the qualifying relative test.

INTERNAL REVENUE CODE

SECTION 152. DEPENDENT DEFINED

. . .

(d) **Qualifying relative.**—For purposes of this section—

. . .

(2) **Relationship.**—..., an individual bears a relationship to the taxpayer described in this paragraph if the individual is any of the following with respect to the taxpayer.

(A) A child or a descendant of a child.

(B) A brother, sister, stepbrother, or stepsister.

(C) The father or mother, or an ancestor of either.

(D) A stepfather or stepmother.

(E) A son or daughter of a brother or sister of the taxpayer.

(F) A brother or sister of the father or mother of the taxpayer.

(G) A son-in-law, daughter-in-law, father-in-law, mother-in-law, brother-in-law, or sister-in-law.

(H) An individual ... who, for the taxable year of the taxpayer, has the same principal place of abode as the taxpayer and is a member of the taxpayer's household.

. . .

Interestingly, the Code defines the relationship requirement so broadly in this context (see Section 152(d)(2)(H) above) that a person technically does not even have to be related to the taxpayer (as we normally think of the meaning of the term "related") to meet the requirements for "qualifying relative."

ii. Gross Income Test

The gross income of the dependent cannot be more than the exemption amount. In 2014, this amount is $3,950. The term "gross income" does not include items of income that the Code specifically excludes from gross income such as gifts, nontaxable scholarships, etc. (see Chapter 10 for a discussion of some of these items).

iii. Support Test

An individual seeking to claim another individual as a dependent must provide over one-half of the other individual's support for the calendar year. As mentioned in the "qualifying child" test, support generally includes amounts spent for food, shelter, clothing, medical expenses, etc. IRS publications address what other items may also be considered "support" for this purpose.

C. Phase-Out of Exemption Deductions

Certain taxpayers in higher tax brackets may have their exemption deductions phased-out. In 2014, the phase-out begins for single individuals with AGI of $254,200 and at $305,050 for married filing jointly.

D. Standard Deduction

In addition to taking deductions for personal and dependency exemptions, a taxpayer is allowed to choose between itemizing his or her "from" AGI deductions or taking the **standard deduction**. As will be discussed in detail in later chapters, itemized deductions are expenditures such as charitable contributions, medical expenses, mortgage interest, state income taxes, and property taxes. Some taxpayers do no incur these expenditures or, if they do, the expenditures are relatively small. Consequently, the Code allows a taxpayer to take the standard deduction when the itemized deductions do not exceed the standard deduction amount. The standard deduction is a fixed amount, usually adjusted upward each year to reflect inflation. For 2014, the following table represents the standard deduction for taxpayers relative to their filing status:

Filing Status:	Standard Deduction:
Single	$ 6,200
Head of household	$ 9,100
Married filing jointly	$12,400
Married filing separately	$ 6,200
Surviving spouse	$12,400

CHAPTER 4: QUESTIONS

1. *Exemption amount.* For the year 2014, what is the personal and dependency exemption amount? What was it for the year 2013?

2. *Dependency exemptions.* What are the two alternative tests to determine if an individual qualifies as a dependent?

3. *Dependency exemptions.* What are the tests an individual must meet to be considered a "qualifying child"?

4. *Dependency exemptions.* What are the tests an individual must meet to be considered a "qualifying relative"?

5. *Dependency exemptions.* Samuel, age 12, lives with his aunt and uncle. Their home is his principal abode and they provide more than one-half of his support for the year. Can Samuel's aunt and uncle claim Samuel as a dependent under the "qualifying child" test?

6. *Dependency exemptions.* Manny, age 84, lives with his grandson, Olaf. Olaf's home is Manny's principal abode and Olaf provides more than one-half of Manny's support for the year. Can Olaf claim Manny as a dependent under the "qualifying relative" test?

7. *Dependency exemptions.* Under what scenario could a 23-year-old qualify as a dependent under the "qualifying child" test?

8. *Phase-out of exemption deductions.* At what income level does the personal and dependency exemption amount begin to phase-out?

9. *Standard deduction vs. itemized deductions.* When is it beneficial for a taxpayer to take the standard deduction instead of itemizing deductions?

10. *Standard deduction.* For the year 2014, what is the standard deduction for a single taxpayer? Head of household? Married filing jointly?

11. *Getting to know IRS Form 1040.* Please refer to the IRS Form 1040 in the Appendix. On what line of Form 1040 does a taxpayer indicate either the standard deduction amount or the itemized deductions amount?

12. *Getting to know IRS Form 1040.* Please refer to the IRS Form 1040 in the Appendix. On what line of Form 1040 does a taxpayer identify his or her personal and dependency exemptions?

Chapter 5

Filing Requirements, Interest and Penalties

The United States tax system relies on individuals to prepare tax returns and submit the returns to the government. In this sense, the tax system is "voluntary" compared to, say, the government knocking on your door and demanding an arbitrary amount of tax. Failure to file a return when required to do so may result in civil and perhaps criminal penalties, however. This chapter discusses the income tax return filing requirements for individuals. We will also cover issues related to interest and penalties that may apply for failure to comply with the tax laws.

A. Filing Requirements

The Code requires that individuals with more than a certain amount of income must timely file an income tax return.

1. Who Must File?

A person's filing status and gross income typically determine whether an individual must file an income tax return. The gross income level at which an individual must file is typically equal to the personal exemption amount plus the standard deduction amounts for the relevant filing status (except for married filing separately, which is only the personal exemption amount). Consequently, this threshold usually increases by a few hundred dollars each year. An individual meeting these thresholds still must file even if the individual has no tax liability. Some special exceptions apply where a taxpayer must file even if the taxpayer's gross income is less than the personal exemption plus the standard deduction. For example, self-employed individuals must file if they have more than $400 of self-employment income even if the remainder of their income does not exceed the gross income threshold.

2. What Form Is Filed?

An individual that files an income tax return must complete one of three forms that the IRS provides. These three forms are: 1040EZ, 1040A, and 1040. The form that the individual completes depends on the complexity of the taxpayer's situation. Although most income tax returns are now filed electronically, you will be at a significant advantage if you familiarize yourself with the hard-copy of the applicable forms.

i. Form 1040EZ

The Form 1040EZ, of course, is the simplest individual income tax return to file. Taxpayers can only use this form, however, if they are single or married filing jointly. Moreover, the taxpayer cannot claim any dependents, cannot itemize deductions, and must have taxable income less than $100,000. A Form 1040EZ is included at the end of the text for your reference. Please refer to the form in the Appendix for additional restrictions on who can file a Form 1040EZ.

ii. Form 1040A

An individual may use Form 1040A no matter the taxpayer's filing status. Moreover, unlike Form 1040EZ, Form 1040A also allows the individual to claim dependency exemptions. But the Form 1040A does not allow a taxpayer to itemize deductions; instead, the taxpayer must take the standard deduction. If a taxpayer wishes to itemize deductions, then the taxpayer must file Form 1040. Please refer to the Form 1040A provided in the Appendix and notice other differences between that form and the Form 1040EZ.

iii. Form 1040

All taxpayers who must file and who do not qualify to use the simpler Forms 1040EZ or 1040A must complete Form 1040. A Form 1040 is also provided in the Appendix for your review. The Form 1040 can appear quite intimidating—especially in relation to the other two forms—but by the time you have completed this course, you will be much more confident with your increased knowledge about the form.

3. When Is the Tax Return Due?

An individual must file his or her income tax return in a timely manner or be subject to possible interest and penalties (discussed later in this chapter). Regarding the due date for individuals to file their income tax returns, the Code provides the following.

INTERNAL REVENUE CODE

SECTION 6072. TIME FOR FILING INCOME TAX RETURNS

(a) **General rule.**—In the case of returns under section 6012, 6013, 6017, or 6031 (relating to income tax under subtitle A), returns made on the basis of the calendar year shall be filed on or before the 15th day of April following the close of the calendar year and returns made on the basis of a fiscal year shall be filed on or before the 15th day of the fourth month following the close of the fiscal year, except as otherwise provided in the following subsections of this section.

. . .

Thus, the due date for individuals (and partnerships) is typically April 15. If April 15th falls on a Saturday, Sunday or holiday then the deadline is moved forward to the next business day. (The due date for corporate income tax returns is generally March 15th for calendar year corporations and the 15th day of the third month after the end of the fiscal year for fiscal year corporations.)

On occasion a taxpayer may not be able to gather all the necessary information to file the tax return by the regular due date. In these situations, the Code allows for a taxpayer to request an extension to file. Individuals can receive an automatic six-month extension to file by filing Form 4868, a copy of which is included in the Appendix for your review. *Important note*: an extension to file is not an extension to pay! An individual that requests an extension to file must still estimate any additional tax liability that may be due or the taxpayer may be subject to interest and the failure-to-pay penalty.

B. Interest

An individual who fails to timely pay his or her income tax liability may be required to pay interest to the government.

INTERNAL REVENUE CODE

SECTION 6601. INTEREST ON UNDERPAYMENT, NONPAYMENT OR EXTENSIONS OF TIME FOR PAYMENT, OF TAX

(a) **General rule.**—If any amount of tax imposed by this title ... is not paid on or before the last date prescribed for payment, interest on such amount at the underpayment rate established under section 6621 shall be paid for the period from such last date to the date paid.

. . .

The interest rate that applies is published by the IRS on a quarterly basis and is calculated by reference to the federal short-term rate. The federal short-term rate takes into consideration fluctuations in market interest rates. Thus, the interest rate that applies can change from quarter-to-quarter. Interest is compounded daily.

What if an individual overpays his or her taxes and is owed a refund? Is the government required to pay interest to the individual? The answer is generally 'yes.'

INTERNAL REVENUE CODE

SECTION 6611. INTEREST ON OVERPAYMENTS

(a) **Rate.**—Interest shall be allowed and paid upon any overpayment in respect of any internal revenue tax at the overpayment rate established under section 6621.

. . .

Thus, in some instances the government may owe the taxpayer for overpaying his or her income tax obligation. One major exception to this rule is provided in Code Section 6611(e).

INTERNAL REVENUE CODE

SECTION 6611. INTEREST ON OVERPAYMENTS

. . .

(e) **Disallowance of interest on certain overpayments.—**
   (1) **Refunds within 45 days after return is filed.**—If any overpayment of tax imposed by this title is refunded within 45 days after the last day prescribed for filing the return of such tax (determined without regard to any extension of time for filing the return) or, in the case of a return filed after such last date, is refunded within 45 days after the date the return is filed, no interest shall be allowed under subsection (a) on such overpayment.

. . .

In accordance with Section 6611(e)(1), if the government refunds an amount that the taxpayer overpaid, then the government owes no interest to the taxpayer as long as the refund was issued within 45 days after the due date of the return or within 45 days after the filing of the return if the return was filed later. If interest is due to the taxpayer because of an overpayment, interest compounds daily.

EXAMPLE 5.1. Alexis files her 2013 return on March 10, 2014. She correctly determines that she overpaid her income taxes by $2,750. To avoid paying interest, when must the government refund the overpayment to Alexis?

Answer: The government has until 45 days after the due date of the return (April 15) to issue the refund to Alexis. Note that the answer in this case is not 45 days after the date she actually filed the return.

C. Civil Penalties

In addition to imposing interest on underpayments of tax, the Code imposes penalties on taxpayers who engage in certain types of behavior in relation to their tax obligations. We will discuss a few of the most common civil penalties (as opposed to *criminal* penalties) here.

1. Failure to File and Failure to Pay Penalties

The Code imposes penalties on individuals who fail to timely file their income tax return and/or fail to pay the amount of tax due.

INTERNAL REVENUE CODE

SECTION 6651. FAILURE TO FILE TAX RETURN OR TO PAY TAX

(a) **Addition to the tax.**—In case of failure

(1) to file any return required under authority of [certain other Code sections], on the date prescribed therefor (determined with regard to any extension of time for filing), unless it is shown that such failure is due to reasonable cause and not due to willful neglect, there shall be added to the amount required to be shown as tax on such return 5 percent of the amount of such tax if the failure is for not more than 1 month, with an additional 5 percent for each additional month or fraction thereof during which such failure continues, not exceeding 25 percent in the aggregate;

(2) to pay the amount shown as tax on any return specified in paragraph (1) on or before the date prescribed for payment of such tax (determined with regard to any extension of time for payment), unless it is shown that such failure is due to reasonable cause and not due to willful neglect, there shall be added to the amount shown as tax on such return 0.5 percent of the amount of such tax if the failure is for not more than 1 month, with an additional 0.5 percent for each additional month or fraction thereof during which such failure continues, not exceeding 25 percent in the aggregate;

. . .

Notice that the taxpayer can avoid the penalties if the taxpayer has "reasonable cause" and the failure was "not due to willful neglect." Also, the Code further provides that if both the failure-to-file penalty and the failure-to-pay penalties apply, then the failure-to-pay penalty reduces the failure-to-file penalty.

2. Accuracy-Related Penalties

In addition to the failure-to-file and failure-to-pay penalties, a taxpayer may be subject to accuracy-related penalties. These penalties apply when a taxpayer substantially understates or overstates a particular item of income or deduction, as the case may be.

INTERNAL REVENUE CODE

SECTION 6662. IMPOSITION OF ACCURACY-RELATED PENALTY ON UNDERPAYMENTS

(a) **Imposition of penalty.**—If this section applies to any portion of an underpayment of tax required to be shown on a return, there shall be added to the tax an amount equal to 20 percent of the portion of the underpayment to which this section applies.

(b) **Portion of underpayment to which section applies.**—This section shall apply to the portion of any underpayment which is attributable to 1 or more of the following:

(1) Negligence or disregard of rules or regulations.

(2) Any substantial understatement of income tax.

(3) Any substantial valuation misstatement ....

(4) Any substantial overstatement of pension liabilities.

(5) Any substantial estate or gift tax valuation understatement.

. . .

We will not discuss the details of each of these accuracy-related penalties here, but a taxpayer should be aware that such penalties exist.

3. Other Civil Penalties

Although the penalties already mentioned are the most common, the Code does provide for other penalties, including a penalty for entering into transactions that lack economic substance and a penalty for civil fraud. The civil fraud penalty carries with it a hefty price.

INTERNAL REVENUE CODE

SECTION 6663. IMPOSITION OF FRAUD PENALTY

(a) **Imposition of penalty.**—If any part of any underpayment of tax required to be shown on a return is due to fraud, there shall be added to the tax an amount equal to 75 percent of the portion of the underpayment which is attributable to fraud.

. . .

Some civil penalties also apply to tax return preparers, but we will address those penalties in Chapter 27.

D. Criminal Penalties

While civil penalties may cause the taxpayer some financial grief, criminal penalties may cause the taxpayer both financial grief and the loss of his or her freedom for a period of time. Perhaps the most common criminal tax penalty is tax evasion.

INTERNAL REVENUE CODE

SECTION 7201. ATTEMPT TO EVADE OR DEFEAT TAX

Any person who willfully attempts in any manner to evade or defeat any tax imposed by this title or the payment thereof shall, in addition to other penalties provided by law, be guilty of a felony and, upon conviction thereof, shall be fined not more than $100,000 ($500,000 in the case of a corporation), or imprisoned not more than 5 years, or both, together with the costs of prosecution.

Other criminal penalties include willful failure to collect or pay over tax, willful failure to file a required return, fraud, and making false statements, among others. Notice that a fraud penalty is among the criminal penalties. Thus, fraud may constitute a civil penalty or a criminal penalty. The distinction lies in the requisite intent of the taxpayer and the higher standard of proof that the government must meet to obtain a guilty verdict in criminal cases (*i.e.*, "beyond a reasonable doubt").

CHAPTER 5: QUESTIONS

1. *U.S. tax system.* Why might the tax system in the United States be referred to as a "voluntary" system?

2. *Filing requirements.* Discuss a situation where an individual is not required to file an income tax return.

3. *Filing requirements.* Name at least one situation where an individual must file an income tax return even though the taxpayer's gross income does not exceed the generally applicable filing threshold.

4. *Form 1040EZ.* May an individual who plans to file as "head of household" file Form 1040EZ?

5. *Form 1040EZ.* May an individual who has dependents file Form 1040EZ?

6. *Form 1040EZ.* May an individual who itemizes deductions file Form 1040EZ?

7. *Form 1040A.* May an individual who plans to file as "head of household" file Form 1040A?

8. *Form 1040A.* May an individual who has dependents file Form 1040A?

9. *Form 1040A.* May an individual who itemizes deductions file Form 1040A?

10. *Form 1040.* On what line of Form 1040 does an individual report his or her business income? Is there a corresponding line for business income on the Form 1040A?

11. *Form 1040.* On what line of Form 1040 does an individual claim a residential energy credit? Is there a corresponding line for residential energy credits on Form 1040A?

12. *Due dates.* On what date must a calendar-year taxpayer file an individual income tax return? May a taxpayer request an extension to file? If so, how long is the extension? Does an extension to file also give the taxpayer an extension to pay the tax?

13. *Interest.* How often does the IRS publish the interest rate that applies to underpayments and overpayments of tax?

14. *Interest.* How long does the government have to issue a refund before the government owes interest to the individual taxpayer on the overpaid tax?

15. *Failure to file penalty.* How much is the failure to file penalty?

16. *Failure to pay penalty.* How much is the failure to pay penalty?

17. *Accuracy-related penalties.* Name at least four accuracy-related penalties.

18. *Civil fraud penalty.* How much is the civil fraud penalty?

19. *Criminal penalties.* Name at least three criminal penalties.

20. *Tax evasion.* How long could a taxpayer be imprisoned if convicted of tax evasion?

TAX RETURN EXERCISE

Tim S. Rossell and Tina A. Rossell are married. Tim's social security number is 111–22–3333. Tina's social security number is 222–33–4444. They live at 555 North Liberty Street, Anytown, USA 10100. They have no children or other dependents. Tim and Tina cannot be claimed as dependents by anyone else. They have decided to file their income tax return as married filing jointly. Tim and Tina choose not to contribute $3 to the presidential election campaign fund.

Tim's Form W-2 shows that he had wages of $27,525 for the year. Tina's Form W-2 shows that she had wages of $31,200 for the year. Tim's employer withheld $3,300 in federal income tax from his pay. Tina's employer withheld $3,900 in federal income tax from her pay. They earned $200 in interest from their bank savings account. Tim and Tina are not eligible for the earned income credit.

Assignment: Prepare an IRS Form 1040EZ for Tim and Tina. Ignore the routing number and account number section if you determine they are due a refund. To determine the amount of tax on Line 10 you will need to refer to the tax tables in the instructions for Form 1040EZ. You can find the instructions on the IRS website at www.irs.gov.

PART 3

Inclusions in Gross Income

Chapter 6

Gross Income Defined, Wages, Salaries, Tips, Business Income, Unemployment Compensation, and Social Security Benefits

As you recall from the individual income tax formula, the concept of "income" is very broad. Also, any income that is not specifically excluded by the Code is included in gross income. In this chapter we explore the definition of "gross income" and discuss some common items of income and how they are treated. First, however, we look at a couple of concepts that are important to remember throughout your study of income taxation—the "assignment of income" doctrine and the "wherewithal to pay" concept.

A. Assignment of Income Doctrine and Wherewithal to Pay Concept

1. Assignment of Income Doctrine

Suppose Ashleigh is employed at ABC, Inc., and that she gets paid $2,000 every other week. Further suppose that Ashleigh has a daughter, Cynthia, and Ashleigh instructs ABC, Inc. to write all her paychecks "to the order of Cynthia" and deposit the $2,000 each time directly into Cynthia's bank account. ABC, Inc. does so. Who is subject to income tax on Ashleigh's wages, Ashleigh or Cynthia? The answer is Ashleigh. Ashleigh earned the income and in accordance with the **assignment of income** doctrine Ashleigh is not allowed to shift the tax burden to someone else. Of course, she can make a gift of the income to Cynthia, but Ashleigh is still subject to income tax on the income she earns. The United States Supreme Court explained in an old, famous case,

Lucas v. Earl, that the fruit (income) is taxed to the tree (person providing services) from which the fruit grew.

The assignment of income doctrine also applies in situations other than just earned income from wages. Suppose that David owns stock in XYZ Corporation. David instructs XYZ Corporation to pay all dividends to his friend Greg. XYZ Corporation does so. Who pays tax on the dividends, David or Greg? The answer is David. The stock is the "tree" and the dividend is the "fruit." The fruit is taxed to the person owning the tree.

2. Wherewithal to Pay Concept

One general concept that underlies many provisions in the Internal Revenue Code is the **wherewithal to pay** concept. This concept basically provides that the law should impose an income tax when the individual is in the best position to pay the tax. For example, when an employee is paid in return for providing services to an employer, the individual is in the position to pay the tax at that point. Thus, the employer is obligated to withhold income tax from the employee's paycheck. Nevertheless, we must follow the dictates of the Internal Revenue Code, and some exceptions exist to the wherewithal to pay concept. To illustrate an exception, suppose an employee is not paid in cash, but is paid with some of the employer's property. Is the employee required to pay tax on the value of the property received? Generally, the answer is 'yes' even though the employee may not have cash to pay the tax upon receipt of the property. As we discuss various tax transactions and concepts throughout the remainder of this text, keep in mind the wherewithal to pay concept and whether it applies in a particular situation. Other issues related to "when" a taxpayer includes income on his or her tax return, including a discussion of the cash method of accounting and the accrual method of accounting, will be covered in Chapter 21.

B. Gross Income Defined

Gross income is basically all income from whatever source derived less any specific exclusions provided by the Code. Consider Code Section 61, which provides a very expansive definition of the term "gross income."

INTERNAL REVENUE CODE

SECTION 61. GROSS INCOME DEFINED

(a) **General definition.**—Except as otherwise provided in this subtitle, gross income means all income from whatever source derived, including (but not limited to) the following items:
  (1) Compensation for services, including fees, commissions, fringe benefits, and similar items;
  (2) Gross income derived from business;
  (3) Gains derived from dealings in property;
  (4) Interest;
  (5) Rents;
  (6) Royalties;
  (7) Dividends;
  (8) Alimony and separate maintenance payments;

(9) Annuities;
(10) Income from life insurance and endowment contracts;
(11) Pensions;
(12) Income from discharge of indebtedness;
(13) Distributive share of partnership gross income;
(14) Income in respect of a decedent; and
(15) Income from an interest in an estate or trust.

. . .

Notice in the gross income definition that the items listed are examples of income, but there are more; hence, the Code says "including (but not limited to)" the items listed. In this and the next couple of chapters we will discuss particular items that are included in gross income.

C. Wages, Salaries, Tips, and Business Income

An individual must include in his or her gross income the wages, salaries, and tips received in return for services provided. Other forms of compensation are included in gross income as well, such as commissions and bonuses. An employer is required to report to an employee shortly after the end of the year (usually by January 31) how much in wages, salary and/or tips the employee earned during the year. The employer does this on Form W-2. Please see the sample form W-2 in the Appendix.

If a taxpayer is self-employed, then the taxpayer's income from the business is also included in gross income. An individual's business income from self-employment is reported on Schedule C of IRS Form 1040. A taxpayer includes both income and expenses on Schedule C. The taxpayer then reports the net income (or loss) from the business on the front page of the Form 1040. Please see the Schedule C in the Appendix. In later chapters we will talk much more in depth about many of the business deductions you see on Schedule C.

1. Employee v. Independent Contractor

One very important issue that an individual should be aware of is whether the individual is an "employee" or an "independent contractor." In some situations, this determination can be a difficult task. Generally, if an employer can control the behavior of an individual (*e.g.*, trains the individual, instructs the individual how to do the work, determines when the individual shows up to work, etc.) and can control the financial aspects of the relationship (*e.g.*, provides the necessary equipment, reimburses costs, etc.) then the relationship looks like an employer-employee relationship. On the other hand, if the relationship indicates that the person has his or her own business where the person can make a profit or loss, the person provides his or her own tools, and determines his or her own hours, etc., then the person is likely an independent contractor.

Given that the classification of a worker as an independent contractor or employee is a very important decision, the IRS offers to assist employers and workers to make the determination if desired. If the employer or worker desires that the IRS make this classification, the proper form to send in to the IRS is Form SS-8. Please see the Appendix for a sample Form SS-8.

2. Reporting Requirements

As discussed earlier, shortly after the end of the year (usually by January 31) an employer is required to send a Form W-2 to an employee to report the wages, salary, and/or tips earned. The Form W-2 also shows how much income tax and other payroll taxes (social security and Medicare) were withheld from the employee's compensation. If the individual is an independent contractor, then the business(es) for whom the individual provided services will send the individual an IRS Form 1099. Remember that the businesses that pay an independent contractor will not withhold income tax or other taxes; therefore, the independent contractor must pay estimated income taxes usually on a quarterly basis using IRS Form 1040-ES. The independent contractor would include his income and expenses on Schedule C (assuming the independent contractor has not formed an entity such as a partnership or corporation in which to conduct the business). Please see the Appendix for a sample Form 1040-ES.

D. Unemployment Compensation

Although people often assume that unemployment compensation is not subject to income tax, the opposite is true. Since unemployment compensation is a substitute for what otherwise would be taxable compensation, unemployment compensation is subject to income tax also.

INTERNAL REVENUE CODE

SECTION 85. UNEMPLOYMENT COMPENSATION

(a) **General rule.**—In the case of an individual, gross income includes unemployment compensation.

(b) **Unemployment compensation defined.**—For purposes of this section, the term "unemployment compensation" means any amount received under a law of the United States or of a State which is in the nature of unemployment compensation.

. . .

E. Social Security Benefits

Should social security benefits be subject to income tax? Some people might say 'no' if the recipient is poor, and 'yes' if the recipient is more wealthy. The provisions of the Code are quite detailed in addressing the taxability of social security benefits.

Generally, an individual's gross income includes social security benefits received by the individual. The amount included, however, is based upon the individual's adjusted gross income (which is modified slightly for this purpose) and filing status. The amount included could be 0%, 50% or 85% of the benefits received. For example, 0% of social security benefits received by a single individual are included in the individual's gross income if the individual's modified adjusted gross income is $25,000 or less. Eighty-five percent of social security benefits could be included in the gross income of a single individual if modified adjusted gross income of that individual exceeds $34,000. For married individuals filing jointly, 85% of the social security benefits could be included if their modified adjusted gross income exceeds $44,000.

CHAPTER 6: QUESTIONS

1. *Assignment of income doctrine.* Discuss the assignment of income doctrine. What is its purpose?

2. *Wherewithal-to-pay concept.* Discuss the wherewithal-to-pay concept. Does it always apply? If not, provide a sample transaction where the concept does not apply.

3. *Reporting requirements.* How does an employee know how much total wages the employee received for the year so that the employee can report it in gross income?

4. *Self-employed.* If a person is self-employed (independent contractor), on what schedule of Form 1040 does the person report his or her business income (or loss)?

5. *Employee v. independent contractor.* Explain the distinction between employee and independent contractor and why the distinction is important.

6. *Reporting requirements.* What is the purpose of IRS Form 1040-ES?

7. *Unemployment compensation.* Is unemployment compensation included in a taxpayer's gross income?

8. *Social security benefits.* Not all the social security benefits an individual receives are included in gross income. What possible percentages of benefits could be included?

9. *Employee v. independent contractor.* Please refer to Form SS-8 in the Appendix and answer the following questions:
   a. Name at least three specific factors relating to behavioral control that the IRS considers in making the employee v. independent contractor determination.
   b. Name at least three specific factors relating to financial control that the IRS considers in making the employee v. independent contractor determination.
   c. Name at least three other factors the IRS considers in making the employee v. independent contractor determination.

10. *Getting to know Schedule C.* Please refer to Schedule C in the Appendix. What is subtracted from gross receipts to arrive at the "gross profit" amount?

11. *Getting to know Schedule C and Form 1040.* If an individual has a net profit from her business as reported on Schedule C, on what line of the individual's Form 1040 is the net profit reported.

12. *Getting to know Form W-2.* Please refer to the Form W-2 in the Appendix and answer the following questions:
    a. In what box on Form W-2 does the employer report to the employee the wages, tips, and other compensation earned by the employee during the year?
    b. In what box on Form W-2 does the employer report to the employee the amount of federal income taxes that the employer withheld from the employee during the year?
    c. In what box on Form W-2 does the employer report to the employee the amount of state income taxes that the employer withheld from the employee during the year?

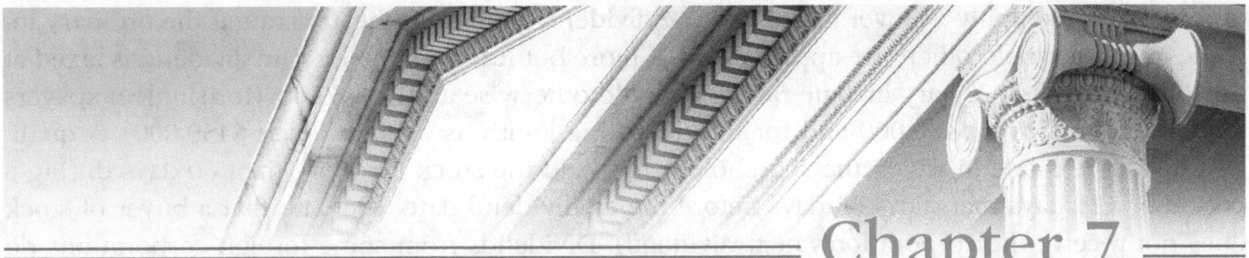

Chapter 7

Interest, Dividends, Capital Gains, Rental, and Royalty Income

We continue our discussion of specific items included in gross income by looking at common types of income from investments.

A. Interest

Interest received by a taxpayer from savings and checking accounts, corporate bonds, federal savings bonds, loans, etc., are included in a taxpayer's gross income. The Code specifically *excludes* from gross income interest received from state and local bonds and a special type of federal savings bond called a **Series EE Savings Bond**. Please see Chapter 10 for a discussion of the special types of interest income that are excluded from a taxpayer's gross income.

An individual reports interest income directly on the individual's Form 1040 (or 1040A or 1040EZ). If a taxpayer has over $1,500 in interest income for the year, however, the taxpayer must complete Schedule B to accompany the taxpayer's Form 1040 or 1040A (Form 1040EZ is unavailable if a taxpayer has over $1,500 in interest income). A Schedule B is provided in the Appendix for your convenience.

A payer of interest generally must send to the recipient a Form 1099-INT shortly after the end of the year (usually by January 31). The Form 1099-INT informs the recipient how much interest the payer paid to the recipient. A sample Form 1099-INT is provided in the Appendix for your convenience.

B. Dividends

A dividend is a distribution from a corporation's earnings and profits to the corporation's shareholders. A dividend is included in the individual's gross income and is taxed at the individual's ordinary income tax rate unless the dividend is a **qualified** dividend. A qualified dividend is taxed at a 0%, 15%, or 20% rate. The dividend is taxed at a 0% rate if the ordinary income rate that otherwise would apply is lower than 25%. The dividend is taxed at the 15% rate if the ordinary income rate that would otherwise apply is 25% or more but less than 39.6%. The dividend is taxed at the 20% rate if the ordinary income rate that would otherwise apply is 39.6% (for single taxpayers that is amounts over $400,000 and for married filing jointly is amounts over $450,000). A qualified dividend is one in which the shareholder has held the stock for more than 60 days during a period of 121 days that starts 60 days before the ex-dividend date (the date that a buyer of stock does not receive the corporation's next dividend). Dividends from some foreign corporations do not qualify as qualified dividends. Also, some other payments may be labeled "dividend" but may not be treated as such for tax purposes (*e.g.*, "dividends" to members of credit unions are treated as interest income to the recipients).

An individual reports dividend income directly on the individual's Form 1040 (or 1040A). If a taxpayer has over $1,500 in dividend income for the year, however, the taxpayer must complete Schedule B to accompany the taxpayer's Form 1040 or 1040A. When reporting dividends on Form 1040 or Form 1040A, the individual reports all dividends on the "ordinary dividends" line and then breaks out the "qualified dividends" on the line provided for qualified dividends. A Schedule B is provided in the Appendix for your reference.

A corporation that issues dividends to shareholders must send to its shareholders a Form 1099-DIV shortly after the end of the year (usually by January 31). The Form 1099-DIV informs the shareholder how much of the distribution constitutes a dividend. A sample Form 1099-DIV is provided in the Appendix for your convenience.

C. Capital Gains and Losses

If a taxpayer disposes of a **capital asset**, the resulting gain or loss realized is a **capital gain** or **capital loss**. If the taxpayer held the asset for longer than one year before the transaction disposing of the asset, the taxpayer's gain or loss will be classified as a **long-term** capital gain or loss. If the taxpayer held the asset for one year or less, the gain or loss on the transaction is classified as a **short-term** capital gain or loss. Once the character of the gains or losses is determined, long-term gains are netted against long-term losses and short-term gains are netted against short-term losses. Then, the separate long-term and short-term net gains and/or losses are netted again to arrive at an overall net long-term or short-term capital gain or loss. If the overall net result is a long-term capital gain, then the individual benefits from the preferential 0%, 15%, and 20% rates rather than the ordinary income tax rates.

EXAMPLE 7.1. Marsha experiences the following capital gains and losses during the year:

Date 1	Long-term capital gain of $2,000
Date 2	Long-term capital loss of $1,500
Date 3	Short-term capital gain of $200
Date 4	Short-term capital loss of $300

How are Marsha's capital gains and losses treated for the year?

Answer: She has a net long-term capital gain of $500 ($2,000 – $1,500) and a net short-term capital loss of $100 ($200 – $300). Marsha then nets the long-term capital gain and short-term capital loss and ends up with an overall $400 net long-term capital gain. This gain will be taxed at the preferential long-term capital gain rates.

If the overall net result is a short-term capital gain, then the individual's ordinary income tax rate applies.

EXAMPLE 7.2. Marsha experiences the following capital gains and losses during the year:

Date 1	Long-term capital gain of $1,000
Date 2	Long-term capital loss of $1,400
Date 3	Short-term capital gain of $800
Date 4	Short-term capital loss of $300

How are Marsha's capital gains and losses treated for the year?

Answer: She has a net long-term capital loss of $400 ($1,000 – $1,400) and a net short-term capital gain of $500 ($800 – $300). Marsha then nets the long-term capital loss and short-term capital gain and ends up with an overall $100 net short-term capital gain. This gain will be taxed at Marsha's ordinary income tax rate.

If the overall net result is a short-term or long-term capital loss, then the individual must carry the loss forward to future years until the individual has capital gains to offset the capital loss. A small exception to this carry-over of losses is that an individual may deduct up to a maximum of $3,000 of the taxpayer's net capital losses against ordinary income each year.

EXAMPLE 7.3. Marsha experiences the following capital gains and losses during the year:

Date 1	Long-term capital gain of $1,500
Date 2	Long-term capital loss of $1,400
Date 3	Short-term capital gain of $100
Date 4	Short-term capital loss of $500

How are Marsha's capital gains and losses treated for the year?

Answer: She has a net long-term capital gain of $100 ($1,500 – $1,400) and a net short-term capital loss of $400 ($100 – $500). Marsha then nets the long-term capital gain and short-term capital loss and ends up with an overall $300 net short-term capital loss. This loss can offset $300 of Marsha's ordinary income.

Capital gains and losses are reported on Schedule D of an individual's Form 1040. A copy of Schedule D is included in the Appendix. In order to properly fill out Schedule D, an individual likely also has to complete Form 8949, a copy of which is also in the Appendix.

Although in most cases the 0%, 15%, and 20% capital gain rates apply, in some cases the applicable rate is 25% (unrecaptured Section 1250 gain) or 28% (collectibles gain). A detailed coverage of these types of gains is beyond the scope of our discussion here. Clearly, the calculation of an individual's tax liability is complicated if the individual has various types of capital gains where multiple tax rates apply. To illustrate this possible complexity, please refer to the Schedule D Tax Worksheet in the Appendix. In short, one must be certain not to forget about the special, lower tax rates that apply to net long-term capital gains.

We have now learned how capital gains and losses are treated. Remember capital gains and losses arise because of the sale or exchange of "capital" assets. The definition of capital asset (as well as other types of assets) is discussed in Chapter 9.

D. Rental Income

An individual that receives rents must include the rents in gross income. Expenses related to generating the rental income typically can offset the rental income. Individuals report rental income from real estate on Schedule E, a copy of which is included in the Appendix.

E. Royalty Income

An individual must include in gross income any royalty income the individual may have. An oil and gas company may pay royalties (usually a percentage of production) to the landowner for allowing drilling to occur on the property. A taxpayer may also license rights in a patent and receive royalties in return. Royalties are reported on Schedule E of an individual's Form 1040. (Note: Self-employed authors who receive royalties on the sale of books typically report the royalties on Schedule C.) A Schedule E is included in the Appendix for your review.

F. Medicare Tax on Net Investment Income

Effective January 1, 2013, Congress imposed a 3.8% Medicare tax on net investment income that applies to certain taxpayers with adjusted gross income over $200,000 (single filers) or $250,000 (married filing jointly). The tax is *in addition to* any other taxes that may apply to the net investment income (*i.e.*, ordinary income tax rate or capital gain tax rate). Net investment income includes interest, dividends, rents, royalties, and capital gains, among other items.

EXAMPLE 7.4. Stefanie is single. She has salary income of $220,000 and dividend income of $10,000. Is Stefanie's dividend income subject to the additional 3.8% Medicare tax on net investment income?

Answer: Yes. Since her adjusted gross income is otherwise over the $200,000 threshold, the dividend income is subject to the 3.8% additional Medicare tax. This tax is in addition to the taxes she would normally be liable for on the dividend income.

CHAPTER 7: QUESTIONS

1. *Interest income.* An individual must file Schedule B to report interest income when the interest income is above what amount?

2. *Interest income.* How does an individual find out how much interest income he or she has received during the year?

3. *Dividend income.* A qualified dividend receives preferential tax rate treatment. What is a qualified dividend?

4. *Dividend income.* At what rate is a dividend taxed if it is not a qualified dividend?

5. *Dividend income.* If a dividend is a qualified dividend, which tax rate(s) may apply?

6. *Dividend income.* How does an individual find out how much dividend income he or she has received during the year?

7. *Dividend income.* An individual must file Schedule B to report dividend income when the dividend income is above what amount?

8. *Capital gains and losses.* What is the tax benefit to an individual for having a gain treated as a net long-term capital gain rather than a net short-term capital gain?

9. *Capital gains and losses.* At what rates could a net long-term capital gain be taxed?

10. *Capital gains and losses.* If an individual experiences a net capital loss, can the capital loss offset the individual's ordinary income? If so, how much?

11. *Capital gains and losses.* On what IRS schedule does an individual report capital gains and losses?

12. *Rental income.* On what IRS schedule does an individual report rental income?

13. *Royalty income.* On what IRS schedule does an individual report royalty income?

14. *Medicare tax on net investment income.* A single individual is subject to the 3.8% Medicare tax on net investment income if the individual's adjusted gross income is at least what amount? What is the amount if the taxpayers' status is married filing jointly?

Chapter 8

Prizes, Awards, Tax Refunds, Alimony, and Other Income

This chapter continues to discuss specific items that are included in an individual's gross income.

A. Prizes and Awards

Ever wondered whether the prize you won at a raffle is taxable? What about prizes that people win on radio shows? Game shows on television? The answer is quite straightforward.

INTERNAL REVENUE CODE

SECTION 74. PRIZES AND AWARDS

(a) **General rule.**—Except as otherwise provided in this section or in section 117 (relating to qualified scholarships), gross income includes amounts received as prizes and awards.

. . .

Notice that the value of prizes and awards is included in an individual's gross income. Section 74 continues on to provide a couple of exceptions to this general rule, however.

INTERNAL REVENUE CODE

SECTION 74. PRIZES AND AWARDS

(b) **Exception for certain prizes and awards transferred to charities.**—Gross income does not include amounts received as prizes and awards made primarily in recognition of religious, charitable, scientific, educational, artistic, literary, or civic achievement, but only if—
  (1) the recipient was selected without any action on his part to enter the contest or proceeding;

(2) the recipient is not required to render substantial future services as a condition to receiving the prize or award; and
(3) the prize or award is transferred by the payor to a governmental unit or [charitable] organization ....

(c) **Exception for certain employee achievement awards.—**
(1) **In general.**—Gross income shall not include the value of an employee achievement award (as defined in section 274(j)) received by the taxpayer if the cost to the employer of the employee achievement award does not exceed the amount allowable as a deduction to the employer for the cost of the employee achievement award.
(2) **Excess deduction award.**—If the cost to the employer of the employee achievement award received by the taxpayer exceeds the amount allowable as a deduction to the employer; then gross income includes the greater of—
(A) an amount equal to the portion of the cost to the employer of the award that is not allowable as a deduction to the employer (but not in excess of the value of the award), or
(B) the amount by which the value of the award exceeds the amount allowable as a deduction to the employer.

. . .

In summary, prizes and awards are included in gross income unless the prize or award was on account of a religious, charitable, etc., activity and the recipient transfers the prize or award to a governmental unit or charitable organization. Regarding *awards*, the award can also be excluded from gross income if the *employee achievement award* exception applies. Section 274(j) indicates that an employer can deduct the cost of an employee achievement award up to $400. Thus, the employee can exclude an employee achievement award up to $400 from gross income. Typically, an employee achievement award is based on the employee's length of service with the employer or the employee's safety record. The Code provides other detailed rules applicable to employee achievement awards and the exclusion of such awards from an individual's gross income, but we will not discuss such details here.

B. Income Tax Refunds

Federal income tax refunds are not included in gross income. State income tax refunds may be included in an individual's gross income depending upon the circumstances. If the individual did not itemize his or her deductions in the tax year the state income tax refund is for, then the individual does not include the refund in his or her gross income in the year the individual receives the refund. This is because the individual received no tax benefit from the deduction of the state income taxes in that year (since the taxpayer did not itemize deductions). If the individual did itemize deductions in the tax year in which the refund is for and the individual included state income taxes paid as an itemized deduction, then the refund is included in the taxpayer's gross income in the year received. This is because the taxpayer in reality benefited from a deduction in the prior tax year that turned out to be too large.

EXAMPLE 8.1. Ned, a single individual, did not itemize his deductions in Year 1; rather, he took the standard deduction. Ned paid a total of $1,700 in state income taxes in Year 1. During the first part of Year 2, Ned completed his state income tax return for Year 1 and he determined his actual state income tax liability was $1,300. He consequently received a $400 state income tax refund from his state in Year 2 for his overpayment of Year 1 state income taxes. When Ned completes his federal income tax return for Year 2, does Ned include the $400 state income tax refund in his gross income?

Answer: No. Since Ned took the standard deduction in Year 1, he received no tax benefit for the $1,700 in state income taxes that he paid.

EXAMPLE 8.2. Marsha, a single individual, itemized her deduction in Year 1. As part of the $26,000 in itemized deductions, $5,400 was for state income taxes that she paid. During the first part of Year 2, Marsha completed her state income tax return for Year 1 and she determined her actual state income tax liability was $4,900. She consequently received a $500 state income tax refund from her state in Year 2 for her overpayment of Year 1 state income taxes. When Marsha completes her federal income tax return for Year 2, does Marsha include the $500 state income tax refund in her gross income?

Answer: Yes. Since Marsha received a tax benefit by deducting $5,400 as an itemized deduction in Year 1, the refund of $500 is included in her gross income in Year 2.

Some unique situations may occur where an individual need only include a partial amount of the refund in her gross income, but we will not discuss those situations here.

This discussion regarding the tax treatment of state income tax refunds is illustrative of the **tax benefit rule**. This rule basically provides that if a taxpayer recovers a previous cost and that cost provided no tax benefit during the year incurred, then the recovery of that cost is not included in gross income. If the previous cost did provide a tax benefit (*i.e.*, reduction in tax liability) in the year paid, then any recovery of that cost is included in the taxpayer's gross income. This concept is broadly applicable and often applies in cases other than just state income tax refunds (*e.g.*, receiving a reimbursement for medical expenses that were previously deducted as itemized deductions).

C. ALIMONY

In many divorce situations, one spouse will pay the other spouse alimony and child support payments. Are the payments for alimony and child support included in the gross income of the recipient spouse?

SECTION 71. ALIMONY AND SEPARATE MAINTENANCE PAYMENTS

(a) **General rule.**—Gross income includes amounts received as alimony or separate maintenance payments.

. . .

(c) **Payments to support children.**—

(1) **In general.**—Subsection (a) shall not apply to that part of any payment which the terms of the divorce or separation instrument fix (in terms of an amount of money or a part of the payment) as a sum which is payable for the support of children of the payor spouse.

. . .

As Section 71 indicates, alimony payments are included in gross income to the recipient but payments representing child support are not included in the recipient's gross income. See Chapter 15 for a discussion of the deductibility of alimony and child support payments by the paying spouse. Property settlements between spouses pursuant to a divorce are not included in gross income.

D. Gambling and Lottery Winnings

Gambling and lottery winnings are included in an individual's gross income. In many situations a payer of gambling winnings must issue a Form W-2G to the winner. This form is included in the Appendix for your convenience. Gambling winnings may be reduced by gambling losses. These losses are generally treated as itemized deductions, however, and may be limited. Clearly, an individual must keep detailed records (diary of transactions, receipts, tickets, etc.) if the individual deducts gambling losses.

E. Cancellation of Indebtedness

If a creditor cancels the debt of a debtor, the general rule is that the amount of debt cancelled is included in the debtor's gross income. After all, the debtor is better off financially because of the discharge of debt. Several exceptions apply to this general rule, however. An individual may be able to exclude a discharge of debt in bankruptcy and insolvency situations, for example. Chapter 10 includes a discussion of these exceptions.

F. Income From Pass-Through Entities

Certain business entities, such as partnerships, limited liability companies, and "S" corporations are not subject to income tax at the entity level. Consequently, these entities are often called "pass-through" entities (or "flow-through" entities). The items of income, losses, expenses, credits, etc., of these pass-through entities are ultimately reported on the respective income tax returns of the owners (*e.g.*, partners, shareholders, etc.) of the entities.

EXAMPLE 8.3. Sheri and Ruperto are partners in a partnership. They have agreed to share the profits and losses of the partnership equally. The partnership earns $1,000 of net business income during the year. Does the *partnership* pay federal income taxes on this amount?

Answer: No. The partnership is a pass-through entity and is not subject to federal income taxes at the entity level.

Do Sheri and Ruperto include the income from the partnership in their respective gross incomes?

Answer: Yes. Both Sheri and Ruperto will each include their $500 respective share (50% × $1,000) of the partnership's net business income in their individual gross income.

The partnership is required to provide each of its partners a Schedule K-1 each year so that the partner knows the items that constitute his or her share of the partnership's income (or loss). The partner then takes the information from the Schedule K-1 and reports the items on the proper line of his or her individual Form 1040. A Schedule K-1 is provided in the Appendix for your convenience.

For a more detailed discussion of the taxation of business entities, please see the *Business Entity Taxation* text by this author.

G. Treasure Finds

Assume that you are walking along a beach and you notice a curious object in the sand. You pick it up and look closely at what appears to be a very old coin from England. Later in the week you take it to an appraiser who specializes in rare coins. The appraiser says it is rare indeed and that it would probably sell for about $7,000 to a coin collector. Nevertheless, you choose to keep the coin rather than sell it. Must you include the value of the coin in your gross income this year?

Regulations issued by the United States Treasury Department help answer this question.

TREASURY REGULATION

Treasury Regulation Section 1.61–14. Miscellaneous Items of Gross Income.—

(a) . . . Treasure trove, to the extent of its value in United States currency, constitutes gross income for the taxable year in which it is reduced to undisputed possession.

. . .

Notice that the value of the treasure trove is included in gross income when it is "reduced to undisputed possession." Determining when the treasure trove has been reduced to undisputed possession can prove difficult in some situations. Also, some questions may arise as to the true value of the treasure trove. Nevertheless, the general rule is that such treasure finds must be included in gross income.

CHAPTER 8: QUESTIONS

1. *Prizes.* A prize is included in an individual's gross income except when?

2. *Awards.* An award is included in an individual's gross income except when?

3. *Income tax refunds.* Are federal income tax refunds included in an individual's gross income?

4. *Income tax refunds.* Are state income tax refunds included in an individual's gross income?

5. *Tax benefit rule.* What is the tax benefit rule? Give an example of when it applies.

6. *Alimony and child support.* Does a recipient of alimony and child support include the amounts received in gross income?

7. *Property settlement pursuant to divorce.* If a spouse receives a property settlement pursuant to a divorce, is the value of the property received included in the spouse's gross income?

8. *Gambling winnings.* Generally, may an individual reduce his or her gambling winnings by gambling loss deductions?

9. *Cancellation of indebtedness.* Mel is having trouble paying his debts. He asks one of his creditors to discharge the $700 he owes to the creditor. The creditor agrees to do so. As a general rule, must Mel include the $700 cancellation of indebtedness in his gross income?

10. *Income from pass-through entities.* Name three entities that are treated as pass-through entities.

11. *Income from pass-through entities.* How is the net income (or loss) of a pass-through entity treated for income tax purposes?

12. *Income from pass-through entities.* How does a partner in a partnership know what his or her share of the partnership's income is for the year?

13. *Treasure trove.* Is a treasure find included in the finder's gross income? If so, when?

Chapter 9

Transactions in Property

In Chapter 7 we discussed that an individual must include income from any net capital gains in his or her gross income. Net long-term capital gains benefit from lower tax rates. Not all sales of property constitute capital gains (or losses), however. Some sales result in ordinary income. In this chapter we discuss the terminology involved in the sale or exchange of assets as well as a discussion of the three major classifications of assets: capital assets, ordinary assets, and Section 1231 assets.

A. TERMINOLOGY

When a taxpayer experiences a **realization event**, the tax consequences of the event must be analyzed. An example of a realization event is the sale or exchange of an asset. Before the tax consequences of a realization event can be determined fully, the taxpayer must calculate the gain or loss on the transaction. The Code informs us how to do that.

INTERNAL REVENUE CODE

SECTION 1001. DETERMINATION OF AMOUNT OF AND RECOGNITION OF GAIN OR LOSS

(a) **Computation of gain or loss.**—The gain from the sale or other disposition of property shall be the excess of the amount realized therefrom over the adjusted basis provided in section 1011 for determining gain, and the loss shall be the excess of the adjusted basis provided in such section for determining loss over the amount realized.

(b) **Amount realized.**—The amount realized from the sale or other disposition of property shall be the sum of any money received plus the fair market value of the property (other than money) received. . . .

(c) **Recognition of gain or loss.**—Except as otherwise provided in this subtitle, the entire amount of the gain or loss, determined under this section, on the sale or exchange of property shall be recognized.

. . .

Thus, to calculate the gain or loss, the taxpayer takes the **amount realized** (total value of money and other property received) from the transaction and subtracts the **adjusted basis** (tax basis) in the asset sold. If the result is positive, the taxpayer has a **gain realized**; if the result is negative, the taxpayer has a **loss realized**. As a general rule, a taxpayer **recognizes** the gain or loss realized and reports it on his or her tax return and pays taxes on the gain or deducts the loss. Not surprisingly, the Code provides several exceptions relating to the general gain/loss recognition rule, however, and in some situations gain or loss is not *recognized* even if gain or loss is *realized*. Some of these exceptions will be discussed throughout this text in various chapters.

To calculate gain or loss, the taxpayer must know his or her tax basis. Taxpayers have a tax basis in every asset they own (*e.g.*, your car, your house, your toothbrush, shares of stock in a corporation, etc.). In most situations the taxpayer's tax basis in an asset is what the taxpayer paid for the asset (*i.e.*, a "cost" basis). In some situations, the taxpayer's tax basis in the asset could be different than what the taxpayer paid for it because, for example, the taxpayer has depreciated the asset and the tax basis has been reduced (see Chapter 12 for a discussion of depreciation). Given the possibility that a taxpayer's tax basis in property could be different than what the taxpayer paid for the property, the Code frequently refers to a taxpayer's tax basis as an "adjusted" basis.

EXAMPLE 9.1. Omar owns a parcel of land. Omar purchased the land ten years ago for $30,000. His tax basis in the land is still $30,000. A buyer, Darla, pays Omar $40,000 in cash for the land. What is Omar's amount realized?

Answer: $40,000. The *amount realized* is the total money received plus the fair market value of any other property received.

What is Omar's gain or loss realized?

Answer: $10,000 gain realized. The *gain or loss realized* on a transaction is determined by taking the amount realized ($40,000 in this case) minus the tax basis of the property Omar transferred ($30,000). Omar has a gain because the amount realized exceeds his tax basis in the property.

What is Omar's gain recognized?

Answer: $10,000 gain recognized. The general rule is that any gain or loss realized must be recognized unless the Code provides otherwise. Given the facts in Omar's situation, the Code does not allow Omar to avoid recognizing this gain.

One important concept that we must cover here is when a property transaction involves a liability. The courts have determined that if a taxpayer is relieved of a liability as part of the transaction, the amount of the debt relief is included in the taxpayer's *amount realized.*

EXAMPLE 9.2. Sandra owns a parcel of land. She purchased the land five years ago for $20,000. Sandra borrowed money from a bank to purchase the land. The amount she now owes the bank is $12,000. Sandra's tax basis in the land is still $20,000. A buyer, Rosa, pays Sandra $23,000 in cash plus Rosa agrees to assume the obligation to pay the $12,000 remaining liability as part of the transaction. What is Sandra's amount realized?

Answer: $35,000. Sandra includes the amount of money received from Rosa ($23,000) plus she includes in her amount realized the relief of the liability ($12,000). Thus, Sandra has an amount realized of $35,000 ($23,000 + $12,000).

What is Sandra's gain realized?

Answer: $15,000. Sandra's amount realized is $35,000 and her tax basis is $20,000. Thus, her gain realized is $15,000 ($35,000 – $20,000).

What is Sandra's gain recognized?

Answer: $15,000. The Code does not allow Sandra to avoid recognizing the $15,000 gain in this situation.

Some situations where a seller's gain *realized* is not *recognized* include, for example, the sale of a personal residence (discussed in detail in Chapter 24) and transferring property in exchange for other property of "like kind" (discussed in detail in Chapter 22).

The purchaser of property has an initial tax basis equal to the amount of money and the fair market value of other property used to purchase the property. The purchaser also includes in his or her initial cost basis the amount of any liabilities of the seller that the purchaser assumed.

B. Classification of Assets

Gains and losses recognized on the sale of assets are classified as either "capital" (*i.e.*, capital gain or capital loss) or "ordinary" (*i.e.*, ordinary income or ordinary loss). Whether gains or losses are classified as "capital" or "ordinary" depends on the type of asset sold or exchanged. The three main classifications of assets are: (1) capital assets; (2) ordinary assets; and (3) Section 1231 assets.

1. Capital Assets

The Code defines "capital asset" in Section 1221.

INTERNAL REVENUE CODE

SECTION 1221. CAPITAL ASSET DEFINED

(a) **In general.**—For purposes of this subtitle, the term "capital asset" means property held by the taxpayer (whether or not connected with his trade or business), but does not include–

(1) stock in trade of the taxpayer or other property of a kind which would properly be included in the inventory of the taxpayer if on hand at the close of the taxable year, or property held by the taxpayer primarily for sale to customers in the ordinary course of his trade or business;

(2) property, used in his trade or business, of a character which is subject to the allowance for depreciation provided in section 167, or real property used in his trade or business;

. . .

(4) accounts or notes receivable acquired in the ordinary course of trade or business for services rendered or from the sale of property described in paragraph (1);

. . .

Notice in Section 1221 that the Code defines a capital asset by defining what is *not* a capital asset. In other words, an asset is a capital asset unless it fits one of the categories listed in Code Section 1221.

2. Ordinary Assets

By reading Section 1221 we can see that inventory, accounts receivable and notes receivable acquired in the ordinary course of business are not capital assets. These assets are **ordinary assets**. The collection of accounts receivable or the sale of inventory will result in ordinary income, or in some cases, ordinary loss.

3. Section 1231 Assets

As a broad statement, a **Section 1231 asset** is an asset that is used in the taxpayer's trade or business, is subject to depreciation, and has been held by the taxpayer for more than one year. Also, land used in a trade or business can be a Section 1231 asset even though land is not subject to depreciation. The Code instructs us how to treat gains and losses from the sale of Section 1231 assets.

INTERNAL REVENUE CODE

SECTION 1231. PROPERTY USED IN THE TRADE OR BUSINESS AND INVOLUNTARY CONVERSIONS

(a) **General rule.**—

(1) **Gains exceed losses.**—If—

(A) the section 1231 gains for any taxable year, exceed

(B) the section 1231 losses for such taxable year, such gains and losses shall be treated as long-term capital gains or long-term capital losses, as the case may be.

(2) **Gains do not exceed losses.**—If—

(A) the section 1231 gains for any taxable year, do not exceed

(B) the section 1231 losses for such taxable year, such gains and losses shall not be treated as gains and losses from sales or exchanges of capital assets.

. . .

Thus, as a general rule, gains on the sale of Section 1231 assets are classified as long-term *capital* gains. Losses on the sale of Section 1231 assets will result in *ordinary* losses. Some exceptions apply to these general rules, however (see the "look-back" rule discussed in this section of the text and also Chapter 22, which discusses the possible recognition of ordinary income due to "depreciation recapture").

At this point, we need to know a bit more detail regarding what a Section 1231 asset is. Code Section 1221 said that it was basically a depreciable asset (or land) used in a trade or business. Fortunately, Code Section 1231 provides a little more detail.

INTERNAL REVENUE CODE

SECTION 1231. PROPERTY USED IN THE TRADE OR BUSINESS AND INVOLUNTARY CONVERSIONS

. . .

(b) **Definition of property used in the trade or business.**—For purposes of this section—

(1) **General rule.**—The term "property used in the trade or business" means property used in the trade or business, of a character which is subject to the allowance for depreciation provided in section 167, held for more than 1 year, and real property used in the trade or business, held for more than 1 year, which is not—

(A) property of a kind which would properly be includible in the inventory of the taxpayer if on hand at the close of the taxable year,

(B) property held by the taxpayer primarily for sale to customers in the ordinary course of his trade or business; ...

Again, notice that in order for an asset to be considered a Section 1231 asset it must be used in the taxpayer's trade or business *and* be held for more than one year. Moreover, inventory and other assets held primarily for sale to customers are not Section 1231 assets.

Consider the following examples in determining the classification of an asset as a capital asset, ordinary asset, or Section 1231 asset.

EXAMPLE 9.3. Rita owns an automobile that she uses strictly for personal use. She purchased the automobile three years ago. Is the automobile a capital asset, ordinary asset, or Section 1231 asset?

Answer: Capital asset. The automobile does not fit any of the classifications in Section 1221 that are listed as *not* capital assets. It is not inventory nor is it used in a trade or business.

EXAMPLE 9.4. Rita owns a small business. One of the assets she owns and uses exclusively in her business is an automobile. She purchased the automobile three years ago and has used it in the business since then. Is the automobile a capital asset, ordinary asset, or Section 1231 asset?

Answer: Section 1231 asset. The automobile is a depreciable asset used in her business and she has held the asset for longer than one year.

EXAMPLE 9.5. Rita owns a small car dealership. The automobiles she sells are considered inventory for the business. Are the automobiles capital assets, ordinary assets, or Section 1231 assets?

Answer: Ordinary assets. Assets that constitute inventory are specifically excluded from both the definition of capital asset and the definition of Section 1231 asset.

As we discussed earlier in this chapter, gains on the sale of Section 1231 assets are generally treated as long-term capital gains. Section 1231 provides a "look-back" rule, however, that could cause some gains to be treated as ordinary income.

INTERNAL REVENUE CODE

SECTION 1231 PROPERTY USED IN THE TRADE OR BUSINESS AND INVOLUNTARY CONVERSIONS

. . .

(c) **Recapture of net ordinary losses.—**

(1) **In general.**—The net section 1231 gain for any taxable year shall be treated as ordinary income to the extent such gain does not exceed the non-recaptured net section 1231 losses.

(2) **Non-recaptured net section 1231 losses.**—For purposes of this subsection, the term "non-recaptured net section 1231 losses" means the excess of—

(A) the aggregate amount of the net section 1231 losses for the 5 most recent preceding taxable years beginning after December 31, 1981, over

(B) the portion of such losses taken into account under paragraph (1) for such preceding taxable years.

. . .

This look-back rule provides that any net Section 1231 gain is considered ordinary income in the current year to the extent that the taxpayer had any net Section 1231 losses in the previous 5 years.

Transactions involving the sale of Section 1231 assets are reported on Form 4797, a copy of which is provided in the Appendix for your convenience.

CHAPTER 9: QUESTIONS

1. *Terminology*. Please explain the meaning of the following terms:
   a. amount realized
   b. gain realized
   c. loss realized
   d. gain or loss recognized
   e. tax ("adjusted") basis

2. *Terminology*. Melinda owns land that is worth $20,000. The land has a liability of $12,000 attached to it. Melinda's tax basis in the land is $17,000. Samantha purchases the land from Melinda for $8,000 cash and also assumes the obligation to pay the liability.
   a. What is Melinda's amount realized?
   b. What is Melinda's gain or loss realized?
   c. What is Samantha's initial tax basis in the land?

3. *Classification of assets*. What are the three classifications of assets?

4. *Capital assets*. A friend of yours asks you what a capital asset is. How would you explain it?

5. *Ordinary assets*. What types of assets typically constitute ordinary assets?

6. *Section 1231 asset*. What is a Section 1231 asset?

7. *Section 1231 assets*. As a general rule, how is a net Section 1231 gain treated for income tax purposes?

8. *Section 1231 assets*. How are net Section 1231 losses treated for income tax purposes?

9. *Section 1231 assets*. If a taxpayer has net Section 1231 losses in the previous five years, how are net Section 1231 gains in the current year treated?

PART 4

Exclusions from Gross Income

Chapter 10

Common Exclusions from Gross Income

In Chapters 10 and 11 we shift focus from specific *inclusions* in gross income to specific *exclusions* from gross income. Remember the general rule is that gross income includes income from whatever source derived unless the Code specifically excludes it.

A. Gifts and Inheritances

Gifts and inheritances are excluded from the recipient's gross income.

INTERNAL REVENUE CODE

SECTION 102. GIFTS AND INHERITANCES

(a) **General rule.**—Gross income does not include the value of property acquired by gift, bequest, devise, or inheritance.

. . .

(c) **Employee gifts.**—

(1) **In general.**—Subsection (a) shall not exclude from gross income any amount transferred by or for an employer to, or for the benefit of, an employee.

. . .

A **bequest** is when someone makes a gift of personal property by will. A **devise** is when someone makes a gift of real property by will. These transfers occur upon the death of the person wishing to make the gift.

In some situations, the *giver* of a gift may be subject to *gift* tax. A discussion of the gift tax (and estate tax) is included in Chapter 26.

B. Life Insurance Proceeds

Life insurance proceeds are excluded from the recipient's gross income.

INTERNAL REVENUE CODE

SECTION 101. CERTAIN DEATH BENEFITS

(a) **Proceeds of life insurance contracts payable by reason of death.**—

(1) **General rule.**—Except as otherwise provided in paragraph (2), subsection (d), subsection (f), and subsection (j), gross income does not include amounts received (whether in a single sum or otherwise) under a life insurance contract, if such amounts are paid by reason of the death of the insured.

. . .

Notice that there are a few exceptions relating to proceeds from life insurance contracts. These exceptions relate to some unique situations involving the sale of life insurance contracts and employer-owned life insurance contracts. We will not discuss these detailed exceptions here.

C. Tax-Exempt Interest

In general, interest income is included in gross income. Section 103 provides that some types of interest, however, are tax-exempt and thus not included in the taxpayer's gross income.

INTERNAL REVENUE CODE

SECTION 103. INTEREST ON STATE AND LOCAL BONDS

(a) **Exclusion.**—Except as provided in subsection (b), gross income does not include interest on any State or local bond.

. . .

(c) **Definitions.**—For purposes of this section and part IV—

(1) State and local bond.—The term "State or local bond" means an obligation of a State or political subdivision thereof.

(2) State.—The term "State" includes the District of Columbia and any possession of the United States.

In accordance with Section 103, the federal government does not tax interest on state and local bonds. Many states, however, do tax interest on state and local bonds for *state* income tax purposes.

Interest on federal Series EE bonds is also excluded from an individual's gross income if the interest earned on the bond is used to pay qualified higher education expenses such as tuition and fees (books and room and board are not qualified expenses). Interest on other federal bonds is included in gross income.

D. SCHOLARSHIPS

As a general rule, the recipient of a qualified scholarship may exclude the amount of the scholarship from the individual's gross income.

INTERNAL REVENUE CODE

SECTION 117. QUALIFIED SCHOLARSHIPS

(a) **General rule.**—Gross income does not include any amount received as a qualified scholarship by an individual who is a candidate for a degree at an educational organization described in section 170(b)(1)(A)(ii).

(b) **Qualified scholarship.**—For purposes of this section—

(1) **In general.**—The term "qualified scholarship" means any amount received by an individual as a scholarship or fellowship grant to the extent the individual establishes that, in accordance with the conditions of the grant, such amount was used for qualified tuition and related expenses.

(2) **Qualified tuition and related expenses.**—For purposes of paragraph (1), the term "qualified tuition and related expenses" means—

(A) tuition and fees required for the enrollment or attendance of a student at an educational organization described in section 170(b)(1)(A)(ii), and

(B) fees, books, supplies, and equipment required for courses of instruction at such an educational organization.

. . .

Notice the reference to Section 170(b)(1)(A)(ii) a couple of times in Section 117. This cross-reference basically provides that the educational organization must be one that maintains a regular faculty and has regularly enrolled students.

Section 117 also clarifies that generally if a student receives payment for teaching, research, or other services, such payment is not excluded from gross income (some exceptions). Moreover, to the extent the scholarship amount covers room and board, the amount is not excluded from gross income.

Benefits of certain tuition reduction plans for employees of educational organizations may also qualify for exclusion from the employee's gross income.

E. Payment on Account of Injury and Sickness

We will divide the discussion of payment on account of injury and sickness into two categories: (1) workers' compensation and (2) other payments on account of personal injury and sickness.

1. Workers' Compensation

An individual may receive payment from a state's workers' compensation plan if the individual is injured while in the scope of his or her employment duties. Such payments are excluded from the individual's gross income.

INTERNAL REVENUE CODE

SECTION 104. COMPENSATION FOR INJURIES OR SICKNESS

(a) **In general.**—Except in the case of amounts attributable to (and not in excess of) deductions allowed under section 213 (relating to medical, etc., expenses) for any prior taxable year, gross income does not include—

(1) amounts received under workmen's compensation acts as compensation for personal injuries or sickness;

. . .

2. Other Payments on Account of Personal Injury or Sickness

Suppose Ally is walking along a sidewalk and someone's dog charges her and bites her, causing her significant personal injury. Ally sues the dog owner. Suppose further Ally and the dog-owner settle the dispute for $10,000. Does Ally include this amount in her gross income?

Suppose in another situation Carson receives a payment of $50,000 as an award from a jury because he won a lawsuit for a defamation claim he had against someone. Does Carson include the amount in his gross income? Section 104 helps us answer these questions.

INTERNAL REVENUE CODE

SECTION 104. COMPENSATION FOR INJURIES OR SICKNESS

(a) **In general.**—Except in the case of amounts attributable to (and not in excess of) deductions allowed under section 213 (relating to medical, etc., expenses) for any prior taxable year, gross income does not include—

. . .

(2) the amount of any damages (other than punitive damages) received (whether by suit or agreement and whether as lump sums or as periodic payments) on account of personal physical injuries or physical sickness;

. . .

Notice that to be excluded from gross income the payment or settlement received must be on account of personal *physical* injuries or *physical* sickness and cannot constitute punitive damages (as opposed to compensatory damages). Punitive damages are awarded in order to punish the defendant for the defendant's conduct. Compensatory damages are to compensate the plaintiff for his or her injury. Thus, in our hypothetical questions posed earlier regarding the dog bite and the defamation case, the settlement for the dog bite would be excluded from Ally's gross income (assuming the settlement did not include punitive damages) but not from Carson's gross income (because the damages he received were not because of a *physical* injury).

F. Income from the Discharge of Debt

We discussed in Chapter 8 that as a general rule a taxpayer's gross income includes any cancellation of indebtedness. Section 108 provides several exceptions to this general rule and allows some discharge of indebtedness to be excluded from the taxpayer's gross income. Note: the terms "cancellation of indebtedness" and "discharge of indebtedness" are often used interchangeably.

INTERNAL REVENUE CODE

Section 108. Income from Discharge of Indebtedness

(a) **Exclusion from gross income.—**

(1) **In general.**—Gross income does not include any amount which (but for this subsection) would be includible in gross income by reason of the discharge (in whole or in part) of indebtedness of the taxpayer if—

(A) the discharge occurs in a title 11 case,

(B) the discharge occurs when the taxpayer is insolvent,

(C) the indebtedness discharged is qualified farm indebtedness,

(D) in the case of a taxpayer other than a C corporation, the indebtedness discharged is qualified real property business indebtedness, or

(E) the indebtedness discharged is qualified principal residence indebtedness which is discharged before January 1, 2014.

. . .

(f) **Student loans.**

(1) **In general.**—In the case of an individual, gross income does not include any amount which (but for this subsection) would be includible in gross income by reason of the discharge (in whole or in part) of any student loan if such discharge was pursuant to a

provision of such loan under which all or part of the indebtedness of the individual would be discharged if the individual worked for a certain period of time in certain professions for any of a broad class of employers.

. . .

Individuals report information related to the exclusion of discharge of indebtedness from gross income on Form 982. Creditors typically send the debtor a Form 1099-A that shows how much debt was cancelled. If the discharged debt was qualified principal residence indebtedness the creditor will typically send a Form 1099-C to the debtor. Forms 982, 1099-A, and Form 1099-C are included in the Appendix text for your convenience. One consequence of being allowed to exclude the cancellation of indebtedness from gross income is that the taxpayer must reduce the taxpayer's tax basis in certain property.

We will discuss four of the Section 108 exclusions here: (1) bankruptcy, (2) insolvency, (3) home mortgages, and (4) student loans.

1. Bankruptcy

Section 108 excludes from gross income amounts that are discharged from Title 11 cases. Remember from Chapter 1 that the United States Code consists of 51 titles. The Internal Revenue Code is Title 26. The Bankruptcy Code is Title 11. Thus, if a debtor's liabilities are discharged pursuant to a court order in a bankruptcy case, such discharge of debt is excluded from the taxpayer's gross income.

2. Insolvency

If the taxpayer is not in bankruptcy, but is insolvent, the cancellation of indebtedness is excluded from the taxpayer's gross income, but only to the extent of the insolvency. The term "insolvency" means the excess of the taxpayer's liabilities over the fair market value of the taxpayer's assets. If the discharge causes the taxpayer to become solvent, then the discharge would be gross income to the taxpayer to the extent of the taxpayer's newfound solvency.

EXAMPLE 10.1. Hunter has assets worth $50,000 and liabilities of $60,000. Assume that one of Hunter's creditors agrees to cancel a $12,000 debt that Hunter owes to the creditor. Can Hunter exclude the full $12,000 from his gross income?

Answer: No. Hunter is allowed to exclude $10,000 of the cancellation because of his insolvency. As a result of the cancellation, Hunter is now *solvent* by $2,000. Thus, Hunter must include $2,000 in his gross income.

3. Home Mortgages

The dramatic downturn in the economy a few years ago caused many people to owe more on their home than their home was worth. When the homeowners could not meet their monthly mortgage payments (*e.g.*, because of job loss, sickness, accumulating debt, etc.), the homeowners could not rely on equity in their homes to help mitigate the situation. This led many homeowners to default on their mortgages and face foreclosure. Lenders would foreclose on the home and discharge the remaining debt that the homeowners owed the lender. Of course, these foreclosures and cancellations of debt still occur.

The maximum amount of qualified principal residence indebtedness that can be excluded from an individual's gross income upon the cancellation of the indebtedness is $2,000,000 (married filing jointly). In order to qualify for the exclusion, the debt must have been secured by the residence and the residence must have been the individual's principal residence. As Code Section 108 indicates, this exclusion expired at the end of 2013. Congress may or may not extend this tax relief provision for future years.

4. Student Loans

Section 108(f) provides that if an individual agrees to provide services for a particular period of time in particular professions, the discharge of student loan indebtedness can be excluded from gross income. For example, if a medical doctor agrees to provide medical services at a hospital in a rural town, the student loan forgiveness may qualify for the exclusion from gross income.

G. Foreign Earned Income Exclusion

As a general rule, the United States requires that U.S. citizens and resident aliens include their worldwide income into gross income. Of course, this brings up the issue of income earned in a foreign country being taxed twice—once in the foreign country and once in the United States. The U.S. tax system attempts to mitigate this double-tax situation by providing foreign tax credits to taxpayers and by addressing the issue through tax treaties with foreign countries. The Code also provides for an election to exclude from gross income foreign earned income up to a certain amount. This exclusion is up to $99,200 for 2014, but is indexed for inflation each year. If the individual elects to exclude the income, the individual foregoes any applicable foreign tax credit (discussed in Chapter 19) that may be available to such income. As you might expect, the taxation of an individual's foreign income can possibly be quite detailed and complex. We will not discuss these details and complexities here.

H. Sale of a Personal Residence

If an individual realizes a gain on the sale of his or her personal residence, the individual may exclude such gain up to $250,000 (single) or $500,000 (married filing jointly). Individuals must meet various tests in order to qualify for this exclusion. A discussion of these tests and the tax consequences of selling a principal residence is included in Chapter 24.

CHAPTER 10: QUESTIONS

1. *Gifts*. Amanda makes a gift of $2,000 to Denzil. Does Denzil include the $2,000 in his gross income?

2. *Inheritances*. Soledad inherits $50,000 from her grandfather who died a few months ago. Does Soledad include the $50,000 in her gross income?

3. *Bequests and devises*. A friend of yours reads Section 102 of the Internal Revenue Code and then asks you, "What do the terms 'bequest' and 'devise' mean?" Please answer your friend's question.

4. *Life insurance proceeds*. Samuel receives $100,000 of life insurance proceeds due to the death of his father. Must Samuel include the $100,000 in his gross income?

5. *Tax-exempt interest*. If an individual receives interest on a federal Series EE bond, is the interest included in gross income?

6. *Tax-exempt interest*. If an individual receives interest on a state or local bond, is the interest included in gross income?

7. *Scholarships*. Camille received a $14,700 scholarship from City University. The scholarship was for $6,000 in tuition, $700 for books, and $8,000 for room and board. How much must Camille include in her gross income as a result of the scholarship?

8. *Personal injuries and sickness*. Shantelle receives a jury award of $125,000 for gender discrimination by her employer. The jury award specified that $50,000 was for compensatory damages and $75,000 was for punitive damages. How much of the award is included in Shantelle's gross income?

9. *Personal injuries and sickness*. Nate works at a construction site. Unfortunately, he was recently injured on the job when he slipped and fell. This past year he received $4,500 in worker's compensation benefits. Must Nate include that amount in his gross income?

10. *Personal injuries and sickness*. Explain the difference between compensatory damages and punitive damages.

11. *Cancellation of indebtedness*. Ritt purchased a set of golf clubs from a local golf shop for $1,500. Ritt paid $300 down and was to pay $300 per year for the next four years. Unfortunately, after Ritt purchased the golf clubs he ran into financial trouble and did not make his remaining payments totaling $1,200 to the golf shop. The golf shop tried to collect the money from Ritt to no avail. The golf shop ultimately decided to cancel Ritt's debt and take the loss rather than sue Ritt. Must Ritt include the $1,200 of cancelled debt into his gross income? Does your answer change if Ritt was insolvent at the time of the debt cancellation?

12. *Cancellation of indebtedness.* What does “insolvent” mean?

13. *Cancellation of indebtedness.* The Bankruptcy Code is Title ______ of the United States Code.

14. *Cancellation of home mortgage indebtedness.* What requirements must be met for an individual to be able to exclude from gross income the cancellation of home mortgage indebtedness?

15. *Cancellation of student loan indebtedness.* What requirements must be met for an individual to be able to exclude from gross income the cancellation of student loan indebtedness?

16. *Foreign earned income.* For the year 2014, an individual can elect to exclude from gross income up to what amount of the individual’s foreign earned income?

Chapter 11

Exclusion of Employer-Provided Employee Benefits

The Code provides for the exclusion from an employee's gross income the value of many employer-provided benefits. This chapter discusses several of them.

A. Accident and Health Plans

Employers increasingly offer health and accident plans that benefit their employees. Employers typically contribute at least some amount toward the cost of premiums for the insurance. Section 106 provides for the tax treatment of these employer-paid premiums.

INTERNAL REVENUE CODE

SECTION 106. CONTRIBUTIONS BY EMPLOYER TO ACCIDENT AND HEALTH PLANS

(a) **General rule**.—Except as otherwise provided in this section, gross income of an employee does not include employer-provided coverage under an accident or health plan.

. . .

Thus, premiums for health and accident insurance as well as benefits received by the employee under such insurance plan are excluded from an employee's gross income. Some exceptions apply to the general rule, but we will not discuss the exceptions here.

Disability insurance is treated a bit differently, even if it is part of a general health and accident insurance plan. As a general rule, although premiums paid by employers for disability insurance for employees are excluded from an employee's gross income, the actual disability benefits are included in the employee's gross income if and when such benefits are received. If an *employee* pays the premiums with after-tax dollars, however, then the benefits are generally not included in the employee's gross income.

B. Cafeteria Plans

An employee's specific needs of certain benefits obviously can vary from one employee to the next. Consequently, employers will often offer a plan that allows employees to select which benefits best fit their needs. These types of plans are called **cafeteria plans** (also sometimes called "flexible spending accounts"). Under a cafeteria plan an employee can choose, for example, between receiving cash or approved fringe benefits such as medical insurance, child care assistance, group-term life insurance, etc. Of course, if the employee chooses the cash option, then the employee includes that amount in gross income. If instead the employee chooses the fringe benefits under the plan then those amounts are excluded from the employee's gross income.

INTERNAL REVENUE CODE

SECTION 125. CAFETERIA PLANS

(a) **General rule.**—Except as provided in subsection (b), no amount shall be included in the gross income of a participant in a cafeteria plan solely because, under the plan, the participant may choose among the benefits of the plan.

. . .

If an employee does not use all of the money set aside for the qualified benefits, then the employee can carry over to the next year an amount up to $500 if the employer's plan allows for it.

C. Dependent Care Assistance

When many employees go to work they often have difficult choices to make regarding care for their dependents. Moreover, paying for such care can be costly. Some employers assist employees in paying for this care. Section 129 indicates whether the employee must include such employer assistance in the employee's gross income.

INTERNAL REVENUE CODE

SECTION 129. DEPENDENT CARE ASSISTANCE PROGRAMS

(a) **Exclusion.**—

(1) **In general.**—Gross income of an employee does not include amounts paid or incurred by the employer for dependent care assistance provided to such employee if the assistance is furnished pursuant to a program which is described in subsection (d).

(2) **Limitation of exclusion.**—

(A) In general.—The amount which may be excluded under paragraph (1) for dependent care assistance with respect to dependent care services provided during a taxable year shall not exceed $5,000 ($2,500 in the case of a separate return by a married individual).

. . .

As indicated, there is a limit of $5,000 that can be excluded per year. Additionally, the plan cannot discriminate in favor of highly compensated employees. As with most tax-favored plans that we discuss in this chapter, an employer must meet strict requirements with respect to the plan (*e.g.*, must be in writing, must inform employees, cannot discriminate, etc.).

D. Educational Assistance

The Internal Revenue Code contains many provisions (*e.g.*, exclusions, deductions and credits) encouraging education. Some employers will pay or reimburse the tuition costs of employees. In these cases, it is possible the amount paid by the employer is excluded from the employee's gross income.

INTERNAL REVENUE CODE

SECTION 127. EDUCATIONAL ASSISTANCE PROGRAMS

(a) **Exclusion from gross income.**—

(1) **In general.**—Gross income of an employee does not include amounts paid or expenses incurred by the employer for educational assistance to the employee if the assistance is furnished pursuant to a program which is described in subsection (b).

(2) **$5,250 maximum exclusion.**—If, but for this paragraph, this section would exclude from gross income more than $5,250 of educational assistance furnished to an individual during a calendar year, this section shall apply only to the first $5,250 of such assistance so furnished.

. . .

The plan cannot discriminate in favor of highly compensated employees and employers must notify employees of the plan. The limit is $5,250 per calendar year per employee. Allowed costs include tuition, fees, books, supplies, and equipment, but not meals, lodging, and transportation.

E. Adoption Assistance

Payments made by an employer for qualified adoption expenses of an employee may be excluded from the employee's gross income.

INTERNAL REVENUE CODE

SECTION 137. ADOPTION ASSISTANCE PROGRAMS

(a) **Exclusion.**—

(1) **In general.**—Gross income of an employee does not include amounts paid or expenses incurred by the employer for qualified adoption expenses in connection with the adoption of a child by an employee if such amounts are furnished pursuant to an adoption assistance program.

. . .

The amount that can be excluded from an employee's income is set at $10,000, but that amount is adjusted each year for inflation ($13,190 for 2014). Also, the plan cannot discriminate in favor of highly compensated employees. The exclusion phases-out for higher income taxpayers.

F. Retirement Plan Contributions

If an employer contributes funds into a qualified retirement plan set up for the benefit of employees, such contributions are excluded (up to certain limits) from the employee's gross income. The growth over time of the value of an employee's savings in a qualified retirement account is also not included in the employee's gross income until the employee withdraws the money. Employers have a wide variety of options in providing additional compensation to employees through pension plans, 401(k) plans, employee stock ownership plans (ESOPs), etc. Plans that do not specifically meet Internal Revenue Code requirements are considered nonqualified plans and typically do not enjoy tax-favored status. We address specific deferred compensation arrangements and retirement plans in Chapter 23.

G. Meals and Lodging

Suppose you accept a job as a hotel manager. Your employer expects you to be available at all hours as much as is reasonably possible to take care of emergencies that may occur. Consequently, your employer indicates that as a condition of your employment, you must live in a hotel suite on site. Is the value of this housing included in your gross income? Section 119 provides the answer.

INTERNAL REVENUE CODE

SECTION 119. MEALS OR LODGING FURNISHED FOR THE CONVENIENCE OF THE EMPLOYER

(a) **Meals and lodging furnished to employee, his spouse, and his dependents, pursuant to employment.**—There shall be excluded from gross income of an employee the value of any meals or lodging furnished to him, his spouse, or any of his dependents by or on behalf of his employer for the convenience of the employer, but only if—

(1) in the case of meals, the meals are furnished on the business premises of the employer, or

(2) in the case of lodging, the employee is required to accept such lodging on the business premises of his employer as a condition of his employment.

. . .

Notice that the exclusion from gross income extends to meals provided by the employer on the employer's premises as long as the meals provided to the employees are for the convenience of the employer.

H. Section 132 Fringe Benefits

Several fringe benefits listed in Section 132 are excluded from an employee's gross income.

INTERNAL REVENUE CODE

SECTION 132. CERTAIN FRINGE BENEFITS

(a) **Exclusion from gross income.**—Gross income shall not include any fringe benefit which qualifies as a—

(1) no-additional-cost service,

(2) qualified employee discount,

(3) working condition fringe,

(4) de minimis fringe,

(5) qualified transportation fringe,

(6) qualified moving expense reimbursement,

(7) qualified retirement planning services,

. . .

A brief discussion of each of these fringe benefits is provided here.

1. No-Additional-Cost Service

If an employer provides a service to an employee and the service is normally offered to customers in the ordinary course of business of the employer, *and* the employer incurs no substantial additional cost, then the value of the service is excluded from the employee's gross income. This happens frequently for airline employees when a flight is not full. The airline may have a policy that allows employees to fly free if there is an available seat that would otherwise go unsold. Hotels may have similar policies for the hotel employees to stay for free in hotel rooms of the employer that may otherwise go unoccupied.

2. Qualified Employee Discount

Employers may offer goods or services to their employees at a discount. Generally, the employee can receive services from the employer at a discount up to 20% of the price the employer would normally charge to customers for the same services. Regarding the sale of products, an employee can exclude the value of a discount equal to the employer's gross profit percentage ((sales price – employer's cost) ÷ sales price). Of course, the goods or services must be of the type that the employer provides to customers in the ordinary course of business.

3. Working Condition Fringe

A working condition fringe includes things like a company car, employer-provided cell phone, and educational benefits the employer may provide (*e.g.*, in-house training). The value of these fringes is excluded from an employee's gross income. Of course, the value of the use of some of these items for *personal* purposes (*e.g.*, personal use of the company car) is generally included in an employee's gross income.

4. De Minimis Fringe

Cups of coffee, company picnics, occasional use of the office copy machine may qualify for exclusion from an employee's gross income because of the small value and administratively cumbersome nature of keeping track of these things for every employee.

5. Qualified Transportation Fringe

An employee can exclude from gross income the value of employer-provided transit passes, parking passes, bicycle expenses, etc. For example, the amount excludable in 2014 for employer-provided parking passes is $250 per month per employee.

6. Qualified Moving Expense Reimbursement

Employers often pay the moving expenses of an employee. If the employee's moving expenses would otherwise qualify as a deduction to the employee (see Chapter 14), then the employee can exclude from the employee's gross income the employer's payment of these expenses.

7. Qualified Retirement Planning Services

An employer may provide retirement planning services to employees in connection with a qualified retirement plan adopted by the employer. The value of such services is excluded from the employee's gross income.

All of these Section 132 fringe benefits as well as the other exclusions discussed in this chapter can be quite detailed. This chapter provides just a general coverage of these topics rather than the particular complexities of each specific exclusion. Consequently, IRS Publication 15-B, *Employer's Tax Guide to Fringe Benefits*, is included in tne Appendix for your convenience. Although Publication 15-B is quite lengthy, it will give you an opportunity to review in more detail the topics covered in this chapter. A tax consultant is wise to have a working knowledge of these fringe benefits and exclusions because both employers and employees frequently ask questions regarding these benefits.

I. Employee Achievement Awards

As we discussed in Chapter 8, awards are generally included in an individual's gross income. The value of the award can be excluded from gross income, however, if the award is an *employee achievement award.* Please refer to the discussion in Chapter 8 for a summary of the employee achievement award exclusion.

J. Group Term Life Insurance Premiums

Employers often are able to contract for favorable life insurance benefits for employees. Typically, the employer will pay all or part of the insurance premium on behalf of an employee. The Code allows for a certain amount of premiums paid on behalf of an employee to be excluded from the employee's gross income.

INTERNAL REVENUE CODE

Section 79. Group-Term Life Insurance Purchased for Employees

(a) **General rule.**—There shall be included in the gross income of an employee for the taxable year an amount equal to the cost of group-term life insurance on his life provided for part or all of such year under a policy (or policies) carried directly or indirectly by his employer (or employers); but only to the extent that such cost exceeds the sum of—

(1) the cost of $50,000 of such insurance, and

(2) the amount (if any) paid by the employee toward the purchase of such insurance.

. . .

Notice that the amount excluded is not $50,000. Rather, the amount excluded is the *cost of providing* up to $50,000 of life insurance proceeds upon the death of the employee. If the proceeds will be greater than $50,000 upon the death of the employee, then the employer includes in the employee's wages the cost of premiums paid by the employer for the excess insurance coverage.

Chapter 11: Questions

1. *Accident and health plans.* Explain the different tax treatment between benefits received under employer-provided health insurance versus disability insurance.

2. *Cafeteria plans.* What is a cafeteria plan?

3. *Cafeteria plans.* What happens to funds that an employee sets aside for use in a cafeteria plan but those funds are not used by the end of the year?

4. *Cafeteria plans.* Sometimes a "cafeteria plan" is referred to as a "______________________ __________ account."

5. *Dependent care assistance.* How much per year can be excluded from an employee's gross income under an employer-sponsored dependent care assistance plan?

6. *Educational assistance.* How much per year can be excluded from an employee's gross income under an employer-sponsored educational assistance plan?

7. *Meals & lodging.* Under what circumstances can employer-provided meals and lodging be excluded from an employee's gross income?

8. *Section 132 fringe benefits.* Explain the "no-additional cost" fringe benefit.

9. *Section 132 fringe benefits.* Explain the "qualified employee discount" fringe benefit.

10. *Section 132 fringe benefits.* Explain the "working condition" fringe benefit.

11. *Section 132 fringe benefits.* Explain the "de minimis" fringe benefit.

12. *Section 132 fringe benefits.* Explain the "qualified transportation" fringe benefit.

13. *Section 132 fringe benefits.* Explain the "qualified moving expense reimbursement" fringe benefit.

14. *Section 132 fringe benefits.* Explain the "qualified retirement planning services" fringe benefit.

15. *Group-term life insurance.* An employee can exclude the value of employer-paid premiums that provide what dollar amount of life insurance benefits to the employee?

PART 5

Deductions in Arriving at Adjusted Gross Income (Deductions "For" AGI)

Chapter 12

Common Business Deductions

We now shift our focus from exclusions from gross income to deductions from *gross income* in arriving at *adjusted gross income* (AGI). These deductions are often called deductions "for AGI" or "above-the-line" deductions (*i.e.*, the "line" being AGI). Now may also be a good time for you to review the individual income tax formula set forth in Chapter 2 and to review the first page of IRS Form 1040. In Chapters 12 through 15 we discuss deductions "for" AGI. This chapter addresses common *business* deductions that are "for" AGI.

A. Ordinary and Necessary Business Expenses

Profits from a business conducted by an individual are subject to income tax. But when determining the amount of income subject to tax, the business subtracts ordinary and necessary expenses incurred by the business.

INTERNAL REVENUE CODE

SECTION 162. TRADE OR BUSINESS EXPENSES

(a) **In general.**—There shall be allowed as a deduction all the ordinary and necessary expenses paid or incurred during the taxable year in carrying on any trade or business.

. . .

The United States Supreme Court has indicated that an "ordinary" expense is one that is *usual or customary* in the context of the type of trade or business the person operates. The term "necessary" is interpreted to mean that the expense is *appropriate and helpful* in the business's attempt to generate revenue.

Code Section 162 does identify some specific expenses as nondeductible for income tax purposes. These expenses include, with some exceptions, illegal payments and kickbacks to government officials, lobbying and political expenditures, fines and penalties levied on the business for violating a law, among others.

B. Travel and Transportation Expenses

A business almost always will incur travel and transportation expenses by its officers and employees in pursuit of business profits. Personal travel and transportation expenses unrelated to business, however, are not tax deductible. Historically, taxpayers have been aggressive as to what constitutes *business* travel and transportation compared to what constitutes *personal* travel and transportation. Consequently, Congress has had to set forth detailed rules as to when travel and transportation expenses are deductible.

1. Travel

Suppose the owner of a business (sole proprietorship) takes a two-week trip to New Zealand solely to rest and relax. She takes her cell phone with her in order to address any critical business issues that may arise back home during her absence from the company. Is her airfare, hotel, meals, etc., deductible for income tax purposes? What if she attends a two-day business seminar while she is there? What if she attends a ten-day business seminar while she is there?

You can see that whether a trip is primarily for business purposes or for personal purposes may be difficult to determine. The tax law provides that if a taxpayer travels "away from home in pursuit of a trade or business," then such expenses are deductible business expenses. Some difficultly arises relating to the definition of "away from home." A person's tax home is the city or general area where his or her trade or business is located, not where his or her personal residence is. A taxpayer must be away from home a length of time that is temporary and is long enough to require sleep or rest while away. If being away from home is due to a permanent or indefinite assignment, then the trip is not "temporary" and the travel expenses would not be deductible.

Once the taxpayer concludes that the travel is temporarily away from home, then the taxpayer must determine whether the travel is for business purposes or personal purposes. If the travel is "primarily related" to business, then the travel costs (*e.g.*, airfare, hotel, etc.) are deductible. If the trip is not primarily related to business, then the travel costs are not deductible, but business expenses that may be incurred while at the destination are deductible. Moreover, in order for the travel expenses to be deductible, the travel normally cannot be extravagant. A specific discussion of the unique rules related to foreign travel, luxury water travel (*e.g.*, cruise ships, etc.), are not presented here.

If an employee incurs business travel costs and is not reimbursed by the employer, these costs are not deductible "for" AGI, but rather the employee treats them as miscellaneous itemized deductions "from" AGI. This is an unfavorable result for the employee since miscellaneous itemized deductions are deductible only to the extent they exceed 2% of the employee's AGI (see Chapter 18). If the employee is reimbursed by the employer, the expenses are "for" AGI deductions and the reimbursement is included in gross income. As a practical matter, however, this produces a "wash" and does not impact the employee for income tax purposes. In most cases in which the employee is reimbursed and the expenses are substantiated (pursuant to a "accountable" plan adopted by the employer), no income or expenses need be reported to the IRS by the employee.

2. Transportation

The term "transportation" is a more narrow term than "travel." Typically, transportation expenses are those incurred to do business locally while the taxpayer is not away from home. A common issue in this area is whether an individual can deduct expenses for commuting to work. The answer is generally 'no.' In some unique cases, however, commuting expenses may be deductible. For example, if an individual drives directly to a client's place of business rather than first driving to the office, the transportation costs incurred to get to the client's place of business may be deductible.

In determining the amount deductible for automobile transportation costs, an individual can use the actual costs incurred (*e.g.*, gas, oil, repairs, depreciation, etc.), or a standard mileage rate per mile. The IRS adjusts the standard mileage rate periodically (usually annually) to reflect gas prices and other related costs. The rate is 56 cents per mile for 2014.

Transportation costs incurred as part of a taxpayer's charitable activities and transportation costs incurred as part of receiving medical treatment may also be deductible subject to limitations (see Chapters 16 and 17).

As with travel expenses, any unreimbursed transportation expenses incurred by an employee for business purposes are deductible as a miscellaneous itemized deduction subject to the 2% of AGI threshold.

C. Expenses for Meals and Entertainment

A common business practice is to meet clients and customers for lunch or to take them to some sporting event or other entertainment. Are such expenses deductible for income tax purposes? Yes, in part. As you might imagine, Congress has imposed strict requirements and limitations with respect to the deductibility of meals and entertainment expenses.

Because of Congress is concerned about abuse of tax deductions for meals and entertainment, only 50% of the cost for business meals and entertainment is deductible. Additionally, strict requirements apply to substantiating the business purpose of the meals and entertainment. In short, the taxpayer must be able to substantiate the date, business purpose, cost, and the identity of the individuals who accompanied the taxpayer. This substantiation requirement is often done through receipts and writing down the necessary information on the back of the receipt. To be deductible, the expenses must not be lavish or extravagant and the taxpayer must generally be able to show that the expenses were "directly related to" or "associated with" a clear business purpose.

D. Depreciation and Amortization

Depreciation typically constitutes a significant deduction for most businesses. Depreciation deductions basically reflect the aging and wear and tear on assets in an attempt to generate profits. Depreciation allowances apply to tangible personal property and real property (except land). To be depreciable, such assets must be used in a trade or business or held for the production of income.

Assets used for personal purposes are not depreciable. *Intangible* personal property is not depreciable; rather, it is amortizable (see discussion on amortization later in this chapter).

INTERNAL REVENUE CODE

SECTION 167. DEPRECIATION

(a) **General rule.**—There shall be allowed as a depreciation deduction a reasonable allowance for the exhaustion, wear and tear (including a reasonable allowance for obsolescence)—
(1) of property used in the trade or business, or
(2) of property held for the production of income.

. . .

As an asset is depreciated, the asset's tax basis is reduced by the amount of the depreciation.

INTERNAL REVENUE CODE

SECTION 1016. ADJUSTMENTS TO BASIS

(a) **General rule.**— Proper adjustment in respect of the property shall in all cases be made—
(2) In respect of any period since February 28, 1913, for exhaustion, wear and tear, obsolescence, amortization, and depletion, to the extent of the amount—
(A) allowed as deductions in computing taxable income under this subtitle or prior income tax laws,

. . .

Since 1986, depreciation deductions have been determined by using the **Modified Accelerated Cost Recovery System (MACRS).**

INTERNAL REVENUE CODE

SECTION 168. ACCELERATED COST RECOVERY SYSTEM

(a) **General rule.**—Except as otherwise provided in this section, the depreciation deduction provided by section 167(a) for any tangible property shall be determined by using—
(1) the applicable depreciation method,
(2) the applicable recovery period, and
(3) the applicable convention.

. . .

Notice that Section 168 provides three key terms that we must understand in order to handle depreciation issues: (1) depreciation method; (2) recovery period; and (3) convention.

1. Depreciation Methods

MACRS provides for three main **depreciation methods**:

- the 200 percent declining balance method switching to the straight line method for the first taxable year for which using the straight line method will provide a larger depreciation allowance
- the 150 percent declining balance method
- the straight line method

One of these three methods is used to depreciate business property. The proper method depends on whether the property is personal property or real property.

i. Tangible Personal Property

The 200% declining balance method applies to personal property with recovery periods of 3, 5, 7, and 10 years (see discussion of recovery periods). With some exceptions, the 150% method applies to property that has a recovery period of 15 or 20 years.

ii. Real Property

Real property except for land is depreciated using the straight line method. Land is not depreciable.

2. Recovery Periods

The taxpayer must also determine the particular asset's **recovery period**. The IRS provides guidance as to which recovery period an asset falls (*e.g.*, 3, 5, 7, 10, 15, 20, 27.5, or 39). The recovery period is based upon an asset's **class life**.

i. Tangible Personal Property

Most business assets fall into the 3-year, 5-year, or 7-year recovery period.

- 3-year property includes assets with a class life of four years or less. Not many assets fall into this category, but small tools are the most common assets in this category.
- 5-year property includes assets with a class life of five to nine years. This includes computers, cars, trucks, and certain research equipment.
- 7-year property includes assets with a class life of ten to 15 years. This includes office furniture, most machinery, horses, and most other assets that don't specifically fall into another category.

ii. Real Property

Depreciable real property basically falls into two categories: nonresidential real property and residential rental property.

- Residential rental property is depreciated over a recovery period of 27.5 years.
- Nonresidential real property is depreciated over a recovery period of 39 years.

3. Conventions

Depreciation is allowed beginning when an asset is "placed in service" (not necessarily when it is purchased). To simplify when depreciation deductions can start, the Code provides for the **half-year convention**, **mid-quarter convention**, and **mid-month convention**.

i. Tangible Personal Property

The half-year convention generally applies to tangible personal property. This means that regardless of when the asset was placed in service during the year, it will be deemed to have been placed in service on July 1 (for a calendar year taxpayer). To prevent manipulation of this provision, the Code requires a mid-quarter provision to apply if more than 40% of the cost of all personal property placed in service during the year was in the last quarter of the year.

ii. Real Property

The mid-month convention applies to real property. This means that regardless of when the asset was placed in service during the month, it will be deemed to have been placed in service on the 15th day of the month.

We have now completed our discussion of the important topics of depreciation method, applicable recovery period, and applicable convention. Fortunately, the IRS has provided depreciation tables to assist in calculating depreciation. These tables already incorporate the applicable method, recovery period, and convention. Some of these tables are provided in the Appendix for your reference.

4. Other Depreciation Issues

i. Property That Cannot Be Depreciated

The Code specifically identifies some assets that are not depreciable (in addition to land). Although there are not many assets that fall into this category, motion picture films, videotape, and sound recordings are examples. Also, as mentioned earlier, intangible assets (*e.g.*, acquired goodwill, trademarks, patents, etc.) are amortized and not depreciated.

ii. The Section 179 Election

Congress frequently modifies the Internal Revenue Code to provide incentives for businesses to invest in assets. Presumably, such incentive helps stimulate manufacturing of such assets and, as a result, provide jobs and business growth in the overall economy. Section 179 is one Code section primarily focused on providing tax incentives to purchase assets.

INTERNAL REVENUE CODE

SECTION 179. ELECTION TO EXPENSE CERTAIN DEPRECIABLE BUSINESS ASSETS

(a) **Treatment as expenses.**—A taxpayer may elect to treat the cost of any section 179 property as an expense which is not chargeable to capital account. Any cost so treated shall be allowed as a deduction for the taxable year in which the section 179 property is placed in service.

. . .

Notice that Section 179 allows the cost of property (subject to some limitations) to be expensed all in the current year rather than capitalized and depreciated over the asset's normal recovery period. This, of course, gives the business more deductions in the current year, which reduces taxable income. The dollar amount of property acquired that is eligible to be expensed changes frequently. For 2013, the deduction amount was capped at $500,000. Unless Congress acts, however, the $500,000 potential deduction amount revert to $25,000 in 2014. The assets that qualify for the Section 179 deduction include computers, office equipment, office furniture, other business equipment and machines, certain vehicles, etc.

iii. Bonus Depreciation

In addition to the Section 179 election to deduct the acquisition cost of qualified property, the Code in 2013 allowed an additional 50% ("bonus") depreciation deduction in the first year the property was placed in service. In other words, Section 179 applied first (if elected), then the taxpayer received a 50% bonus depreciation deduction to the extent of the remaining tax basis of the asset, then the normal depreciation rules applied.

EXAMPLE 12.1. Assume in 2013 Neil purchase one new asset for use in his business. The cost of the asset is $600,000. He places the asset in service in 2013. What deductions can Neil take in 2013 related to the purchase of this asset?

Answer: First, Neil can expense $500,000 in 2013 because of the Section 179 election. At that point the tax basis remaining is $100,000. Of this amount, Neil can expense $50,000 due to "bonus" depreciation. The remaining $50,000 tax basis is depreciated using the applicable MACRS depreciation method, recovery period, and convention.

The bonus depreciation provision expired at the end of 2013. Congress may or may not renew this provision for future years.

iv. Listed Property

Significant complication to the depreciation rules arises when an asset is used for both business and personal reasons. Assets that are most subject to this dual-use are identified as "listed property." Of course, depreciation is only allowed on the business use of an asset and not personal use. Thus, a taxpayer must keep records as to the business use versus personal use of the asset. The Code identifies listed property as follows:

INTERNAL REVENUE CODE

SECTION 280F. LIMITATION ON DEPRECIATION FOR LUXURY AUTOMOBILES; LIMITATION WHERE CERTAIN PROPERTY USED FOR PERSONAL PURPOSES

. . .

(d) **Definitions and special rules.**—For purposes of this section—

. . .

(4) Listed property.—

(A) In general.—Except as provided in subparagraph (B), the term "listed property" means—

(i) any passenger automobile,

(ii) any other property used as a means of transportation,

(iii) any property of a type generally used for purposes of entertainment, recreation, or amusement,

(iv) any computer or peripheral equipment ..., and

(v) any other property of a type specified by the Secretary by regulations.

. . .

If the asset is used more than 50% for business purposes, then the regular depreciation schedules apply (but only to the portion that is used for business purposes). If the asset is used 50% or less for business purposes, then the straight line depreciation method must be used (but only to the portion that is used for business purposes).

v. Other Terminology and Special Rules

In addition to all the depreciation issues we have discussed so far, we should be familiar with some other terminology and special rules.

MACRS was instituted in 1986. Between 1981 and 1986 the system was called **ACRS** (Accelerated Cost Recovery System). Prior to 1981, general depreciation principles contained in Section 167 applied, which are based on financial accounting depreciation rules. Nevertheless, you might often see references to the **General Depreciation System (GDS)**. Basically, the General Depreciation System is comprised of ACRS and MACRS, and is what you will use nearly all of the time. The **Alternative Depreciation System (ADS)** basically allows only straight line depreciation and applies to property used outside the United States. Moreover, a taxpayer may elect to use the ADS instead of the typical MACRS depreciation methods. A taxpayer may want to do this if accelerated depreciation deductions will not benefit the taxpayer (*e.g.*, taxpayer anticipates net operating losses and additional depreciation deductions will not reduce the taxpayer's income tax liability).

Businesses engaged in extracting natural resources (*e.g.,* oil, gas, iron ore, etc.) have *special* rules that apply. Rather than *depreciating* certain assets, these businesses follow the **depletion** rules that apply to certain drilling and mining costs that such businesses frequently encounter. A detailed discussion of depletion and related costs is not presented here.

5. Amortization

As mentioned earlier, intangible assets are not depreciated. Rather, intangible assets are **amortized**. Amortization is similar to straight line depreciation—the same amount is deducted for each time interval over the entire recovery period. Assets that are typically amortized are organizational costs, start-up costs, and other purchased intangible assets such as trademarks, patents, and goodwill, etc. (sometimes these intangible assets are called "Section 197 intangibles"). Intangible assets are typically amortized over a 15-year period.

6. IRS Form 4562

Not surprisingly, tax professionals deal with depreciation issues all the time. Nearly all businesses utilize depreciation deductions in ultimately determining the taxpayer's taxable income. Hence, becoming familiar with IRS Form 4562 (Depreciation and Amortization) is a good idea. This form is included in the Appendix for your convenience.

E. Other Common Business Expenses

While we have already discussed such common business expenses as travel, transportation, meals, entertainment, and depreciation, a business frequently has many more expenses that are deducted for income tax purposes. Such common expenses include advertising, utilities, rent, wages, insurance, repairs, supplies, and employee benefit programs. A detailed explanation of each of these expenses is not presented here. For sole proprietors, such expenses are listed on Schedule C of IRS Form 1040. A Schedule C is provided in the Appendix for your reference.

F. Home Office Expenses

Self-employed individuals and some employees often incur expenses because they have an office in their home. If certain requirements are met, these individuals may be able to deduct home office expenses. Not surprisingly, the rules applicable to home offices can be quite detailed because this is an area that taxpayers can often abuse.

1. In General

Code Section 280A sets forth some of the rules for home office deductions.

SECTION 280A. DISALLOWANCE OF CERTAIN EXPENSES IN CONNECTION WITH BUSINESS USE OF HOME, RENTAL OF VACATION HOMES, ETC.

(a) **General rule.**—Except as otherwise provided in this section, in the case of a taxpayer who is an individual or an S corporation, no deduction otherwise allowable under this chapter shall be allowed with respect to the use of a dwelling unit which is used by the taxpayer during the taxable year as a residence.

. . .

(c) **Exceptions for certain business or rental use; limitation on deductions for such use.**—

(1) Certain business use.—Subsection (a) shall not apply to any item to the extent such item is allocable to a portion of the dwelling unit which is exclusively used on a regular basis—

(A) as the principal place of business for any trade or business of the taxpayer,

(B) as a place of business which is used by patients, clients, or customers in meeting or dealing with the taxpayer in the normal course of his trade or business, or

(C) in the case of a separate structure which is not attached to the dwelling unit, in connection with the taxpayer's trade or business.

In the case of an employee, the preceding sentence shall apply only if the exclusive use referred to in the preceding sentence is for the convenience of his employer. For purposes of subparagraph (A), the term "principal place of business" includes a place of business which is used by the taxpayer for the administrative or management activities of any trade or business of the taxpayer if there is no other fixed location of such trade or business where the taxpayer conducts substantial administrative or management activities of such trade or business.

. . .

Notice that to be eligible for home office deductions, the office must be "exclusively" used as a place of business, etc. Thus, taxpayers should be careful not to use the particular room in the house for personal purposes in addition to business purposes. Moreover, the Code limits the deductions applicable to a home office to the extent of the gross income earned in the business (*i.e.*, the taxpayer cannot use losses generated by the home office expenses to offset income from other sources).

Expenses that are typically deducted for home offices are utilities, depreciation, property taxes, insurance, etc. Of course, only the portions of these expenses that apply to the business are deductible under the home office rules. Thus, the taxpayer must determine the percentage of the home that is used for business purposes. This is typically determined by square footage. IRS Form 8829 is the form in which a taxpayer claims deductions for home office use. Such form is included in the Appendix for your reference. Myriad other rules apply to home offices, such as particular provisions for day care services, storage use, and certain rental arrangements. Given the administrative burden for taxpayers to comply with the home office use rules, the IRS has issued a "safe harbor" rule to assist taxpayers in dealing with the complexity.

2. Safe Harbor

Effective January 1, 2013, the IRS provides a "safe harbor" for home office expenses. The safe harbor contains, in part, the following provisions:

IRS REVENUE PROCEDURE 2013-13

SECTION 1. PURPOSE

This revenue procedure provides an optional safe harbor method that individual taxpayers may use to determine the amount of deductible expenses attributable to certain business use of a residence during the taxable year. This safe harbor method is an alternative to the calculation, allocation, and substantiation of actual expenses for purposes of satisfying the requirements of § 280A of the Internal Revenue Code. This revenue procedure is effective for taxable years beginning on or after January 1, 2013.

. . .

SECTION 4. APPLICATION

(a) *Computation of the safe harbor amount*

(1) A taxpayer determines the amount of deductible expenses for a qualified business use of the home for the taxable year under the safe harbor method by multiplying the allowable square footage by the prescribed rate.

(2) The allowable square footage is the portion of a home used in a qualified business use of the home, but not to exceed 300 square feet.

(3) The prescribed rate is $5.00. The Service and the Treasury Department may update this rate from time to time as warranted.

(4) This safe harbor method is an alternative to the calculation and allocation of actual expenses otherwise required by § 280A. Accordingly, except as provided in section 4.04 of this revenue procedure, a taxpayer electing the safe harbor method for a taxable year cannot deduct any actual expenses related to the qualified business use of that home for that taxable year.

. . .

Notice that the safe harbor allows $5.00 per square foot with a maximum of 300 square feet of qualified business use. You can locate Revenue Procedure 2013–13 on the IRS website if you need further detail regarding the safe harbor.

CHAPTER 12: QUESTIONS

1. *Business expenses.* How has the United States Supreme Court interpreted the term "ordinary" in the context of business expenses?

2. *Business expenses.* How has the United States Supreme Court interpreted the term "necessary" in the context of business expenses?

3. *Business expenses.* Identify at least three types of business expenses that are specifically identified by Section 162 as nondeductible.

4. *Travel expenses.* A friend asks you whether he can deduct certain travel expenses. Please explain to your friend the general rules applicable to the deductibility of travel expenses.

5. *Transportation expenses.* Explain whether the expenses incurred to commute to work are deductible. What is the current rate per-mile that applies to business mileage?

6. *Travel and transportation expenses.* What is the disadvantage to an employee that incurs deductible travel and/or transportation expenses but is not reimbursed by her employer?

7. *Meals & entertainment.* The deductibility of the cost of meals and entertainment is limited. What is that limitation?

8. *Depreciation.* Explain what the following terms mean in the depreciation context:
   a. MACRS
   b depreciation method
   c. recovery period
   d. convention
   e. ADS
   f. GDS
   g. ACRS

9. *Depreciation.* Name the three main depreciation methods under MACRS.

10. *Depreciation.* What recovery periods are the most common for tangible personal property?

11. *Depreciation.* Typically, what convention is used for the depreciation of tangible personal property? What alternative convention is used if the taxpayer acquires more than 40% of the year's assets during the last quarter of the year?

12. *Depreciation.* What depreciation method is used for nonresidential real property?

13. *Depreciation.* What recovery period is used for nonresidential real property?

14. *Depreciation.* What depreciation method is used for residential rental property?

15. *Depreciation.* What recovery period is used for residential rental property?

16. *Depreciation.* What is "listed" property? What is unique about the depreciation treatment of listed property?

17. *Depreciation.* Your client purchases some office furniture (7-year recovery period) for $10,000 and places it in service this year. What is the client's depreciation deduction for Year 1? Year 5? Please use the applicable table in the Appendix to calculate the depreciation amount.

18. *Depreciation*. Your client purchases an apartment building that qualifies as residential rental property. The purchase price was on May 1 for $500,000, and the apartment building was placed in service immediately. What is the client's depreciation deduction for Year 1? Year 15? Please use the applicable table in the Appendix to calculate the depreciation amount.

19. *Depreciation and amortization*. What is the difference between depreciation and amortization?

20. *Section 179 election*. Please explain the benefits to a taxpayer if the taxpayer makes a Section 179 election.

21. *Bonus depreciation*. What is bonus depreciation? Is it available even after a Section 179 deduction? Conduct an Internet search to see if congress extended the bonus depreciation provision past 2013.

22. *Home office expenses*. Name some expenses that are typically deductible under the home office rules. Explain, in general, how a taxpayer determines how much the deductions are.

23. *Home office expenses*. The IRS has issued a "safe harbor" relating to home office expenses. Explain what the safe harbor is.

Chapter 13

Losses and Bad Debts

Taxpayers are likely to experience some losses from time to time. The question from a tax standpoint is whether such losses are deductible. This chapter covers a variety of losses and how the Internal Revenue Code treats such losses.

A. Losses on Personal-Use Assets

Suppose you have a garage sale and sell an old couch for $100. You paid $400 for the couch ten years ago. Can you deduct your $300 realized loss? Code Section 165 provides the answer.

INTERNAL REVENUE CODE

SECTION 165. LOSSES

(a) **General rule.**—There shall be allowed as a deduction any loss sustained during the taxable year and not compensated for by insurance or otherwise.

(b) **Amount of deduction.**—For purposes of subsection (a), the basis for determining the amount of the deduction for any loss shall be the adjusted basis provided in section 1011 for determining the loss from the sale or other disposition of property.

(c) **Limitation on losses of individuals.**—In the case of an individual, the deduction under subsection (a) shall be limited to—

(1) losses incurred in a trade or business;

(2) losses incurred in any transaction entered into for profit, though not connected with a trade or business; and

(3) except as provided in subsection (h), losses of property not connected with a trade or business or a transaction entered into for profit, if such losses arise from fire, storm, shipwreck, or other casualty, or from theft.

. . .

(e) **Theft losses.**—For purposes of subsection (a), any loss arising from theft shall be treated as sustained during the taxable year in which the taxpayer discovers such loss.

. . .

Notice that Section 165 allows deductions for losses incurred in a trade or business or transactions entered into for profit. Nonbusiness-related losses are deductible for individuals if the loss relates to fire, storm, shipwreck, or other casualty, or from theft, but these losses are "from" AGI deductions rather than "for" AGI deductions and can be limited to a significant extent. We discuss casualty losses in more detail in Chapter 18.

Losses on the sale of personal-use assets are not deductible. This includes cars, furniture, clothes, pianos, homes, etc., used for personal purposes. Thus, you cannot deduct the $300 loss on the couch you sold at a garage sale. Interestingly, however, *gains* on the sale of these items are included in an individual's gross income as capital gains (with some exceptions like gains on the sale of a personal residence, which are often excluded from gross income (see Chapter 24)).

In addition to disallowing losses on personal-use assets, the Code disallows deductions for personal, living, and family expenses.

INTERNAL REVENUE CODE

SECTION 262. PERSONAL, LIVING, AND FAMILY EXPENSES

(a) **General rule.**—Except as otherwise expressly provided in this chapter, no deduction shall be allowed for personal, living, or family expenses.

. . .

Thus, household expenses such as groceries, furniture, utilities, and other expenses associated with personal and family use are not deductible.

B. Net Operating Losses

Taxpayers' businesses often experience net income in some years and net losses in others. Congress has tried to even-out these fluctuations by allowing a taxpayer to carry forward and carry back losses from one year to another.

INTERNAL REVENUE CODE

SECTION 172. NET OPERATING LOSS DEDUCTION

(a) **Deduction allowed.**—There shall be allowed as a deduction for the taxable year an amount equal to the aggregate of (1) the net operating loss carryovers to such year, plus (2) the net operating loss carrybacks to such year. For purposes of this subtitle, the term "net operating loss deduction" means the deduction allowed by this subsection.

(b) **Net operating loss carrybacks and carryovers.**—

(1) **Years to which loss may be carried.**—

(A) General rule.—Except as otherwise provided in this paragraph, a net operating loss for any taxable year—

(i) shall be a net operating loss carryback to each of the 2 taxable years preceding the taxable year of such loss, and

(ii) shall be a net operating loss carryover to each of the 20 taxable years following the taxable year of the loss.

. . .

Of course, **net operating losses** (NOLs) occur when expenses exceed income. Notice the general rule is that NOLs may be carried back to the previous two years from the year the NOL occurred and forward to the next 20 years after the NOL occurred. A taxpayer may elect to forego the carryback period and choose to carry the NOL forward only. The Code also requires certain adjustments to be made if taxpayers have an NOL. For example, individual taxpayers must "add back" their personal exemption deduction (*i.e.*, no NOL deduction *and* personal exemption deduction). Other "add-backs" must be made also, but such details are not discussed here. An individual uses IRS Form 1045 to determine any potential refund because of the carryback or carryover of NOLs to other years. Form 1045 is included in the Appendix for your reference.

C. Bad Debts

Taxpayers frequently lend other people money. These transactions can be in the course of business or outside the scope of a person's business. When these loans go bad, a question of deductibility arises.

INTERNAL REVENUE CODE

SECTION 166. BAD DEBTS

(a) **General rule.**—

(1) **Wholly worthless debts.**—There shall be allowed as a deduction any debt which becomes worthless within the taxable year.

(2) **Partially worthless debts.**—When satisfied that a debt is recoverable only in part, the Secretary may allow such debt, in an amount not in excess of the part charged off within the taxable year, as a deduction.

(b) **Amount of deduction.**—For purposes of subsection (a), the basis for determining the amount of the deduction for any bad debt shall be the adjusted basis provided in section 1011 for determining the loss from the sale or other disposition of property.

. . .

(d) **Nonbusiness debts.**—

(1) **General rule.**—In the case of a taxpayer other than a corporation—

(A) subsection (a) shall not apply to any nonbusiness debt; and

(B) where any nonbusiness debt becomes worthless within the taxable year, the loss resulting therefrom shall be considered a loss from the sale or exchange, during the taxable year, of a capital asset held for not more than 1 year.

(2) **Nonbusiness debt defined.**—For purposes of paragraph (1), the term "nonbusiness debt" means a debt other than—

(A) a debt created or acquired (as the case may be) in connection with a trade or business of the taxpayer; or

(B) a debt the loss from the worthlessness of which is incurred in the taxpayer's trade or business.

. . .

A *business* bad debt is allowed as an ordinary deduction when it becomes partially or wholly worthless. A *nonbusiness* bad debt is treated as a short-term capital loss and is deductible only when it becomes wholly worthless. Thus, the classification of the debt as business or nonbusiness is critical. The amount of the deduction is equal to the taxpayer's tax basis in the debt.

Notice that a nonbusiness bad debt is a debt that arises in any context other than in connection with the taxpayer's trade or business. Importantly, the focus is on whether the *lender* made the loan as part of the lender's trade or business and not whether the *borrower* is engaged in a trade or business or uses the debt proceeds in the course of the borrower's trade or business. Of course, the taxpayer seeking to deduct a bad debt loss should have adequate documentation to show the amount of the loss and that there was a bona fide debtor-creditor relationship (*e.g.*, the "loan" was not, for example, in reality a gift).

D. Hobby Losses

Assume your client, Jen, enjoys making crafts. She likes to make unique Santa Clauses for Christmas, turkeys for Thanksgiving, skeletons for Halloween, etc. She also sells her crafts at craft fairs held around her local area. These craft fairs occur several times a year, usually in the summer and early fall. Suppose this year she sells $2,000 worth of crafts, but incurred $2,400 of expenses in creating the crafts. Are Jen's expenses deductible for income tax purposes?

The answer lies primarily on whether Jen's craft-making is "engaged in for profit" or is a "hobby." Section 183 provides the law in this area.

INTERNAL REVENUE CODE

SECTION 183. ACTIVITIES NOT ENGAGED IN FOR PROFIT

(a) **General rule.**—In the case of an activity engaged in by an individual or an S corporation, if such activity is not engaged in for profit, no deduction attributable to such activity shall be allowed under this chapter except as provided in this section.

. . .

(c) **Activity not engaged in for profit defined.**—For purposes of this section, the term "activity not engaged in for profit" means any activity other than one with respect to which deductions are allowable for the taxable year under section 162 or under paragraph (1) or (2) of section 212.

(d) **Presumption.**—If the gross income derived from an activity for 3 or more of the taxable years in the period of 5 consecutive taxable years which ends with the taxable year exceeds the deductions attributable to such activity (determined without regard to whether or not such activity is engaged in for profit), then, unless the Secretary establishes to the contrary, such activity shall be presumed for purposes of this chapter for such taxable year to be an activity engaged in for profit. . . .

If the activity constitutes an activity engaged in for profit, then Jen can deduct all her expenses and she has a $400 loss that may offset other income. If the activity is a "hobby," then she can only deduct her expenses to the extent of her income. Moreover, some expenses that she incurs may be treated as miscellaneous itemized deductions and deductible only to the extent she itemizes deductions and only to the extent that the expenses (in combination with other miscellaneous itemized deductions) exceed 2% of her adjusted gross income.

Notice the presumption that if the activity generates a profit for at least 3 out of the last 5 years, the activity is presumed to be an activity engaged in for profit. But it's not quite that easy. The IRS can rebut this presumption even though the taxpayer may have made a profit for at least 3 out of the last 5 years. The IRS looks at several factors to determine if the activity is profit-motivated. Such factors include:

- The time and effort expended by the taxpayer in carrying on the activity
- The expertise of the taxpayer or the taxpayer's advisors
- Manner in which the taxpayer carries on the activity
- The success of the taxpayer in carrying on other similar or dissimilar activities
- The taxpayer's history of income or losses with respect to the activity

If the IRS is able to rebut the presumption, then the burden of proof shifts to the taxpayer to show that the activity is engaged in for profit.

E. At-Risk Losses

Congress is concerned about taxpayers entering into transactions where tax losses could be generated with no associated economic losses. For example, depreciation deductions could cause a taxpayer to have a tax loss, but those depreciation deductions do not necessarily result in economic losses (in fact, the property being depreciated could go *up* in value). Consequently, Congress enacted Section 465, which allows a taxpayer to deduct losses only to the extent the taxpayer is economically "at risk."

INTERNAL REVENUE CODE

SECTION 465. DEDUCTIONS LIMITED TO AMOUNT AT RISK

(a) **Limitation to amount at risk.**—
(1) **In general.**—In the case of—
(A) an individual, and
(B) a C corporation with respect to which the stock ownership requirement of paragraph (2) of section 542(a) is met,
engaged in an activity to which this section applies, any loss from such activity for the taxable year shall be allowed only to the extent of the aggregate amount with respect to which the

taxpayer is at risk (within the meaning of subsection (b)) for such activity at the close of the taxable year.

. . .

(b) **Amounts considered at risk.**—

(1) **In general.**—For purposes of this section, a taxpayer shall be considered at risk for an activity with respect to amounts including—

(A) the amount of money and the adjusted basis of other property contributed by the taxpayer to the activity, and

(B) amounts borrowed with respect to such activity (as determined under paragraph (2)).

(2) **Borrowed amounts.**—For purposes of this section, a taxpayer shall be considered at risk with respect to amounts borrowed for use in an activity to the extent that he—

(A) is personally liable for the repayment of such amounts, or

(B) has pledged property, other than property used in such activity, as security for such borrowed amount (to the extent of the net fair market value of the taxpayer's interest in such property).

. . .

In short, the amount of money plus the adjusted basis of other property contributed to an activity is considered at risk. Additionally, any *recourse* debt (*i.e.*, lender can demand repayment by the taxpayer or repossess taxpayer's other pledged property) also counts as amounts at risk.

Nonrecourse debt does not count in the taxpayer's amount at risk unless the debt meets the definition of **qualified nonrecourse financing**. This type of financing applies to real property financing and must meet the following requirements:

- the financing must be secured by the real property;
- the financing is borrowed by the taxpayer with respect to the activity of holding real property;
- the financing is borrowed by the taxpayer from a "qualified person";
- no person is personally liable for repayment (with some narrow exceptions); and
- the financing is not convertible debt.

A "qualified person" is basically any person that is actively engaged in the trade or business of lending money and is not a related person to the borrower.

Any loss that is disallowed due to the fact that the taxpayer has insufficient amount at risk is carried forward to subsequent years until the taxpayer does have enough at risk. A taxpayer is able to deduct unused at-risk losses when the taxpayer disposes of the activity. A taxpayer reports at-risk losses on IRS Form 6198, a copy of which is provided in the Appendix.

F. Passive Losses

In addition to the at-risk loss limitation just discussed, a taxpayer seeking to deduct losses must also survive the passive loss limitation.

SECTION 469. PASSIVE ACTIVITY LOSSES AND CREDITS LIMITED

(a) **Disallowance.**—

(1) **In general.**—If for any taxable year the taxpayer is described in paragraph (2), neither—

(A) the passive activity loss, nor

(B) the passive activity credit,

for the taxable year shall be allowed.

(2) **Persons described.**—The following are described in this paragraph:

(A) any individual, estate, or trust,

(B) any closely held C corporation, and

(C) any personal service corporation

. . .

(c) **Passive activity defined.**—For purposes of this section—

(1) **In general.**—The term "passive activity" means any activity—

(A) which involves the conduct of any trade or business, and

(B) in which the taxpayer does not materially participate.

. . .

Thus, if a taxpayer is involved in a passive activity, any net loss from the activity is not deductible. Such loss can be carried forward and deducted in future years. The Code provides that passive losses can be deducted only against passive income (*i.e.*, and not against the taxpayer's portfolio income or active income). Unused passive losses can also be deducted in the year the taxpayer disposes of the activity.

A critical issue relating to an activity is whether the activity is considered "passive." Notice in Code Section 469(c)(1), an activity is passive if the taxpayer does not **materially participate**. The Treasury Regulations provide seven ways to meet the material participation test.

- The individual participates in the activity for more than 500 hours during such year;
- The individual's participation in the activity for the taxable year constitutes substantially all of the participation in such activity of all individuals (including individuals who are not owners of interests in the activity) for such year;
- The individual participates in the activity for more than 100 hours during the taxable year, and such individual's participation in the activity for the taxable year is not less than the participation in the activity of any other individual (including individuals who are not owners of interests in the activity) for such year;
- The activity is a significant participation activity for the taxable year, and the individual's aggregate participation in all significant participation activities during such year exceeds 500 hours;
- The individual materially participated in the activity for any five taxable years during the ten taxable years that immediately precede the taxable year;
- The activity is a personal service activity and the individual materially participated in the activity for any three taxable years preceding the taxable year; or
- Based on all of the facts and circumstances, the individual participates in the activity on a regular, continuous, and substantial basis during such year.

A taxpayer need meet only one of the above tests to materially participate in an activity. The regulations provide significantly more detail with respect to these tests, but such detail will not be presented here.

Although any rental activity is generally considered a passive activity, special rules apply to rental *real estate* activities. For example, a rental real estate activity is not presumed to be a passive activity if the taxpayer in question is a real estate professional and spends at least 750 hours per year in real property trades or businesses in which the professional materially participates. Another exception is for taxpayers that own rental real estate and have adjusted gross income of less than $150,000. These taxpayers need only *actively* participate (a lesser standard than material participation) in the real estate rental activity and own at least 10% of the activity. Passive losses generated from the rental activity for these taxpayers are deductible up to $25,000 each year. Such allowable deduction begins to phase-out once the taxpayer's adjusted gross income exceeds $100,000 and is completely phased-out when the taxpayer's adjusted gross income is $150,000.

Losses from passive activities are reported on IRS Form 8582, a copy of which is provided in the Appendix.

G. Losses on Transactions with a Related Party

Whenever a taxpayer enters into a transaction with a related party, special tax issues may arise particularly if the transaction results in a loss to one of the parties. Congress has specifically disallowed losses on transactions between related parties.

INTERNAL REVENUE CODE

SECTION 267. LOSSES, EXPENSES, AND INTEREST WITH RESPECT TO TRANSACTIONS BETWEEN RELATED TAXPAYERS

(a) **In general.**—

(1) **Deduction for losses disallowed.**—No deduction shall be allowed in respect of any loss from the sale or exchange of property, directly or indirectly, between persons specified in any of the paragraphs of subsection (b). ...

(b) **Relationships.**—The persons referred to in subsection (a) are:

(1) Members of a family, as defined in subsection (c)(4);

(2) An individual and a corporation more than 50 percent in value of the outstanding stock of which is owned, directly or indirectly, by or for such individual;

. . .

(4) A grantor and a fiduciary of any trust;

. . .

(11) An S corporation and another S corporation if the same persons own more than 50 percent in value of the outstanding stock of each corporation;

. . .

The definition of related party is very broad (including related individuals, partnerships, corporations, trusts, etc.). Section 267 sets forth many more relationships that are considered related parties than what is presented here. Consequently, care must be taken to determine if a transaction is between related parties and a look at Section 267 is in order.

As mentioned, if a transaction between related parties results in a loss, the loss is disallowed. Nevertheless, if a purchasing related party (Party B, for example) later sells the property at a gain, the initial disallowed loss (to related Party A) can be used by Party B to offset Party B's later gain.

H. OTHER LOSSES

We explained in Chapter 7 that capital losses are netted against capital gains. To the extent gains exceed losses, a net capital gain results. To the extent capital losses exceed capital gains, a net capital loss results. Net capital losses are deductible against an individual's ordinary income up to a maximum of $3,000 per year. The remaining net capital loss is carried forward to subsequent years.

Individual taxpayers may also experience losses on the worthlessness of securities. Such losses are treated as capital losses (unless the individual is a dealer in securities) on the last day of the taxable year in which the security becomes worthless.

Certain stock issued by small businesses may qualify as "Section 1244 stock." Such small business stock is tax-favored in that if a seller of Section 1244 stock realizes a loss, such loss can be recognized as an *ordinary* loss rather than a capital loss. This is an incentive from Congress for people to invest in small corporations. Not surprisingly, there are strict requirements for stock to qualify as Section 1244 stock, and the ordinary loss that a taxpayer may recognize on the sale of Section 1244 stock is limited to $50,000 ($100,000 married filing jointly). Any excess loss is treated as a capital loss.

CHAPTER 13: QUESTIONS

1. *Personal-use assets.* You sell your car that you use solely for personal purposes. The sales price was $7,000. You paid $18,000 for it five years ago. Is your loss deductible for income tax purposes?

2. *Net operating losses.* An individual taxpayer can carry back an NOL for how many years?

3. *Net operating losses.* An individual taxpayer can carry forward an NOL for how many years?

4. *Bad debts.* How is an individual's nonbusiness bad debt treated for income tax purposes?

5. *Bad debts.* Explain when a *partially* worthless bad debt can be deducted.

6. *Hobby losses.* Explain the presumption related to whether an activity is a hobby or whether the activity is engaged in for profit.

7. *Hobby losses.* If an activity is deemed to be a hobby, are the expenses incurred in the hobby deductible? If so, how much?

8. *Hobby losses.* Name at least three factors involved in determining whether a taxpayer has a profit motive in relation to a particular activity.

9. *At-risk losses.* You have a client that hears about the at-risk loss limitation, but the client really does not know what it means. Explain the at-risk loss limitation to your client.

10. *At-risk losses.* What is qualified nonrecourse financing?

11. *Passive losses.* Passive losses are deductible against what type of income?

12. *Passive losses.* What does "material participation" mean? Discuss at least two material participation tests.

13. *Passive losses.* As an exception to the general passive activity loss limitation rules, an individual who *actively* participates in a rental real estate activity can deduct up to how much against the individual's ordinary income?

14. *Related party losses.* Explain the rules regarding losses on transactions with related parties.

Chapter 14

Alimony, Moving Expenses, Educational Expenses, Student Loan Interest, and Tuition and Fees

In this chapter we continue our discussion of deductions allowed in calculating adjusted gross income (*i.e.*, deductions "for" AGI).

A. Alimony

You may recall from Chapter 8, the recipient of alimony must include the amount received in gross income. The payer of alimony is allowed a deduction for AGI as is easily ascertained by reading Code Section 215.

INTERNAL REVENUE CODE

Section 215. Alimony, etc., payments

(a) **General rule.**—In the case of an individual, there shall be allowed as a deduction an amount equal to the alimony or separate maintenance payments paid during such individual's taxable year.

(b) **Alimony or separate maintenance payments defined.**—For purposes of this section, the term "alimony or separate maintenance payment" means any alimony or separate maintenance payment (as defined in section 71(b)) which is includible in the gross income of the recipient under section 71.

. . .

While alimony payments are deductible, child support payments are not.

B. Moving Expenses

Employees may frequently relocate due to a change in employment. Moving expenses incurred because of a change in employment are deductible if the taxpayer is not reimbursed by his or her employer. If, in fact, the employee is reimbursed by the employer, the reimbursement is excluded from the employee's gross income. For the moving expenses to be deductible, the taxpayer must meet certain requirements contained in Section 217.

INTERNAL REVENUE CODE

SECTION 217. MOVING EXPENSES

(a) **Deduction allowed.**—There shall be allowed as a deduction moving expenses paid or incurred during the taxable year in connection with the commencement of work by the taxpayer as an employee or as a self-employed individual at a new principal place of work.

(b) **Definition of moving expenses.**—

(1) **In general.**—For purposes of this section, the term "moving expenses" means only the reasonable expenses—

(A) of moving household goods and personal effects from the former residence to the new residence, and

(B) of traveling (including lodging) from the former residence to the new place of residence.

Such term shall not include any expenses for meals.

. . .

(c) **Conditions for allowance.**—No deduction shall be allowed under this section unless—

(1) the taxpayer's new principal place of work—

(A) is at least 50 miles farther from his former residence than was his former principal place of work, or

(B) if he had no former principal place of work, is at least 50 miles from his former residence, and

(2) either—

(A) during the 12-month period immediately following his arrival in the general location of his new principal place of work, the taxpayer is a full-time employee, in such general location, during at least 39 weeks, or

(B) during the 24-month period immediately following his arrival in the general location of his new principal place of work, the taxpayer is a full-time employee or performs services as a self-employed individual on a full-time basis, in such general location, during at least 78 weeks, of which not less than 39 weeks are during the 12-month period referred to in subparagraph (A).

. . .

The moving expense deduction applies to both employees and self-employed individuals. Regarding travel expenses, the taxpayer can choose to deduct the actual expenses incurred (*e.g.*, gas and oil, but not depreciation or repairs) or 23.5 cents per mile in 2014 (24 cents in 2013). Notice also that the move must meet certain distance requirements (*e.g.*, the "50-mile" test) and the individual must be employed for a certain period of time following the move. Moving expenses are reported on IRS Form 3903, a copy of which is provided in the Appendix.

C. EDUCATIONAL EXPENSES

The IRS has acknowledged that expenses paid for education can qualify as ordinary and necessary business expenses. Of course, there are several other Code provisions that allow certain tax deductions or credits for educational expenses (*e.g.,* exclusion of employer educational assistance, deduction for tuition and fees, deduction for student loan interest, American Opportunity Credit, Lifetime Learning Credit, etc.), but here we will limit our discussion as to the extent the expenses can qualify as *business expenses* for an employee or self-employed individual.

The Treasury regulations provide guidance as to the requirements that need to be met for educational expenses to be deductible as business expenses.

TREASURY REGULATION

TREASURY REGULATION § 1.162–5. EXPENSES FOR EDUCATION

(a) **General rule**. Expenditures made by an individual for education ... which are not expenditures of a type described in paragraph (b)(2) or (3) of this section are deductible as ordinary and necessary business expenses (even though the education may lead to a degree) if the education—

(1) Maintains or improves skills required by the individual in his employment or other trade or business, or

(2) Meets the express requirements of the individual's employer, or the requirements of applicable law or regulations, imposed as a condition to the retention by the individual of an established employment relationship, status, or rate of compensation.

(b) **Nondeductible educational expenditures—**

. . .

(2) Minimum educational requirements. (i) The first category of nondeductible educational expenses ... are expenditures made by an individual for education which is required of him in order to meet the minimum educational requirements for qualification in his employment or other trade or business. . . .

(3) Qualification for new trade or business. (i) The second category of nondeductible educational expenses within the scope of subparagraph (1) of this paragraph are expenditures made by an individual for education which is part of a program of study being pursued by him which will lead to qualifying him in a new trade or business. . . .

Notice that there are really two prongs to this issue. First, the education must meet at least one of two specific tests, and second, the education must *not* meet *either* of two other tests. In short, the education must:

- Maintain or improve skills required by the individual in his employment or other trade or business; or

- Meet the express requirements of the individual's employer or the requirements of applicable law or regulations, imposed as a condition to the retention by the individual of an established employment relationship, status, or rate of compensation.

and must not

- be required of him in order to meet the minimum educational requirements for qualification in his employment or other trade of business; or
- be part of a program of study that qualifies the taxpayer for a new trade or business.

If the educational expenses qualify as business expenses, then a self-employed individual can deduct them as a "for" AGI deduction. If the taxpayer is an employee such expenses, if unreimbursed by the employer, are treated as miscellaneous itemized deductions, which are deductible only to the extent the expenses (when combined with other miscellaneous itemized deductions) exceed 2% of the taxpayer's AGI (see Chapter 18).

D. Student Loan Interest Deduction

Among the many tax incentives for taxpayers to further their education, Congress has provided a deduction for student loan interest paid.

INTERNAL REVENUE CODE

SECTION 221. INTEREST ON EDUCATION LOANS

(a) **Allowance of deduction.**—In the case of an individual, there shall be allowed as a deduction for the taxable year an amount equal to the interest paid by the taxpayer during the taxable year on any qualified education loan.

. . .

The student loan interest deduction is limited to $2,500 per year and begins to phase-out when an individual's adjusted gross income exceeds a particular threshold, which varies based on filing status. As indicated in Section 221, the interest paid must be on a "qualified" education loan. A qualified loan is one that is not a loan from a related person and that is used to pay qualified educational expenses. Such expenses include tuition, books, room and board and other necessary expenses like transportation. If the student loan was taken out to pay the education expenses of a qualifying dependent (*e.g.*, child), the student loan interest is deductible by the payer (*e.g.*, parent). The interest is deductible (subject to the $2,500 limit and related phase-out) until the loan is paid off.

A deduction for student loan interest is not available if the taxpayer deducts the amount of interest paid because of another provision of the Code (*e.g.*, home mortgage interest). Individuals that pay student loan interest will receive an IRS Form 1098-E from the lending institution. A copy of this form is included in the Appendix.

E. Tuition and Fees Deduction

Yet another provision to give individuals an incentive to further their education is the tuition and fees deduction.

INTERNAL REVENUE CODE

SECTION 222. QUALIFIED TUITION AND RELATED EXPENSES

(a) **Allowance of deduction.**—In the case of an individual, there shall be allowed as a deduction an amount equal to the qualified tuition and related expenses paid by the taxpayer during the taxable year.

. . .

The amount of the deduction can be up to $4,000 of qualified tuition and fees paid to an eligible institution each year. A taxpayer can take this deduction for expenses paid on behalf of the taxpayer's dependent. This deduction also phases-out once the taxpayer's adjusted gross income reaches a certain threshold based on filing status.

If the taxpayer chooses to use other provisions of the Code with respect to the tuition and fees paid (*e.g.*, the American Opportunity Credit or Lifetime Learning Credit) the tuition deduction discussed here is not available. Amounts paid for tuition and related expenses are deductible, but room and board, transportation, etc., are not deductible. The institution to which the tuition was paid will send the student IRS Form 1098-T shortly after the end of the year. Form 1098-T is included at the end of the text for your reference. This deduction expired at the end of 2013. Congress may or may not extend it.

CHAPTER 14: QUESTIONS

1. *Alimony and child support*. Which one of the following statements is true?
   a. Child support paid is deductible and alimony paid is not deductible.
   b. Child support paid is not deductible and alimony paid is deductible.

2. *Moving expenses*. Explain what requirements a taxpayer must meet in order to deduct moving expenses.

3. *Moving expenses*. If a taxpayer chooses to deduct automobile expenses on a per-mile basis, what is the current rate per-mile allowed by the IRS?

4. *Educational expenses as business expenses*. Explain to your fellow student what requirements must be met for educational expenses to be considered deductible business expenses.

5. *Educational expenses*. How does an employee treat educational expenses that qualify as business expenses if the employer does not reimburse the employee?

6. *Student loan interest deduction.* Up to how much of qualified student loan interest can an individual deduct each year? Is there a phase-out?

7. *Tuition and fees deduction.* Up to how much of qualified tuition and fees can an individual deduct each year? Is there a phase-out? Conduct an Internet search to see if Congress has extended this provision past 2013.

Chapter 15

Individual Retirement Account Contributions, One-Half Self-Employment Tax, and Other "For" AGI Deductions

This chapter concludes our discussion of deductions "for" AGI.

A. Individual Retirement Account Contributions

Subject to some limitations, the Code allows an individual to deduct contributions to an **individual retirement account (IRA)** (sometimes called a "traditional" IRA).

INTERNAL REVENUE CODE

SECTION 219. RETIREMENT SAVINGS

(a) **Allowance of deduction.**—In the case of an individual, there shall be allowed as a deduction an amount equal to the qualified retirement contributions of the individual for the taxable year.

. . .

The contribution limit is $5,500 per year (2014) unless the individual is age 50 or older and eligible for the "catch-up" provisions that allow such individuals to contribute up to $6,500 per year. The amount deductible is phased-out for individuals who are active participants in an employer-sponsored retirement plan and the individual has adjusted gross income over a certain threshold. The 2014 phase-out thresholds begin at AGI of $60,000 (single) and $96,000 (married filing jointly). An individual can continue to make contributions to IRA until the age of 70½. A penalty applies if an individual contributes more than the allowed limit or makes a contribution after age 70½. In such a situation, the taxpayer should correct the problem as soon as possible. An individual can make a contribution to an IRA even though the contribution may not be deductible because of the phase-out thresholds or other applicable limitations.

Earnings on the contributions to IRAs continue to grow tax-deferred for the years the funds remain in the IRA. This is true both for deductible and nondeductible IRA contributions. Of course, this allows the IRA to increase in value much faster over time than if tax were impose on the income each year. Most individuals place their IRA contributions in an account at a financial institution or mutual fund company. Some individuals, however, like to exercise greater control over their IRA contributions and, if the individual meets strict requirements imposed by tax regulations, can set up a **self-directed** IRA. A detailed explanation of self-directed IRAs will not be presented here.

An individual can begin to withdraw funds from his or her IRA at the age of 59½ and must start receiving minimum distributions by age 70½. If an individual withdraws funds early, there is a 10% penalty tax on the amount withdrawn, with some exceptions (*e.g.*, withdrawal of a limited amount of funds for a down payment on a home if the individual is a first-time homebuyer). Funds distributed from a traditional IRA are included in the individual's gross income as ordinary income. However, if the individual made any nondeductible contributions to the IRA, then the individual will not be taxed on a fraction of each distribution over the course of the distribution period to the extent of the nondeductible contributions the individual made to the account.

A second-type of IRA is called a **Roth IRA**. The Code contains the provision for Roth IRAs in Section 408A.

INTERNAL REVENUE CODE

SECTION 408A. ROTH IRAS

(a) **General rule.**—Except as provided in this section, a Roth IRA shall be treated for purposes of this title in the same manner as an individual retirement plan.

. . .

(c) **Treatment of contributions.**—

(1) **No deduction allowed.**—No deduction shall be allowed under section 219 for a contribution to a Roth IRA.

. . .

(d) **Distribution rules.**—For purposes of this title—

(1) **Exclusion.**—Any qualified distribution from a Roth IRA shall not be includible in gross income.

. . .

Notice that for a Roth IRA contributions are not deductible, but distributions are excluded from the individual's gross income. Moreover, the increase in value of the Roth IRA escapes taxation each year. Like traditional IRAs, there are contribution limits and phase-outs based on AGI. The Roth

IRA contribution limit in 2014 is $5,500 ($6,500 for individuals 50 and older). Unlike the applicable rules to a traditional IRA, however, the Roth IRA rules allow an individual to contribute even if the individual actively participates in an employer-sponsored retirement plan. The amount allowed to be contributed to a Roth IRA may be limited based on a taxpayer's adjusted gross income, however.

Occasionally an individual may want to switch (*i.e.*, **rollover**) his or her IRA from one institution to another. An individual may rollover IRAs and Roth IRAs without incurring the 10% early withdrawal penalty and without incurring income tax if strict requirements are met. Typically, the taxpayer must rollover any distribution into another qualified account within 60 days of receiving the distribution. Of course, a safer approach would be to have the old institution send the funds directly to the new institution. Many other detailed rules can apply to traditional and Roth IRA rollovers that are not presented here.

An individual should receive an IRS Form 5498 reporting the amount of traditional IRA and Roth IRA contributions for the year. A copy of this form is included in the Appendix. If an individual receives a distribution from a traditional IRA or Roth IRA, the payer will send the individual an IRS Form 1099-R, a copy of which is in the Appendix. An individual reports distributions from a Roth IRA (and nondeductible contributions to a traditional IRA) on IRS Form 8606, a copy of which is included in the Appendix.

B. Health Savings Accounts

Some individuals may be covered by health plans that have high deductibles. Thus, whenever these individuals incur medical costs, they may have to cover much of the cost out of their own pockets with after-tax dollars. To assist individuals in these situations, Congress enacted provisions relating to tax-favored health savings accounts.

INTERNAL REVENUE CODE

SECTION 223. HEALTH SAVINGS ACCOUNTS

(a) **Deduction allowed.**—In the case of an individual who is an eligible individual for any month during the taxable year, there shall be allowed as a deduction for the taxable year an amount equal to the aggregate amount paid in cash during such taxable year by or on behalf of such individual to a health savings account of such individual.

. . .

(c) **Definitions and special rules.**—For purposes of this section—

(1) **Eligible individual.**—

(A) In general.—The term "eligible individual" means, with respect to any month, any individual if—

(i) such individual is covered under a high deductible health plan as of the 1st day of such month, . . .

. . .

(f) **Treatment of distributions.**—

(1) **Amounts used for qualified medical expenses.**—Any amount paid or distributed out of a health savings account which is used exclusively to pay qualified medical expenses of any account beneficiary shall not be includible in gross income.

(2) **Inclusions of amounts not used for qualified medical expenses.**—Any amount paid or distributed out of a health savings account which is not used exclusively to pay the qualified medical expenses of the account beneficiary shall be included in the gross income of such beneficiary.

. . .

Of course, the Code is quite complex in defining what constitutes a "high deductible plan." We will not discuss the details here nor delve into the contribution limits and phase-out limits that always seem to apply to tax-favored provisions such as this.

C. Certain Retirement Plans for Self-Employed Individuals

A sole proprietor obviously has no employer to contribute to the sole proprietor's retirement fund. The sole proprietor *is* the employer. Consequently, the Code allows the sole proprietor to set up qualified retirement programs benefitting the sole proprietor and his or her employees. One such program is called a **simplified employee pension (SEP)**. Under an SEP, the sole proprietor can make contributions directly to an IRA set up for the sole proprietor and directly to IRAs set up for each individual employee. These arrangements are sometimes called SEP-IRAs. The employer receives a deduction for the amount contributed to the IRAs. Of course, there is a limit to the total amount the sole proprietor can deduct. This limit is 25% of the compensation (with a ceiling of $260,000 in 2014) paid to the participants during the year (but not more than $52,000 per employee).

Another retirement plan arrangement often used by sole proprietors is a **Savings Incentive Match Plan for Employees (SIMPLE)**. SIMPLE plans allow employees to voluntarily reduce their salary and have the amount of the reduction be contributed to a SIMPLE IRA or SIMPLE 401(k). The employer also matches the contribution up to a certain amount. As expected, the amount an employee can contribute is limited, as is the deduction for the employer match.

Sole proprietors and partnerships can also set up other common retirement plan arrangements such as defined contribution plans and defined benefit plans that other businesses (*e.g.*, corporations) have. See Chapter 23 for more detail on defined contribution and defined benefit plans. These plans can be quite complex and costly to set up and manage. Consequently, many small businesses organize SEP or SIMPLE plans instead.

D. One-Half of Self-Employment Tax

Since self-employed individuals have no employer to withhold income tax or payroll taxes (*i.e.*, FICA tax (social security and Medicare)), these individuals must satisfy these tax payment obligations themselves. In an employer-employee situation, the employer is required to match the employee's portion of social security and Medicare taxes. Thus, a self-employed individual must pay what an employer would normally have withheld from the employee's paycheck plus the employer's match.

The Code imposes a 6.2% social security tax on an employee's wages up to a ceiling of $117,000 (in 2014). The Medicare tax is 1.45% on all an employee's wages (no ceiling). Thus, a self-employed person is responsible for paying 7.65% (representing the employee's portion) plus another 7.65% (representing the employer's match). Consequently, the total self-employment tax is 15.3% (7.65% plus 7.65%).

To lessen some of the pain for the self-employed individual, the Code allows a deduction for one-half of the social security and Medicare amounts.

INTERNAL REVENUE CODE

SECTION 164. TAXES

. . .

(f) **Deduction for one-half of self-employment taxes.—**

(1) **In general.**—In the case of an individual . . . there shall be allowed as a deduction for the taxable year an amount equal to one-half of the taxes imposed by section 1401 for such taxable year.

. . .

The Code also imposes an additional 0.9% Medicare tax on individuals earning over a certain amount. These amounts are $200,000 (single individuals) and $250,000 (married filing jointly). A self-employed individual may not deduct half of this additional amount. A self-employed individual calculates the amount of self-employment tax owed as well as the deduction for one-half that amount on Schedule SE, a copy of which is included in the Appendix for your reference.

E. Domestic Production Activities Deduction

To encourage manufacturing and production activities in the United States, Congress has enacted the **domestic production activities** deduction.

INTERNAL REVENUE CODE

SECTION 199. INCOME ATTRIBUTABLE TO DOMESTIC PRODUCTION ACTIVITIES

(a) **Allowance of deduction.—**

(1) **In general.**—There shall be allowed as a deduction an amount equal to 9 percent of the lesser of—

(A) the qualified production activities income of the taxpayer for the taxable year, or

(B) taxable income (determined without regard to this section) for the taxable year.

. . .

(b) **Deduction limited to wages paid.**—

(1) **In general.**—The amount of the deduction allowable under subsection (a) for any taxable year shall not exceed 50 percent of the W-2 wages of the taxpayer for the taxable year.

. . .

Notice the deduction is equal to 9% of the taxpayer's taxable income or "qualified production activities" income, whichever is less. The deduction is capped at 50% of wages paid by the taxpayer. Activities qualifying under this Code section are construction, engineering, film production, production of tangible personal property manufactured, produced, grown, or extracted by the taxpayer in the United States, and several other similar activities. Section 199 provides many detailed definitions and narrow exceptions. A taxpayer calculates the domestic production activities deduction on IRS Form 8903. Form 8903 is included in the Appendix for your reference.

F. Penalty on Early Withdrawal of Savings

If a taxpayer has invested money in a certificate of deposit, the taxpayer is usually not able to withdraw the money for a period of time without incurring a penalty. If the taxpayer does withdraw the money early and incurs a penalty, such penalty is deductible for income tax purposes.

INTERNAL REVENUE CODE

SECTION 62. ADJUSTED GROSS INCOME DEFINED

(a) **General rule.**—For purposes of this subtitle, the term "adjusted gross income" means, in the case of an individual, gross income minus the following deductions:

. . .

(9) Penalties forfeited because of premature withdrawal of funds from time savings accounts or deposits.—The deductions allowed by section 165 for losses incurred in any transaction entered into for profit, though not connected with a trade or business to the extent that such losses include amounts forfeited to a bank, mutual savings bank, savings and loan association, building and loan association, cooperative bank or homestead association as a penalty for premature withdrawal of funds from a time savings account, certificate of deposit, or similar class of deposit.

. . .

The financial institution reports the amount of the penalty to the taxpayer on IRS Form 1099-INT.

G. Teachers' Classroom Expenses

Teachers frequently purchase materials for the classroom with their own money. The Code provides a small tax break for these purchases.

INTERNAL REVENUE CODE

SECTION 62. ADJUSTED GROSS INCOME DEFINED

(a) **General rule.**—For purposes of this subtitle, the term "adjusted gross income" means, in the case of an individual, gross income minus the following deductions:

. . .

(2) (D) Certain expenses of elementary and secondary school teachers.—In the case of taxable years beginning during 2002, 2003, 2004, 2005, 2006, 2007, 2008, 2009, 2010, 2011, 2012, or 2013 the deductions allowed by section 162 which consist of expenses, not in excess of $250, paid or incurred by an eligible educator in connection with books, supplies (other than nonathletic supplies for courses of instruction in health or physical education), computer equipment (including related software and services) and other equipment, and supplementary materials used by the eligible educator in the classroom.

. . .

This provision is frequently scheduled to expire, but Congress just tags on another year or two to keep the deduction alive. Congress may or may not extend this provision past 2013.

CHAPTER 15: QUESTIONS

1. *Traditional IRAs.* Are contributions to IRAs deductible? Are there any limits on contributions to IRAs? If so, how much?
2. *Traditional IRAs.* Is the increase in earnings within an IRA taxed each year? If the IRA goes down in value during the year is the taxpayer entitled to a deduction?
3. *Traditional IRAs.* At what age can an individual withdraw IRA funds without a penalty? What is the penalty for early withdrawal? Are IRA distributions subject to income tax?
4. *Traditional IRAs.* At what age must an individual start receiving distributions from the individual's IRA?
5. *Roth IRAs.* Are contributions to Roth IRAs deductible? Are there any limits on contributions to Roth IRAs? If so, how much?
6. *Roth IRAs.* Is the increase in earnings within a Roth IRA taxed each year?
7. *Roth IRAs.* Are distributions from Roth IRAs subject to income tax?
8. *IRA rollovers.* What is a "rollover" in the context of IRAs?
9. *Health savings account.* Explain generally the purpose of a health savings account. Who is eligible to participate?

10. *SEP and SIMPLE plans.* What does SEP stand for in the retirement plan context? What does SIMPLE stand for in the retirement plan context? Explain generally how these plans work.

11. *One-half SE tax deduction.* Explain what amount a self-employed individual may deduct with respect to the payment of social security and Medicare taxes.

12. *Domestic production activities deduction.* What is the purpose of the domestic production activities deduction?

13. *Domestic production activities deduction.* Explain generally how this deduction is determined.

14. *Teachers' classroom expenses.* Up to how much of classroom expenses a teacher may deduct for 2013?

TAX RETURN EXERCISE

Your client, Heather R. Calibrini, is not married. She was born August 26, 1978. She has two children, Shawn Calibrini and Alyssa Calibrini, who live with her full time and she provides all of their support. Her son Shawn is 12 years-old and her daughter Alyssa is 5 years-old. Shawn's social security number is 111-11-1111. Alyssa's social security number is 222-22-2222. Heather's address is 111 Constitution Ave., Liberty, NY 11110. Heather's social security number is 444-44-4444. Heather does not wish to contribute to the Presidential Election Campaign fund.

Heather works as an office administrator. The Form W-2 that she received from her employer showed that she received $53,400 in wages for the year. Her employer withheld $3,100 in federal income taxes. Heather earned $100 in taxable interest income on her savings account at Savings Bank. Heather also received a dividend of $800 from ABC Corporation. The dividend is a qualified dividend.

Heather is still paying on her student loans. She paid $300 in student loan interest for the year.

Assignment: Please complete a Form 1040A for Heather for the most recent calendar year.

Important Note: Remember that qualified dividends are taxed a lower rate than ordinary income. In order to make sure you determine the proper tax on Line 28, you will need to complete the Qualified Dividend and Capital Gain Tax Worksheet. You can find this in the Instructions for Form 1040A on the IRS website at www.irs.gov. Please attach this worksheet to your tax return. Also, remember to list the dividends on Line 9a and Line 9b. (The total amount of dividends a taxpayer receives—whether qualified or not— is reported on Line 9a. The amount of qualified dividends is reported on Line 9b.)

Another Important Note: Heather's children qualify for the child tax credit. Remember the child tax credit ($1,000 per child unless the phase-out applies) on Line 33. Refer to the instructions to Form 1040A for assistance. You can assume that Heather does not qualify for the additional child tax credit or the earned income credit.

PART 6

Itemized Deductions (Deductions "From" AGI)

Chapter 16

Medical Expenses, Taxes, and Interest Expense

In Chapters 16 through 18 we turn our focus to allowable itemized deductions "from" AGI. Remember that these deductions only benefit the taxpayer if the taxpayer itemizes deductions rather than takes the standard deduction. In this chapter we discuss medical expenses, taxes, and interest expenses. Additionally, we explain the potential overall reduction to itemized deductions for higher-income taxpayers.

A. Medical Expenses

Medical expenses can be a significant part of an individual's or family's costs during the year. Consequently, Congress enacted Code Section 213 to allow medical expenses as an itemized deduction.

INTERNAL REVENUE CODE

SECTION 213. MEDICAL, DENTAL, ETC., EXPENSES

(a) **Allowance of deduction.**—There shall be allowed as a deduction the expenses paid during the taxable year, not compensated for by insurance or otherwise, for medical care of the taxpayer, his spouse, or a dependent . . . to the extent that such expenses exceed 10 percent of adjusted gross income.

(b) **Limitation with respect to medicine and drugs.**—An amount paid during the taxable year for medicine or a drug shall be taken into account under subsection (a) only if such medicine or drug is a prescribed drug or is insulin.

. . .

For medicine and drugs to be deductible, a physician must prescribe them to the taxpayer (except for insulin). This means that expenses related to the purchase of over-the-counter medicine such as cold and allergy remedies, aspirin, etc., are not deductible medical expenses. Vitamins, weight loss programs, health magazine subscriptions, club memberships, and vacations, are also nondeductible as medical expenses even though they may contribute to the overall health of the individual.

Notice that medical expenses are only deductible to the extent they exceed 10% of the taxpayer's AGI. This is, of course, a significant limitation that often prevents a lot of taxpayers from benefiting from this deduction at all. Congress did provide a slight break to older taxpayers, however, by keeping the limitation at 7.5% of AGI through 2016.

INTERNAL REVENUE CODE

SECTION 213. MEDICAL, DENTAL, ETC., EXPENSES

(f) **Special rule for 2013, 2014, 2015, and 2016.**—In the case of any taxable year beginning after December 31, 2012, and ending before January 1, 2017, subsection (a) shall be applied with respect to a taxpayer by substituting "7.5 percent" for "10 percent" if such taxpayer or such taxpayer's spouse has attained age 65 before the close of such taxable year.

Perhaps the most critical part of Section 213 is the definition of "medical care." The Code provides the definition as follows:

INTERNAL REVENUE CODE

SECTION 213. MEDICAL, DENTAL, ETC., EXPENSES

. . .

(d) **Definitions.**—For purposes of this section—
  (1) The term "medical care" means amounts paid—
    (A) for the diagnosis, cure, mitigation, treatment, or prevention of disease, or for the purpose of affecting any structure or function of the body,
    (B) for transportation primarily for and essential to medical care referred to in subparagraph (A),
    (C) for qualified long-term care services . . .,

. . .

(9) **Cosmetic surgery.**—
  (A) In general. The term "medical care" does not include cosmetic surgery or other similar procedures, unless the surgery or procedure is necessary to ameliorate a deformity arising from, or directly related to, a congenital abnormality, a personal injury resulting from an accident or trauma, or disfiguring disease.
  (B) Cosmetic surgery defined. For purposes of this paragraph, the term "cosmetic surgery" means any procedure which is directed at improving the patient's appearance and does not meaningfully promote the proper function of the body or prevent or treat illness or disease.

. . .

Medical insurance premiums are also considered medical expenses.

Automobile transportation expenses for medical care are deductible at 23.5 cents per mile in 2014. Other transportation expenses that may qualify are parking fees and tolls, bus, taxi, airfare, etc. Lodging expenses necessarily incurred as part of the treatment for medical care may also be deductible, but only to the extent of $50 per night (per individual) and only if there is no significant element of personal pleasure, recreation, or vacation as part of the trip.

Amounts paid for long-term care services are deductible as medical expenses. "Long-term" care is defined as at least 90-days. Such care must be part of a prescribed plan to diagnose, prevent, cure, treat, rehabilitate, etc., injuries or diseases an individual may have.

Notice in Section 213 that "cosmetic surgery" is specifically identified as not constituting medical care unless the procedure is necessary to correct a congenital abnormality, a personal injury, or disfiguring disease.

Some amounts paid for the modification of an individual's home may be deductible (*e.g.*, ramps, cost to remove barriers, etc.). Also, even a swimming pool may be partially deductible if it is installed in the yard of an individual's home for medical purposes (*e.g.*, a doctor prescribes regularly swimming activities for someone with arthritis). The amount deductible in such a case would be the cost of the installation less the increase in value of the person's home.

Medical expenses are reported on Schedule A of the individual's Form 1040. A Schedule A is provided in the Appendix for your reference.

B. Taxes

Certain taxes paid by individuals may also qualify as itemized deductions.

INTERNAL REVENUE CODE

SECTION 164. TAXES

(a) **General rule.**—Except as otherwise provided in this section, the following taxes shall be allowed as a deduction for the taxable year within which paid or accrued:

(1) State and local, and foreign, real property taxes.

(2) State and local personal property taxes.

. . .

(b) **Definitions and special rules.**—For purposes of this section—

(1) **Personal property taxes.**—The term "personal property tax" means an ad valorem tax which is imposed on an annual basis in respect of personal property.

. . .

The most common taxes that are deductible for federal income tax purposes are state income taxes and property taxes.

Most states impose income taxes, but some do not. Congress has allowed individuals to choose to deduct state income taxes or general sales taxes that an individual pays during the year. If the individual chooses to deduct sales taxes, the individual must have receipts documenting the amount of tax paid, or in the alternative, the taxpayer can use a specific amount determined by the IRS and published on tables provided by the IRS. The option to deduct sales taxes instead of state income taxes expired at the end of 2013. *Federal* income taxes are not deductible.

Notice that for a property tax to be deductible it must be an "ad valorem" tax. This means the tax must be based on the value of the property. Thus, fees imposed by some states on vehicles based on the year the vehicle was manufactured (rather than on the value of the vehicle), for example, are not a deductible property tax.

An individual deducts taxes as an itemized deduction on Schedule A, a copy of which is included in the Appendix.

C. Interest Expenses

Taxpayers often borrow money to accomplish a variety of business and nonbusiness objectives. Of course, interest incurred as part of a trade or business is deductible. Interest paid for nonbusiness reasons, however, may or may not be deductible depending upon the purpose of the indebtedness. For example, an individual may be paying interest on a loan to acquire a personal residence (a "from" AGI deduction), educational loans (a "for" AGI deduction discussed in Chapter 14), and personal credit card balances (not deductible). We will discuss specifically personal residence interest, investment interest, and other personal interest over the next couple of pages.

1. Personal Residence Interest

A major deduction for many homeowners is the mortgage interest deduction.

INTERNAL REVENUE CODE

SECTION 163. INTEREST

. . .

(h) (3) **Qualified residence interest.**—For purposes of this subsection—

(A) In general.—The term "qualified residence interest" means any interest which is paid or accrued during the taxable year on—

(i) acquisition indebtedness with respect to any qualified residence of the taxpayer, or

(ii) home equity indebtedness with respect to any qualified residence of the taxpayer.

. . .

(h) (4) **Other definitions and special rules.—**

(A) Qualified residence.—For purposes of this subsection—

(i) In general.—The term "qualified residence" means—

(I) the principal residence (within the meaning of section 121) of the taxpayer, and

(II) 1 other residence of the taxpayer which is selected by the taxpayer for the taxable year and which is used by the taxpayer as a residence (within the meaning of section 280A(d)(1)).

. . .

To qualify as acquisition indebtedness, the personal residence must secure the loan. Moreover, interest is deductible only on a total acquisition indebtedness of $1 million. But notice that the taxpayer can deduct interest on two residences—the principal residence and one other residence. Interest paid on home equity indebtedness is also deductible. This interest deduction is limited to interest paid on indebtedness not exceeding $100,000. If the individual does not have $100,000 of equity in his or her home, then the amount of interest that is deductible is limited to the amount of the loan that represents equity in the home. The interest on home equity indebtedness is deductible without regard to how the taxpayer uses the loan proceeds.

In many situations, when a taxpayer obtains a loan to purchase a home, the taxpayer will pay "points" to the lender. A "point" is one percentage point of the loan proceeds (*i.e.*, one point of $200,000 is $2,000). Points paid must generally be capitalized and deducted over the term of the loan (because points are viewed as prepaid interest), but in many situations points can be deducted entirely in the year paid. Customarily, if the borrower provides a down payment on the loan at least equal to the amount charged as points, the amount charged for points is currently deductible.

Sometimes lenders will require a borrower to obtain mortgage insurance to protect the lender against a potential default by the borrower. Mortgage insurance premiums paid by the borrower were treated as qualified residence interest and were deductible (this provision expired at the end of 2013 and may or may not be renewed). The deduction for mortgage insurance premiums phased-out for higher-income taxpayers.

A lender uses IRS Form 1098 to report to an individual the amount of mortgage interest, points paid, and mortgage insurance premiums paid by the individual. Form 1098 is included in the Appendix for your convenience. The individual includes these amounts as itemized deductions on Schedule A.

2. Investment Interest

If an individual borrows money and then invests the money, is the interest on the borrowed amount deductible? The answer is yes, but the deduction is limited.

INTERNAL REVENUE CODE

SECTION 163. INTEREST

(a) **General rule.**—There shall be allowed as a deduction all interest paid or accrued within the taxable year on indebtedness.

. . .

(d) **Limitation on investment interest.**—

(1) **In general.**—In the case of a taxpayer other than a corporation, the amount allowed as a deduction under this chapter for investment interest for any taxable year shall not exceed the net investment income of the taxpayer for the taxable year.

. . .

The deduction for investment interest expense is limited to the individual's net investment income. Net investment income is income from property held for investment less expenses which are directly connected with the production of the investment income. Investment income usually consists of interest, dividends, royalties, annuities, and in some cases, capital gains. Remember from Chapter 7 that long-term capital gains and qualified dividends benefit from a lower tax rate than ordinary income. The taxpayer may elect to include the long-term capital gains and qualified dividends in the "investment income" total (so that that taxpayer can deduct more investment interest), but the taxpayer would have to give up the benefit of the lower applicable tax rates on long-term capital gains and qualified dividends.

An individual calculates his or her investment interest expense deduction on IRS Form 4952, a copy of which is in the Appendix for your reference.

3. Personal Interest

What about interest paid on an auto loan? Other consumer loans? Personal loans? Section 163 provides the answer.

INTERNAL REVENUE CODE

SECTION 163. INTEREST

. . .

(h) **Disallowance of deduction for personal interest.**—

(1) **In general.**—In the case of a taxpayer other than a corporation, no deduction shall be allowed under this chapter for personal interest paid or accrued during the taxable year.

(2) **Personal interest.**—For purposes of this subsection, the term "personal interest" means any interest allowable as a deduction under this chapter other than—

(A) interest paid or accrued on indebtedness properly allocable to a trade or business (other than the trade or business of performing services as an employee),

(B) any investment interest (within the meaning of subsection (d)),

(C) any interest which is taken into account under section 469 in computing income or loss from a passive activity of the taxpayer,

(D) any qualified residence interest (within the meaning of paragraph (3)),

. . .

(F) any interest allowable as a deduction under section 221 (relating to interest on educational loans).

. . .

Thus, except for the types of personal interest identified in Section 163(h) (*e.g.*, primarily business interest, qualified residence interest, investment interest, and student loan interest), all other interest paid by an individual is not deductible.

D. Potential Reduction of Overall Itemized Deductions

Higher-income individuals may have their overall itemized deductions reduced due to what is often called the "Pease" limitation (named after the late congressman, Donald J. Pease, who authored the legislation). Section 68 sets forth this limitation.

INTERNAL REVENUE CODE

SECTION 68. Overall limitation on itemized deductions

(a) **General rule.**—In the case of an individual whose adjusted gross income exceeds the applicable amount, the amount of the itemized deductions otherwise allowable for the taxable year shall be reduced by the lesser of—
   (1) 3 percent of the excess of adjusted gross income over the applicable amount, or
   (2) 80 percent of the amount of the itemized deductions otherwise allowable for such taxable year.

. . .

Notice the reference to "applicable amount." This amount, of course, varies depending upon filing status. In 2014, for example, the applicable amount is $305,050 for married filing jointly and $254,200 for a single individual. For purposes of the 80%-of-itemized-deductions calculation, medical expenses, casualty and theft losses, and investment interest expenses are not included as itemized deductions.

Chapter 16: Questions

1. *Medical expenses.* Medical expenses are deductible only if the aggregate amount of medical expenses exceeds ______% of a taxpayer's AGI. If the taxpayer is age 65 or older, only the medical expenses that exceed _______% of the taxpayer's AGI are deductible.

2. *Medical expenses.* Transportation necessary to obtain medical care is deductible at _______ cents per mile.

3. *Medical expenses.* Long-term care expenses are deductible as medical expenses. How long is "long-term" care?

4. *Medical expenses.* The Code provides that cosmetic surgery is not considered "medical care." How is cosmetic surgery defined?

5. *Taxes.* Are federal income taxes paid deductible for federal income tax purposes?

6. *Taxes.* Are state *income* taxes paid deductible for federal income tax purposes?

7. *Taxes.* Are state *sales* taxes paid deductible for federal income tax purposes?

8. *Interest.* A taxpayer is allowed to deduct personal residence interest on acquisition indebtedness up to what amount?

9. *Interest.* A taxpayer is allowed to deduct home equity interest on a home equity loan up to what amount?

10. *Interest.* Are "points" deductible?

11. *Interest.* Are private mortgage insurance premiums deductible?

12. *Interest.* A taxpayer is allowed to deduct investment interest up to what amount?

13. *Interest.* If a taxpayer chooses to treat long-term capital gains and qualified dividends as investment income (for purposes of calculating the investment interest deduction), what benefit does the taxpayer give up?

14. *Interest.* Sheila borrows $2,000 to purchase a computer for personal use. Is the interest she pays on the loan deductible for income tax purposes?

15. *Pease limitation.* If an individual's AGI exceeds a certain amount, the individual's overall itemized deductions may be reduced by how much?

Chapter 17
Charitable Contributions

Congress encourages taxpayers to donate to charitable organizations by allowing a tax deduction for the donations. Unfortunately, the tax law pertaining to charitable contributions can be quite complex. We address the core issues in this chapter.

A. CHARITABLE CONTRIBUTIONS IN GENERAL

Congress has specifically defined “charitable contribution” in Code Section 170.

INTERNAL REVENUE CODE

SECTION 170. CHARITABLE, ETC., CONTRIBUTIONS AND GIFTS

(a) **Allowance of deduction.**—

(1) **General rule.**—There shall be allowed as a deduction any charitable contribution (as defined in subsection (c)) payment of which is made within the taxable year. A charitable contribution shall be allowable as a deduction only if verified under regulations prescribed by the Secretary.

. . .

(c) **Charitable contribution defined.**—For purposes of this section, the term “charitable contribution” means a contribution or gift to or for the use of—

(1) A State, a possession of the United States, or any political subdivision of any of the foregoing, or the United States or the District of Columbia, but only if the contribution or gift is made for exclusively public purposes.

(2) A corporation, trust, or community chest, fund, or foundation—

(A) created or organized in the United States or in any possession thereof, or under the law of the United States, any State, the District of Columbia, or any possession of the United States.

(B) organized and operated exclusively for religious, charitable, scientific, literary, or educational purposes, or to foster national or international amateur sports competition (but only if no part of its activities involve the provision of athletic facilities or equipment), or for the prevention of cruelty to children or animals.

(C) no part of the net earnings of which inures to the benefit of any private shareholder or individual; and

(D) which is not disqualified for tax exemption under section 501(c)(3) by reason of attempting to influence legislation, and which does not participate in, or intervene in (including the publishing or distributing of statements), any political campaign on behalf of (or in opposition to) any candidate for public office.

. . .

Notice that deductions are allowed for contributions to state and local governments as well as corporations, trust, community chest, fund, or foundation that engages in certain activities. *Important note*: the use of the term "corporation" in this context means a *nonprofit* corporation. The recipient organization, if it is not a governmental organization, generally must be organized and operated exclusively for religious, charitable, scientific, literary, or educational purposes, or to foster amateur sports competition or to prevent cruelty to children or animals. These types of organizations are often called "501(c)(3)" organizations because they must meet the requirements of Code Section 501(c)(3) in order to be exempt from income taxation and to allow donors to qualify for charitable contribution deductions.

B. Public Charities and Private Foundations

As just discussed, charitable contributions are deductible (subject to some limitations discussed later) if the donor makes the contribution to certain types of organizations, the most common of which are Section 501(c)(3) organizations. Section 501(c)(3) organizations include two major types of classifications—public charities and private nonoperating foundations (we will just refer to them as "private foundations" from here forward, but there is also a distinct form of organization called private *operating* foundations). Deductions for donations to private foundations may be limited to a greater extent than are donations to public charities. Typical organizations that automatically qualify for *public charity* status are:

- a church or a convention or association of churches;
- most educational organizations with regular faculty and curriculum and regularly enrolled students;
- hospitals and medical research organizations; and
- governmental entities

Other organizations can qualify for public charity status if they are broadly supported by the public or by governmental entities.

Private foundations are usually organized by an individual or a few individuals who wish to have significant control over the charitable, educational, etc., activities of the organization. As a general rule, these organizations also are typically funded by only a few individuals rather than by the general public. Private foundations are also subject to strict regulations and face penalty taxes for violating those regulations. After reviewing an organization's application for tax-exempt status, the IRS determines whether the organization qualifies as a public charity or private foundation. The IRS then sends the organization a **determination letter**, which indicates the organization's status. A potential donor can ask the organization for a copy of its determination letter so that the donor knows if the organization is a public charity or private foundation. For further discussion relating to tax-exempt entities, public charities, private foundations, etc., please see the *Business Entity Taxation* textbook by this author.

C. Limitations on Deductibility of Donations to Public Charities

Although donations may otherwise qualify as tax deductible charitable contributions, the Code imposes limits on how much an individual can deduct in any one year.

INTERNAL REVENUE CODE

SECTION 170. CHARITABLE, ETC., CONTRIBUTIONS AND GIFTS

. . .

(b) **Percentage limitations.—**

(1) **Individuals.**—In the case of an individual, the deduction provided in subsection (a) shall be limited as provided in the succeeding subparagraphs.

(A) General rule.—Any charitable contribution to—

(i) a church or a convention or association of churches,

(ii) [most educational organizations]

(iii) [hospitals and medical research organizations]

. . .

(v) [governmental units]

(vi) [publicly supported organizations]

. . .

shall be allowed to the extent that the aggregate of such contributions does not exceed 50 percent of the taxpayer's contribution base for the taxable year.

. . .

(G) Contribution base defined.—For purposes of this section, the term "contribution base" means adjusted gross income (computed without regard to any net operating loss carryback to the taxable year under section 172).

. . .

Notice, then, that the general limitation on donations to public charities is 50% of the individual's "contribution base." An individual's contribution base is equal to the individual's adjusted gross income (computed without regard to any net operating loss carrybacks, if any, to the current year).

If the individual's charitable contribution deductions to public charities exceed the 50% limitation, the excess can be carried forward for up to five years.

The Code contains a special rule that could reduce the amount deductible for contributions to public charities if the contribution is of **capital gain property**. Capital gain property is any property to the extent it would produce a long-term capital gain if the property were sold. Although the fair market value of the capital gain property is generally allowed as the contribution amount, the Code limits the overall amount of deductible capital gain property to 30% of the individual's contribution base rather than 50%. The taxpayer may elect that the 50% limitation apply instead of the 30% limitation on the contribution of capital gain property, but in such a case the taxpayer may only deduct the tax basis of the property and not the fair market value. The Code generally allows an individual to deduct only the property's tax basis if the property donated is **ordinary income property** *(e.g., inventory)* rather than capital gain property.

D. Limitations on Deductibility of Donations to Private Foundations

Deductions for contributions to private foundations are limited to 30% of the individual's contribution base. Deductions for contributions of capital gain property to private foundations are limited to 20% of the individual's contribution base. Moreover, in most situations an individual is allowed to deduct only the basis of the property contributed to private foundations and not the property's fair market value. Thus, you can see that the Code allows an individual to deduct potentially more contributions to public charities during a given year than contributions to private foundations.

E. Reporting, Documentation, and Other Special Rules

To conclude this chapter we discuss briefly some reporting and documentation requirements as well as some other special rules relating to common charitable contribution issues.

1. Reporting and Documentation

Individuals report their charitable contribution deductions on Schedule A. If the individual makes cash donations of $250 or more then the individual generally needs to obtain a statement from the charitable organization showing the amount of money contributed. If an individual makes a donation of non-cash property of any amount to a charitable organization, the individual must obtain a written acknowledgement from the organization describing the property. The organization does not need to state the *value* of any property contributed, however. If the individual deducts more than $500 for a contribution of non-cash property to a charitable organization, the individual must file IRS Form 8283 with his or her tax return. This form, of course, asks for a bit more detail regarding the property contributed. If the individual deducts more than $5,000 for property contributed to a charitable organization, the individual must obtain an appraisal of the property and report certain information relating to the appraisal on Form 8283. In some cases, the appraisal may need to be attached to the individual's tax return and submitted to the IRS. A copy of Form 8283 is provided in the Appendix. In short, a tax advisor should make sure his or her clients are properly substantiating any charitable contributions.

A common charitable contribution is that of an old vehicle. Given some past abuses by taxpayers relating to the value of those vehicles, the IRS now has strict documentation requirements for vehicle donations. If, for example, the charity shortly after receiving a donated car sells the car in an arm's-length transaction, the charity must inform the IRS and the individual donor of the sales price. The donor's deduction is then limited to the sales price. With respect to vehicle donations, the charitable organization must provide the donor an IRS Form 1098-C. A Form 1098-C is included in the Appendix for your reference.

2. Other Special Rules

An individual may deduct transportation expenses incurred in connection with volunteering for charitable activities. Rather than deducting actual costs, however, the IRS allows the taxpayer to elect to deduct 14 cents per mile. The value of the taxpayer's *time* is not deductible.

If a taxpayer makes a donation to a charitable organization and receives something of value in return (*e.g.*, food, entertainment, merchandise, etc.), then the taxpayer's charitable contribution deduction is decreased by the value of what the taxpayer received unless the value is of a token amount. These contributions are sometimes called *quid pro quo* contributions. Special rules also apply if the donor receives tickets (or the right to purchase tickets) to athletic events in return for a donation to a college or university.

CHAPTER 17: QUESTIONS

1. *Deductible contributions.* In order for a taxpayer's donation to an organization to qualify for a tax deduction, the contribution has to be made to certain types of organizations. What types of organizations are they?

2. *Public charities.* What types of organizations automatically qualify for "public charity" status?

3. *Public charities vs. private foundations.* What advantage(s) are there to being a public charity as opposed to a private foundation?

4. *Public charities vs. private foundations.* What advantage(s) are there to being a private foundation as opposed to a public charity?

5. *Deduction limitations.* What general deduction limitation applies to charitable contributions made to public charities? What if the contributions are of capital gain property?

6. *Deduction limitations.* What general deduction limitation applies to charitable contributions made to private foundations? What if the contributions are of capital gain property?

7. *Reporting requirements.* When must an individual receive a written acknowledgement from a charitable organization describing the donation? What must a taxpayer do if the taxpayer

deducts an amount in excess of $500 for non-cash property contributed to a charitable organization? What if the deduction exceeds $5,000?

8. *Reporting requirements.* What special reporting requirements are involved if a taxpayer takes a charitable contribution deduction for the donation of a vehicle?

9. *Other special rules.* May an individual deduct as a charitable contribution the value of his or her time?

10. *Other special rules.* How much per mile can an individual deduct for transportation expenses in connection with volunteer charitable service?

11. *Other special rules.* Generally, how is an individual's charitable contribution deduction impacted if the individual receives something in return for the charitable contribution?

Chapter 18

Casualty and Theft Losses and Miscellaneous Itemized Deductions

In this chapter we conclude our discussion of itemized deductions. In particular, we discuss casualty and theft losses and then miscellaneous itemized deductions.

A. Casualty and Theft Losses

Individuals and businesses may be able to deduct losses that occur as a result of a casualty or theft. Section 165 provides the law in this area.

INTERNAL REVENUE CODE

SECTION 165. LOSSES

(a) **General rule.**—There shall be allowed as a deduction any loss sustained during the taxable year and not compensated for by insurance or otherwise.

(b) **Amount of deduction.**—For purposes of subsection (a), the basis for determining the amount of the deduction for any loss shall be the adjusted basis provided in section 1011 for determining the loss from the sale or other disposition of property.

(c) **Limitation on losses of individuals.**—In the case of an individual, the deduction under subsection (a) shall be limited to—

(1) losses incurred in a trade or business;

(2) losses incurred in any transaction entered into for profit, though not connected with a trade or business; and

(3) except as provided in subsection (h), losses of property not connected with a trade or business or a transaction entered into for profit, if such losses arise from fire, storm, shipwreck, or other casualty, or from theft.

. . .

(e) **Theft losses.**—For purposes of subsection (a), any loss arising from theft shall be treated as sustained during the taxable year in which the taxpayer discovers such loss.

. . .

Losses incurred in business or in transactions entered into for profit are "for" AGI deductions. Losses on personal use assets are not deductible. Personal losses due to *casualty* or *theft*, however, are deductible as an itemized deduction for individuals.

There can be some uncertainty as to the meaning of "casualty." The IRS defines the term as some identifiable event that is sudden, unexpected or unusual. What if termites feast upon a home for ten years causing extensive damage? Is this a casualty? Courts have ruled that this is not sudden enough to constitute a casualty. On the other hand, a sudden infestation of beetles that destroyed a taxpayer's trees was held to be a "casualty." A theft loss is deductible in the year the individual discovers that a theft occurred.

Notice that casualty and theft losses are deductible only to the extent the loss was not compensated for by insurance. The Code, in fact, requires the taxpayer to file a claim for insurance (if the taxpayer has insurance) before the casualty or theft loss can be deducted.

The amount of a casualty or theft loss that is deductible is limited. First, these losses can only be claimed if the loss exceeds $100 (per loss). Second, in addition to the $100 threshold, casualty or theft losses can only be deducted to the extent the losses (in aggregate) exceed 10% of the individual's adjusted gross income. These limitations can cause many casualty and theft losses to provide no reduction in tax liability to the taxpayer. Casualty and theft losses are reported on Form 4684, a copy of which is provided in the Appendix for your reference.

B. Miscellaneous Itemized Deductions

Afew itemized deductions are classified as "miscellaneous" itemized deductions. These deductions are typically deductible only to the extent the individual's aggregate miscellaneous itemized deductions exceed 2% of the taxpayer's AGI. Sometimes the 2% limitation is called the "2% floor" or even the "2% haircut." Section 67 sets forth this limitation.

INTERNAL REVENUE CODE

SECTION 67. 2-PERCENT FLOOR ON MISCELLANEOUS ITEMIZED DEDUCTIONS

(a) **General rule.**—In the case of an individual, the miscellaneous itemized deductions for any taxable year shall be allowed only to the extent that the aggregate of such deductions exceeds 2 percent of adjusted gross income.

(b) **Miscellaneous itemized deductions.**—For purposes of this section, the term "miscellaneous itemized deductions" means the itemized deductions other than—

(1) the deduction under section 163 (relating to interest),

(2) the deduction under section 164 (relating to taxes),

(3) the deduction under section 165(a) for casualty or theft losses described in paragraph (2) or (3) of section 165(c) or for losses described in section 165(d),

(4) the deductions under section 170 (relating to charitable, etc., contributions and gifts) and section 642(c)(relating to deduction for amounts paid or permanently set aside for a charitable purpose),

(5) the deduction under section 213 (relating to medical, dental, etc., expenses),

. . .

The most common miscellaneous itemized deductions are unreimbursed employee expenses, investment expenses, and tax return preparation fees. We discuss these deductions and a couple of others throughout the rest of this chapter.

1. Unreimbursed Employee Expenses

Suppose you occasionally use your personal vehicle for business purposes for your employer (*e.g.*, deliver a package, drive to meet with a client away from the office, etc.). Suppose further that your employer does not reimburse you for the cost of gasoline. Are these and similar expenses you incur deductible to you? The answer is yes, subject to the 2% floor.

Common business expenses that employees may incur but not get reimbursed by the employer are transportation expenses for business-related activity, uniforms and other special clothing required to be worn by the employee by the employer, dues to professional organizations, subscriptions to professional journals, meals and entertainment, and travel expenses. All these employee expenses are subject to the 2% floor. For vehicle expenses, the employee can elect to deduct the actual costs (*e.g.*, gas, oil, depreciation, etc.) or 56 cents per mile (in 2014).

Note: Even if the employer does reimburse an employee for the employee's business expenses, the reimbursement is included in the employee's gross income and the expenses are miscellaneous itemized deductions (subject to the 2% floor) if the employer's plan is not an **accountable** plan. An accountable plan is one in which the employer reimburses the employee, but the employee must meet strict documentation requirements and be required to return to the employer any reimbursement that exceeds the expenses. Under an accountable plan, the employer's reimbursement is technically included in the employee's gross income but at the same time the employee's deduction is a "for" AGI deduction, thus resulting in a wash. As a practical matter, then, the employer will not report the reimbursement in the employee's gross income and the employee will not report the "for" AGI deduction. Under an accountable plan, some of the strict documentation requirements are waived if the employer uses the per-diem tables established by the IRS, which allows deductions for a certain set amount for meals and lodging depending upon the location the employee incurs the expenses (*e.g.*, New York City, Dallas, Omaha, etc.).

An employee calculates and reports unreimbursed business expenses (or reimbursed business expenses under a non-accountable plan) on IRS Form 2106. This form is included in the Appendix for your reference. Ultimately, the amount on Form 2106 is transferred to Schedule A as part of the individual's itemized deductions.

2. Investment Expenses

Individuals often incur expenses associated with investments. Of course, the investment income is subject to inclusion in the individual's gross income and ultimately taxed. The Code allows taxpayers to deduct expenses incurred to generate the taxable income. Nevertheless, the deduction is limited by the 2% floor. Some common investment expenses are investment adviser fees, custodial fees, costs for clerical help, safe deposit boxes, subscriptions to investment journals, and perhaps office rent and state or local transfer tax fees.

3. Tax Return Preparation Fees and Other Miscellaneous Itemized Deductions

Expenses an individual incurs to have his or her individual income tax return prepared qualify as miscellaneous itemized deductions. If the individual is also a sole proprietor, however, a common practice is to split the tax return preparation fees into two parts: the cost for preparing the tax return related to the business and the cost for the remaining personal items reflected on the return. This separation is beneficial to the individual because the tax return preparation fees charged for the business part of the return are treated as business expenses and thus not subject to the 2% floor.

An individual may incur accounting, legal or other professional fees related to the individual's production of income activities or activities related to the management, conservation, or maintenance of income-producing property. These expenses can also qualify as miscellaneous itemized deductions as do fees paid for tax advice relating to these activities. Accounting and/or legal fees incurred for purposes other than for business or other income-producing activities are considered personal, nondeductible expenses.

The instructions to IRS Form 1040, Schedule A list a few more very narrow expenses that may also qualify as miscellaneous itemized deductions, but we will not go into detail here regarding those items.

CHAPTER 18: QUESTIONS

1. *Casualty and theft losses.* Casualty and theft losses are deductible only when they exceed what amount?

2. *Casualty and theft losses.* What is a "casualty"?

3. *Itemized deductions.* Name four itemized deductions that are not *miscellaneous* itemized deductions.

4. *Miscellaneous itemized deductions.* Why might it be disadvantageous for an expense to be classified as a "miscellaneous" itemized deduction?

5. *Miscellaneous itemized deductions.* Name some common miscellaneous itemized deductions.

6. *Employee expenses.* Explain the difference between an accountable plan and a non-accountable plan and what difference it might make to an employee's deduction of business expenses.

7. *Investment expenses.* Name some common investment expenses an individual may incur.

8. *Other miscellaneous deductions.* Are tax return preparation fees deductible? If so, are they subject to the 2% floor?

PART 7

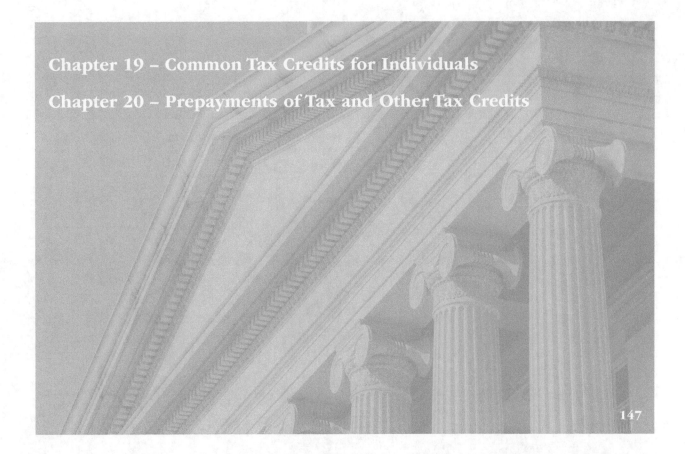

Tax Credits

Chapter 19

Common Tax Credits for Individuals

Once taxable income is determined, the applicable tax rate is applied. The result is the individual's gross income tax liability. From that point, the individual subtracts any prepaid taxes and any tax **credits** the individual may be entitled to. In this chapter we discuss common tax credits for individuals and in Chapter 20 we discuss tax prepayments and other tax credits for which an individual may qualify.

A. Earned Income Credit

Lower-income individuals that have earned income up to a certain amount may qualify for the **earned income credit (EIC)**. Section 32 provides for this credit.

INTERNAL REVENUE CODE

SECTION 32. EARNED INCOME

(a) **Allowance of credit.—**

(1) **In general.**—In the case of an eligible individual, there shall be allowed as a credit against the tax imposed by this subtitle for the taxable year an amount equal to the credit percentage of so much of the taxpayer's earned income for the taxable year as does not exceed the earned income amount.

. . .

Section 32 is quite detailed in its definitions and formulas to determine the amount of the credit. In short, the amount of the tax credit depends on the amount of earned income and the number of qualifying children the taxpayer has. Of course, the intent of the EIC is basically to give a tax break to lower-income individuals who are working and have children (although some lower-income individuals with no children may also qualify for a small credit). The table below shows the limits on earned income and the maximum credit for 2014:

Earned income and AGI must each be less than:

- $46,997 ($52,427 married filing jointly) with three or more qualifying children
- $43,756 ($49,186 married filing jointly) with two qualifying children
- $38,511 ($43,941 married filing jointly) with one qualifying child
- $14,590 ($20,020 married filing jointly) with no qualifying children

Maximum credit =

- $6,143 with three or more qualifying children
- $5,460 with two qualifying children
- $3,305 with one qualifying child
- $496 with no qualifying children

The amount of the credit may be disallowed if the taxpayer has over $3,350 of *investment* income for the year. Unlike most credits, the EIC is a *refundable* credit. This means the taxpayer receives a refund to the extent of the EIC even if the taxpayer's net tax liability is already zero.

B. Child Tax Credit

Separate from the earned income tax credit, the Code also allows a tax credit of a set amount for each qualifying child of a taxpayer.

INTERNAL REVENUE CODE

SECTION 24. CHILD TAX CREDIT

(a) **Allowance of credit.**—There shall be allowed as a credit against the tax imposed by this chapter for the taxable year with respect to each qualifying child of the taxpayer . . . an amount equal to $1,000.

. . .

Thus, the current credit is $1,000 per child that is under age 17 and meets certain relationship, support, and other tests. The child tax credit begins to phase-out at certain income levels. For example, the phase-out begins for single individuals at an AGI of $75,000 and for married individuals filing jointly at an AGI of $110,000. In some narrow situations, a certain portion of the child tax credit may be treated as a refundable credit.

C. American Opportunity Credit and Lifetime Learning Credit

The Code contains many provisions giving tax breaks to individuals seeking higher education (*e.g.*, tuition and fees deduction, student loan interest deduction, employer-provided exclusions, etc.) Two education-related tax *credits* that may be available to taxpayers are the American Opportunity Tax Credit (AOTC) and the lifetime learning credit (LLC).

INTERNAL REVENUE CODE

SECTION 25A. HOPE AND LIFETIME LEARNING CREDITS

(a) **Allowance of credit.**—In the case of an individual, there shall be allowed as a credit against the tax imposed by this chapter for the taxable year the amount equal to the sum of—

(1) the Hope Scholarship Credit, plus

(2) the Lifetime Learning Credit.

. . .

Notice that Section 25A refers to the Hope Scholarship Credit. The Hope Scholarship Credit was temporarily expanded (through 2018) and is now called the American Opportunity Tax Credit. We will refer to it as the AOTC in our discussion.

1. American Opportunity Tax Credit

This credit is allowed up to a maximum of $2,500 per year for each qualifying student (thus, a credit for more than $2,500 may be available to a taxpayer who pays for the qualifying expenses of more than one student in the family, for example). The credit is calculated as 100% of the first $2,000 plus 25% of up to a maximum of $2,000 in additional expenses. The credit is only available for the first four years of post-secondary education. Qualified expenses include mainly tuition, fees, and textbooks paid for the taxpayer, the taxpayer's spouse, or any dependent of the taxpayer. Room and board do not qualify. The student must be enrolled at least for one-half of a full load.

As with many other deductions and credits, the benefits of the credit begin to phase-out for individuals with income over a certain threshold. For example, the threshold is $160,000 for married individuals filing jointly. In some situations, a portion of the AOTC may qualify as a refundable credit.

2. Lifetime Learning Credit

This credit is different in a couple of respects from the AOTC. The LLC is allowed up to a maximum of $2,000 credit per year for each *taxpayer* (not for each student). This is calculated by taking 20% of the qualified tuition expenses up to $10,000. The credit is available for qualified expenses beyond the student's first four years of post-secondary education, and the student need not be attending at least half-time. The LLC also phases out for taxpayers who have income over a certain threshold. Also, a taxpayer is not allowed to claim both the AOTC and LLC in the same year. The AOTC and LLC are claimed on IRS Form 8863, a copy of which is included in the Appendix.

D. Credit for Child and Dependent Care Expenses

For individuals incurring expenses for child and dependent care, the Code allows a credit up to a certain amount for qualified expenses.

INTERNAL REVENUE CODE

SECTION 21. EXPENSES FOR HOUSEHOLD AND DEPENDENT CARE SERVICES NECESSARY FOR GAINFUL EMPLOYMENT

(a) **Allowance of credit.**—

(1) **In general.**—In the case of an individual for which there are 1 or more qualifying individuals . . . with respect to such individual, there shall be allowed as a credit against the tax imposed by this chapter for the taxable year an amount equal to the applicable percentage of the employment-related expenses . . . paid by such individual during the taxable year.

. . .

This credit is intended to give a tax break to allow individuals with dependents to be gainfully employed and who incur expenses related to care for their children or other qualifying dependents. The dependent(s) must be under 13 years-old, or if the dependent(s) are 13 or over, the dependent(s) must be physical or mentally incapable of caring for themselves. The amount of the credit ranges from 20% to 35% of the applicable employment-related expenses (with such expenses capped at $3,000 for one qualifying individual and $6,000 for two or more qualifying individuals). The percentage that applies depends upon the taxpayer's adjusted gross income. The credit phases out for taxpayers with AGI over a certain threshold. The credit is calculated on IRS Form 2441, a copy of which is included in the Appendix.

E. Adoption Credit

To assist individuals who undergo the often-expensive process of adopting a child, the Code provides for an adoption credit.

INTERNAL REVENUE CODE

SECTION 23. ADOPTION EXPENSES

(a) **Allowance of credit.**—

(1) **In general.**—In the case of an individual, there shall be allowed as a credit against the tax imposed by this chapter the amount of the qualified adoption expenses paid or incurred by the taxpayer.

. . .

Qualified adoption expenses include adoption fees, attorney fees, court costs, etc. The amount of the credit is limited to $13,190 for 2014, subject to phase-out for higher-income taxpayers. The credit is claimed on IRS Form 8839, a copy of which is included in the Appendix.

F. Foreign Tax Credit

The United States has the jurisdiction to tax United States citizens and residents on their worldwide income. This raises the issue of double-taxation for a taxpayer's foreign-sourced income (*i.e.*, the income being taxed in the foreign country and in the United States). Congress has lessened this concern by allowing a taxpayer a credit against his or her U.S. income tax by the amount of income tax paid in the foreign country.

INTERNAL REVENUE CODE

SECTION 27. TAXES OF FOREIGN COUNTRIES AND POSSESSIONS OF THE UNITED STATES; POSSESSION TAX CREDIT

(a) **Foreign tax credit.**—The amount of taxes imposed by foreign countries and possessions of the United States shall be allowed as a credit against the tax imposed by this chapter to the extent provided in section 901.

. . .

INTERNAL REVENUE CODE

SECTION 901. TAXES OF FOREIGN COUNTRIES AND OF POSSESSIONS OF UNITED STATES

(a) **Allowance of credit.**—If the taxpayer chooses to have the benefits of this subpart, the tax imposed by this chapter shall, subject to the limitation of section 904, be credited with the amounts provided in the applicable paragraph of subsection (b) . . .

(b) **Amount allowed.**—Subject to the limitation of section 904, the following amounts shall be allowed as the credit under subsection (a):

(1) **Citizens and domestic corporations.**—In the case of a citizen of the United States and of a domestic corporation, the amount of any income, war profits, and excess profits taxes paid or accrued during the taxable year to any foreign country or to any possession of the United States . . ..

. . .

The United States also enters into tax treaties with foreign countries to try to eliminate or at least reduce the potential for double-taxation. Technically, a taxpayer may elect to *deduct* the foreign taxes paid or claim the foreign tax *credit*. Of course, the credit is usually more beneficial because it is a dollar-for-dollar reduction in the taxpayer's overall tax liability. As a general rule, the taxpayer is only allowed to claim a foreign tax credit that is equal to or less than the amount of tax the United States imposes on the income. In other words, if the tax rate is higher in the foreign country than in the United States, the taxpayer cannot deduct the amount of tax paid in excess of the tax that would have been paid to the United States government on the income. Such disallowed excess amount can be carried back one year and forward ten years, however.

CHAPTER 19: QUESTIONS

1. *Earned income credit.* What is the purpose of the earned income credit?

2. *Earned income credit.* The earned income credit is a refundable credit. Explain what that means.

3. *Earned income credit.* Is it possible for a taxpayer to qualify for the earned income credit if the taxpayer has no children?

4. *Child tax credit.* How much is the child tax credit per child? Is this amount subject to phase-out?

5. *American Opportunity Tax Credit.* What is the maximum credit an individual can receive under the AOTC?

6. *American Opportunity Tax Credit.* Is the maximum AOTC amount applicable per taxpayer or per student?

7. *American Opportunity Tax Credit.* To qualify for the AOTC, does the student have to be attending at least half of a full load of classes?

8. *Lifetime Learning Credit.* What is the maximum credit an individual can receive under the LLC?

9. *Lifetime Learning Credit.* Is the maximum LLC amount applicable per taxpayer or per student?

10. *Lifetime Learning Credit.* To qualify for the LLC, does the student have to be attending at least half of a full load of classes?

11. *Child and dependent care credit.* What is the purpose of the child and dependent care credit?

12. *Child and dependent care credit.* Generally, qualifying dependent care expenses must be for a dependent under what age? If the dependent is older than that age, what conditions must exist for that person to be a qualifying dependent?

13. *Adoption credit.* What is the maximum adoption credit for the year 2014?

14. *Foreign tax credit.* The foreign tax credit is limited. Explain. To the extent the foreign tax credit is limited can the excess foreign taxes paid by a taxpayer be carried back or carried forward? If so, for how many years?

Chapter 20

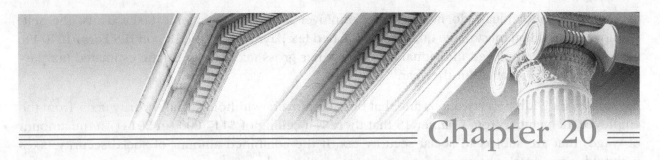

Prepayments of Tax and Other Tax Credits

We conclude our discussion of tax credits in this chapter by looking at prepayment of taxes as well as a few more available tax credits in addition to those discussed in Chapter 19.

A. Prepayment of Taxes

Employers are required to withhold income taxes from an employee's paycheck. The employer determines how much to withhold based upon an employee's furnishing the employer an IRS Form W-4 upon which the employee informs the employer the employee's filing status and how many "personal allowances" (similar to personal and dependency exemptions) the employee is claiming. The employer can then look at IRS tables to determine how much income tax to withhold from an employee's paycheck based upon the number of personal allowances and filing status. An IRS Form W-4 is included in the Appendix for your reference.

Of course, the amount of income tax the employer withholds is usually not equal to the exact amount of the employee's tax liability each year. Thus, a taxpayer may be entitled to a refund or owe more in taxes after the individual calculates the actual amount of tax liability for the year. The employee may have the employer withhold more income taxes in order to compensate for the fact that the employee may have other income that is not subject to withholding (*e.g.*, interest and dividend income). Nevertheless, the individual is allowed to subtract from his or her gross tax liability the amount of taxes he or she prepaid through employer withholding.

INTERNAL REVENUE CODE

SECTION 31. TAX WITHHELD ON WAGES

(a) **Wage withholding for income tax purposes.—**

(1) **In general.**—The amount withheld as tax under chapter 24 shall be allowed to the recipient of the income as a credit against the tax imposed by this subtitle.

. . .

Self-employed individuals do not have an employer to withhold income taxes. Thus, the self-employed individual must make quarterly estimated tax payments to the IRS on IRS Form 1040-ES. Of course, a self-employed individual can reduce her gross tax liability by the estimated tax payments she makes throughout the year.

Assume an individual has two jobs and that both employers withhold social security taxes from the employee. Remember from Chapter 15 that there is a ceiling of $117,000 (in 2014) on the amount of wages that are subject to social security tax. If the combined amount of social security taxes withheld is too much, the employee can take a credit for the excess.

B. Business Credits

The Code contains an abundant number of tax credits that are broadly referred to as "business credits." These credits are available not just to individuals engaged in business activity (*i.e.*, a sole proprietor), but also corporations, partnerships, and limited liability companies that engage in those activities. Many chapters could be written describing each credit in detail, but that is not our purpose here.

Section 38 sets forth the general rule for an allowance of the general business credit.

INTERNAL REVENUE CODE

SECTION 38. GENERAL BUSINESS CREDIT

(a) **Allowance of credit.**—There shall be allowed as a credit against the tax imposed by this chapter for the taxable year an amount equal to the sum of—
   (1) the business credit carryforwards carried to such taxable year,
   (2) the amount of the current year business credit, plus
   (3) the business credit carrybacks carried to such taxable year.

(b) **Current year business credit.**—For purposes of this subpart, the amount of the current year business credit is the sum of the following credits determined for the taxable year:
   (1) the investment credit determined under section 46,
   (2) the work opportunity credit determined under section 51(a),
   (3) the alcohol fuels credit determined under section 40(a),
   (4) the research credit determined under section 41(a),
   (5) the low-income housing credit determined under section 42(a),
   (6) the enhanced oil recovery credit under section 43(a),
   (7) in the case of an eligible small business . . ., the disabled access credit determined under section 44(a),

. . .

   (23) the new energy efficient home credit determined under section 45L(a),
   (24) the energy efficient appliance credit determined under section 45M(a),

. . .

   (35) the portion of the new qualified plug-in electric drive motor vehicle credit to which Section 30D(c)(1) applies, plus

(36) the small employer health insurance credit determined under section 45R.

(c) **Limitation based on amount of tax.**—

(1) **In general.**—The credit under subsection (a) for any taxable year shall not exceed the excess (if any of the taxpayer's net income tax over the greater of—

(A) the tentative minimum tax for the taxable year, or

(B) 25 percent of so much of the taxpayer's net regular tax liability as exceeds $25,000.

. . .

Notice that the "general business credit" is comprised of many smaller credits. The total amount of business tax credits a taxpayer can take is limited. To the extent the business tax credits for which a taxpayer is eligible goes unused for a particular year due to the limitation, the taxpayer can carry the excess credits back one year and forward 20 years. A taxpayer reports the general business credits on IRS Form 3800, a copy of which is included in the Appendix.

C. Residential Energy Credits

Congress has given taxpayers a tax incentive to invest in some items that make homes more energy efficient. We will discuss two credits here: (1) the nonbusiness energy property credit, and (2) the residential energy efficient property credit.

1. Nonbusiness Energy Property Credit

An individual is eligible for a tax credit for installing energy efficient windows, doors, insulation, furnaces, central air conditioners, etc.

INTERNAL REVENUE CODE

SECTION 25C. NONBUSINESS ENERGY PROPERTY

(a) **Allowance of credit.**—In the case of an individual, there shall be allowed as a credit against the tax imposed by this chapter for the taxable year an amount equal to the sum of—

(1) 10 percent of the amount paid or incurred by the taxpayer for qualified energy efficiency improvements installed during such taxable year, and

(2) the amount of the residential energy property expenditures paid or incurred by the taxpayer during such taxable year.

. . .

There is a $500 lifetime limit for this credit. This credit is claimed on IRS Form 5695, a copy of which is included in the Appendix. This credit expired at the end of 2013. Congress may or may not extend the credit to future years.

2. Residential Energy Efficient Property Credit

Congress continues to encourage expenditures on energy efficient property.

INTERNAL REVENUE CODE

SECTION 25D. RESIDENTIAL ENERGY EFFICIENT PROPERTY

(a) **Allowance of credit.**—In the case of an individual, there shall be allowed as a credit against the tax imposed by this chapter for the taxable year an amount equal to the sum of—
   (1) 30 percent of the qualified solar electric property expenditures made by the taxpayer during such year,
   (2) 30 percent of the qualified solar water heating property expenditures made by the taxpayer during such year,
   (3) 30 percent of the qualified fuel cell property expenditures made by the taxpayer during such year,
   (4) 30 percent of the qualified small wind energy property expenditures made by the taxpayer during such year, and
   (5) 30 percent of the qualified geothermal heat pump property expenditures made by the taxpayer during such year.

. . .

As you can see, this credit encourages individuals to install in their residences items such as solar electric property, solar water heating property, fuel cell property, wind energy property, and geothermal heat pump property. This credit is claimed on IRS Form 5695, a copy of which is included in the Appendix. There are some limitations to this credit also, but to the extent a credit is not allowed to be used in the current year, the credit carries over to the next year.

D. Qualified Retirement Savings Contributions Credit ("Saver's Credit")

The Code allows a tax credit for lower-income and moderate-income taxpayers who make contributions to retirement accounts (such as IRAs, 401(k)'s, etc.). The credit is in addition to any deduction the individual may receive from the contribution. The credit is limited to a maximum of $1,000 and the amount of the credit could be less than that based upon the individual's adjusted gross income and amount of eligible contributions to qualified retirement plans. This credit is calculated by using IRS Form 8880, a copy of which is included in the Appendix.

E. Other Credits

In addition to the many credits we have identified and discussed in Chapter 19 and this chapter, there are still more less-common credits that may be available to a particular taxpayer. A tax advisor is wise to become more familiar with these credits as he or she gets to know the needs of particular clients. A detailed discussion of the several additional credits is will not be presented here, however.

CHAPTER 20: QUESTIONS

1. *Prepayment of taxes.* How does an employer determine how much income tax to withhold from an employee's paycheck?

2. *Prepayment of taxes.* How does a self-employed individual go about paying estimated taxes?

3. *Prepayment of taxes.* What can an individual do if an employee has two jobs and the two employers withhold too much social security tax?

4. *Business credits.* Name four credits that fall under the business tax credit umbrella.

5. *Business credits.* If a taxpayer's business tax credits are limited in a particular year, is the taxpayer allowed to use the excess credits in another year? If so, which year(s)?

6. *Residential energy credits.* What types of expenditures are eligible for the nonbusiness energy property credit?

7. *Residential energy credits.* What types of expenditures are eligible for the residential energy efficient property credit?

8. *Saver's credit.* What is the maximum credit amount an individual may qualify for under the retirement savings contribution credit?

TAX RETURN EXERCISE

Your new clients, Roger K. and Bradi G. Westerfield have hired you to prepare their income tax return for the most recently completed calendar year. Roger and Bradi are married and will file a joint return. They live at 777 South Garfield Avenue, Paradise, UT 84303.

Roger's social security number:	888-88-8888
Bradi's social security number:	555-55-5555

Roger and Bradi have two children, Samantha (age 15) and Josh (age 7). Both children lived with them for the entire year and Roger and Bradi provided all of their support.

Samantha's social security number:	333-33-3333
Josh's social security number:	777-77-7777

Roger and Bradi provide you with the following information:

Roger

Roger is a self-employed electrician. He started the business in 2008 and named it "Lightning-Fast Electrician Services." Roger is a cash method taxpayer and he materially participated in the business during the year. According to the IRS instructions to Form 1040, Schedule C, his business code is 238210. He did not make any payments that required him to file Form 1099. Roger's books show the following for the year:

Revenue from services provided	$100,000
Advertising expense	($2,000)
Car and truck expenses	($8,000)
Legal and professional services	($1,500)
Supplies	($500)
Meals and entertainment	($2,000)
Wages paid to employees	($37,000)

Roger made $6,000 of *federal* estimated income tax payments on Form 1040-ES throughout the year.

Bradi

Bradi works as a loan specialist at MNO Bank. Bradi's Form W-2 that she received from MNO Bank shows that she had $58,000 in wages. MNO Bank withheld $7,000 in federal income taxes and $2,000 in state income taxes for the year.

Other information provided to you by Roger and Bradi

Taxable interest income from a savings account:	$200
Mortgage interest paid on their principal residence:	$18,000
Charitable contributions to their church:	$1,500
Charitable contributions to the United Way:	$500
Property taxes paid on their principal residence:	$1,700
Qualified medical expenses:	$5,200
State income tax refund received:	$400
Federal income tax refund received:	$2,100

Please prepare an IRS Form 1040 (and appropriate schedules) for Roger and Bradi for the most recent calendar year. They do not wish to contribute to the Presidential Election Campaign fund. Roger and Bradi itemized deductions on their previous year's return. You will need to complete the Form 1040, Schedule A, Schedule C, and Schedule SE.

PART 8

Timing of Recognizing Income and Deductions

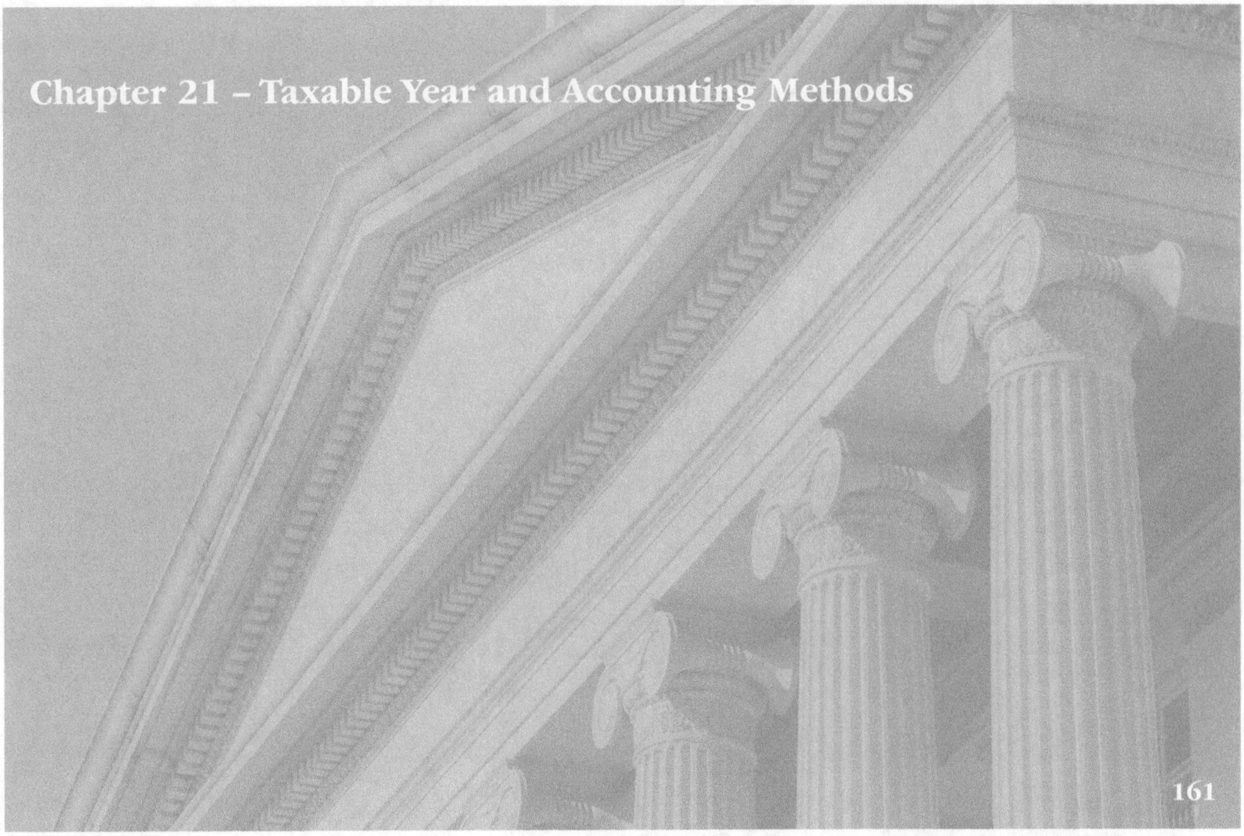

Chapter 21

Taxable Year and Accounting Methods

Throughout the textbook so far, we have primarily discussed the tax law relating to items that are included and excluded from a taxpayer's gross income, deductions "for" and "from" AGI, and various tax credits. Of course, these issues are all important in calculating the individual's net tax liability (or refund). Rather than focusing on "what" is income, this chapter focuses on the question of "when" to include items into income and "when" to allow expenses as tax deductions. Of course, generally accepted accounting principles (GAAP) do not override the Internal Revenue Code for income tax purposes. Thus, accountants and other tax consultants should not automatically assume that complying with GAAP is the same as complying with the Code.

A. Taxable Year

Every taxpayer (*e.g.*, individuals, corporations, etc.) has a **taxable year**. For individuals, the taxable year is usually a calendar year.

INTERNAL REVENUE CODE

SECTION 441. PERIOD FOR COMPUTATION OF TAXABLE INCOME

(a) **Computation of taxable income.**—Taxable income shall be computed on the basis of the taxpayer's taxable year.

(b) **Taxable year.**—For purposes of this subtitle, the term "taxable year" means—

(1) the taxpayer's annual accounting period, if it is a calendar year or a fiscal year;

(2) the calendar year, if subsection (g) applies;

. . .

(c) **Annual accounting period.**—For purposes of this subtitle, the term "annual accounting period" means the annual period on the basis of which the taxpayer regularly computes his income in keeping his books.
(d) **Calendar year.**—For purposes of this subtitle, the term "calendar year" means a period of 12 months ending on December 31.
(e) **Fiscal year.**—For purposes of this subtitle, the term "fiscal year" means a period of 12 months ending on the last day of any month other than December.

. . .

(g) **No books kept; no accounting period.**—Except as provided in section 443 (relating to returns for periods of less than 12 months), the taxpayer's taxable year shall be the calendar year if—
  (1) the taxpayer keeps no books;
  (2) the taxpayer does not have an annual accounting period; or
  (3) the taxpayer has an annual accounting period, but such period does not qualify as a fiscal year.

. . .

Corporations have the flexibility to select a fiscal year end (*e.g.*, the taxable year ends on the last day of a month other than December) if it is consistent with the corporation's annual accounting period. Other taxable year ends may be available to taxpayers if certain requirements are met. Of course, the taxable year end is important because the taxpayer's income tax return is due within a certain time after the end of the year. The Code allows a special "52–53 week" year-end for some taxpayers (usually corporations) when the taxpayer desires the year-end to always be on the same day of the week (*e.g.*, the last Friday in June). Special rules also apply to partnerships, S corporations, and personal service corporations. A detailed discussion of these issues is not presented here.

B. Accounting Methods

A taxpayer's **method of accounting** determines when a taxpayer includes an item in gross income or is allowed to deduct an expense.

INTERNAL REVENUE CODE

SECTION 446. GENERAL RULE FOR METHODS OF ACCOUNTING

(a) **General rule.**—Taxable income shall be computed under the method of accounting on the basis of which the taxpayer regularly computes his income in keeping his books.
(b) **Exceptions.**—If no method of accounting has been regularly used by the taxpayer, or if the method used does not clearly reflect income, the computation of taxable income shall be made under such method as, in the opinion of the Secretary, does clearly reflect income.

(c) **Permissible methods.**—Subject to the provisions of subsections (a) and (b), a taxpayer may compute taxable income under any of the following methods of accounting—
   (1) the cash receipts and disbursements method;
   (2) an accrual method;
   (3) any other method permitted by this chapter; or
   (4) any combination of the foregoing methods permitted under regulations prescribed by the Secretary.

. . .

By far the two most common methods of accounting are the **cash method** and **accrual method**.

1. Cash Method

Most individuals use the cash method of accounting. The Treasury regulations inform us as to when income is recognized and when expenses are deductible under the cash method.

TREASURY REGULATION

TREASURY REGULATION §1.446-1. GENERAL RULE FOR METHODS OF ACCOUNTING

. . .

(c) **Permissible methods.**—(1) In general. Subject to the provisions of paragraphs (a) and (b) of this section, a taxpayer may compute his taxable income under any of the following methods of accounting:
   (i) **Cash receipts and disbursements method**. Generally, under the cash receipts and disbursements method in the computation of taxable income, all items which constitute gross income (whether in the form of cash, property, or services) are to be included for the taxable year in which actually or constructively received. Expenditures are to be deducted for the taxable year in which actually made.

. . .

In short, under the cash method of accounting:

- Income is recognized when it is actually or constructively received.
- Expenses are deductible when made.

Some explanation is warranted relating to the meaning of **constructive receipt**. The Treasury regulations again provide guidance on this issue.

TREASURY REGULATION

TREASURY REGULATION §1.451-2. CONSTRUCTIVE RECEIPT OF INCOME

(a) **General rule**. Income although not actually reduced to a taxpayer's possession is constructively received by him in the taxable year during which it is credited to his account, set apart for him, or otherwise made available so that he may draw upon it at any time, or so that he could have drawn upon it during the taxable year if notice of intention to withdraw had been given. However, income is not constructively received if the taxpayer's control of its receipt is subject to substantial limitations or restrictions.

. . .

Thus, an individual cannot avoid including an item in his or her income in the current year merely by delaying actual receipt of the income if the income is otherwise readily available to the taxpayer without substantial limitations or restrictions.

The Code limits some taxpayers' use of the cash method of accounting. For example, C corporations (except for certain corporations with gross receipts of not more than $5,000,000 and qualified personal service corporations), partnerships with C corporations as a partner, and tax shelters cannot use the cash method of accounting. A more detailed explanation of these limitations is discussed here.

2. Accrual Method

Most large businesses use the accrual method of accounting. The Treasury regulations inform us as to when income is recognized and when expenses are deductible under the accrual method.

TREASURY REGULATION

TREASURY REGULATION §1.446-1. GENERAL RULE FOR METHODS OF ACCOUNTING

. . .

(c) **Permissible methods.**—(1) In general. Subject to the provisions of paragraphs (a) and (b) of this section, a taxpayer may compute his taxable income under any of the following methods of accounting:

. . .

(ii) **Accrual method**. (A) Generally, under an accrual method, income is to be included for the taxable year when all the events have occurred that fix the right to receive the income and the amount of the income can be determined with reasonable accuracy. Under such a method, a liability is incurred, and generally is taken into account for Federal income tax purposes, in the taxable year in which all the events have occurred that establish the fact of the liability, the amount of the liability can be determined with reasonable accuracy, and economic performance has occurred with respect to the liability. . . .

In sum, under the accrual method of accounting:

- Income is recognized when all the events have occurred to fix the right to receive the income and the amount of income can be determined with reasonable accuracy.
- A liability is incurred in the taxable year in which all the events have occurred that establish the fact of the liability, the amount of the liability can be determined with reasonable accuracy, and economic performance has occurred.

Notice that "economic performance" must occur before a liability incurred by an accrual method taxpayer is deductible. This means that the services or goods (as the case may be) must be provided to the taxpayer.

3. Inventories

The tax rules applicable to inventories are worthy of a separate discussion here.

INTERNAL REVENUE CODE

SECTION 471. GENERAL RULE FOR INVENTORIES

(a) **General rule.**—Whenever in the opinion of the Secretary the use of inventories is necessary in order clearly to determine the income of any taxpayer, inventories shall be taken by such taxpayer on such basis as the Secretary may prescribe as conforming as nearly as may be to the best accounting practice in the trade or business and as most clearly reflecting the income.

. . .

Notice that the critical point of Section 471 is that accounting for inventories must "clearly reflect" the income of the taxpayer.

A taxpayer is allowed to use the first-in first-out (FIFO) or last-in first-out (LIFO) methods for tax purposes. Taxpayers generally may value their inventory at cost or at the lower of cost or market under the FIFO method, but only at cost if the LIFO method is used.

For large manufacturing and merchandising businesses with average gross receipts exceeding $10 million per year the Code requires that some costs that may otherwise be expensed be included in the cost of inventory or be capitalized. Such expenses are costs directly or indirectly related to manufacturing or purchasing the inventory. Examples include packaging and warehousing costs, salaries of administrative employees relating to inventory management, overhead, and warehousing costs. These rules are found in Section 263A of the Code and are frequently referred to as the **UNICAP** ("uniform capitalization") rules.

4. Other Accounting Method and Timing Issues

Other issues arise in accounting for income and expenses. For example, a seller may agree to sell property to a buyer in installments. If this occurs, the taxpayer then accounts for the transaction on the installment method of accounting. The installment method only applies for accounting for gains and applies if at least one payment is received by the taxpayer in a year after the sale occurs.

The installment method allows the taxpayer to recognize gains into income when the taxpayer actually receives the payments rather than recognizing the entire gain in the year of sale. In short, the installment method requires the taxpayer to calculate a gross profit percentage on the sale, and then each installment payment is treated partially as a return of capital and partially as a gain. The installment method is not applicable to sales of marketable securities or inventory or for sales at a loss. Taxpayers may elect out of the installment method.

Special rules apply to accounting for **long-term contracts** (*e.g.*, projects that will not be completed within the same tax year in which the project began). These contracts typically apply to businesses involved in construction, manufacturing, and building/installation activities. Most companies use the **percentage of completion** method, but some others are allowed to use the **completed contract** method. Under the percentage of completion method, the taxpayer recognizes income in intervals along the way until the project is complete. Under the completed contract method, the taxpayer just recognizes the income when the project is complete. The detailed rules, calculations, and limitations relating to these contracts are not discussed here.

Sometimes taxpayers will loan money to other taxpayers at an interest rate that is below the market rate of interest. In these cases, the IRS is concerned that tax on foregone interest income is being avoided. Consequently, the tax law provides that unless some narrow exceptions apply, a market rate of interest is **imputed** on the transaction. This means the lender will be deemed to have received a market rate of interest and the borrower will be deemed to have paid the interest. Additional rules apply depending upon the lender's motivation for entering into a transaction with an interest rate below market (*e.g.*, the lender-parent wanted the foregone interest to be a gift to the borrower-child). The IRS publishes the interest rates at which it considers a market rate. These rates published by the IRS are called **applicable federal rates (AFRs)**. A tax consultant should be able to identify below market or interest-free loans and then advise the client whether the imputed interest rules will apply. A full coverage of the exceptions and detailed rules applicable to imputed interest is not discussed here.

Special technical rules also apply to taxpayers who sell property (or issue financial instruments) at a discount and receive, for example, a lump sum payment at a later date that represents both principal and interest. For example, suppose a corporation issues a bond for $7,500 and agrees to pay the bondholder $10,000 in five years. Furthermore, no interest is paid during the five year period. Tax law will treat the $2,500 difference between $7,500 and $10,000 effectively as interest over the five year period. Consequently, the bondholder must recognize interest income gradually over the five year period rather than all $2,500 at the end of year five when it is actually received. These rules are called the **original issue discount (OID)** rules and can be quite complicated in certain transactions as you might expect.

CHAPTER 21: QUESTIONS

1. *Taxable year.* How does the Code define "fiscal year"?

2. *Taxable year.* What is a 52–53 week taxable year?

3. *Accounting methods.* Under the cash method of accounting, when is income recognized by a taxpayer?

4. *Accounting methods.* Under the cash method of accounting, what does "constructive receipt" mean?

5. *Accounting methods.* Under the cash method of accounting, when is an expense deductible?

6. *Accounting methods.* Under the accrual method of accounting, when is income recognized by a taxpayer?

7. *Accounting methods.* Under the accrual method of accounting, when is a liability deductible?

8. *Inventories.* Evaluate this statement: If a taxpayer complies with GAAP, then the taxpayer complies with the Internal Revenue Code.

9. *Inventories.* Discuss briefly what the UNICAP rules are and when they apply.

10. *Installment method.* When does the installment method of accounting apply?

11. *Long-term contracts.* What are the two primary methods to account for long-term contracts?

12. *Imputed interest.* What does AFR stand for? When does the AFR apply to a transaction?

13. *Original issue discount.* When do the OID rules apply?

PART 9

Special Topics

Chapter 22

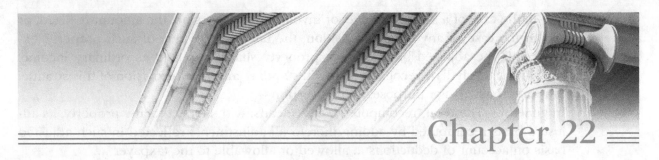

Special Issues in Property Transactions

In this chapter we look at three issues involving property transactions that warrant separate attention: (1) depreciation recapture; (2) like-kind exchanges; and (3) involuntary conversions.

A. Depreciation Recapture

You may recall from Chapter 9 that we classify assets into three broad categories: (1) capital assets; (2) ordinary assets; and (3) Section 1231 assets. Remember also that Section 1231 assets are depreciable assets (and land) held longer than a year and used in a trade or business. As a general rule, gains on the sale of Section 1231 assets generate capital gains and the sale of Section 1231 assets at a loss generates ordinary losses. A major exception to this rule, is that on the sale of a Section 1231 asset that has been depreciated, the Code requires that any gain on the sale of that asset be classified as *ordinary income* to the extent of the depreciation previously taken. This is called **depreciation recapture**.

1. Depreciation Recapture on Sale of Depreciable Personal Property

Section 1245 sets forth the depreciation recapture rules as applicable to personal property (and to some narrow situations involving real property).

INTERNAL REVENUE CODE

SECTION 1245. GAIN FROM DISPOSITIONS OF CERTAIN DEPRECIABLE PROPERTY

(a) **General rule.—**

(1) **Ordinary income.**—Except as otherwise provided in this section if section 1245 property is disposed of the amount by which the lower of—

(A) the recomputed basis of the property, or

(B)

(i) in the case of a sale, exchange, or involuntary conversion, the amount realized, or
(ii) in the case of any other disposition, the fair market value of such property, exceeds the adjusted basis of such property shall be treated as ordinary income. Such gain shall be recognized notwithstanding any other provision of this subtitle.

(2) **Recomputed basis.**—For purposes of this section—

(A) In general.—The term "recomputed basis" means, with respect to any property, its adjusted basis recomputed by adding thereto all adjustments reflected in such adjusted basis on account of deductions ... allowed or allowable to the taxpayer ....

. . .

Given that most depreciable personal property declines in value over time, the depreciation recapture provisions in Section 1245 effectively cause most gains on the sale of Section 1231 assets to be treated as ordinary income. The sale of business property and calculation of depreciation recapture is reported on IRS Form 4797, a copy of which is included in the Appendix.

If depreciable property is inherited, the depreciation recapture potential disappears. This is not the case if the property is gifted, however (*i.e.*, although depreciation recapture is not recognized immediately upon receiving the gift, the donee could recognized depreciation recapture income on the subsequent sale of the gifted property).

2. Depreciation Recapture on Sale of Depreciable Real Property

Section 1250 sets forth the depreciation recapture rules as applicable to real property (except for a few narrow situations in which some depreciable real property is classified under Section 1245). These rules are similar to the Section 1245 with a few exceptions. If depreciable real property is sold for a gain, the gain is considered ordinary income *only to the extent the property was depreciated faster than under the straight-line method.* Since real property placed in service after 1986 is subject to the straight-line method for depreciation, the recapture of this "additional depreciation" is now not as common.

To the extent the gain on the sale of Section 1250 property is not recaptured because of "additional depreciation," the gain is considered **unrecaptured Section 1250 gain** *to the extent of straight-line depreciation taken.* This gain is taxed at a maximum rate of 25% (for individuals). Any gain beyond unrecaptured Section 1250 gain is considered a long-term capital gain that is taxed at the applicable long-term capital gain rate.

EXAMPLE 22.1. Lu owns a sole proprietorship. She sells a building that she purchased many years ago and that is classified as a Section 1250 asset for depreciation recapture purposes. Her basis in the building at the time of sale is $100,000. The sale price was $900,000. She has taken $550,000 in depreciation deductions on the building. If she would have used the straight line method of depreciation she would have been entitled to $500,000 in depreciation deductions. What are the income tax consequences to Lu on the sale of the building?

Answer: Lu has an overall gain of $800,000 (sale price of $900,000 minus her $100,000 tax basis in the property). She must recognize ordinary income of $50,000 due to "additional depreciation." She has unrecaptured Section 1250 gain of $500,000 (taxed at a maximum rate of 25%), and a long-term capital gain of $250,000 (taxed at normally applicable long-term capital gain rates).

B. LIKE-KIND EXCHANGES

In Chapter 9 we discussed the general rule that any gain or loss realized on the "sale or exchange" of property must be recognized unless the Code provides otherwise. Section 1031 is one provision where the Code does, in fact, provide otherwise. This Code section allows taxpayers to exchange property without recognizing gain or loss if the property is of "like-kind."

INTERNAL REVENUE CODE

SECTION 1031. EXCHANGE OF PROPERTY HELD FOR PRODUCTIVE USE OR INVESTMENT

(a) **Nonrecognition of gain or loss from exchanges solely in kind.—**

(1) **In general.**—No gain or loss shall be recognized on the exchange of property held for productive use in a trade or business or for investment if such property is exchanged solely for property of like kind which is to be held either for productive use in a trade or business or for investment.

(2) **Exception.**—This subsection shall not apply to any exchange of—

(A) stock in trade or other property held primarily for sale,

(B) stocks, bonds, or notes,

(C) other securities or evidences of indebtedness or interest,

(D) interests in a partnership,

. . .

(3) Requirement that property be identified and that exchange be completed not more than 180 days after transfer of exchanged property.—For purposes of this subsection, any property received by the taxpayer shall be treated as property which is not like-kind property if—

(A) such property is not identified as property to be received in the exchange on or before the day which is 45 days after the date on which the taxpayer transfers the property relinquished in the exchange, or

(B) such property is received after the earlier of—

(i) the day which is 180 days after the date on which the taxpayer transfers the property relinquished in the exchange, or

(ii) the due date (determined with regard to extension) for the transferor's return of the tax imposed by this chapter for the taxable year in which the transfer of the relinquished property occurs.

. . .

Transactions that satisfy the requirements of Section 1031 are called **Section 1031 exchanges** or **like-kind exchanges**. The requirements are very strict. Notice that the taxpayer must identify the **replacement property** within 45 days after giving up the **relinquished property**. The taxpayer must further actually acquire the replacement property within 180 days after giving up the relinquished property. Of course, these time frames are not applicable if the taxpayer enters into a simultaneous exchange of the properties rather than a deferred exchange.

The IRS provides extensive guidance as to what assets are considered "like-kind." For example, an exchange of real estate for real estate is considered like-kind (even if it is raw land for an apartment building). Thus, the definition of like-kind is very broad when it relates to real property (although real property in foreign countries is not considered like-kind with real property in the United States). With respect to personal property, however, the rules are much more detailed. To be like-kind the assets have to be in a "like class." A like class is defined as those identified as within the same General Asset Class *or* Product Class. The "General Asset Classes" include, for example, the following:

- Class 00.11 (office furniture, fixtures and equipment)
- Class 00.22 (automobiles and taxis)
- Class 00.23 (buses)
- Class 00.241 (light general purpose trucks)
- Class 00.242 (heavy general purpose trucks)

Thus, an exchange of an automobile for a heavy general purpose truck would not be in the same class and not like-kind. An office desk for an office chair, however, would be in the same class and be considered like-kind. The IRS has published these General Asset Classes for taxpayers' convenience. "Product Classes" are identified in a publication by the United States Office of Management and Budget. That publication is the North American Industry Classification System Manual (NAICS Manual). A discussion of Product Classes is beyond the scope of our coverage here.

An important component of a qualifying deferred like-kind exchange is that the taxpayer relinquishing his or her property cannot directly receive the funds from the buyer of the relinquished property. Such funds should be directed to and held by a third party, called a **qualified intermediary (QI)**. The QI is often a real estate title company, but it does not have to be. Then, within 180 days of giving up the relinquished property, the taxpayer instructs the QI to acquire the replacement property on behalf of the taxpayer. (Note: the taxpayer would have within 45 days of giving up the relinquished property, identified the replacement property by giving the QI, or some other party who is not a "disqualified" party, written notification of the identification.)

Reverse like-kind exchanges are also possible. This type of an exchange occurs when the taxpayer acquires the replacement property before giving up the relinquished property. These transactions must comply with strict requirements, but basically the taxpayer must sell the relinquished property within 180 days of acquiring the replacement property. Like "forward" exchanges, qualified third parties must usually be involved to accommodate a reverse exchange (called "qualified exchange accommodation arrangements," or QEAAs).

As you might expect, the fair market values of the properties involved in like-kind exchanges are not always the same. Thus, sometimes money (*i.e.*, "boot") must exchange hands to make the exchange equal in value. If the taxpayer relinquishing property also receives boot in addition to the replacement property, the amount of any gain realized is recognized to the extent of the boot.

A taxpayer's basis in the replacement property is usually equal to his or her basis in the relinquished property minus any boot received plus any gain recognized.

EXAMPLE 22.2. Kristen owns Parcel K (tax basis of $70, fair market value $100). Melanie owns Parcel M (tax basis of $50, fair market value $120). Kristen and Melanie desire to enter into a simultaneous like-kind exchange wherein Kristen will acquire Parcel M from Melanie and Melanie will acquire Parcel K from Kristen. Parcels K and M are like-kind properties. Since Parcel M is worth $20 more than Parcel K, Kristen also pays $20 in cash to Melanie as part of the deal. What are the income tax consequences to Melanie and Kristen?

Answer: Melanie's *amount realized* is $120 (value of Parcel K received plus $20 cash received). Melanie's *gain realized* is $70 ($120 minus her $50 basis in Parcel M that she relinquished). Melanie's *gain recognized* is $20 (the lesser of gain realized or boot received). Melanie's tax basis in Parcel K is $50 (her $50 basis in Parcel M minus the $20 in boot received plus $20 gain recognized).

Kristen's amount realized is $120 (value of Parcel M she received). She has a $30 gain realized ($120 minus her $70 basis in Parcel K plus $20 in cash she paid). She has no gain recognized because she received no boot. Her tax basis in Parcel M is $90 (her $70 basis in Parcel K plus the $20 she paid in cash).

Care must also be taken if a like-kind exchange is entered into with a related party. If the related party disposes of the exchanged property within two years of the exchange, the original like-kind exchange would no longer qualify for nonrecognition and gain realized in the original transaction would then be recognized in the year the related party disposed of the exchanged property.

Like-kind exchanges are reported on IRS Form 8824, a copy of which is included in the Appendix.

C. Involuntary Conversions

Sometimes a taxpayer may have property involuntarily taken due to condemnation, casualty, theft, etc. The Code provides a way to replace such property without the recognition of gain if certain requirements are met.

INTERNAL REVENUE CODE

SECTION 1033. INVOLUNTARY CONVERSIONS

(a) **General rule.**—If property (as a result of its destruction in whole or in part, theft, seizure, or requisition or condemnation or threat or imminence thereof) is compulsorily or involuntarily converted—

(1) **Conversion into similar property.**—Into property similar or related in service or use to the property so converted, no gain shall be recognized.

(2) **Conversion into money.**—Into money or into property not similar or related in service or use to the converted property, the gain (if any) shall be recognized except to the extent hereinafter provided in this paragraph:

(A) Nonrecognition of gain. If the taxpayer during the period specified in subparagraph (B), for the purpose of replacing the property so converted, purchases other property similar or related in service or use to the property so converted . . . at the election of the taxpayer the gain shall be recognized only to the extent that the amount realized upon such conversion . . . exceeds the cost of such other property. . . .

. . .

(B) Period within which property must be replaced. The period referred to in subparagraph (A) shall be the period beginning with the date of the disposition of the converted property, or the earliest date of the threat or imminence of requisition or condemnation of the converted property, whichever is the earlier, and ending—

(i) 2 years after the close of the first taxable year in which any part of the gain upon the conversion is realized, or

(ii) subject to such terms and conditions as may be specified by the Secretary, at the close of such later date as the Secretary may designate on application by the taxpayer.

. . .

Notice that in order to avoid the recognition of gain on the involuntary conversion, the taxpayer must generally replace the property by two years after the close of the taxable year in which any part of the gain is realized (three years in some narrow situations). Also, the property ultimately replacing the property that was subject to the involuntary conversion must be "property similar or related in service or use to the property so converted." This requirement is quite restrictive. The IRS has ruled, for example, that replacing a bowling alley destroyed by fire with a billiards center is not "similar or related in service or use."

If the involuntary conversion is due to casualty or theft, it is reported on IRS Form 4684. Otherwise, it is report on IRS Form 4797. Both forms are included in the Appendix for your convenience.

CHAPTER 22: QUESTIONS

1. *Depreciation recapture.* Explain the significance of the depreciation recapture provisions.

2. *Depreciation recapture.* Section 1245 mainly applies to what type of property?

3. *Depreciation recapture.* Section 1250 mainly applies to what type of property?

4. *Depreciation recapture.* What is "unrecaptured Section 1250 gain"? At what maximum rate is such gain taxed?

5. *Like-kind exchanges.* What Code Section governs "like-kind" exchanges?

6. *Like-kind exchanges.* How many days after giving up the relinquished property does a taxpayer have to identify the replacement property?

7. *Like-kind exchanges.* How many days after giving up the relinquished property does a taxpayer have to acquire the replacement property?

8. *Like-kind exchanges.* What is the importance of a qualified intermediary?

9. *Like-kind exchanges.* How does a taxpayer determine whether personal property is "like-kind"?

10. *Like-kind exchanges.* Explain generally how a reverse like-kind exchange occurs.

11. *Like-kind exchanges.* What special rule applies if the like-kind exchange occurs between related parties?

12. *Involuntary conversions.* What is an "involuntary conversion"?

13. *Involuntary conversions.* Typically, if a taxpayer wishes to avoid gain on an involuntary conversion (because insurance proceeds received by the taxpayer exceed the tax basis of the property involuntarily converted), how long does a taxpayer have to the replace property that was the subject of the involuntary conversion?

Chapter 23

Qualified Retirement Plans and Deferred Compensation Arrangements

Among the important factors for an individual to consider when deciding if to accept a job offer is whether the employer offers health benefits, a retirement plan, and other possible compensation arrangements. In this chapter we discuss various qualified retirement plans as well as a few common deferred compensation arrangements.

A. Qualified Retirement Plans

The Internal Revenue Code recognizes certain retirement plans as being tax-favored. In Chapter 15 we discussed individual retirement accounts (both traditional IRAs and Roth IRAs). In this chapter we cover the fundamentals of certain other qualified retirement plans.

Qualified retirement plans enjoy significant tax benefits. For example, the employer receives a tax deduction for amounts contributed to the plan. The employee does not recognize into gross income the amount contributed by the employer or the amount contributed by the employee. Moreover, the funds in the plan grow tax-free until the employee withdraws the funds at a later time. The amount that employers and employees can contribute to the plans each year is limited, however.

Section 401 of the Code provides the fundamental law allowing for qualified retirement plans. This section is quite complex and provides a plethora of rules relating to establishment of a qualified trust to administer the retirement funds, maximum contributions, minimum withdrawals at a certain age, no discrimination in favor of highly compensated employees, minimum participation standards, minimum vesting standards, etc. If the plan meets these requirements, then the plan is "qualified" and receives the tax-favored status. Usually an employer must hire specialists in this area to make sure these retirement plans are set up properly and meet all IRS requirements. Not only are retirement plans regulated by the IRS, but retirement plans are also regulated by the Department of Labor. The Department of Labor enforces the **Employee Retirement Income Security Act (ERISA)** portion of retirement plans while the IRS enforces the tax aspects. An in-depth discussion of ERISA is not presented here, but ERISA basically requires the employer to provide pertinent information to employees about the plans, gives participants the right to sue for benefits and breaches of fiduciary duty by the employer/administrator of the plan, and also sets minimum standards for participation, vesting, etc.

1. Pension Plans

A **pension plan** is an arrangement where the employer contributes a certain amount (not based on the profitability of the employer) according to a formula set forth in the plan. A pension plan can be set up in two fundamentally distinct ways: (1) as a **defined benefit** plan, or (2) as a **defined contribution** plan.

i. Defined Benefit

A defined benefit plan is structured so that upon retirement an employee receives a certain fixed amount (*e.g.*, an exact amount of money each month or an amount equal to x% of the employee's average salary over the last five years before retirement). The amounts contributed by the employer to the plan must **vest** to the employee-participant after 5 years of employment (*i.e.*, "cliff" vesting). This means that even if the employee terminates employment with the employer after five years, the employee can take the vested amount and roll it over into another plan. An alternative vesting schedule is that 20% of the amount contributed by the employer vests to the employee after the third year of employment, and 20% each year thereafter until after 7 years of employment the employee is 100% vested.

ii. Defined Contribution

In contrast to a defined benefit plan, a defined contribution plan is set up so that the employer regularly contributes to the plan a certain amount (*e.g.*, 6% of the employee's salary). The plan does not guarantee a certain benefit upon retirement. The amounts contributed by the employer to the plan must vest to the employee-participant after 3 years of employment or 20% each year after the second year until the employee-participant is 100% vested after six years of service. Of course, the employee is 100% vested in any amounts the employee personally contributes.

2. Profit-sharing Plans, Stock Bonus Plans, etc.

Other qualified plans may allow the employee to receive cash or *elect* to have that amount contributed to a retirement plan. This type of arrangement is called a Section 401(k) plan. Although a Section 401(k) plan may often be referred to as a **profit-sharing plan**, the employer does not necessarily have to make profits to contribute to the plan. In fact, in order to qualify as a 401(k) plan, the employer must make "substantial and recurring" contributions. The employer may set up a qualified plan that does truly share profits with employees also.

Sometimes an employer may wish to allow employees to invest in the company's own stock as part of the retirement plan. These plans are called **Employee Stock Ownership Plans (ESOPs)**.

Of course, as with all qualified retirement plans, strict requirements must be met for the plan to withstand IRS scrutiny and receive tax-favored status. Plans such as ESOPs are called **stock bonus plans.**

Generally, the minimum age a person can start withdrawing funds from a qualified plan is age 59½ and an individual must start withdrawing minimum distributions at age 70½. Withdrawals are included in the individual's gross income and subject to income tax. Also, with a few exceptions, an individual incurs a 10% penalty tax if the funds are withdrawn early.

B. DEFERRED COMPENSATION ARRANGEMENTS

In addition to a qualified retirement plan that an employer may wish to adopt for employees, an employer can set up compensation arrangements to entice individuals to accept a job offer or to give current employees an incentive to work hard and benefit from a rise in the value of a corporation's stock (or the value of a membership interest in an limited liability company or partnership interest in a partnership). The myriad arrangements that can be entered into by employer and employee often are called **deferred compensation arrangements**. Of course, this basically means that the employee has an opportunity to earn additional income in the future through some way other than a straight salary.

1. Restricted Stock

Assume that you are offered a position at a corporation and the corporation offers to compensate you $100,000 annual salary plus 1,000 shares of stock upon signing the employment contract. Assume further, however, that the offer states that if you voluntarily leave the corporation within the first three years of employment, you forfeit the 1,000 shares of stock and must give them back to the corporation. What are the income tax consequences to you upon receiving the stock?

The scenario just presented illustrates a situation involving **restricted stock**. Section 83 of the Code provides the law in this situation.

INTERNAL REVENUE CODE

SECTION 83. PROPERTY TRANSFERRED IN CONNECTION WITH PERFORMANCE OF SERVICES

(a) **General rule.**—If, in connection with the performance of services, property is transferred to any person other than the person for whom such services are performed, the excess of—

(1) the fair market value of such property ... at the first time the rights of the person having the beneficial interest in such property are transferable or are not subject to a substantial risk of forfeiture, whichever occurs earlier, over

(2) the amount (if any) paid for such property, shall be included in the gross income of the person who performed the services in the first taxable year in which the rights of the person having the beneficial interest in such property are transferable or are not subject to a substantial risk of forfeiture, whichever is applicable. ...

. . .

Notice according to Section 83 that the person receiving property in return for services does not include the value of the property in gross income when the property is received if the property is nontransferable or is subject to a substantial risk of forfeiture. Once the property becomes transferable or not subject to forfeiture, then the value of the property is included in the person's gross income at that time. Consequently, in our scenario where you receive 1,000 shares of stock that you may forfeit if you terminate employment within three years, you would not have gross income until the three year time period elapses. You would have ordinary income after the expiration of three years to the extent of whatever the value of the stock is at that time.

The Code does allow a person to *elect* to include the value of restricted property when received rather than when the restriction is removed. This is called a **Section 83(b) election.**

INTERNAL REVENUE CODE

SECTION 83. PROPERTY TRANSFERRED IN CONNECTION WITH PERFORMANCE OF SERVICES

. . .

(b) **Election to include in gross income in year of transfer.—**

(1) **In general.**—Any person who performs services in connection with which property is transferred to any person may elect to include in his gross income, for the taxable year in which such property is transferred, the excess of—

(A) the fair market value of such property at the time of transfer ..., over

(B) the amount (if any) paid for such property.

If such election is made, subsection (a) shall not apply with respect to the transfer of such property, and if such property is subsequently forfeited, no deduction shall be allowed in respect of such forfeiture.

(2) **Election.**—An election under paragraph (1) with respect to any transfer of property shall be made in such manner as the Secretary prescribes and shall be made not later than 30 days after the date of such transfer. Such election may not be revoked except with the consent of the Secretary.

. . .

If a taxpayer makes a Section 83(b) election, the taxpayer includes the value of the property in gross income in the year the property is received rather than in the year the restrictions lapse. Notice, however, that this can be somewhat risky in that no deduction is allowed if the individual includes the amount in gross income but then later forfeits the property. On the other hand, a Section 83(b) election may be worthwhile if the value of the property now is relatively low and the individual anticipates that the value of the property will be quite high when the restrictions lapse.

2. Stock Options

Another compensation mechanism a corporation can adopt is a stock option plan. These plans are of two fundamental types: (1) **incentive stock option plans**, and (2) **nonqualified stock option plans**.

i. Incentive Stock Option Plans

An incentive stock option (ISO) plan (sometimes called a "statutory" stock option plan) receives special treatment under the Code. If the Code's requirements are met an employee does not recognize income on the receipt of the option (the "grant" date). When the employee exercises the option and purchases the stock (the "exercise" date), no income is recognized even though the value of the stock exceeds the purchase price. When the employee sells the stock (the "sale" date) the employee recognizes a long-term capital gain. The employer receives no deduction on the grant date, exercise date or sale date.

Some of the requirements of an ISO plan are that the employee must hold on to the stock for a certain period of time, the option price is not less than the fair market value of the stock at the time the option is granted, the option is not transferable, and among other things, the option cannot be exercised after 10 years from the grant date. An employee should receive from the employer an IRS Form 3921 for the year in which the ISO was exercised. This form is included in the Appendix for your reference.

ii. Nonqualified Stock Option Plans

If a stock option plan does not meet the requirements of an ISO, then different tax consequences to the employee and corporation result. On the grant date, the employee does not recognize income. On the exercise date, the employee has ordinary income to the extent of the difference between the fair market value of the stock and the exercise price (*i.e.*, the "spread"). The employer receives an ordinary deduction at this time. The employee's tax basis in the stock is the amount paid for the stock plus the amount included in gross income on the exercise date. When the employee later sells the stock, the employee will have a capital gain. The employer receives no additional deduction on the sale date. The tax consequences would differ if we assume that the option itself has a readily ascertainable fair market value on the grant date, but we will not discuss that here.

3. Other Arrangements

Other deferred compensation arrangements may be entered into by employers and employees. Common incentive plans may reward executives a bonus based upon the performance of the stock or profitability of the company. Companies may also provide retirement plans for executives above and beyond the qualified plans we have discussed. As indicated earlier, this chapter contains the fundamentals of retirement plans and deferred compensation arrangements, but these plans and arrangements typically are quite complex and warrant further study once a student has mastered the concepts presented here.

CHAPTER 23: QUESTIONS

1. *Qualified retirement plans.* Explain the main tax benefits that qualified retirement plans enjoy.

2. *Qualified retirement plans.* What does ERISA stand for?

3. *Defined benefit plan.* Explain the fundamentals of a defined benefit pension plan.

4. *Defined contribution plan.* Explain the fundamentals of a defined contribution plan.

5. *Vesting.* Explain what "vesting" means.

6. *Restricted stock.* What makes stock "restricted"?

7. *Restricted stock.* What are the default tax consequences when someone receives restricted stock?

8. *Restricted stock.* What are the income tax consequences to an individual who makes a Section 83(b) election with respect to restricted stock?

9. *Stock options.* Explain the differences in tax treatment between incentive stock options and nonqualified stock options.

Chapter 24

Vacation Homes and Sale of a Principal Residence

A common tax issue that every tax consultant should be familiar with is the consequences of selling a personal residence. Many taxpayers also have a second home that they may use as a vacation home or rent out for all or part of the year. This chapter covers the tax treatment of vacation home rentals and the sale of a personal residence.

A. Vacation Homes

Vacation homes are frequently rented for a period of time during the year when the owner is not using the home. This raises tax issues such as:

- Can the taxpayer depreciate the vacation home?
- Can the taxpayer deduct insurance, maintenance, and other expenses?

The answer to these questions depends on whether the home is used for rental only, used as a personal residence only, or a combination of personal residence and rental. Code Section 280A sets forth the fundamental statutory authority for how to handle these issues.

INTERNAL REVENUE CODE

SECTION 280A. DISALLOWANCE OF CERTAIN EXPENSES IN CONNECTION WITH BUSINESS USE OF HOME, RENTAL OF VACATION HOMES, ETC.

(a) **General rule.**—Except as otherwise provided in this section, in the case of a taxpayer who is an individual or an S corporation, no deduction otherwise allowable under this chapter shall be allowed with respect to the use of a dwelling unit which is used by the taxpayer during the taxable year as a residence.

(b) **Exception for interest, taxes, casualty losses, etc.**—Subsection (a) shall not apply to any deduction allowable to the taxpayer without regard to its connection with his trade or business (or with his income-producing activity).

. . .

(d) **Use as residence.**—

(1) **In general.**—For purposes of this section, a taxpayer uses a dwelling unit during the taxable year as a residence if he uses such unit (or portion thereof) for personal purposes for a number of days which exceeds the greater of

(A) 14 days, or

(B) 10 percent of the number of days during such year for which such unit is rented at a fair value.

. . .

Notice that if the vacation home is used as a *personal residence only* (*i.e.*, no rental use), no expenses are deductible except those that are otherwise deductible through other provisions of the Code (*e.g.*, qualified interest and property taxes as itemized deductions).

If the vacation home used for *rental purposes only*, then the taxpayer can depreciate it and deduct maintenance expenses as would a taxpayer with any other rental.

If the vacation home is used *partly for rental purposes and partly as a personal residence*, then the analysis must go a bit further. If the taxpayer does not use the vacation home for personal use more than 14 days during the year or more than 10% of the number of days the home was rented, then the taxpayer is treated as not using the home as a personal residence. If the taxpayer does exceed these thresholds then the fraction of the associated expenses (depreciation, maintenance, utilities, etc.) related to personal use are not deductible. We will not go into the details of the calculation here.

The Code provides a special rule for vacation homes not rented for more than 14 days during the year.

INTERNAL REVENUE CODE

SECTION 280A. DISALLOWANCE OF CERTAIN EXPENSES IN CONNECTION WITH BUSINESS USE OF HOME, RENTAL OF VACATION HOMES, ETC.

. . .

(g) **Special rule for certain rental use.**—Notwithstanding any other provision of this section or section 183, if a dwelling unit is used during the taxable year by the taxpayer as a residence and such dwelling unit is actually rented for less than 15 days during the taxable year, then—

(1) no deduction otherwise allowable under this chapter because of the rental use of such dwelling unit shall be allowed, and

(2) the income derived from such use for the taxable year shall not be included in the gross income of such taxpayer under section 61.

Thus, the taxpayer is not required to include any rental income into gross income if the home is rented for less than 15 days during the year. No deductions are allowed, however.

Income and expenses attributable to rental properties, including vacation homes, are reported on an individual's Schedule E, a copy of which is provided in the Appendix.

B. Sale of a Principal Residence

Homeowners enjoy tax deductions for qualified interest on a home mortgage or home equity loan (discussed in Chapter 16). Taxpayers also benefit from an exclusion of gain on the sale of their principal residence.

INTERNAL REVENUE CODE

SECTION 121. EXCLUSION OF GAIN FROM SALE OF PRINCIPAL RESIDENCE

(a) **Exclusion.**—Gross income shall not include gain from the sale or exchange of property if, during the 5-year period ending on the date of the sale or exchange, such property has been owned and used by the taxpayer as the taxpayer's principal residence for periods aggregating 2 years or more.

(b) **Limitations.**—

(1) **In general.**—The amount of gain excluded from gross income under subsection (a) with respect to any sale or exchange shall not exceed $250,000.

(2) **Special rules for joint returns.**—In the case of a husband and wife who make a joint return for the taxable year of the sale or exchange of the property—

(A) $500,000 limitation for certain joint returns.—Paragraph (1) shall be applied by substituting $500,000" for "$250,000" if—

(i) either spouse meets the ownership requirements of subsection (a) with respect to such property,

(ii) both spouses meet the use requirements of subsection (a) with respect to such property, and

(iii) neither spouse is ineligible for the benefits of subsection (a) with respect to such property by reason of paragraph (3).

. . .

(3) Application to only 1 sale or exchange every 2 years.—

(A) In general.—Subsection (a) shall not apply to any sale or exchange by the taxpayer if, during the 2-year period ending on the date of such sale or exchange, there was any other sale or exchange by the taxpayer to which subsection (a) applied.

. . .

This exclusion protects most homeowners from including gain into gross income because most taxpayers do not experience a gain of more than $250,000 (single) or $500,000 (married filing jointly) on the sale of their personal residence. But taxpayers must meet the ownership and use requirements to take advantage of the exclusion.

1. Ownership and Use Requirements

To be eligible for the exclusion, a taxpayer must own and use the residence as the taxpayer's *principal* residence for at least two of the last five years (with some narrow exceptions discussed later). A taxpayer has only one principal residence. Although all the facts and circumstances may be pertinent, the residence that the taxpayer uses the majority of the time is usually considered the taxpayer's principal residence. The exclusion is available only once every two years.

For married couples filing jointly, both spouses must meet the use requirement in order for the $500,000 exclusion to apply (rather than the $250,000 exclusion). Also, the $500,000 exclusion cannot be used if either spouse has sold or exchanged a principal residence within the past two years.

Since a personal residence is a capital asset, any sale of the principal residence that produces a taxable gain would ultimately be reported on IRS Form 8949 and Schedule D of the individual's Form 1040 (see the end of Chapter 8 for Form 8949 and Schedule D). Any sale of a principal residence that results in a loss, however, is not deductible at all since the residence is a personal-use asset.

2. Exceptions to Ownership and Use Requirements

Sometimes individuals may be required to sell their principal residence due to some unforeseen circumstance such as a job transfer. In these situations, the Code relaxes the two year ownership and use requirement in certain situations. For example, if an individual becomes incapacitated or is either physically or mentally unable to care for themselves and moves to a licensed care facility, then the individual need only meet the ownership and use requirements for one year instead of two years.

An individual may be eligible for partial exclusion of gain even if the individual fails to meet the ownership and use requirements. The following may be reasons to allow a partial exclusion (*e.g.*, not the full $250,000 or $500,000) of the gain from a principal residence:

- Change of employment
- Health Reasons
- Unforeseen Circumstances
    - involuntary conversion of the home
    - damage to the home from natural or man-made disasters or terrorism
    - death
    - divorce
    - multiple births resulting from the same pregnancy

If any of these reasons apply, then the taxpayer may be eligible for a reduced exclusion based upon the fraction of time out of two years the taxpayer otherwise owned and used the principal residence.

3. Gain Due to Depreciation

Recall that a portion of a personal residence can be used as a home office. If so, depreciation deductions are available to the taxpayer. If the homeowner has depreciated a portion of the home, the taxpayer's tax basis in the home is reduced. Upon sale of the home, gain *due to the depreciation* is not eligible for the exclusion. Thus, a taxpayer could end up with somewhat of a surprise when that depreciation is recaptured upon the sale of the principal residence.

CHAPTER 24: QUESTIONS

1. *Vacation homes.* For how many days can a taxpayer rent a vacation home without having to include the rent in gross income?

2. *Vacation homes.* Explain to what extent tax deductions (*e.g.*, depreciation, maintenance, utilities, etc.) are available to a taxpayer who rents out a vacation home for one-half the year and uses it for personal purposes the other half of the year.

3. *Sale of a principal residence.* What is the maximum amount of gain exclusion for a single individual on the qualified sale of a principal residence? Married filing jointly?

4. *Sale of a principal residence.* Generally, how long must a taxpayer own and use a principal residence in order for the exclusion of gain on the sale of the residence to apply?

5. *Sale of a principal residence.* For purposes of the gain exclusion on the sale of a principal residence, may a taxpayer have more than one principal residence?

6. *Sale of a principal residence.* Is the gain exclusion on the sale of a principal residence available only once-in-a-lifetime for a taxpayer? If not, how often may a taxpayer utilize the gain exclusion?

7. *Sale of a principal residence.* Under what circumstances may a partial exclusion of gain be available to a taxpayer who fails to meet the ownership and use tests?

8. *Sale of a principal residence.* If a taxpayer has depreciated a portion of his or her principal residence because part of it was used as a home office, how does the taxpayer treat the gain that is attributable to the depreciation when selling his or her home?

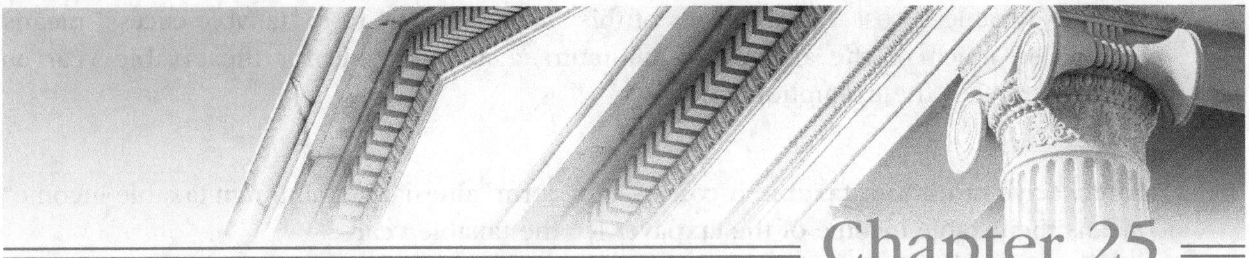

Chapter 25

Alternative Minimum Tax

Historically, many taxpayers have thought it unfair that some wealthy taxpayers could take advantage of certain tax deductions and, even though their economic income was quite high, taxable income for those wealthy taxpayers was quite low or even zero. Consequently, Congress has enacted the **alternative minimum tax (AMT)** with the overriding purpose to ensure that higher-income taxpayers pay at least a minimum amount of tax.

A. Imposition of the AMT

However noble Congress' attempt at fairness may have been by enacting the AMT, most taxpayers many tax consultants view the AMT as a complicated mess. The AMT is one area of the Code where many people think it should be repealed just because of its complication and burden it puts on taxpayers to figure out. While the AMT applies to both individuals and corporations, we will focus on the AMT as it applies to individuals. Our coverage of this topic here will be limited to the broad fundamentals rather than specific details.

INTERNAL REVENUE CODE

SECTION 55. ALTERNATIVE MINIMUM TAX IMPOSED

(a) **General rule**.—There is hereby imposed (in addition to any other tax imposed by this subtitle) a tax equal to the excess (if any) of—

(1) the tentative minimum tax for the taxable year, over

(2) the regular tax for the taxable year.

(b) **Tentative minimum tax**.—For purposes of this part—

(1) **Amount of tentative tax**.—

(A) Noncorporate taxpayers.—

(i) In general. In the case of a taxpayer other than a corporation, the tentative minimum tax for the taxable year is the sum of—

(I) 26 percent of so much of the taxable excess as does not exceed $175,000, plus

(II) 28 percent of so much of the taxable excess as exceeds $175,000.

. . .

(ii) Taxable excess. For purposes of this subsection, the term "taxable excess" means so much of the alternative minimum taxable income for the taxable year as exceeds the exemption amount.

. . .

(2) **Alternative minimum taxable income.**—The term "alternative minimum taxable income" means the taxable income of the taxpayer for the taxable year—
(A) determined with the adjustments provided in section 56 and section 58, and
(B) increased by the amount of items of tax preference described in section 57.

. . .

(d) **Exemption amount.**—For purposes of this section—
(1) **Exemption amount for taxpayers other than corporations.**—In the case of a taxpayer other than a corporation, the term "exemption amount" means—
(A) $78,750 in the case of—
(i) a joint return, or
(ii) a surviving spouse,
(B) $50,600 in the case of an individual who—
(i) is not a married individual, and
(ii) is not a surviving spouse,

. . .

In short, the AMT calculation starts with the taxpayer's regular taxable income calculated without regard to the AMT rules. Then, certain AMT **preference items** are added to the taxpayer's regular taxable income and then some AMT **adjustments** are either added or subtracted (as the case may be). The result is **alternative minimum taxable income**. The taxpayer then subtracts an **exemption** amount to arrive at the **AMT base**. The AMT base is then multiplied by the applicable tax rate (26% up to $175,000 and 28% over $175,000). The result is the **tentative minimum tax**. The regular tax is then subtracted to determine whether there is any alternative minimum tax.

A summary of the AMT formula is as follows:

Regular taxable income

+	AMT preference items
+/−	AMT adjustments
=	Alternative minimum taxable income
−	Exemption amount
=	Alternative minimum tax base
×	26% on the first $175,000 plus 28% on the amount over $175,000
=	Tentative minimum tax
−	Regular income tax
=	Alternative minimum tax

B. Preference Items

The following list is a partial summary of *preference items* that are added to an individual's regular taxable income as part of the calculation of the AMT:

- certain depletion deductions
- some intangible drilling costs
- certain interest on private activity bonds that is tax-exempt under regular tax
- certain accelerated depreciation deductions on property placed in service before 1987
- certain exclusions of gains on the sale of qualified small business stock

AMT preference items are not all that common for individuals. AMT *adjustments* (rather than *preference items*) are much more common and typically impact many more taxpayers.

C. Adjustments

The following list is a partial summary of *adjustments* that are made to an individual's regular taxable income as part of the calculation of the AMT:

- a possible recalculation of depreciation deductions under a slower method
- a possible recalculation of permissible net operating losses
- no deduction for miscellaneous itemized deductions
- no deduction for state, local, or foreign income taxes or sales taxes
- no deduction for state, local, or foreign real or personal property taxes
- no deduction for the standard deduction
- no personal exemption deductions are allowed
- different treatment of incentive stock options than under regular tax calculation

As you can see, the items that can possibly hit taxpayers hard are the disallowance of personal exemptions and itemized deductions such as state and local income taxes, state and local property taxes, and miscellaneous itemized deductions.

D. Exemption Amount

After a taxpayer's regular taxable income is modified by AMT preference items and adjustments, then the taxpayer subtracts an exemption amount. The exemption amount for 2014 is $52,800 (2013 was $51,900) for unmarried individuals and $82,100 for married filing jointly (2013 was $80,800). These amounts are adjusted for inflation.

Once the exemption amount is subtracted, a 26% tax rate applies to the first $182,500 over and a 28% tax rate applies to the amount over $182,500. A taxpayer then applies any AMT credits against tax that may be available. Ultimately, the taxpayer pays the higher of the AMT or the regular tax. The AMT is calculated and reported on IRS Form 6251, a copy of which is included in the Appendix.

Obviously, taxpayers do not usually calculate the AMT by hand. Although software programs are capable of calculating an individual's AMT, tax consultants should still be familiar enough with AMT issues to recognize when an individual may incur the tax and how to advise clients as to any planning opportunities.

CHAPTER 25: QUESTIONS

1. *AMT in general.* For what policy purpose was the AMT enacted?
2. *AMT in general.* Does the AMT apply to both individuals and corporations?
3. *AMT in general.* What is the starting point for the AMT calculation?
4. *Preference items.* Name at least two AMT preference items.
5. *Adjustments.* Name at least four AMT adjustments.
6. *Exemption amount.* What is the AMT exemption amount for 2014?
7. *AMT rates.* What are the two tax rates that apply in calculating an individual's alternative income tax liability?

Chapter 26

Overview of Other Taxes

This textbook focuses on federal *income* taxation of individuals. Of course, the tax system in the United States (including state and local taxes) contains many more types of taxes. This chapter provides an overview of such taxes.

A. Gift Taxes

We discussed in Chapter 10 that a recipient of a gift (*i.e.*, the "donee") does not include the amount of the gift in his or her gross income and thus is not subject to *income* tax. Nevertheless the *giver* (*i.e.*, the "donor") may be subject to the *gift* tax regime.

INTERNAL REVENUE CODE

SECTION 2501. IMPOSITION OF TAX

(a) **Taxable transfers.**—

(1) **General rule.**—A tax, computed as provided in section 2502, is hereby imposed for each calendar year on the transfer or property by gift during such calendar year by any individual, resident or nonresident.

. . .

The gift tax rate that applies to the donor on a **taxable gift** is as high as 40%. A giver of a gift is allowed to exclude up to a gift of $14,000 *per donee* each year, however. This amount is called the **annual exclusion**. Thus, for example, an individual could make gifts of $14,000 each to ten different people for a total of $140,000 and not be subject to the gift tax. The $14,000 is indexed for inflation and adjusts upward every few years, but only in increments of $1,000.

Married individuals may elect to **gift-split**. Thus, a donor individual can make a gift to each individual donee in an amount up to $28,000 per year if the donor's spouse consents. Gifts made to spouses are not subject to the gift tax because of an **unlimited marital deduction**. Donations to qualified charities are also not subject to the gift tax.

Even if a gift is a taxable gift (*i.e.*, the gift is in excess of the annual exclusion), the taxpayer may still be able to avoid the gift tax. Each taxpayer has a $5,000,000 unified gift and estate tax **exclusion amount**. This amount is indexed for inflation, however. The 2014 exclusion amount is $5,340,000. This means that a taxpayer can elect to use all or any portion of this $5,340,000 during his or her lifetime by making taxable gifts and then electing for those gifts not to be taxed. Whatever amount of the $5,340,000 is remaining when the taxpayer dies can be used to reduce his or her estate taxes. Gift taxes are calculated and reported on IRS Form 709, a copy of which is included in the Appendix.

B. Estate Taxes

You may have heard a saying similar to, "There's nothing more certain in life as death and taxes." Well, for some individuals it is possible for both to apply at the same time. The Code imposes a tax on the value of an individual's taxable estate.

INTERNAL REVENUE CODE

SECTION 2001. IMPOSITION AND RATE OF TAX

(a) **Imposition.**—A tax is hereby imposed on the transfer of the taxable estate of every decedent who is a citizen or resident of the United States.

. . .

The estate tax rate that applies to the taxable estate is as high as 40%. The **executor** of the estate (*i.e.*, the person that handles the affairs of the decedent's estate) is responsible to determine the value of all the assets the decedent owned. These assets are included in the decedent's **gross estate**. The gross estate is then reduced by allowable deductions such as funeral expenses, liabilities of the decedent, and gifts to charity. An **unlimited marital deduction** is also allowed. The gross estate is further reduced by the remaining portion of the unified gift and estate tax exclusion amount ($5,000,000 plus inflation adjustment). Moreover, if the decedent's spouse preceded the decedent in death, the decedent can also reduce his or her gross estate by the unused portion of the exclusion amount of his or her deceased spouse. This is called the exclusion amount **portability** between spouses. Thus, together spouses can exclude from their collective gross estates up to $10,000,000 (plus inflation adjustment).

As you might surmise, the $5,340,000 (in 2014) exclusion amount for each spouse allows many individuals to escape the reach of the estate tax. The estate tax has been a hot political topic over the years and the exclusion amount has varied (*e.g.*, $600,000 in 1997, $1,000,000 in 2003, $5,000,000 in 2011 and indexed for inflation each year thereafter). One should be careful, however, because some items can be included in a decedent's gross estate that may quickly cause the value of the estate to increase. For example, if a deceased person owned a life insurance policy upon his or her death, the proceeds from the policy are in most cases included in the decedent's gross estate even if the named beneficiary was someone other than the decedent's estate. Estate taxes are calculated and reported on IRS Form 706, a copy of which is included in the Appendix.

Another tax related to gift and estate taxes is called the **generation-skipping tax**. This tax exists to prevent taxpayers from avoiding potential gift and estate taxes at each generation by making transfers to grandchildren (or great-grandchildren), thus skipping a generation (or two). Details of this tax are not presented here.

C. Payroll Taxes

Employers are required to withhold income taxes from their employees' paychecks. In addition to *income* tax withholding, employers must also withhold *social security* tax and *Medicare* tax. The social security tax and Medicare tax are together called "FICA" taxes or "payroll" taxes. FICA stands for **Federal Insurance Contributions Act**. In 2014, the employer withholds 6.2% of the first $117,000 of an employee's wages. The employer also withholds 1.45% of the employee's wages (no ceiling). An employer is also required to match the amount of social security and Medicare taxes withheld from an employee. As mentioned in Chapter 15, if an individual has wages exceeding $200,000 (single) or $250,000 (married filing jointly), the individual is subject to an additional 0.9% Medicare tax.

D. Business Entity Taxation

One of the first decisions an individual is faced with when going into business is which type of business entity to form. Of course, a sole proprietorship is an option, but sole proprietorships do not offer the owner any liability protection from the debts and obligations of the business. This section briefly discusses the tax treatment of various business entities.

1. Partnerships

A partnership exists when two or more persons join together to carry on a business with the intent to make a profit. There are several varieties of partnerships: (1) general partnerships, (2) limited partnerships, (3) limited liability partnerships, and (4) limited liability limited partnerships. All of these variations are treated as "pass-through" (sometimes called "flow-through") entities for federal income tax purposes. This means that the entities themselves are not subject to income tax; rather, the *partners* are subject to income tax on their respective shares of the partnership's income. Each partner receives a Schedule K-1 from the partnership informing the partner of his or her share of partnership income. The partner then takes the amounts from the Schedule K-1 and reports them in the appropriate place on the partner's income tax return.

2. Limited Liability Companies

Limited liability companies (LLCs) are a separate statutory creature under state law but are treated like partnerships for federal income tax law. Thus, they are "pass-through" entities and the owners (called "members") of the LLC are taxed on the income.

3. C Corporations

Unlike partnerships and LLCs, corporations are subject to income tax at the entity level. Then, when the income is distributed to shareholders, the income is taxed again as a dividend. Thus, corporations are often referred to as being "double-taxed." Subchapter "C" of the Internal Revenue Code governs the taxation of regular corporations. Consequently, these corporations are often called "C" corporations.

4. S Corporations

If a corporation meets the requirements of a "small business corporation," the corporation can make an election to be an "S" corporation. Subchapter S governs the tax treatment of these corporations. The advantage of an S corporation is that it is a "flow-through" entity much like a partnership and avoids the double-layer of taxation. S corporations have to live with many restrictions, however. For example, S corporations can only have a maximum of 100 shareholders, can generally only have individuals, trusts, and estates as shareholders, and can only have one class of stock outstanding.

5. The "Check-the-Box" Rules

The IRS allows partnerships and LLCs to elect to be treated as C corporations. This election is made by checking a box on an IRS form. Hence, you may occasionally hear that a partnership or LLC has "checked-the-box" to be treated as a corporation. Corporations, on the other hand, are not allowed to check-the-box to be treated as a partnership or LLC. Corporations do have the option to make an "S" election, however, and be treated as a pass-through entity. Even partnerships and LLCs that make an election to be treated as a corporation under the check-the-box rules can also make an "S" election and be treated as an S corporation for income tax purposes.

E. Income Taxation of Trusts and Estates

Individuals frequently set up trusts to hold and manage assets. The person establishing the trust is called the **grantor** (or settlor). Responsibility for managing the trust falls upon the **trustee** (who may or may not also be the grantor). The trust also identifies **beneficiaries** who may often receive income from the trust and/or may be scheduled to receive property at a later date. In many cases, a trust is treated as a pass-through entity and is not subject to income tax at the entity level. Nevertheless, if the trust does not distribute income, the trust may be classified as a "complex" trust (as opposed to a "simple" trust) and be subject to income taxation.

Estates are created when an individual dies. The **executor** of the estate identifies the assets, collects income, pays liabilities of the decedent, and winds up the affairs of the estate. If an estate distributes income earned during this time, the estate is typically not subject to income tax, but it may be subject to income tax if it accumulates the income.

F. International Taxation

The United States has the jurisdiction to tax the worldwide income of its citizens and residents. This creates the possibility of individuals being double-taxed on their income earned in foreign countries—once in the United States and once in the foreign country. The United States has tried to mitigate this potential double-taxation by providing a **foreign tax credit** to U.S. citizens and residents who pay foreign income taxes. The Code also provides a **foreign-earned income exclusion** that shields up to a certain amount from taxation in the United States if a person chooses to exclude the income rather than utilize the foreign tax credit. The United States has also entered into income tax treaties with many foreign countries. These treaties also try to mitigate the impact of double-taxation.

Of course, international taxation can be quite complex, both for individuals and business entities. One major issue for individuals, however, is whether the individual is a **U.S. person**. If so, the United States has jurisdiction to tax the person's worldwide income (subject to allowance for the foreign tax credit and treaty provisions). A "U.S. person" is a U.S. citizen, resident alien, or a domestic corporation, domestic partnership, and domestic trusts and estates. A resident alien is someone who has a green card or meets a "substantial presence" test where they are present in the United States for a particular amount of time. If a person is not a U.S. person, they are a **foreign person** and are taxed in the United States only on their United States-sourced income rather than on their worldwide income.

U.S. corporations operating in foreign countries also have to be aware of international tax issues. For example, a U.S. corporation should be familiar with the **transfer pricing** issues if it sells goods to a foreign subsidiary. Moreover, some income earned by a foreign subsidiary (called "**Subpart F income**") may be taxed in the United States in the current year while other types of income is not taxed in the United States until such income is **repatriated** to the United States.

G. Excise Taxes

When you pay for a gallon of gasoline you may occasionally notice a sticker on the gas pump informing you how much in fuel taxes you pay on a per-gallon basis. In addition to fuel taxes, other excise tax examples are taxes on telecommunications, air transportation services, and tanning bed businesses. Basically, **excise tax** is a broad term that connotes a tax on the provision of certain services (*e.g.*, tanning bed services) or on a transactions involving particular items (*e.g.*, fuel). Federal excise taxes are generally reported on IRS Form 720, a copy of which is provided in the Appendix.

H. State and Local Taxation

Most states have enacted a number of different taxes. Typical taxes include income taxes, sales taxes, property taxes, and excise taxes. Some cities and counties also add additional taxes on top of state taxes. Some individuals consider a state's overall tax burden when they are deciding where to live when they retire. Businesses also consider the tax burden when determining where to locate headquarters and where to have warehouses.

Similar to a multi-*national* business, a multi-*state* business has to worry about the potential of getting taxed twice on the same income. Fortunately, states recognize this problem and provide formulas for apportioning business income among the states in which the business is subject to taxes. A taxpayer is subject to taxation in a state only when the taxpayer has sufficient **nexus** with the state. As a general rule, a taxpayer has nexus with a state when the taxpayer has established a **nontrivial physical presence** in the state. Nevertheless, states have their own nexus rules and some states now claim that a mere *economic* presence (as opposed to a *physical* presence) is sufficient to establish nexus. Additionally, a state's nexus rules for *income* tax purposes can be different than for *sales* tax purposes.

CHAPTER 26: QUESTIONS

1. *Gift taxes*. How much is an individual's annual exclusion for gift tax purposes?
2. *Gift taxes*. How many times can a taxpayer use the annual exclusion each year?
3. *Gift taxes*. What does gift-splitting mean?
4. *Gift taxes*. How much may an individual give to his or her spouse without incurring a gift tax?
5. *Gift taxes*. Explain how an individual may still avoid gift taxes even if a gift exceeds the annual exclusion.
6. *Estate taxes*. How much is the lifetime exclusion amount for the unified gift and estate tax system (ignoring adjustments for inflation)?
7. *Estate taxes*. What is a decedent's "gross estate"?
8. *Estate taxes*. What does "portability" of the exclusion amount mean?
9. *Payroll taxes*. What does FICA stand for?
10. *Payroll taxes*. What is the social security tax withholding rate?
11. *Payroll taxes*. What is the Medicare tax withholding rate?
12. *Business entity taxation*. Generally, how are partnerships treated for income tax purposes?
13. *Business entity taxation*. Generally, how are limited liability companies treated for income tax purposes?

14. *Business entity taxation*. Generally, how are C corporations treated for income tax purposes?

15. *Business entity taxation*. Generally, how are S corporations treated for income tax purposes?

16. *Business entity taxation*. What are the "check-the-box" rules?

17. *Income taxation of trusts and estates*. Generally, if a trust or estate distributes current income to the grantor or to the beneficiaries, is the trust or estate subject to income tax on the income?

18. *International taxation*. How does the United States address the potential double-taxation problem of a U.S. person that has foreign-sourced income?

19. *International taxation*. Who is a "U.S. person"? Explain the importance for U.S. income tax purposes of whether a person is a U.S. person or a foreign person.

20. *Excise taxes*. What is an excise tax? Give some examples.

21. *State and local taxation*. Name some common taxes imposed by state and local governments.

22. *State and local taxation*. What does "nexus" mean?

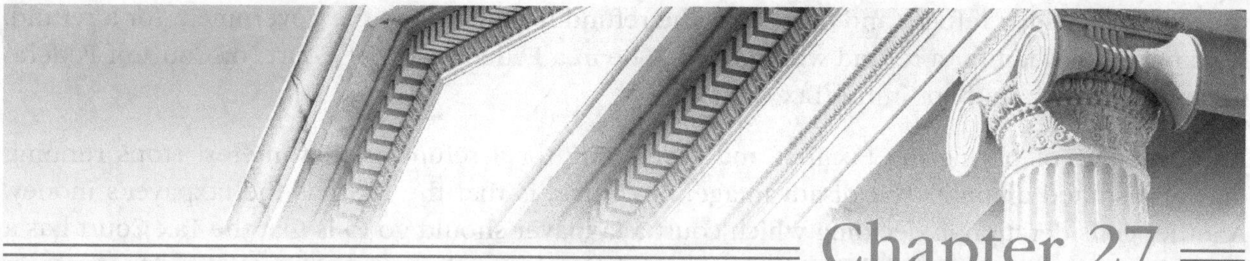

Chapter 27

Tax Audits and Appeals

Getting audited by the IRS is a scary thought for a lot of people. But some would argue that if the government did not have a tax enforcement agency, then the government would not be able to collect the revenue it needs to provide services to the public. This chapter discusses broadly the audit process and the taxpayer appeal process.

A. IRS Audits and Appeals

A taxpayer is usually notified of an audit by receiving a letter in the mail. The letter will explain what years are involved and will often ask the taxpayer to provide additional information. There are a few different ways that the IRS can conduct an audit. A **correspondence audit** is one conducted through the mail. An **office audit** is where the IRS requests the taxpayer to come in and meet an agent at the IRS office. A **field audit** is where the IRS agent comes out to the taxpayer's place of business.

Once the agent is finished auditing the taxpayer, the agent will issue a report reflecting the agent's findings. The agent's report will be accompanied by what is called a **30-day letter**. The 30-day letter states that the taxpayer has 30 days to submit a protest and request an appeal with the IRS appeals office if the taxpayer disagrees with the agent's findings. If the taxpayer does not request an appeal within the 30 days, the taxpayer will then receive a **Statutory Notice of Deficiency** ("90-day letter"). The Statutory Notice of Deficiency indicates that the taxpayer has 90 days to file a petition in Tax Court if the taxpayer wants to challenge the IRS's findings in court without first paying the tax.

If the taxpayer does go to the IRS appeals office, the taxpayer states his or her case before someone who may have a different view of the issue than the agent who audited the taxpayer. The appeals office also can settle issues with the taxpayer instead of going to court. The agent who audits the taxpayer usually has no authority to settle the case by accepting an offer from a taxpayer. If a taxpayer cannot settle the issues involved in the audit in the appeals conference, then the taxpayer will receive a Statutory Notice of Deficiency. If the taxpayer does not want to pay the tax first, the taxpayer has 90 days to file a petition in the U.S. Tax Court. The Tax Court is the only court that will hear a tax case if the taxpayer has not yet paid the tax. The taxpayer could pay the tax first, claim a refund, and then, after the refund is denied, sue the government for a refund. A taxpayer's lawsuit for a refund would have to be in a Federal District Court (or Court of Federal Claims), however, and not in the Tax Court.

An advantage of paying the tax first and then suing for a refund is that interest stops running on the disputed amount. The disadvantage, of course, is that the IRS has the taxpayer's money. Another consideration in deciding which court a taxpayer should go to is that the Tax Court has a specialist tax judge. In Federal District Court the judge is usually not a tax specialist. Moreover, in Federal District Court, the taxpayer has the right to request a jury. In Tax Court, no jury is available. Some lawyers might think a jury would be more favorable to a taxpayer in certain cases.

The party that loses at the Tax Court or Federal District Court level has the right of an automatic appeal to the Circuit Court of Appeals wherein the taxpayer resides. For example, California is in the Ninth Circuit Court of Appeals. New York is in the Second Circuit Court of Appeals. If a taxpayer or the IRS loses the case at the circuit court level, they can request for the United States Supreme Court to hear the case. Whether the Supreme Court hears the case is up to the Supreme Court to determine. The Supreme Court reviews very few, if any, tax cases each year.

Here is a broad summary of the process:

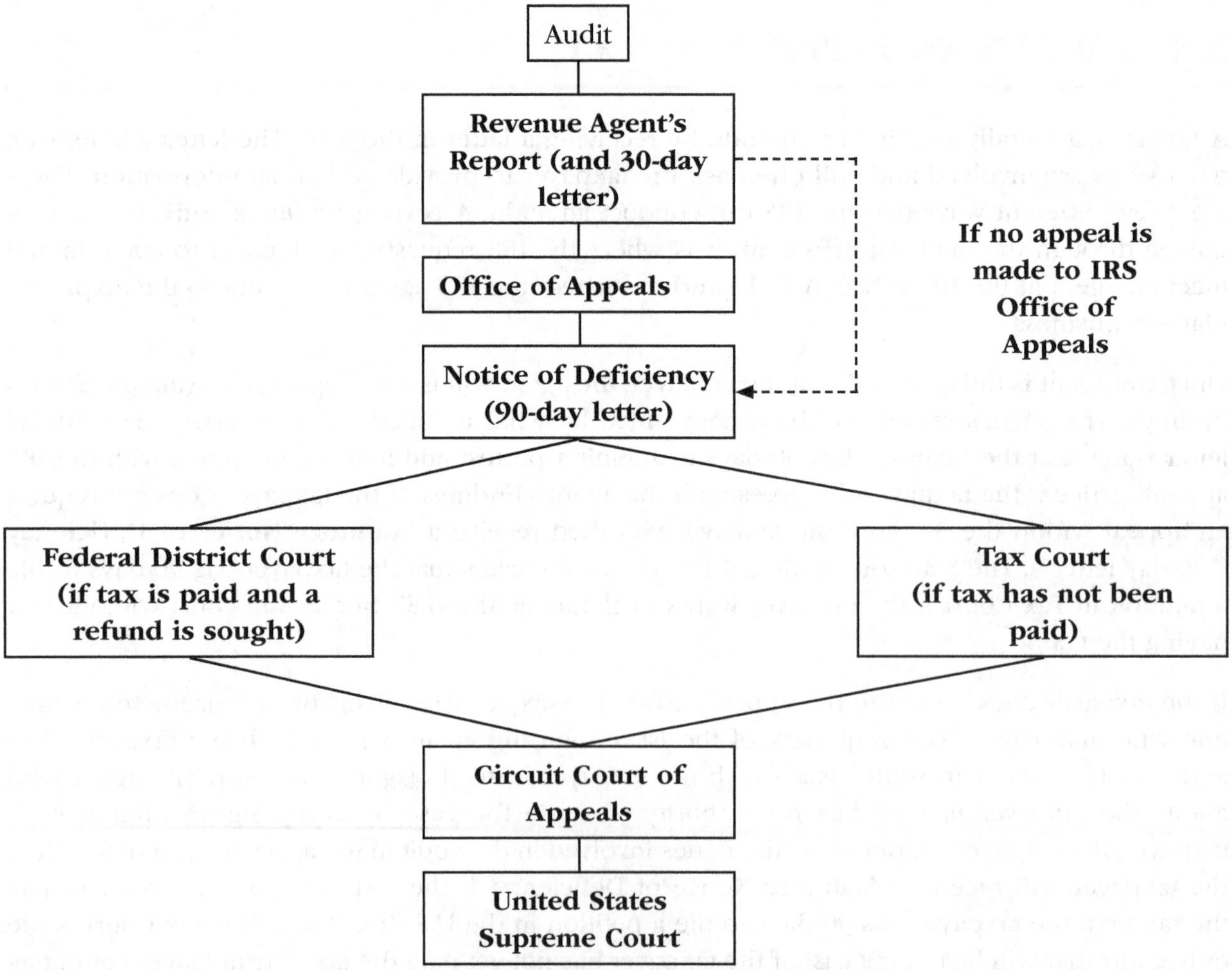

Again, this diagram is not a comprehensive illustration of the entire process, but shows the overall appeal system. A few additional items of discussion are warranted, however. The disputed amount of tax technically can be paid earlier than after receiving a 90-day letter. A suit could then commence in Federal District Court if the taxpayer claims a refund and the IRS denies the claim. Also, if a taxpayer desires to pursue the Tax Court route, a taxpayer can make a "deposit" and stop the interest from running. A taxpayer can also pay the tax and sue for refund (if the refund claim is denied) in the U.S. Court of Federal Claims, which is a court similar to District Court. Any appeal from this court goes to the Federal Circuit Court of Appeals.

B. Statute of Limitations

How long does the IRS have to audit your income tax return and assess additional taxes and perhaps interest and penalties?

INTERNAL REVENUE CODE

SECTION 6501. LIMITATIONS ON ASSESSMENT AND COLLECTION

(a) **General rule.**—Except as otherwise provided in this section, the amount of any tax imposed by this title shall be assessed within 3 years after the return was filed (whether or not such return was filed on or after the date prescribed) . . .

(b) **Time return deemed filed.**—

(1) **Early return.**—For purposes of this section, a return of tax imposed by this title . . . filed before the last day prescribed by law or by regulations promulgated pursuant to law for the filing thereof, shall be considered as filed on such last day.

. . .

Thus, the IRS generally has three years to assess an additional tax. Similarly, a taxpayer also typically has three years to amend a return and request a refund (See Code Section 6511).

INTERNAL REVENUE CODE

SECTION 6511. LIMITATIONS ON CREDIT OR REFUND

(a) **Period of limitation on filing claim.**— Claim for credit or refund of an overpayment of any tax imposed by this title in respect of which tax the taxpayer is required to file a return shall be filed by the taxpayer within 3 years from the time the return was filed or 2 years from the time the tax was paid, whichever of such periods expires the later, or if no return was filed by the taxpayer, within 2 years from the time the tax was paid.

. . .

The statute of limitations for the IRS to assess a tax deficiency can extend to six years if a taxpayer omits an amount of gross income in excess of 25% of the gross income stated on the return. There is no statute of limitations if the taxpayer fails to file a return when required to do so or if the taxpayer files a fraudulent return. Section 6501 provides these rules.

INTERNAL REVENUE CODE

SECTION 6501. LIMITATIONS ON ASSESSMENT AND COLLECTION

. . .

(c) **Exceptions.**—

(1) **False return.**—In the case of a false or fraudulent return with the intent to evade tax, the tax may be assessed, or a proceeding in court for collection of such tax may be begun without assessment, at any time.

(2) **Willful attempt to evade tax.**—In case of a willful attempt in any manner to defeat or evade tax imposed by this title . . ., the tax may be assessed, or a proceeding in court for the collection of such tax may be begun without assessment, at any time.

(3) **No return.**—In the case of failure to file a return, the tax may be assessed, or a proceeding in court for the collection of such tax may be begun without assessment, at any time.

. . .

(e) **Substantial omission of items.**—Except as otherwise provided in subsection (c)—

(1) **Income taxes.**—In the case of any tax imposed by subtitle A—

(A) General rule.—If the taxpayer omits from gross income an amount properly includible therein which is in excess of 25 percent of the amount of gross income stated in the return, the tax may be assessed, or a proceeding in court for the collection of such tax may be begun without assessment, at any time within 6 years after the return was filed.

. . .

C. BURDEN OF PROOF

If a tax controversy goes to court, who has the burden of proof to show that they are correct? The taxpayer? The IRS? Section 7491 addresses this issue.

INTERNAL REVENUE CODE

SECTION 7491. BURDEN OF PROOF

(a) **Burden shifts where taxpayer produces credible evidence.**—

(1) **General rule.**—If, in any court proceeding, a taxpayer introduces credible evidence with respect to any factual issue relevant to ascertaining the liability of the taxpayer for any tax imposed by subtitle A or B, the Secretary shall have the burden of proof with respect to such issues.

(2) **Limitations.**—Paragraph (1) shall apply with respect to an issue only if—

(A) the taxpayer has complied with the requirements under this title to substantiate any item,

(B) the taxpayer has maintained all records required under this title and has cooperated with reasonable requests by the Secretary for witnesses, information, documents, meetings, and interviews, and

(C) in the case of partnership, corporation, or trust, the taxpayer is described in section 7430(c)(4)(A)(ii).

(3) **Coordination.**—Paragraph (1) shall not apply to any issue if any other provision of this title provides for a specific burden of proof with respect to such issue.

(b) **Use of statistical information on unrelated taxpayers.**—In the case of an individual taxpayer, the Secretary shall have the burden of proof in any court proceeding with respect to any item of income which was reconstructed by the Secretary solely through the use of statistical information on unrelated taxpayers.

. . .

Thus, the taxpayer has the burden of proof unless the taxpayer produces credible evidence, maintains adequate records, and cooperates with the IRS during the audit process. If a taxpayer meets these requirements, then the burden of proof shifts to the IRS. One exception to this is if a corporation, partnership, or trust has a net worth in excess of $7 million, the burden of proof does not shift even if these requirements are met.

When it comes to penalties, the IRS has the burden of proof.

D. PRIVILEGED COMMUNICATIONS

Communications between a taxpayer and an attorney are in most cases "privileged," meaning that the lawyer cannot be compelled to disclose what the client has communicated to the lawyer. In a tax context, does the same privilege extend to accountants and other tax practitioners? Section 7525 addresses this issue.

INTERNAL REVENUE CODE

SECTION 7525. CONFIDENTIALITY PRIVILEGES RELATING TO TAXPAYER COMMUNICATIONS

(a) **Uniform application to taxpayer communications with federally authorized practitioners.**

(1) **General rule.**—With respect to tax advice, the same common law protections of confidentiality which apply to a communication between a taxpayer and an attorney shall also apply to a communication between a taxpayer and any federally authorized tax practitioner to the extent the communication would be considered a privileged communication if it were between a taxpayer and an attorney.

(2) **Limitations.**—Paragraph (1) may only be asserted in—
   (A) Any noncriminal tax matter before the Internal Revenue Service; and
   (B) Any noncriminal tax proceeding in Federal court brought by or against the United States.
(3) **Definitions.**—For purposes of this subsection—
   (A) Federally authorized tax practitioner. The term "federally authorized tax practitioner" means any individual who is authorized under Federal law to practice before the Internal Revenue Service if such practice is subject to Federal regulation under section 330 of title 31 United States Code.
   (B) Tax advice. The term "tax advice" means advice given by an individual with respect to a matter which is within the scope of the individual's authority to practice described in subparagraph (A).

. . .

The term **federally authorized tax practitioner** includes lawyers, certified public accountants, enrolled agents, and some other individuals in unique situations. This particular privilege does not apply in criminal matters or in matters unrelated to a client's tax obligations. Also, if the communication is made solely for the purpose of preparing a tax return or in connection with any written communication in furtherance of a tax shelter, such communication is not privileged.

E. Regulation of Tax Return Preparers

Given actual and perceived abuses and incompetence of some tax return preparers, the Treasury Department has tried to implement new regulations to govern paid tax return preparers. These new regulations basically provide that paid tax return preparers must register with the IRS and obtain a **practitioner tax identification number** (a "PTIN"). Even attorneys, CPAs, and enrolled agents must obtain a PTIN. As part of the new regulations, paid tax return preparers will also need to pass a competency exam and complete continuing education requirements. Attorneys, CPAs, and enrolled agents are exempt from the exam and continuing education requirements. Other individuals may be exempt from these requirements also (*e.g.*, certain supervised individuals who only assist in preparing returns). Recently, some taxpayers have challenged the authority of the IRS to issue these regulations. The courts are addressing the issue and the future of these regulations is currently uncertain. So far the courts have ruled that the IRS lacks the authority to impose continuing education requirements and to demand the taking of competency exams for tax return preparers.

Tax return preparers are also subject to potential civil and criminal penalties. For example, disclosing or using information about a client's financial information in an unauthorized manner could lead to penalties on the tax return preparer. Of course, knowingly filing fraudulent or frivolous returns could also lead to penalties. Conspiring with a taxpayer to defraud the government is also a crime. Many other civil penalties and crimes apply to tax return preparers, but we will not discuss them in detail here.

CHAPTER 27: QUESTIONS

1. *IRS audit.* What are the different types of IRS audits?

2. *30-day letter.* When a taxpayer receives a 30-day letter at the conclusion of an audit, the letter will say that the taxpayer has 30 days to do what?

3. *Statutory Notice of Deficiency.* When a taxpayer receives a 90-day letter (Statutory Notice of Deficiency), the taxpayer has 90 days to do what?

4. *Tax Court.* If a taxpayer pays the tax and sues the government for a refund, can the taxpayer be heard in Tax Court? If not, what court(s) can hear the case?

5. *Tax Court.* If a taxpayer does not pay the tax and wants to take the government to court over the dispute, can the taxpayer be heard in Tax Court? If not, what court(s) can hear the case?

6. *Federal court system.* Explain some differences between the Tax Court and United States District Court.

7. *Litigation strategy.* Why would a taxpayer deliberately choose to go to a district court rather than to Tax Court?

8. *Appellate courts.* If a taxpayer loses a case in Tax Court or U.S. District Court, can the taxpayer appeal the case? If the taxpayer wants to take the case all the way to the U.S. Supreme Court, does the U.S Supreme Court have to hear the case?

9. *Burden of proof.* Explain who has the burden of proof in a tax controversy.

10. *Burden of proof.* Who has the burden of proof when it comes to the assessment of penalties?

11. *Statute of limitations.* How long does the IRS have generally to audit a taxpayer's return before the statute of limitations runs out? What if the taxpayer omits a substantial amount of income? What if the taxpayer files a fraudulent return? What if the taxpayer files no return at all (assuming the taxpayer was required to file a return)?

12. *Privileged communications.* Under what circumstances are a client's conversations with a non-attorney tax practitioner considered a privileged communication?

13. *Internet activity.* Go to the IRS website and find Publication 556 (Examination of Returns, Appeal Rights, and Claims for Refund).
    a. How many days advance notice must you give the IRS if you plan to make an audio recording of the examination interview?
    b. What is the "fast track mediation" process?
    c. How does the IRS say a taxpayer can stop interest from accruing?

d. Can a taxpayer represent himself at an appeals conference?
e. Is it possible to recover litigation costs and administrative costs from the government if the taxpayer is the prevailing party? What conditions must be met?
f. How much time does a taxpayer have to file a claim for refund?

14. *Internet activity.* Go to the U.S. Tax Court website at www.ustaxcourt.gov. Click on the "Forms" tab. Find the link to a simplified form for a Petition.
    a. If a taxpayer chooses to have the "small tax case" procedures apply, can the taxpayer or IRS appeal the decision?
    b. If a taxpayer wants the small tax case procedures to apply, the amount of tax in dispute must generally be below what amount?
    c. How much is the filing fee when filing the petition with the Tax Court?
    d. Does the Tax Court hear cases in your state? If so, what city or cities? If not, what is the closest city to you where the Tax Court hears cases?

Chapter 28

Overview of Tax Research

As you recall from your early study of American government, the U.S. Constitution establishes three branches of government: (1) legislative branch; (2) executive branch; and (3) judicial branch. Tax laws, regulations, rules, and court decisions come from these branches of government. An indispensable skill for every tax consultant is the ability to find answers. Obviously, the tax laws can change frequently and memorizing changes in every area of taxation from year to year is usually impractical and nearly impossible.

In this chapter we will discuss the fundamentals of tax research. We will look at each branch of government and how each branch impacts the tax law. Ultimately, we will mention a few tax research resources and common forms of citation for references to the law.

A. Legislative Branch

Congress is the legislative branch of the Federal government. In short, a bill is introduced either in the House of Representatives or in the Senate. Often the bill is referred to a subcommittee that holds hearings and ultimately decides whether to approve the bill and move it on for a vote of the whole House or Senate. The **Ways and Means Committee** is the subcommittee that deals with tax bills in the House of Representatives. The **Finance Committee** is the subcommittee that deals with tax bills in the Senate. Frequently, the House will pass a bill and send it to the Senate for a vote and the Senate will change it. Whenever the two bills (*e.g.*, the one from the House and the one from the Senate) are not identical, the bill typically goes to the **Joint Committee on Taxation** (JCT) for reconciliation. Then, the reconciled bill goes back to the House and Senate for approval. If approved, the bill goes to the President of the United States for signature or veto.

When a tax bill becomes law, the law is housed in the Internal Revenue Code, which is Title 26 of the United States Code. The United States Code has 51 titles.

A record of the deliberations in the House and Senate can be consulted by a tax researcher if the researcher is interested in the **legislative history** of a particular law. These deliberations can be found in the ***Congressional Record***. Also, the JCT periodically publishes a report explaining new tax laws. These reports are commonly compiled and published as the JCT's ***Blue Book***.

B. Executive Branch

The executive branch consists of the President and the various departments of government (*e.g.*, Departments of Defense, Homeland Security, Transportation, Treasury, Energy, and Education, etc.). Of course, the Internal Revenue Service is housed within the Treasury Department. The Treasury Department, just like other departments, has authority from Congress to issue regulations interpreting the law. The Treasury Department and IRS have issued many regulations and rulings interpreting the Internal Revenue Code.

1. Treasury Regulations

A **Treasury regulation** is the highest authoritative document the IRS can issue (technically, the regulations come from the Treasury Department). It is very close to having the same authority as the Code—but not quite. Indeed, if a taxpayer takes a position contrary to a Treasury regulation, the probability of winning in court is very low.

Regulations can be designated as "proposed," "temporary," or "final." To become final a regulation must go through a hearing process and the public must have an opportunity to comment. The IRS can issue temporary regulations in some situations where guidance on an issue is needed quickly, but a temporary regulation typically expires after three years (with some exceptions). A proposed regulation is one that is going through the hearing process and may eventually become a final regulation. A tax advisor is wise to observe the proposed regulation process to be aware of what may become a final regulation in the near future.

2. Revenue Rulings, Revenue Procedures

Revenue Rulings and **Revenue Procedures** address tax issues in more detail than do Treasury regulations. Taxpayers can rely on these documents when giving tax advice or preparing returns. Revenue Rulings and Revenue Procedures are not as authoritative as Treasury regulations, but they do represent the position of the IRS on the matters discussed and they should be respected as authority and not ignored by taxpayers.

3. Private Letter Rulings

When a taxpayer desires certainty regarding the tax treatment of a future transaction, the taxpayer can request an advance ruling by the IRS. The taxpayer must disclose the facts of the proposed transaction to the IRS and pay a fee for the advance ruling. These rulings are called **private letter rulings** (PLRs). They are binding only on the specific taxpayer involved. No other taxpayers can rely specifically on the ruling, but PLRs can provide helpful insight to other taxpayers on how the IRS might handle similar transactions.

4. Determination Letters

When a taxpayer has already entered into a transaction, the taxpayer may need to receive confirmation that the transaction was done properly. For example, a charity would receive a **determination**

letter from the IRS after charity has applied for tax-exempt status. Also, a retirement plan may be set up and then seek a determination letter from the IRS stating that the plan qualifies for tax-favored status.

5. Technical Advice Memoranda

Occasionally, an IRS agent or employee who is working on an issue in an audit may seek guidance internally from IRS personnel higher up the organizational ladder. The agent would request a **technical advice memorandum** (TAM) from the IRS national office to give guidance on how to handle a particular issue in question.

C. Judicial Branch

As we discussed in Chapter 27, if the IRS and a taxpayer cannot resolve a conflict, the parties can take the case to Tax Court or a federal district court. If a taxpayer (or the IRS) loses at this level, the losing party can appeal the case to a court of appeal. The United States has a number of circuit courts of appeal based on geographic boundaries. The Tax Court judge or district court judge is bound to follow the circuit court of appeals rulings in whatever circuit the taxpayer resides or does business. Of course, appeals from the circuit court of appeal may be appealed to the United States Supreme Court, but the chances of the Supreme Court hearing the case are very small. Court cases decided within the taxpayer's circuit should be given greater weight than those outside the taxpayer's circuit, but decisions outside the taxpayer's circuit can still be very persuasive to a court in the taxpayer's circuit.

D. Tax Research Resources

When engaging in tax research, a tax consultant should be cognizant of whether the authority on which he or she is relying is either **primary** authority or **secondary** authority. Primary authority consists of the U.S. Constitution, Internal Revenue Code, Treasury Regulations, IRS Revenue Rulings and Procedures, and court cases. Secondary authority consists of treatises and journal articles written by respected authors, textbooks, explanations by editors of tax services, and other tax periodicals. Of course, the goal of the tax researcher is to find primary authority that is right on point. Secondary authority can assist the researcher in learning more about the subject and pointing the researcher to the relevant primary authority. In some situations where primary authority does not specifically address the issue at hand, secondary authority can be very valuable to the researcher.

In today's technological age, many people try to find tax answers by using popular search engines on the internet for free. While this approach can help, a tax researcher should be very careful when relying on information found in this manner because such information could be wrong or out-of-date. The IRS website (www.irs.gov), however, is a common place to find information. The website has forms, instructions, publications, and guidance for various tax issues. Most courts also have their own websites. For example, the Tax Court's is www.ustaxcourt.gov.

Many public accounting firms and other tax consulting firms rely on private, for-profit businesses to provide up-to-date tax information. Some of these tax information providers include:

- CCH
- RIA
- Lexis-Nexis
- Westlaw
- BNA

These providers stay on top of tax law changes and usually have updates on their websites within 24 hours if not sooner. Of course, these providers charge a fee for access to their services. Although most tax research information is now online, some companies provide summaries of the tax law in hardcopy form so that a tax practitioner has a handy "quick reference." Colleges and universities usually subscribe to one or more of the tax services listed above. Your instructor can help you locate your library's online subscription (if applicable).

E. Common Forms of Citation

When a tax researcher drafts a memorandum to a supervisor, the researcher is wise to cite his or her authority for the analysis, conclusions, etc. The following is a summary of common forms of citations to primary authority. Sometimes accountants, lawyers, and other tax practitioners prefer one form of citation over another. Of course, you should follow your instructor's (or supervisor's) preferred form if it is different from the forms below. Also, this is not meant to be a comprehensive explanation of tax citation forms. When you take a course specifically in tax research, you will have much more exposure to both primary and secondary authority and forms of citation. Here are some examples.

1. Internal Revenue Code

The Code is often cited as follows (using Code Section 121 as an example):

- IRC Section 121
- Section 121
- Code Section 121
- Sec. 121
- IRC §121
- 26 U.S.C. §121

2. Treasury Regulations

Treasury Regulations are often cited as follows:

- Treas. Reg. 1.121-1
- Reg. 1.121-1
- Treas. Reg. §1.121-1
- Reg. §1.121-1
- Reg. Sec. 1.121-1

The number before the period identifies the type of Treasury regulation it is:

- 1 = income tax
- 20 = estate tax
- 25 = gift tax
- 301 = administrative/procedural matters

The number immediately after the period identifies the Code Section that the regulation applies to. The number after the dash refers to whether the regulation is the first, second, third, etc., regulation interpreting that particular Code section. If a regulation is a temporary regulation, the citation will usually have a capital "T" at the end. If it is a proposed regulation, the citation will usually have "Prop." before the citation. When the Treasury Department makes a decision that modifies a regulation, the document that is issued is called a **Treasury Decision** and is abbreviated "T.D." followed by the date of the decision.

3. Revenue Rulings and Revenue Procedures

Revenue Rulings and Revenue Procedures are often cited as follows:

- Rev. Rul. 2012-36
- Rev. Proc. 2007-6

Of course, the first number is the year the ruling or procedure was issued. For example, referring to the above citation, the revenue ruling was the 36th revenue ruling issued in 2012.

Sometimes revenue rulings and revenue procedures will have a citation that includes an "I.R.B." in it. That citation stands for the ***Internal Revenue Bulletin***, which typically is issued weekly by the IRS and contains all the revenue rulings, revenue procedures, and other IRS issuances. Twice per year the IRS typically combines all the Internal Revenue Bulletins into a ***Cumulative Bulletin***, which if cited is abbreviated "C.B."

4. Private Letter Rulings and Technical Advice Memoranda

Private Letter Rulings are often cited as follows:

- Private Letter Ruling 200735021
- Priv. Ltr. Rul. 200735021
- PLR 200735021

Technical Advice Memoranda are often cited as follows:

- Technical Advice Memorandum 9505002
- TAM 9505002

For both private letter rulings and technical advice memoranda, you can draw certain conclusions from the numbers. For example, in PLR 200735021, this is the 21st private letter ruling issued in the 35th week of the year 2007. In TAM 9505002, this is the second TAM issued in the 5th week of 1995 (notice that prior to 2000, the years do not include the first two numbers of the year). Sometimes the exact date a PLR or TAM was issued will follow the citation.

5. Court Cases

Common court case citations are presented next.

i. Tax Court

Tax Court decisions are either **regular** decisions or **memorandum** decisions. Regular decisions tend to address new or different legal issues than what the Tax Court has addressed in the past. Memorandum decisions tend to be cases that address factual issues that may be different than what the Tax Court has addressed in the past, but the applicable law, analysis, and conclusions are not significantly new or different from past cases.

- *Anthony J. Kadillak*, 127 T.C. 184 (2006)
- *Anthony J. Kadillak v. Commissioner*, 127 T.C. 184 (2006)
- *Kadillak*, 127 T.C. 184 (2006)

Some tax service providers (*e.g.*, RIA and CCH) have slightly different ways of citing cases, but you will become familiar with those as you gain experience in tax research. If a Tax Court decision is a memorandum decision, you will often see "T.C. Memo" or "T.C.M." in the citation.

Occasionally at the end of a Tax Court case you will see the statement, "Entered under Rule 155." This means that the court made the decision regarding the tax issue in controversy, but leaves the mathematical calculation of the tax, interest and penalties for the taxpayer and the IRS to work out. Also, prior to 1943, the **Board of Tax Appeals** was the predecessor to the Tax Court. If you see a decision from the Board of Tax Appeals you should be aware that it is a very old case perhaps dealing with law that is now out of date. Of course, you should determine whether a case you are relying on was overturned on appeal. A tax **citator** can help you do this. Most popular tax service companies (*e.g.*, RIA and CCH) have citators. Citators can also help you with determining whether a revenue ruling or revenue procedure has been superseded or is now obsolete.

ii. U.S. District Court

Cases from U.S. District Court are commonly cited as follows:

- *Johnson v. U.S.*, 861 F. Supp. 2d 609 (D. Md. 2012)

Notice this citation indicates the case was decided in the District of Maryland. This citation format (and the format illustrated in the following examples relating to the U.S Court of Federal Claims, U.S. Circuit Court of Appeals, and U.S. Supreme Court) is the format used by West Publishing Company and has become the primary form of citation in these courts. In tax cases, RIA and CCH have also developed their form of citation that is a bit different from this. RIA's is the *American Federal Tax Reports* (AFTR) and CCH's is *United States Tax Cases* (USTC). Notice also that the case name is italicized (*i.e.*, *Johnson* in the above citation). Sometimes case names will be underlined instead of italicized.

iii. U.S. Court of Federal Claims

Cases from the U.S. Court of Federal Claims are commonly cited as follows:

- *Smith v. U.S.*, 101 Fed. Cl. 474 (2012)

iv. U.S. Circuit Court of Appeals

Cases from the U.S. Circuit Courts of Appeal are commonly cited as follows:

- *Ourisman v. Commissioner*, 760 F.2d 541 (4th Cir. 1985)

Notice the citation indicates that this case was decided by the 4th Circuit Court of Appeals.

v. United States Supreme Court

Cases from the United States Supreme Court are commonly cited as follows:

- *O'Gilvie v. U.S.*, 519 U.S. 79 (1996)

Obviously, it takes a little time to get use to the forms of citation. Nevertheless, a successful tax researcher needs to be able to use the citations to find documents and also cite to the documents properly when preparing a memorandum or other correspondence in which the tax researcher is citing the Code, IRS issuances, and court cases.

CHAPTER 28: QUESTIONS

1. *Branches of government.* What are the three branches of the U.S. government?
2. *Legislative branch.* What committee in the House of Representatives is primarily responsible for tax legislation?
3. *Legislative branch.* What committee in the Senate is primarily responsible for tax legislation?
4. *Legislative branch.* If a tax bill passed in the Senate is not identical to the tax bill passed in the House, how are the bills reconciled?
5. *Executive branch.* The IRS is an agency in what governmental department?
6. *Executive branch.* Name the three different types of regulations.
7. *Executive branch.* Distinguish between a revenue ruling and a private letter ruling.
8. *Executive branch.* What is a TAM?
9. *Executive branch.* What is a determination letter?
10. *Judicial branch.* A Tax Court judge is bound to follow what decisions from other courts?
11. *Judicial branch.* What is the difference between a Tax Court regular decision and a memorandum decision?

12. *Tax research*. Explain the difference between primary authority and secondary authority.

13. *Tax research*. What does the abbreviation I.R.B. stand for? What does the abbreviation C.B. stand for?

14. *Citations*. What is a Treasury Decision?

Appendix of Forms

Appendix of Forms

Various IRS Forms and Publications are included in this Appendix in the following order:

Form 706	United States Estate Tax (and Generation-Skipping Transfer) Tax Return
Form 709	United States Gift (and Generation-Skipping Transfer) Tax Return
Form 720	Quarterly Federal Excise Tax Return
Form 982	Reduction of Tax Attributes Due to Discharge of Indebtedness
Form 1040	U.S. Individual Income Tax Return
Schedule A	Itemized Deductions
Schedule B	Interest and Ordinary Dividends
Schedule C	Profit or Loss From Business
Schedule D	Capital Gains and Losses
Schedule D	Tax Worksheet
Schedule E	Supplemental Income and Loss
Schedule SE	Self-Employment Tax
Form 1040A	U.S. Individual Income Tax Return
Form 1040EZ	Income Tax Return for Single and Joint Filers With No Dependents
Form 1040-ES	Estimated Tax
Form 1045	Application for Tentative Refund
Form 1098	Mortgage Interest Statement
Form 1098-C	Contributions of Motor Vehicles, Boats, and Airplanes
Form 1098-E	Student Loan Interest Statement
Form 1098-T	Tuition Statement
Form 1099-A	Acquisition or Abandonment of Secured Property
Form 1099-C	Cancellation of Debt
Form 1099-DIV	Dividends and Distributions
Form 1099-INT	Interest Income
Form 1099-MISC	Miscellaneous Income
Form 1099-R	Distributions From Pensions, Annuities, Retirement or Profit-Sharing Plans, IRAs, Insurance Contracts, etc.
Form 1116	Foreign Tax Credit
Form 2106	Employee Business Expenses
Form 2441	Child and Dependent Care Expenses
Form 3800	General Business Credit
Form 3903	Moving Expenses
Form 3921	Exercise of an Incentive Stock Option Under Section 422(b)
Form 4562	Depreciation and Amortization
Form 4684	Casualties and Thefts

Form 4797	Sales of Business Property
Form 4868	Application for Automatic Extension of Time To File U.S. Individual Income Tax Return
Form 4952	Investment Interest Expense Deduction
Form 5498	IRA Contribution Information
Form 5695	Residential Energy Credits
Form 6198	At-Risk Limitations
Form 6251	Alternative Minimum Tax—Individuals
Form 8283	Noncash Charitable Contributions
Form 8582	Passive Activity Loss Limitations
Form 8606	Nondeductible IRAs
Form 8615	Tax for Certain Children Who Have Unearned Income
Form 8824	Like-Kind Exchanges
Form 8829	Expenses for Business Use of Your Home
Form 8839	Qualified Adoption Expenses
Form 8863	Education Credits
Form 8880	Credit for Qualified Retirement Savings Contributions
Form 8903	Domestic Production Activities Deduction
Form 8949	Sales and Other Dispositions of Capital Assets
Form SS-8	Determination of Worker Status for Purposes of Federal Employment Taxes and Income Tax Withholding
Form SSA-1099	Social Security Benefit Statement
Form W-2	Wage and Tax Statement
Form W-2G	Certain Gambling Winnings
Form W-4	Employee's Withholding Allowance Certificate
Organizational Chart of the IRS	
Publication 15-B	Employer's Tax Guide to Fringe Benefits
Schedule K-1	Partner's Share of Income, Deductions, Credits (from Form 1065)
Tables A-1 through A-7 (for depreciation calculation)	

Form **706**

(Rev. August 2013)

Department of the Treasury
Internal Revenue Service

United States Estate (and Generation-Skipping Transfer) Tax Return

▶ Estate of a citizen or resident of the United States (see instructions). To be filed for decedents dying after December 31, 2012.

▶ Information about Form 706 and its separate instructions is at *www.irs.gov/form706.*

OMB No. 1545-0015

Part 1—Decedent and Executor

1a Decedent's first name and middle initial (and maiden name, if any)	**1b** Decedent's last name			**2** Decedent's social security no.
3a City, town, or post office; county; state or province; country; and ZIP or foreign postal code.	**3b** Year domicile established	**4** Date of birth		**5** Date of death
	6b Executor's address (number and street including apartment or suite no.; city, town, or post office; state or province; country; and ZIP or foreign postal code) and phone no.			
6a Name of executor (see instructions)				
6c Executor's social security number (see instructions)				Phone no.

6d If there are multiple executors, check here ☐ and attach a list showing the names, addresses, telephone numbers, and SSNs of the additional executors.

7a Name and location of court where will was probated or estate administered | **7b** Case number

8 If decedent died testate, check here ▶ ☐ and attach a certified copy of the will. **9** If you extended the time to file this Form 706, check here ▶ ☐

10 If Schedule R-1 is attached, check here ▶ ☐ **11** If you are estimating the value of assets included in the gross estate on line 1 pursuant to the special rule of Reg. section 20.2010-2T(a) (7)(ii), check here ▶ ☐

Part 2—Tax Computation

1	Total gross estate less exclusion (from Part 5—Recapitulation, item 13)			**1**	
2	Tentative total allowable deductions (from Part 5—Recapitulation, item 24)			**2**	
3a	Tentative taxable estate (subtract line 2 from line 1)			**3a**	
b	State death tax deduction			**3b**	
c	Taxable estate (subtract line 3b from line 3a)			**3c**	
4	Adjusted taxable gifts (see instructions)			**4**	
5	Add lines 3c and 4			**5**	
6	Tentative tax on the amount on line 5 from Table A in the instructions			**6**	
7	Total gift tax paid or payable (see instructions)			**7**	
8	Gross estate tax (subtract line 7 from line 6)			**8**	
9a	Basic exclusion amount	**9a**			
9b	Deceased spousal unused exclusion (DSUE) amount from predeceased spouse(s), if any (from Section D, Part 6—Portability of Deceased Spousal Unused Exclusion)	**9b**			
9c	Applicable exclusion amount (add lines 9a and 9b)	**9c**			
9d	Applicable credit amount (tentative tax on the amount in 9c from Table A in the instructions)	**9d**			
10	Adjustment to applicable credit amount (May not exceed $6,000. See instructions.)	**10**			
11	Allowable applicable credit amount (subtract line 10 from line 9d)			**11**	
12	Subtract line 11 from line 8 (but do not enter less than zero)			**12**	
13	Credit for foreign death taxes (from Schedule P). (Attach Form(s) 706-CE.)	**13**			
14	Credit for tax on prior transfers (from Schedule Q)	**14**			
15	Total credits (add lines 13 and 14)			**15**	
16	Net estate tax (subtract line 15 from line 12)			**16**	
17	Generation-skipping transfer (GST) taxes payable (from Schedule R, Part 2, line 10)			**17**	
18	Total transfer taxes (add lines 16 and 17)			**18**	
19	Prior payments (explain in an attached statement)			**19**	
20	Balance due (or overpayment) (subtract line 19 from line 18)			**20**	

Under penalties of perjury, I declare that I have examined this return, including accompanying schedules and statements, and to the best of my knowledge and belief, it is true, correct, and complete. Declaration of preparer other than the executor is based on all information of which preparer has any knowledge.

Sign Here

▶ Signature of executor ▶ Date

▶ Signature of executor ▶ Date

Paid Preparer Use Only

Print/Type preparer's name	Preparer's signature	Date	Check ☐ if self-employed	PTIN
Firm's name ▶			Firm's EIN ▶	
Firm's address ▶			Phone no.	

For Privacy Act and Paperwork Reduction Act Notice, see instructions. Cat. No. 20548R Form **706** (Rev. 8-2013)

Estate of:	Decedent's social security number

Part 3—Elections by the Executor

Note. For information on electing portability of the decedent's DSUE amount, including how to opt out of the election, see Part 6—Portability of Deceased Spousal Unused Exclusion.

Note. Some of the following elections may require the posting of bonds or liens.

Please check "Yes" or "No" box for each question (see instructions).		Yes	No
1 Do you elect alternate valuation?	1		
2 Do you elect special-use valuation? If "Yes," you must complete and attach Schedule A-1	2		
3 Do you elect to pay the taxes in installments as described in section 6166? If "Yes," you must attach the additional information described in the instructions. **Note. By electing section 6166 installment payments, you may be required to provide security for estate tax deferred under section 6166 and interest in the form of a surety bond or a section 6324A lien.**	3		
4 Do you elect to postpone the part of the taxes due to a reversionary or remainder interest as described in section 6163?	4		

Part 4—General Information

Note. Please attach the necessary supplemental documents. **You must attach the death certificate.** (See instructions)

Authorization to receive confidential tax information under Reg. section 601.504(b)(2)(i); to act as the estate's representative before the IRS; and to make written or oral presentations on behalf of the estate:

Name of representative (print or type)	State	Address (number, street, and room or suite no., city, state, and ZIP code)

I declare that I am the ☐ attorney/ ☐ certified public accountant/ ☐ enrolled agent (check the applicable box) for the executor. I am not under suspension or disbarment from practice before the Internal Revenue Service and am qualified to practice in the state shown above.

Signature	CAF number	Date	Telephone number

1 Death certificate number and issuing authority (attach a copy of the death certificate to this return).

2 Decedent's business or occupation. If retired, check here ▶ ☐ and state decedent's former business or occupation.

3a Marital status of the decedent at time of death:
☐ Married ☐ Widow/widower ☐ Single ☐ Legally separated ☐ Divorced

3b For all prior marriages, list the name and SSN of the former spouse, the date the marriage ended, and whether the marriage ended by annulment, divorce, or death. Attach additional statements of the same size if necessary.

4a Surviving spouse's name	4b Social security number	4c Amount received (see instructions)

5 Individuals (other than the surviving spouse), trusts, or other estates who receive benefits from the estate (do not include charitable beneficiaries shown in Schedule O) (see instructions).

Name of individual, trust, or estate receiving $5,000 or more	Identifying number	Relationship to decedent	Amount (see instructions)
All unascertainable beneficiaries and those who receive less than $5,000 ▶			
Total			

If you answer "Yes" to any of the following questions, you must attach additional information as described.	Yes	No
6 Is the estate filing a protective claim for refund? If "Yes," complete and attach two copies of Schedule PC for each claim.		
7 Does the gross estate contain any section 2044 property (qualified terminable interest property (QTIP) from a prior gift or estate)? (see instructions)		
8a Have federal gift tax returns ever been filed? If "Yes," attach copies of the returns, if available, and furnish the following information:		
b Period(s) covered / c Internal Revenue office(s) where filed		
9a Was there any insurance on the decedent's life that is not included on the return as part of the gross estate?		
b Did the decedent own any insurance on the life of another that is not included in the gross estate?		

Page 2

Estate of: | **Decedent's social security number**

Part 4—General Information *(continued)*

If you answer "Yes" to any of the following questions, you must attach additional information as described.		Yes	No
10	Did the decedent at the time of death own any property as a joint tenant with right of survivorship in which **(a)** one or more of the other joint tenants was someone other than the decedent's spouse, and **(b)** less than the full value of the property is included on the return as part of the gross estate? If "Yes," you must complete and attach Schedule E		
11a	Did the decedent, at the time of death, own any interest in a partnership (for example, a family limited partnership), an unincorporated business, or a limited liability company; or own any stock in an inactive or closely held corporation?		
b	If "Yes," was the value of **any** interest owned (from above) discounted on this estate tax return? If "Yes," see the instructions on reporting the total accumulated or effective discounts taken on Schedule F or G		
12	Did the decedent make any transfer described in sections 2035, 2036, 2037, or 2038? (see instructions) If "Yes," you must complete and attach Schedule G		
13a	Were there in existence at the time of the decedent's death any trusts created by the decedent during his or her lifetime?		
b	Were there in existence at the time of the decedent's death any trusts not created by the decedent under which the decedent possessed any power, beneficial interest, or trusteeship?		
c	Was the decedent receiving income from a trust created after October 22, 1986, by a parent or grandparent?		
	If "Yes," was there a GST taxable termination (under section 2612) on the death of the decedent?		
d	If there was a GST taxable termination (under section 2612), attach a statement to explain. Provide a copy of the trust or will creating the trust, and give the name, address, and phone number of the current trustee(s).		
e	Did the decedent at any time during his or her lifetime transfer or sell an interest in a partnership, limited liability company, or closely held corporation to a trust described in lines 13a or 13b?		
	If "Yes," provide the EIN for this transferred/sold item. ▶		
14	Did the decedent ever possess, exercise, or release any general power of appointment? If "Yes," you must complete and attach Schedule H		
15	Did the decedent have an interest in or a signature or other authority over a financial account in a foreign country, such as a bank account, securities account, or other financial account?		
16	Was the decedent, immediately before death, receiving an annuity described in the "General" paragraph of the instructions for Schedule I or a private annuity? If "Yes," you must complete and attach Schedule I		
17	Was the decedent ever the beneficiary of a trust for which a deduction was claimed by the estate of a predeceased spouse under section 2056(b)(7) and which is not reported on this return? If "Yes," attach an explanation		

Part 5—Recapitulation.

Note. If estimating the value of one or more assets pursuant to the special rule of Reg. section 20.2010-2T(a)(7)(ii), enter on both lines 10 and 23 the amount noted in the instructions for the corresponding range of values. (See instructions for details.)

Item no.	Gross estate		Alternate value	Value at date of death
1	Schedule A—Real Estate	1		
2	Schedule B—Stocks and Bonds	2		
3	Schedule C—Mortgages, Notes, and Cash	3		
4	Schedule D—Insurance on the Decedent's Life (attach Form(s) 712)	4		
5	Schedule E—Jointly Owned Property (attach Form(s) 712 for life insurance)	5		
6	Schedule F—Other Miscellaneous Property (attach Form(s) 712 for life insurance)	6		
7	Schedule G—Transfers During Decedent's Life (att. Form(s) 712 for life insurance)	7		
8	Schedule H—Powers of Appointment	8		
9	Schedule I—Annuities	9		
10	Estimated value of assets subject to the special rule of Reg. section 20.2010-2T(a)(7)(ii)	10		
11	Total gross estate (add items 1 through 10)	11		
12	Schedule U—Qualified Conservation Easement Exclusion	12		
13	Total gross estate less exclusion (subtract item 12 from item 11). Enter here and on line 1 of Part 2—Tax Computation	13		

Item no.	Deductions		Amount
14	Schedule J—Funeral Expenses and Expenses Incurred in Administering Property Subject to Claims	14	
15	Schedule K—Debts of the Decedent	15	
16	Schedule K—Mortgages and Liens	16	
17	Total of items 14 through 16	17	
18	Allowable amount of deductions from item 17 (see the instructions for item 18 of the Recapitulation)	18	
19	Schedule L—Net Losses During Administration	19	
20	Schedule L—Expenses Incurred in Administering Property Not Subject to Claims	20	
21	Schedule M—Bequests, etc., to Surviving Spouse	21	
22	Schedule O—Charitable, Public, and Similar Gifts and Bequests	22	
23	Estimated value of deductible assets subject to the special rule of Reg. section 20.2010-2T(a)(7)(ii)	23	
24	Tentative total allowable deductions (add items 18 through 23). Enter here and on line 2 of the Tax Computation	24	

Estate of:	Decedent's social security number

Part 6—Portability of Deceased Spousal Unused Exclusion (DSUE)

Portability Election

A decedent with a surviving spouse elects portability of the deceased spousal unused exclusion (DSUE) amount, if any, by completing and timely-filing this return. No further action is required to elect portability of the DSUE amount to allow the surviving spouse to use the decedent's DSUE amount.

Section A. Opting Out of Portability

The estate of a decedent with a surviving spouse may opt out of electing portability of the DSUE amount. Check here and do not complete Sections B and C of Part 6 only if the estate opts **NOT** to elect portability of the DSUE amount. ☐

Section B. QDOT

	Yes	No
Are any assets of the estate being transferred to a qualified domestic trust (QDOT)?		

If "Yes," the DSUE amount portable to a surviving spouse (calculated in Section C, below) is preliminary and shall be redetermined at the time of the final distribution or other taxable event imposing estate tax under section 2056A. See instructions for more details.

Section C. DSUE Amount Portable to the Surviving Spouse (To be completed by the estate of a decedent making a portability election.)

Complete the following calculation to determine the DSUE amount that can be transferred to the surviving spouse.

1	Enter the amount from line 9c, Part 2—Tax Computation	1		
2	Reserved	2		
3	Enter the value of the cumulative lifetime gifts on which tax was paid or payable (see instructions)	3		
4	Add lines 1 and 3	4		
5	Enter amount from line 10, Part 2—Tax Computation	5		
6	Divide amount on line 5 by 40% (0.40) (do not enter less than zero)	6		
7	Subtract line 6 from line 4	7		
8	Enter the amount from line 5, Part 2- Tax Computation	8		
9	Subtract line 8 from line 7 (do not enter less than zero)	9		
10	DSUE amount portable to surviving spouse (Enter lesser of line 9 or line 9a, Part 2 - Tax Computation) . .	10		

Section D. DSUE Amount Received from Predeceased Spouse(s) (To be completed by the estate of a deceased surviving spouse with DSUE amount from predeceased spouse(s))

Provide the following information to determine the DSUE amount received from deceased spouses.

A Name of Deceased Spouse (dates of death after December 31, 2010, only)	B Date of Death (enter as mm/dd/yy)	C Portability Election Made?		D If "Yes," DSUE Amount Received from Spouse	E DSUE Amount Applied by Decedent to Lifetime Gifts	F Year of Form 709 Reporting Use of DSUE Amount Listed in col E	G Remaining DSUE Amount, if any (subtract col. E from col. D)
		Yes	No				
Part 1 — DSUE RECEIVED FROM LAST DECEASED SPOUSE							
Part 2 — DSUE RECEIVED FROM OTHER PREDECEASED SPOUSE(S) AND USED BY DECEDENT							
Total (for all DSUE amounts from predeceased spouse(s) applied)							

Add the amount from Part 1, column D and the total from Part 2, column E. Enter the result on line 9b, Part 2—Tax Computation . . . . ▶ ________

Form **709**

Department of the Treasury
Internal Revenue Service

United States Gift (and Generation-Skipping Transfer) Tax Return

► **Information about Form 709 and its separate instructions is at *www.irs.gov/form709*.**

(For gifts made during calendar year 2013)

► **See instructions.**

OMB No. 1545-0020

2013

Part 1—General Information

1 Donor's first name and middle initial	2 Donor's last name	3 Donor's social security number
4 Address (number, street, and apartment number)		5 Legal residence (domicile)
6 City or town, state or province, country, and ZIP or foreign postal code		7 Citizenship (see instructions)

		Yes	No
8	If the donor died during the year, check here ► ☐ and enter date of death ______________ , ______		
9	If you extended the time to file this Form 709, check here ► ☐		
10	Enter the total number of donees listed on Schedule A. Count each person only once. ►		
11a	Have you (the donor) previously filed a Form 709 (or 709-A) for any other year? If "No," skip line 11b		
b	Has your address changed since you last filed Form 709 (or 709-A)?		
12	**Gifts by husband or wife to third parties.** Do you consent to have the gifts (including generation-skipping transfers) made by you and by your spouse to third parties during the calendar year considered as made one-half by each of you? (see instructions.) (If the answer is "Yes," the following information must be furnished and your spouse must sign the consent shown below. **If the answer is "No," skip lines 13–18.**)		
13	Name of consenting spouse — 14 SSN		
15	Were you married to one another during the entire calendar year? (see instructions)		
16	If 15 is "No," check whether ☐ married ☐ divorced or ☐ widowed/deceased, and give date (see instructions) ►		
17	Will a gift tax return for this year be filed by your spouse? (If "Yes," mail both returns in the same envelope.)		
18	**Consent of Spouse.** I consent to have the gifts (and generation-skipping transfers) made by me and by my spouse to third parties during the calendar year considered as made one-half by each of us. We are both aware of the joint and several liability for tax created by the execution of this consent.		
	Consenting spouse's signature ► **Date ►**		
19	Have you applied a DSUE amount received from a predeceased spouse to a gift or gifts reported on this or a previous Form 709? If "Yes," complete Schedule C		

Part 2—Tax Computation

1	Enter the amount from Schedule A, Part 4, line 11	1	
2	Enter the amount from Schedule B, line 3	2	
3	Total taxable gifts. Add lines 1 and 2	3	
4	Tax computed on amount on line 3 (see *Table for Computing Gift Tax* in instructions)	4	
5	Tax computed on amount on line 2 (see *Table for Computing Gift Tax* in instructions)	5	
6	Balance. Subtract line 5 from line 4	6	
7	Applicable credit amount. If donor has DSUE amount from predeceased spouse(s), enter amount from Schedule C, line 4; otherwise, see instructions	7	
8	Enter the applicable credit against tax allowable for all prior periods (from Sch. B, line 1, col. C)	8	
9	Balance. Subtract line 8 from line 7. Do not enter less than zero	9	
10	Enter 20% (.20) of the amount allowed as a specific exemption for gifts made after September 8, 1976, and before January 1, 1977 (see instructions)	10	
11	Balance. Subtract line 10 from line 9. Do not enter less than zero	11	
12	Applicable credit. Enter the smaller of line 6 or line 11	12	
13	Credit for foreign gift taxes (see instructions)	13	
14	Total credits. Add lines 12 and 13	14	
15	Balance. Subtract line 14 from line 6. Do not enter less than zero	15	
16	Generation-skipping transfer taxes (from Schedule D, Part 3, col. H, Total)	16	
17	Total tax. Add lines 15 and 16	17	
18	Gift and generation-skipping transfer taxes prepaid with extension of time to file	18	
19	If line 18 is less than line 17, enter **balance due** (see instructions)	19	
20	If line 18 is greater than line 17, enter **amount to be refunded**	20	

Attach check or money order here.

Sign Here

Under penalties of perjury, I declare that I have examined this return, including any accompanying schedules and statements, and to the best of my knowledge and belief, it is true, correct, and complete. Declaration of preparer (other than donor) is based on all information of which preparer has any knowledge.

May the IRS discuss this return with the preparer shown below (see instructions)? ☐ **Yes** ☐ **No**

► Signature of donor — Date

Paid Preparer Use Only

Print/Type preparer's name	Preparer's signature	Date	Check ☐ if self-employed	PTIN
Firm's name ►			Firm's EIN ►	
Firm's address ►			Phone no.	

For Disclosure, Privacy Act, and Paperwork Reduction Act Notice, see the instructions for this form. Cat. No. 16783M Form **709** (2013)

SCHEDULE A Computation of Taxable Gifts (Including transfers in trust) (see instructions)

A Does the value of any item listed on Schedule A reflect any valuation discount? If "Yes," attach explanation . . . . Yes ☐ No ☐

B ☐ ◄ Check here if you elect under section 529(c)(2)(B) to treat any transfers made this year to a qualified tuition program as made ratably over a 5-year period beginning this year. See instructions. Attach explanation.

Part 1—Gifts Subject Only to Gift Tax. Gifts less political organization, medical, and educational exclusions. (see instructions)

A Item number	B • Donee's name and address • Relationship to donor (if any) • Description of gift • If the gift was of securities, give CUSIP no. • If closely held entity, give EIN	C	D Donor's adjusted basis of gift	E Date of gift	F Value at date of gift	G For split gifts, enter 1/2 of column F	H Net transfer (subtract col. G from col. F)
1							
Gifts made by spouse —*complete* ***only*** *if you are splitting gifts with your spouse and he/she also made gifts.*							
Total of Part 1. Add amounts from Part 1, column H . . . . ▶							

Part 2—Direct Skips. Gifts that are direct skips and are subject to both gift tax and generation-skipping transfer tax. You must list the gifts in chronological order.

A Item number	B • Donee's name and address • Relationship to donor (if any) • Description of gift • If the gift was of securities, give CUSIP no. • If closely held entity, give EIN	C 2632(b) election out	D Donor's adjusted basis of gift	E Date of gift	F Value at date of gift	G For split gifts, enter 1/2 of column F	H Net transfer (subtract col. G from col. F)
1							
Gifts made by spouse —*complete* ***only*** *if you are splitting gifts with your spouse and he/she also made gifts.*							
Total of Part 2. Add amounts from Part 2, column H . . . . ▶							

Part 3—Indirect Skips. Gifts to trusts that are currently subject to gift tax and may later be subject to generation-skipping transfer tax. You must list these gifts in chronological order.

A Item number	B • Donee's name and address • Relationship to donor (if any) • Description of gift • If the gift was of securities, give CUSIP no. • If closely held entity, give EIN	C 2632(c) election	D Donor's adjusted basis of gift	E Date of gift	F Value at date of gift	G For split gifts, enter 1/2 of column F	H Net transfer (subtract col. G from col. F)
1							
Gifts made by spouse —*complete* ***only*** *if you are splitting gifts with your spouse and he/she also made gifts.*							
Total of Part 3. Add amounts from Part 3, column H . . . . ▶							

(If more space is needed, attach additional statements.)

Form **709** (2013)

Part 4—Taxable Gift Reconciliation

1	Total value of gifts of donor. Add totals from column H of Parts 1, 2, and 3			1	
2	Total annual exclusions for gifts listed on line 1 (see instructions)			2	
3	Total included amount of gifts. Subtract line 2 from line 1			3	
Deductions (see instructions)					
4	Gifts of interests to spouse for which a marital deduction will be claimed, based on item numbers ______ of Schedule A	4			
5	Exclusions attributable to gifts on line 4	5			
6	Marital deduction. Subtract line 5 from line 4	6			
7	Charitable deduction, based on item nos. ______ less exclusions	7			
8	Total deductions. Add lines 6 and 7			8	
9	Subtract line 8 from line 3			9	
10	Generation-skipping transfer taxes payable with this Form 709 (from Schedule D, Part 3, col. H, Total)			10	
11	**Taxable gifts.** Add lines 9 and 10. Enter here and on page 1, Part 2—Tax Computation, line 1			11	

Terminable Interest (QTIP) Marital Deduction. (see instructions for Schedule A, Part 4, line 4)

If a trust (or other property) meets the requirements of qualified terminable interest property under section 2523(f), and:

a. The trust (or other property) is listed on Schedule A, and

b. The value of the trust (or other property) is entered in whole or in part as a deduction on Schedule A, Part 4, line 4, then the donor shall be deemed to have made an election to have such trust (or other property) treated as qualified terminable interest property under section 2523(f).

If less than the entire value of the trust (or other property) that the donor has included in Parts 1 and 3 of Schedule A is entered as a deduction on line 4, the donor shall be considered to have made an election only as to a fraction of the trust (or other property). The numerator of this fraction is equal to the amount of the trust (or other property) deducted on Schedule A, Part 4, line 6. The denominator is equal to the total value of the trust (or other property) listed in Parts 1 and 3 of Schedule A.

If you make the QTIP election, the terminable interest property involved will be included in your spouse's gross estate upon his or her death (section 2044). See instructions for line 4 of Schedule A. If your spouse disposes (by gift or otherwise) of all or part of the qualifying life income interest, he or she will be considered to have made a transfer of the entire property that is subject to the gift tax. See *Transfer of Certain Life Estates Received From Spouse* in the instructions.

12 Election Out of QTIP Treatment of Annuities

☐ ◀Check here if you elect under section 2523(f)(6) **not** to treat as qualified terminable interest property any joint and survivor annuities that are reported on Schedule A and would otherwise be treated as qualified terminable interest property under section 2523(f). See instructions. Enter the item numbers from Schedule A for the annuities for which you are making this election ▶ ______

SCHEDULE B Gifts From Prior Periods

If you answered "Yes," on line 11a of page 1, Part 1, see the instructions for completing Schedule B. If you answered "No," skip to the Tax Computation on page 1 (or Schedules C or D, if applicable). Complete Schedule A before beginning Schedule B. See instructions for recalculation of the column C amounts. Attach calculations.

A Calendar year or calendar quarter (see instructions)	**B** Internal Revenue office where prior return was filed	**C** Amount of applicable credit (unified credit) against gift tax for periods after December 31, 1976	**D** Amount of specific exemption for prior periods ending before January 1, 1977	**E** Amount of taxable gifts
1 Totals for prior periods	1			

2	Amount, if any, by which total specific exemption, line 1, column D is more than $30,000	2	
3	Total amount of taxable gifts for prior periods. Add amount on line 1, column E and amount, if any, on line 2. Enter here and on page 1, Part 2—Tax Computation, line 2	3	

(If more space is needed, attach additional statements.)

Form **709** (2013)

SCHEDULE C **Deceased Spousal Unused Exclusion (DSUE) Amount**

Provide the following information to determine the DSUE amount and applicable credit received from prior spouses. Complete Schedule A before beginning Schedule C.

A Name of Deceased Spouse (dates of death after December 31, 2010 only)	B Date of Death	C Portability Election Made?		D If "Yes," DSUE Amount Received from Spouse	E DSUE Amount Applied by Donor to Lifetime Gifts (list current and prior gifts)	F Date of Gift(s) (enter as mm/dd/yy for Part 1 and as yyyy for Part 2)
		Yes	No			
Part 1—DSUE RECEIVED FROM LAST DECEASED SPOUSE						
Part 2—DSUE RECEIVED FROM PREDECEASED SPOUSE(S)						
TOTAL (for all DSUE amounts applied for Part 1 and Part 2)						

1	Donor's basic exclusion amount (see instructions)	1	
2	Total from column E, Parts 1 and 2	2	
3	Add lines 1 and 2	3	
4	Applicable credit on amount in line 3 (See *Table for Computing Gift Tax* in the instructions). Enter here and on line 7, Part 2—Tax Computation	4	

SCHEDULE D **Computation of Generation-Skipping Transfer Tax**

Note. Inter vivos direct skips that are completely excluded by the GST exemption must still be fully reported (including value and exemptions claimed) on Schedule D.

Part 1—Generation-Skipping Transfers

A Item No. (from Schedule A, Part 2, col. A)	B Value (from Schedule A, Part 2, col. H)	C Nontaxable Portion of Transfer	D Net Transfer (subtract col. C from col. B)
1			
Gifts made by spouse (for gift splitting only)			

(If more space is needed, attach additional statements.) Form **709** (2013)

Part 2—GST Exemption Reconciliation (Section 2631) and Section 2652(a)(3) Election

Check here ▶ ☐ if you are making a section 2652(a)(3) (special QTIP) election (see instructions)

Enter the item numbers from Schedule A of the gifts for which you are making this election ▶ ____________

1	Maximum allowable exemption (see instructions)	1	
2	Total exemption used for periods before filing this return	2	
3	Exemption available for this return. Subtract line 2 from line 1	3	
4	Exemption claimed on this return from Part 3, column C total, below	4	
5	Automatic allocation of exemption to transfers reported on Schedule A, Part 3 (see instructions)	5	
6	Exemption allocated to transfers not shown on line 4 or 5, above. **You must attach a "Notice of Allocation."** (see instructions)	6	
7	Add lines 4, 5, and 6	7	
8	Exemption available for future transfers. Subtract line 7 from line 3	8	

Part 3—Tax Computation

A Item No. (from Schedule D, Part 1)	B Net Transfer (from Schedule D, Part 1, col. D)	C GST Exemption Allocated	D Divide col. C by col. B	E Inclusion Ratio (Subtract col. D from 1.000)	F Maximum Estate Tax Rate	G Applicable Rate (multiply col. E by col. F)	H Generation-Skipping Transfer Tax (multiply col. B by col. G)
1					40% (.40)		
					40% (.40)		
					40% (.40)		
					40% (.40)		
					40% (.40)		
					40% (.40)		
Gifts made by spouse (for gift splitting only)							
					40% (.40)		
					40% (.40)		
					40% (.40)		
					40% (.40)		
					40% (.40)		
					40% (.40)		
Total exemption claimed. Enter here and on Part 2, line 4, above. May not exceed Part 2, line 3, above			**Total generation-skipping transfer tax.** Enter here; on page 3, Schedule A, Part 4, line 10; and on page 1, Part 2—Tax Computation, line 16				

(If more space is needed, attach additional statements.) Form **709** (2013)

Form **720** (Rev. January 2014) Department of the Treasury Internal Revenue Service

Quarterly Federal Excise Tax Return

▶ See the Instructions for Form 720.
▶ Information about Form 720 and its instructions is at *www.irs.gov/form720.*

OMB No. 1545-0023

Check here if:
☐ Final return
☐ Address change

Name | Quarter ending

Number, street, and room or suite no. (If you have a P.O. box, see the instructions.) | Employer identification number

City or town, state or province, country, and ZIP or foreign postal code

FOR IRS USE ONLY	
T	
FF	
FD	
FP	
I	
T	

Part I

IRS No.	Environmental Taxes (attach Form 6627)			Tax	IRS No.
18	Domestic petroleum oil spill tax				18
21	Imported petroleum products oil spill tax				21
98	Ozone-depleting chemicals (ODCs)				98
19	ODC tax on imported products				19
	Communications and Air Transportation Taxes (see instructions)			Tax	
22	Local telephone service and teletypewriter exchange service				22
26	Transportation of persons by air				26
28	Transportation of property by air				28
27	Use of international air travel facilities				27
	Fuel Taxes	Number of gallons	Rate	Tax	
60	(a) Diesel, tax on removal at terminal rack		$.244		60
	(b) Diesel, tax on taxable events other than removal at terminal rack		.244		
	(c) Diesel, tax on sale or removal of biodiesel mixture (not at terminal rack)		.244		
104	Diesel-water fuel emulsion		.198		104
105	Dyed diesel, LUST tax		.001		105
107	Dyed kerosene, LUST tax		.001		107
119	LUST tax, other exempt removals (see instructions)		.001		119
35	(a) Kerosene, tax on removal at terminal rack (see instructions)		.244		35
	(b) Kerosene, tax on taxable events other than removal at terminal rack		.244		
69	Kerosene for use in aviation (see instructions)		.219		69
77	Kerosene for use in commercial aviation (other than foreign trade)		.044		77
111	Kerosene for use in aviation, LUST tax on nontaxable uses		.001		111
79	Other fuels (see instructions)				79
62	(a) Gasoline, tax on removal at terminal rack		.184		62
	(b) Gasoline, tax on taxable events other than removal at terminal rack		.184		
13	Any liquid fuel used in a fractional ownership program aircraft		.141		13
14	Aviation gasoline		.194		14
112	Liquefied petroleum gas (LPG)		.183		112
118	"P Series" fuels		.184		118
120	Compressed natural gas (CNG) (GGE = 126.67 cu. ft.)		.183		120
121	Liquefied hydrogen		.184		121
122	Fischer-Tropsch process liquid fuel from coal (including peat)		.244		122
123	Liquid fuel derived from biomass		.244		123
124	Liquefied natural gas (LNG)		.243		124
33	**Retail Tax**—Truck, trailer, and semitrailer chassis and bodies, and tractor		12% of sales price		33
	Ship Passenger Tax	Number of persons	Rate	Tax	
29	Transportation by water		$3 per person		29
	Other Excise Tax	Amount of obligations	Rate	Tax	
31	Obligations not in registered form		$ .01		31
	Foreign Insurance Taxes— Policies issued by foreign insurers	Premiums paid	Rate	Tax	IRS No.
30	Casualty insurance and indemnity bonds		$ .04		30
	Life insurance, sickness and accident policies, and annuity contracts		.01		
	Reinsurance		.01		

For Privacy Act and Paperwork Reduction Act Notice, see the separate instructions. Cat. No. 10175Y Form **720** (Rev. 1-2014)

IRS No.	Manufacturers Taxes	Number of tons	Sales price	Rate	Tax	IRS No.
36	Coal—Underground mined			$1.10 per ton		36
37				4.4% of sales price		37
38	Coal—Surface mined			$ .55 per ton		38
39				4.4% of sales price		39
				Number of tires	Tax	IRS No.
108	Taxable tires other than bias ply or super single tires					108
109	Taxable bias ply or super single tires (other than super single tires designed for steering)					109
113	Taxable tires, super single tires designed for steering					113
40	Gas guzzler tax. Attach Form 6197. Check if one-time filing . . . . ☐					40
97	Vaccines (see instructions)					97
			Sales price			
136	Taxable medical devices			2.3% of sales price		136
1	**Total.** Add all amounts in Part I. Complete Schedule A unless one-time filing ▶				$	

Part II

IRS No.	Patient-Centered Outcomes Research Fee (see instructions)	(a) Avg. number of lives covered	(b) Rate for avg. covered life	Col. (a) x Col. (b)	Tax	IRS No.
133	Specified health insurance policies		$1.00			133
	Applicable self-insured health plans		$1.00			
				Rate		
41	Sport fishing equipment (other than fishing rods and fishing poles)			10% of sales price		41
110	Fishing rods and fishing poles (limits apply, see instructions)			10% of sales price		110
42	Electric outboard motors			3% of sales price		42
114	Fishing tackle boxes			3% of sales price		114
44	Bows, quivers, broadheads, and points			11% of sales price		44
106	Arrow shafts			$ .48 per shaft		106
140	Indoor tanning services			10% of amount paid		140
			Number of gallons	Rate	Tax	
64	Inland waterways fuel use tax			$ .20		64
125	LUST tax on inland waterways fuel use (see instructions)			.001		125
51	Alcohol and cellulosic biofuel sold as but not used as fuel					51
117	Biodiesel sold as but not used as fuel					117
20	**Floor Stocks Tax—** Ozone-depleting chemicals (floor stocks). Attach Form 6627.					20
2	**Total.** Add all amounts in Part II ▶				$	

Part III

3	Total tax. Add Part I, line 1, and Part II, line 2 . . . . ▶			3	
4	Claims (see instructions; complete Schedule C) . . . . . . ▶		4		
5	Deposits made for the quarter . . . . ▶	5			
	☐ Check here if you used the safe harbor rule to make your deposits.				
6	Overpayment from previous quarters . . ▶	6			
7	Enter the amount from Form 720X included on line 6, if any . . . . ▶	7			
8	Add lines 5 and 6 . . . . ▶		8		
9	Add lines 4 and 8 . . . . ▶			9	
10	**Balance Due.** If line 3 is greater than line 9, enter the difference. Pay the full amount with the return (see instructions) ▶			10	
11	**Overpayment.** If line 9 is greater than line 3, enter the difference. Check if you want the overpayment: ☐ **Applied to your next return, or** ☐ **Refunded to you.**			11	

Third Party Designee

Do you want to allow another person to discuss this return with the IRS (see instructions)? ☐ **Yes.** Complete the following. ☐ **No**

Designee name ▶ Phone no. ▶ Personal identification number (PIN) ▶

Sign Here

Under penalties of perjury, I declare that I have examined this return, including accompanying schedules and statements, and to the best of my knowledge and belief, it is true, correct, and complete. Declaration of preparer (other than taxpayer) is based on all information of which preparer has any knowledge.

▶ Signature Date ▶ Title

Type or print name below signature. ▶ Telephone number ▶

Paid Preparer Use Only

Print/Type preparer's name	Preparer's signature	Date	Check ☐ if self-employed	PTIN
Firm's name ▶			Firm's EIN ▶	
Firm's address ▶			Phone no.	

Form **720** (Rev. 1-2014)

Form **982** (Rev. July 2013) Department of the Treasury Internal Revenue Service

Reduction of Tax Attributes Due to Discharge of Indebtedness (and Section 1082 Basis Adjustment)

▶ Attach this form to your income tax return.
▶ Information about Form 982 and its instructions is at *www.irs.gov/form982*.

OMB No. 1545-0046
Attachment Sequence No. **94**

Name shown on return	Identifying number

Part I General Information (see instructions)

1	Amount excluded is due to (check applicable box(es)):		
a	Discharge of indebtedness in a title 11 case		☐
b	Discharge of indebtedness to the extent insolvent (not in a title 11 case)		☐
c	Discharge of qualified farm indebtedness		☐
d	Discharge of qualified real property business indebtedness		☐
e	Discharge of qualified principal residence indebtedness		☐
2	Total amount of discharged indebtedness excluded from gross income	2	
3	Do you elect to treat all real property described in section 1221(a)(1), relating to property held for sale to customers in the ordinary course of a trade or business, as if it were depreciable property?		☐ Yes ☐ No

Part II Reduction of Tax Attributes.
You must attach a description of any transactions resulting in the reduction in basis under section 1017. See Regulations section 1.1017-1 for basis reduction ordering rules, and, if applicable, required partnership consent statements. (For additional information, see the instructions for Part II.)

Enter amount excluded from gross income:

4	For a discharge of qualified real property business indebtedness applied to reduce the basis of depreciable real property	4	
5	That you elect under section 108(b)(5) to apply first to reduce the basis (under section 1017) of depreciable property	5	
6	Applied to reduce any net operating loss that occurred in the tax year of the discharge or carried over to the tax year of the discharge	6	
7	Applied to reduce any general business credit carryover to or from the tax year of the discharge	7	
8	Applied to reduce any minimum tax credit as of the beginning of the tax year immediately after the tax year of the discharge	8	
9	Applied to reduce any net capital loss for the tax year of the discharge, including any capital loss carryovers to the tax year of the discharge	9	
10a	Applied to reduce the basis of nondepreciable and depreciable property if not reduced on line 5. *DO NOT use in the case of discharge of qualified farm indebtedness*	10a	
b	Applied to reduce the basis of your principal residence. *Enter amount here ONLY if line 1e is checked*	10b	
11	For a discharge of qualified farm indebtedness applied to reduce the basis of:		
a	Depreciable property used or held for use in a trade or business or for the production of income if not reduced on line 5	11a	
b	Land used or held for use in a trade or business of farming	11b	
c	Other property used or held for use in a trade or business or for the production of income	11c	
12	Applied to reduce any passive activity loss and credit carryovers from the tax year of the discharge	12	
13	Applied to reduce any foreign tax credit carryover to or from the tax year of the discharge	13	

Part III Consent of Corporation to Adjustment of Basis of Its Property Under Section 1082(a)(2)

Under section 1081(b), the corporation named above has excluded $ ______________ from its gross income for the tax year beginning ______________ and ending ______________. Under that section, the corporation consents to have the basis of its property adjusted in accordance with the regulations prescribed under section 1082(a)(2) in effect at the time of filing its income tax return for that year. The corporation is organized under the laws of ______________.

(State of incorporation)

Note. *You must attach a description of the transactions resulting in the nonrecognition of gain under section 1081.*

For Paperwork Reduction Act Notice, see page 5 of this form. Cat. No. 17066E Form **982** (Rev. 7-2013)

Form **1040** Department of the Treasury—Internal Revenue Service (99)
U.S. Individual Income Tax Return **2013** OMB No. 1545-0074 IRS Use Only—Do not write or staple in this space.

For the year Jan. 1–Dec. 31, 2013, or other tax year beginning , 2013, ending , 20 See separate instructions.

Your first name and initial	Last name	**Your social security number**
If a joint return, spouse's first name and initial	Last name	**Spouse's social security number**
Home address (number and street). If you have a P.O. box, see instructions.	Apt. no.	▲ Make sure the SSN(s) above and on line 6c are correct.
City, town or post office, state, and ZIP code. If you have a foreign address, also complete spaces below (see instructions).		**Presidential Election Campaign** Check here if you, or your spouse if filing jointly, want $3 to go to this fund. Checking a box below will not change your tax or refund. ☐ You ☐ Spouse
Foreign country name	Foreign province/state/county · Foreign postal code	

Filing Status

Check only one box.

1 ☐ Single
2 ☐ Married filing jointly (even if only one had income)
3 ☐ Married filing separately. Enter spouse's SSN above and full name here. ▶
4 ☐ Head of household (with qualifying person). (See instructions.) If the qualifying person is a child but not your dependent, enter this child's name here. ▶
5 ☐ Qualifying widow(er) with dependent child

Exemptions

6a ☐ **Yourself.** If someone can claim you as a dependent, **do not** check box 6a . . . .
b ☐ **Spouse** . . . .

Boxes checked on 6a and 6b
No. of children on 6c who:
• lived with you
• did not live with you due to divorce or separation (see instructions)
Dependents on 6c not entered above
Add numbers on lines above ▶

c **Dependents:**

(1) First name Last name	(2) Dependent's social security number	(3) Dependent's relationship to you	(4) ✓ if child under age 17 qualifying for child tax credit (see instructions)
			☐
			☐
			☐
			☐

If more than four dependents, see instructions and check here ▶☐

d Total number of exemptions claimed

Income

Attach Form(s) W-2 here. Also attach Forms W-2G and 1099-R if tax was withheld.

If you did not get a W-2, see instructions.

7	Wages, salaries, tips, etc. Attach Form(s) W-2		7	
8a	**Taxable** interest. Attach Schedule B if required		8a	
b	**Tax-exempt** interest. **Do not** include on line 8a . . .	8b		
9a	Ordinary dividends. Attach Schedule B if required		9a	
b	Qualified dividends	9b		
10	Taxable refunds, credits, or offsets of state and local income taxes . . .		10	
11	Alimony received		11	
12	Business income or (loss). Attach Schedule C or C-EZ		12	
13	Capital gain or (loss). Attach Schedule D if required. If not required, check here ▶ ☐		13	
14	Other gains or (losses). Attach Form 4797		14	
15a	IRA distributions . 15a	b Taxable amount . . .	15b	
16a	Pensions and annuities 16a	b Taxable amount . . .	16b	
17	Rental real estate, royalties, partnerships, S corporations, trusts, etc. Attach Schedule E		17	
18	Farm income or (loss). Attach Schedule F		18	
19	Unemployment compensation		19	
20a	Social security benefits 20a	b Taxable amount . . .	20b	
21	Other income. List type and amount		21	
22	Combine the amounts in the far right column for lines 7 through 21. This is your **total income** ▶		22	

Adjusted Gross Income

23	Educator expenses	23		
24	Certain business expenses of reservists, performing artists, and fee-basis government officials. Attach Form 2106 or 2106-EZ	24		
25	Health savings account deduction. Attach Form 8889 .	25		
26	Moving expenses. Attach Form 3903	26		
27	Deductible part of self-employment tax. Attach Schedule SE .	27		
28	Self-employed SEP, SIMPLE, and qualified plans . .	28		
29	Self-employed health insurance deduction	29		
30	Penalty on early withdrawal of savings	30		
31a	Alimony paid b Recipient's SSN ▶	31a		
32	IRA deduction	32		
33	Student loan interest deduction	33		
34	Tuition and fees. Attach Form 8917	34		
35	Domestic production activities deduction. Attach Form 8903	35		
36	Add lines 23 through 35		36	
37	Subtract line 36 from line 22. This is your **adjusted gross income** . . . . . ▶		37	

For Disclosure, Privacy Act, and Paperwork Reduction Act Notice, see separate instructions. Cat. No. 11320B Form **1040** (2013)

Tax and Credits	38	Amount from line 37 (adjusted gross income)		38
	39a	Check if: { ☐ **You** were born before January 2, 1949, ☐ Blind. } **Total boxes** / { ☐ **Spouse** was born before January 2, 1949, ☐ Blind. } **checked ▶ 39a** ☐		
	b	If your spouse itemizes on a separate return or you were a dual-status alien, check here ▶ 39b☐		
Standard Deduction for—	40	**Itemized deductions** (from Schedule A) **or** your **standard deduction** (see left margin)		40
• People who check any box on line 39a or 39b **or** who can be claimed as a dependent, see instructions.	41	Subtract line 40 from line 38		41
• All others:	42	**Exemptions.** If line 38 is $150,000 or less, multiply $3,900 by the number on line 6d. Otherwise, see instructions		42
Single or Married filing separately, $6,100	43	**Taxable income.** Subtract line 42 from line 41. If line 42 is more than line 41, enter -0-		43
Married filing jointly or Qualifying widow(er), $12,200	44	**Tax** (see instructions). Check if any from: **a** ☐ Form(s) 8814 **b** ☐ Form 4972 **c** ☐ ______		44
Head of household, $8,950	45	**Alternative minimum tax** (see instructions). Attach Form 6251		45
	46	Add lines 44 and 45 ▶		46
	47	Foreign tax credit. Attach Form 1116 if required	47	
	48	Credit for child and dependent care expenses. Attach Form 2441	48	
	49	Education credits from Form 8863, line 19	49	
	50	Retirement savings contributions credit. Attach Form 8880	50	
	51	Child tax credit. Attach Schedule 8812, if required	51	
	52	Residential energy credits. Attach Form 5695	52	
	53	Other credits from Form: **a** ☐ 3800 **b** ☐ 8801 **c** ☐ ______	53	
	54	Add lines 47 through 53. These are your **total credits**		54
	55	Subtract line 54 from line 46. If line 54 is more than line 46, enter -0- ▶		55
Other Taxes	56	Self-employment tax. Attach Schedule SE		56
	57	Unreported social security and Medicare tax from Form: **a** ☐ 4137 **b** ☐ 8919		57
	58	Additional tax on IRAs, other qualified retirement plans, etc. Attach Form 5329 if required		58
	59a	Household employment taxes from Schedule H		59a
	b	First-time homebuyer credit repayment. Attach Form 5405 if required		59b
	60	Taxes from: **a** ☐ Form 8959 **b** ☐ Form 8960 **c** ☐ Instructions; enter code(s) ______		60
	61	Add lines 55 through 60. This is your **total tax** ▶		61
Payments	62	Federal income tax withheld from Forms W-2 and 1099	62	
	63	2013 estimated tax payments and amount applied from 2012 return	63	
If you have a qualifying child, attach Schedule EIC.	64a	**Earned income credit (EIC)**	64a	
	b	Nontaxable combat pay election 64b		
	65	Additional child tax credit. Attach Schedule 8812	65	
	66	American opportunity credit from Form 8863, line 8	66	
	67	Reserved	67	
	68	Amount paid with request for extension to file	68	
	69	Excess social security and tier 1 RRTA tax withheld	69	
	70	Credit for federal tax on fuels. Attach Form 4136	70	
	71	Credits from Form: **a** ☐ 2439 **b** ☐ Reserved **c** ☐ 8885 **d** ☐	71	
	72	Add lines 62, 63, 64a, and 65 through 71. These are your **total payments** ▶		72
Refund	73	If line 72 is more than line 61, subtract line 61 from line 72. This is the amount you **overpaid**		73
	74a	Amount of line 73 you want **refunded to you.** If Form 8888 is attached, check here ▶ ☐		74a
Direct deposit? See instructions.	▶ b	Routing number ▶ **c** Type: ☐ Checking ☐ Savings		
	▶ d	Account number		
	75	Amount of line 73 you want **applied to your 2014 estimated tax** ▶	75	
Amount You Owe	76	**Amount you owe.** Subtract line 72 from line 61. For details on how to pay, see instructions ▶		76
	77	Estimated tax penalty (see instructions)	77	

Third Party Designee

Do you want to allow another person to discuss this return with the IRS (see instructions)? ☐ **Yes.** Complete below. ☐ **No**

Designee's name ▶ | Phone no. ▶ | Personal identification number (PIN) ▶

Sign Here

Joint return? See instructions. Keep a copy for your records.

Under penalties of perjury, I declare that I have examined this return and accompanying schedules and statements, and to the best of my knowledge and belief, they are true, correct, and complete. Declaration of preparer (other than taxpayer) is based on all information of which preparer has any knowledge.

Your signature	Date	Your occupation	Daytime phone number
Spouse's signature. If a joint return, **both** must sign.	Date	Spouse's occupation	If the IRS sent you an Identity Protection PIN, enter it here (see inst.)

Paid Preparer Use Only

Print/Type preparer's name	Preparer's signature	Date	Check ☐ if self-employed	PTIN
Firm's name ▶		Firm's EIN ▶		
Firm's address ▶		Phone no.		

Form **1040** (2013)

SCHEDULE A (Form 1040)

Department of the Treasury
Internal Revenue Service (99)

Itemized Deductions

▶ Information about Schedule A and its separate instructions is at *www.irs.gov/schedulea.*
▶ Attach to Form 1040.

OMB No. 1545-0074

2013

Attachment Sequence No. **07**

Name(s) shown on Form 1040 | **Your social security number**

Medical and Dental Expenses		**Caution.** Do not include expenses reimbursed or paid by others.			
	1	Medical and dental expenses (see instructions)	1		
	2	Enter amount from Form 1040, line 38 [2]			
	3	Multiply line 2 by 10% (.10). But if either you or your spouse was born before January 2, 1949, multiply line 2 by 7.5% (.075) instead	3		
	4	Subtract line 3 from line 1. If line 3 is more than line 1, enter -0-		4	
Taxes You Paid	5	State and local **(check only one box):** a ☐ Income taxes, **or** b ☐ General sales taxes	5		
	6	Real estate taxes (see instructions)	6		
	7	Personal property taxes	7		
	8	Other taxes. List type and amount ▶	8		
	9	Add lines 5 through 8		9	
Interest You Paid	10	Home mortgage interest and points reported to you on Form 1098	10		
Note. Your mortgage interest deduction may be limited (see instructions).	11	Home mortgage interest not reported to you on Form 1098. If paid to the person from whom you bought the home, see instructions and show that person's name, identifying no., and address ▶	11		
	12	Points not reported to you on Form 1098. See instructions for special rules	12		
	13	Mortgage insurance premiums (see instructions)	13		
	14	Investment interest. Attach Form 4952 if required. (See instructions.)	14		
	15	Add lines 10 through 14		15	
Gifts to Charity	16	Gifts by cash or check. If you made any gift of $250 or more, see instructions	16		
If you made a gift and got a benefit for it, see instructions.	17	Other than by cash or check. If any gift of $250 or more, see instructions. You **must** attach Form 8283 if over $500	17		
	18	Carryover from prior year	18		
	19	Add lines 16 through 18		19	
Casualty and Theft Losses	20	Casualty or theft loss(es). Attach Form 4684. (See instructions.)		20	
Job Expenses and Certain Miscellaneous Deductions	21	Unreimbursed employee expenses—job travel, union dues, job education, etc. Attach Form 2106 or 2106-EZ if required. (See instructions.) ▶	21		
	22	Tax preparation fees	22		
	23	Other expenses—investment, safe deposit box, etc. List type and amount ▶	23		
	24	Add lines 21 through 23	24		
	25	Enter amount from Form 1040, line 38 [25]			
	26	Multiply line 25 by 2% (.02)	26		
	27	Subtract line 26 from line 24. If line 26 is more than line 24, enter -0-		27	
Other Miscellaneous Deductions	28	Other—from list in instructions. List type and amount ▶		28	
Total Itemized Deductions	29	Is Form 1040, line 38, over $150,000? ☐ **No.** Your deduction is not limited. Add the amounts in the far right column for lines 4 through 28. Also, enter this amount on Form 1040, line 40. ☐ **Yes.** Your deduction may be limited. See the Itemized Deductions Worksheet in the instructions to figure the amount to enter.		29	
	30	If you elect to itemize deductions even though they are less than your standard deduction, check here ▶ ☐			

For Paperwork Reduction Act Notice, see Form 1040 instructions. Cat. No. 17145C **Schedule A (Form 1040) 2013**

SCHEDULE B
(Form 1040A or 1040)

Department of the Treasury
Internal Revenue Service (99)

Interest and Ordinary Dividends

► Attach to Form 1040A or 1040.
► Information about Schedule B (Form 1040A or 1040) and its instructions is at *www.irs.gov/scheduleb*.

OMB No. 1545-0074
2013
Attachment Sequence No. **08**

Name(s) shown on return | **Your social security number**

Part I Interest

(See instructions on back and the instructions for Form 1040A, or Form 1040, line 8a.)

Note. If you received a Form 1099-INT, Form 1099-OID, or substitute statement from a brokerage firm, list the firm's name as the payer and enter the total interest shown on that form.

			Amount
1	List name of payer. If any interest is from a seller-financed mortgage and the buyer used the property as a personal residence, see instructions on back and list this interest first. Also, show that buyer's social security number and address ►	1	
2	Add the amounts on line 1	2	
3	Excludable interest on series EE and I U.S. savings bonds issued after 1989. Attach Form 8815	3	
4	Subtract line 3 from line 2. Enter the result here and on Form 1040A, or Form 1040, line 8a . . . . ►	4	

Note. If line 4 is over $1,500, you must complete Part III.

Part II Ordinary Dividends

(See instructions on back and the instructions for Form 1040A, or Form 1040, line 9a.)

Note. If you received a Form 1099-DIV or substitute statement from a brokerage firm, list the firm's name as the payer and enter the ordinary dividends shown on that form.

			Amount
5	List name of payer ►	5	
6	Add the amounts on line 5. Enter the total here and on Form 1040A, or Form 1040, line 9a . . . . ►	6	

Note. If line 6 is over $1,500, you must complete Part III.

Part III Foreign Accounts and Trusts

(See instructions on back.)

You must complete this part if you **(a)** had over $1,500 of taxable interest or ordinary dividends; **(b)** had a foreign account; or **(c)** received a distribution from, or were a grantor of, or a transferor to, a foreign trust.

		Yes	No
7a	At any time during 2013, did you have a financial interest in or signature authority over a financial account (such as a bank account, securities account, or brokerage account) located in a foreign country? See instructions		
	If "Yes," are you required to file FinCEN Form 114, Report of Foreign Bank and Financial Accounts (FBAR), formerly TD F 90-22.1, to report that financial interest or signature authority? See FinCEN Form 114 and its instructions for filing requirements and exceptions to those requirements		
b	If you are required to file FinCEN Form 114, enter the name of the foreign country where the financial account is located ►		
8	During 2013, did you receive a distribution from, or were you the grantor of, or transferor to, a foreign trust? If "Yes," you may have to file Form 3520. See instructions on back		

For Paperwork Reduction Act Notice, see your tax return instructions. Cat. No. 17146N **Schedule B (Form 1040A or 1040) 2013**

SCHEDULE C (Form 1040)

Department of the Treasury
Internal Revenue Service (99)

Profit or Loss From Business

(Sole Proprietorship)

▶ **For information on Schedule C and its instructions, go to *www.irs.gov/schedulec*.**
▶ **Attach to Form 1040, 1040NR, or 1041; partnerships generally must file Form 1065.**

OMB No. 1545-0074
2013
Attachment Sequence No. **09**

Name of proprietor | **Social security number (SSN)**

A Principal business or profession, including product or service (see instructions) | **B Enter code from instructions** ▶

C Business name. If no separate business name, leave blank. | **D Employer ID number (EIN),** (see instr.)

E Business address (including suite or room no.) ▶
City, town or post office, state, and ZIP code

F Accounting method: **(1)** ☐ Cash **(2)** ☐ Accrual **(3)** ☐ Other (specify) ▶

G Did you "materially participate" in the operation of this business during 2013? If "No," see instructions for limit on losses . ☐ **Yes** ☐ **No**

H If you started or acquired this business during 2013, check here . . . . ▶ ☐

I Did you make any payments in 2013 that would require you to file Form(s) 1099? (see instructions) . . . . ☐ **Yes** ☐ **No**

J If "Yes," did you or will you file required Forms 1099? . . . . ☐ **Yes** ☐ **No**

Part I Income

1	Gross receipts or sales. See instructions for line 1 and check the box if this income was reported to you on Form W-2 and the "Statutory employee" box on that form was checked . . . . ▶ ☐	1	
2	Returns and allowances	2	
3	Subtract line 2 from line 1	3	
4	Cost of goods sold (from line 42)	4	
5	**Gross profit.** Subtract line 4 from line 3	5	
6	Other income, including federal and state gasoline or fuel tax credit or refund (see instructions) . . .	6	
7	**Gross income.** Add lines 5 and 6 . . . . ▶	7	

Part II Expenses

Enter expenses for business use of your home only on line 30.

8	Advertising	8		18	Office expense (see instructions)	18	
9	Car and truck expenses (see instructions)	9		19	Pension and profit-sharing plans .	19	
10	Commissions and fees .	10		20	Rent or lease (see instructions):		
11	Contract labor (see instructions)	11		a	Vehicles, machinery, and equipment	20a	
12	Depletion	12		b	Other business property . . .	20b	
13	Depreciation and section 179 expense deduction (not included in Part III) (see instructions)	13		21	Repairs and maintenance . . .	21	
				22	Supplies (not included in Part III) .	22	
				23	Taxes and licenses	23	
				24	Travel, meals, and entertainment:		
14	Employee benefit programs (other than on line 19) . .	14		a	Travel	24a	
15	Insurance (other than health)	15		b	Deductible meals and entertainment (see instructions) .	24b	
16	Interest:			25	Utilities	25	
a	Mortgage (paid to banks, etc.)	16a		26	Wages (less employment credits) .	26	
b	Other	16b		27a	Other expenses (from line 48) . .	27a	
17	Legal and professional services	17		b	**Reserved for future use** . . .	27b	

28	**Total expenses** before expenses for business use of home. Add lines 8 through 27a . . . . . . ▶	28	
29	Tentative profit or (loss). Subtract line 28 from line 7	29	
30	Expenses for business use of your home. Do not report these expenses elsewhere. Attach Form 8829 unless using the simplified method (see instructions). **Simplified method filers only:** enter the total square footage of: (a) your home: ________ and (b) the part of your home used for business: ________. Use the Simplified Method Worksheet in the instructions to figure the amount to enter on line 30	30	
31	**Net profit or (loss).** Subtract line 30 from line 29. • If a profit, enter on both **Form 1040, line 12** (or **Form 1040NR, line 13**) and on **Schedule SE, line 2.** (If you checked the box on line 1, see instructions). Estates and trusts, enter on **Form 1041, line 3.** • If a loss, you **must** go to line 32.	31	
32	If you have a loss, check the box that describes your investment in this activity (see instructions). • If you checked 32a, enter the loss on both **Form 1040, line 12,** (or **Form 1040NR, line 13**) and on **Schedule SE, line 2.** (If you checked the box on line 1, see the line 31 instructions). Estates and trusts, enter on **Form 1041, line 3.** • If you checked 32b, you **must** attach **Form 6198.** Your loss may be limited.	32a ☐ All investment is at risk. 32b ☐ Some investment is not at risk.	

For Paperwork Reduction Act Notice, see the separate instructions. Cat. No. 11334P **Schedule C (Form 1040) 2013**

Part III **Cost of Goods Sold** (see instructions)

33 Method(s) used to value closing inventory: a ☐ Cost b ☐ Lower of cost or market c ☐ Other (attach explanation)

34 Was there any change in determining quantities, costs, or valuations between opening and closing inventory? If "Yes," attach explanation . . . ☐ Yes ☐ No

35	Inventory at beginning of year. If different from last year's closing inventory, attach explanation	35	
36	Purchases less cost of items withdrawn for personal use	36	
37	Cost of labor. Do not include any amounts paid to yourself	37	
38	Materials and supplies	38	
39	Other costs	39	
40	Add lines 35 through 39	40	
41	Inventory at end of year	41	
42	**Cost of goods sold.** Subtract line 41 from line 40. Enter the result here and on line 4	42	

Part IV **Information on Your Vehicle.** Complete this part **only** if you are claiming car or truck expenses on line 9 and are not required to file Form 4562 for this business. See the instructions for line 13 to find out if you must file Form 4562.

43 When did you place your vehicle in service for business purposes? (month, day, year) ▶ ____ / ____ / ____

44 Of the total number of miles you drove your vehicle during 2013, enter the number of miles you used your vehicle for:

a Business ____________ b Commuting (see instructions) ____________ c Other ____________

45 Was your vehicle available for personal use during off-duty hours? . . . ☐ Yes ☐ No

46 Do you (or your spouse) have another vehicle available for personal use? . . . ☐ Yes ☐ No

47a Do you have evidence to support your deduction? . . . ☐ Yes ☐ No

b If "Yes," is the evidence written? . . . ☐ Yes ☐ No

Part V **Other Expenses.** List below business expenses not included on lines 8–26 or line 30.

48 **Total other expenses.** Enter here and on line 27a	48	

Schedule C (Form 1040) 2013

SCHEDULE D (Form 1040)	Capital Gains and Losses	OMB No. 1545-0074
Department of the Treasury Internal Revenue Service (99)	▶ Attach to Form 1040 or Form 1040NR. ▶ Information about Schedule D and its separate instructions is at *www.irs.gov/scheduled*. ▶ Use Form 8949 to list your transactions for lines 1b, 2, 3, 8b, 9, and 10.	**2013** Attachment Sequence No. **12**

Name(s) shown on return | **Your social security number**

Part I Short-Term Capital Gains and Losses—Assets Held One Year or Less

See instructions for how to figure the amounts to enter on the lines below. This form may be easier to complete if you round off cents to whole dollars.	**(d)** Proceeds (sales price)	**(e)** Cost (or other basis)	**(g)** Adjustments to gain or loss from Form(s) 8949, Part I, line 2, column (g)	**(h) Gain or (loss)** Subtract column (e) from column (d) and combine the result with column (g)
1a Totals for all short-term transactions reported on Form 1099-B for which basis was reported to the IRS and for which you have no adjustments (see instructions). However, if you choose to report all these transactions on Form 8949, leave this line blank and go to line 1b .				
1b Totals for all transactions reported on Form(s) 8949 with **Box A** checked				
2 Totals for all transactions reported on Form(s) 8949 with **Box B** checked				
3 Totals for all transactions reported on Form(s) 8949 with **Box C** checked				

4 Short-term gain from Form 6252 and short-term gain or (loss) from Forms 4684, 6781, and 8824 .	**4**	
5 Net short-term gain or (loss) from partnerships, S corporations, estates, and trusts from Schedule(s) K-1	**5**	
6 Short-term capital loss carryover. Enter the amount, if any, from line 8 of your **Capital Loss Carryover Worksheet** in the instructions	**6**	( )
7 **Net short-term capital gain or (loss).** Combine lines 1a through 6 in column (h). If you have any long-term capital gains or losses, go to Part II below. Otherwise, go to Part III on the back	**7**	

Part II Long-Term Capital Gains and Losses—Assets Held More Than One Year

See instructions for how to figure the amounts to enter on the lines below. This form may be easier to complete if you round off cents to whole dollars.	**(d)** Proceeds (sales price)	**(e)** Cost (or other basis)	**(g)** Adjustments to gain or loss from Form(s) 8949, Part II, line 2, column (g)	**(h) Gain or (loss)** Subtract column (e) from column (d) and combine the result with column (g)
8a Totals for all long-term transactions reported on Form 1099-B for which basis was reported to the IRS and for which you have no adjustments (see instructions). However, if you choose to report all these transactions on Form 8949, leave this line blank and go to line 8b .				
8b Totals for all transactions reported on Form(s) 8949 with **Box D** checked				
9 Totals for all transactions reported on Form(s) 8949 with **Box E** checked				
10 Totals for all transactions reported on Form(s) 8949 with **Box F** checked.				

11 Gain from Form 4797, Part I; long-term gain from Forms 2439 and 6252; and long-term gain or (loss) from Forms 4684, 6781, and 8824	**11**	
12 Net long-term gain or (loss) from partnerships, S corporations, estates, and trusts from Schedule(s) K-1	**12**	
13 Capital gain distributions. See the instructions	**13**	
14 Long-term capital loss carryover. Enter the amount, if any, from line 13 of your **Capital Loss Carryover Worksheet** in the instructions	**14**	( )
15 **Net long-term capital gain or (loss).** Combine lines 8a through 14 in column (h). Then go to Part III on the back	**15**	

For Paperwork Reduction Act Notice, see your tax return instructions. Cat. No. 11338H **Schedule D (Form 1040) 2013**

Part III **Summary**

16	Combine lines 7 and 15 and enter the result	16	
	• If line 16 is a **gain,** enter the amount from line 16 on Form 1040, line 13, or Form 1040NR, line 14. Then go to line 17 below. • If line 16 is a **loss,** skip lines 17 through 20 below. Then go to line 21. Also be sure to complete line 22. • If line 16 is **zero,** skip lines 17 through 21 below and enter -0- on Form 1040, line 13, or Form 1040NR, line 14. Then go to line 22.		
17	Are lines 15 and 16 **both** gains? ☐ **Yes.** Go to line 18. ☐ **No.** Skip lines 18 through 21, and go to line 22.		
18	Enter the amount, if any, from line 7 of the **28% Rate Gain Worksheet** in the instructions . . ▶	18	
19	Enter the amount, if any, from line 18 of the **Unrecaptured Section 1250 Gain Worksheet** in the instructions . . . . ▶	19	
20	Are lines 18 and 19 **both** zero or blank? ☐ **Yes.** Complete the **Qualified Dividends and Capital Gain Tax Worksheet** in the instructions for Form 1040, line 44 (or in the instructions for Form 1040NR, line 42). **Do not** complete lines 21 and 22 below. ☐ **No.** Complete the **Schedule D Tax Worksheet** in the instructions. **Do not** complete lines 21 and 22 below.		
21	If line 16 is a loss, enter here and on Form 1040, line 13, or Form 1040NR, line 14, the **smaller** of: • The loss on line 16 or • ($3,000), or if married filing separately, ($1,500) . . . . **Note.** When figuring which amount is smaller, treat both amounts as positive numbers.	21	( )
22	Do you have qualified dividends on Form 1040, line 9b, or Form 1040NR, line 10b? ☐ **Yes.** Complete the **Qualified Dividends and Capital Gain Tax Worksheet** in the instructions for Form 1040, line 44 (or in the instructions for Form 1040NR, line 42). ☐ **No.** Complete the rest of Form 1040 or Form 1040NR.		

Schedule D (Form 1040) 2013

Schedule D Tax Worksheet

Keep for Your Records

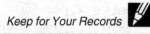

Complete this worksheet only if line 18 or line 19 of Schedule D is more than zero. Otherwise, complete the Qualified Dividends and Capital Gain Tax Worksheet in the Instructions for Form 1040, line 44 (or in the Instructions for Form 1040NR, line 42) to figure your tax. Before completing this worksheet, complete Form 1040 through line 43 (or Form 1040NR through line 41).

Exception: Do not use the Qualified Dividends and Capital Gain Tax Worksheet **or** this worksheet to figure your tax if:

- Line 15 or line 16 of Schedule D is zero or less **and** you have no qualified dividends on Form 1040, line 9b (or Form 1040NR, line 10b); **or**
- Form 1040, line 43 (or Form 1040NR, line 41) is zero or less.

Instead, see the instructions for Form 1040, line 44 (or Form 1040NR, line 42).

1. Enter your taxable income from Form 1040, line 43 (or Form 1040NR, line 41). (However, if you are filing Form 2555 or 2555-EZ (relating to foreign earned income), enter instead the amount from line 3 of the Foreign Earned Income Tax Worksheet in the Instructions for Form 1040, line 44) . . . . . 1. ______
2. Enter your qualified dividends from Form 1040, line 9b (or Form 1040NR, line 10b) . . . . . 2. ______
3. Enter the amount from Form 4952 (used to figure investment interest expense deduction), line 4g . . . . . 3. ______
4. Enter the amount from Form 4952, line 4e* . . . . . 4. ______
5. Subtract line 4 from line 3. If zero or less, enter -0- . . . . . 5. ______
6. Subtract line 5 from line 2. If zero or less, enter -0-** . . . . . 6. ______
7. Enter the **smaller** of line 15 or line 16 of Schedule D . . . . . 7. ______
8. Enter the **smaller** of line 3 or line 4 . . . . . 8. ______
9. Subtract line 8 from line 7. If zero or less, enter -0-** . . . . . 9. ______
10. Add lines 6 and 9 . . . . . 10. ______
11. Add lines 18 and 19 of Schedule D** . . . . . 11. ______
12. Enter the **smaller** of line 9 or line 11 . . . . . 12. ______
13. Subtract line 12 from line 10 . . . . . 13. ______
14. Subtract line 13 from line 1. If zero or less, enter -0- . . . . . 14. ______
15. Enter:
    - $36,250 if single or married filing separately;
    - $72,500 if married filing jointly or qualifying widow(er); or
    - $48,600 if head of household

    . . . . . 15. ______
16. Enter the **smaller** of line 1 or line 15 . . . . . 16. ______
17. Enter the **smaller** of line 14 or line 16 . . . . . 17. ______
18. Subtract line 10 from line 1. If zero or less, enter -0- . . . . . 18. ______
19. Enter the **larger** of line 17 or line 18 . . . . . 19. ______
20. Subtract line 17 from line 16. This amount is taxed at 0%. . . . . . 20. ______

    If lines 1 and 16 are the same, skip lines 21 through 41 and go to line 42. Otherwise, go to line 21.
21. Enter the **smaller** of line 1 or line 13 . . . . . 21. ______
22. Enter the amount from line 20 (if line 20 is blank, enter -0-) . . . . . 22. ______
23. Subtract line 22 from line 21. If zero or less, enter -0- . . . . . 23. ______
24. Enter:
    - $400,000 if single;
    - $225,000 if married filing separately;
    - $450,000 if married filing jointly or qualifying widow(er); or
    - $425,000 if head of household

    . . . . . 24. ______
25. Enter the smaller of line 1 or line 24 . . . . . 25. ______
26. Add lines 19 and 20 . . . . . 26. ______
27. Subtract line 26 from line 25. If zero or less, enter -0- . . . . . 27. ______
28. Enter the **smaller** of line 23 or line 27 . . . . . 28. ______
29. Multiply line 28 by 15% (.15) . . . . . 29. ______
30. Add lines 22 and 28 . . . . . 30. ______

    If lines 1 and 30 are the same, skip lines 31 through 41 and go to line 42. Otherwise, go to line 31.

SCHEDULE E (Form 1040)

Department of the Treasury
Internal Revenue Service (99)

Supplemental Income and Loss

(From rental real estate, royalties, partnerships, S corporations, estates, trusts, REMICs, etc.)

▶ Attach to Form 1040, 1040NR, or Form 1041.

▶ Information about Schedule E and its separate instructions is at *www.irs.gov/schedulee*.

OMB No. 1545-0074

2013

Attachment Sequence No. **13**

Name(s) shown on return | **Your social security number**

Part I **Income or Loss From Rental Real Estate and Royalties** **Note.** If you are in the business of renting personal property, use **Schedule C** or **C-EZ** (see instructions). If you are an individual, report farm rental income or loss from **Form 4835** on page 2, line 40.

A Did you make any payments in 2013 that would require you to file Form(s) 1099? (see instructions) ☐ Yes ☐ No

B If "Yes," did you or will you file required Forms 1099? ☐ Yes ☐ No

1a	Physical address of each property (street, city, state, ZIP code)
A	
B	
C	

1b	Type of Property (from list below)	**2** For each rental real estate property listed above, report the number of fair rental and personal use days. Check the **QJV** box only if you meet the requirements to file as a qualified joint venture. See instructions.		**Fair Rental Days**	**Personal Use Days**	**QJV**
A			**A**			☐
B			**B**			☐
C			**C**			☐

Type of Property:

1 Single Family Residence
2 Multi-Family Residence
3 Vacation/Short-Term Rental
4 Commercial
5 Land
6 Royalties
7 Self-Rental
8 Other (describe)

Income:	**Properties:**		**A**	**B**	**C**
3	Rents received	**3**			
4	Royalties received	**4**			
Expenses:					
5	Advertising	**5**			
6	Auto and travel (see instructions)	**6**			
7	Cleaning and maintenance	**7**			
8	Commissions	**8**			
9	Insurance	**9**			
10	Legal and other professional fees	**10**			
11	Management fees	**11**			
12	Mortgage interest paid to banks, etc. (see instructions)	**12**			
13	Other interest	**13**			
14	Repairs	**14**			
15	Supplies	**15**			
16	Taxes	**16**			
17	Utilities	**17**			
18	Depreciation expense or depletion	**18**			
19	Other (list) ▶	**19**			
20	Total expenses. Add lines 5 through 19	**20**			
21	Subtract line 20 from line 3 (rents) and/or 4 (royalties). If result is a (loss), see instructions to find out if you must file **Form 6198**	**21**			
22	Deductible rental real estate loss after limitation, if any, on **Form 8582** (see instructions)	**22**	( )	( )	( )

23a	Total of all amounts reported on line 3 for all rental properties	**23a**	
b	Total of all amounts reported on line 4 for all royalty properties	**23b**	
c	Total of all amounts reported on line 12 for all properties	**23c**	
d	Total of all amounts reported on line 18 for all properties	**23d**	
e	Total of all amounts reported on line 20 for all properties	**23e**	
24	**Income.** Add positive amounts shown on line 21. **Do not** include any losses	**24**	
25	**Losses.** Add royalty losses from line 21 and rental real estate losses from line 22. Enter total losses here	**25**	( )
26	**Total rental real estate and royalty income or (loss).** Combine lines 24 and 25. Enter the result here. If Parts II, III, IV, and line 40 on page 2 do not apply to you, also enter this amount on Form 1040, line 17, or Form 1040NR, line 18. Otherwise, include this amount in the total on line 41 on page 2	**26**	

For Paperwork Reduction Act Notice, see the separate instructions. Cat. No. 11344L **Schedule E (Form 1040) 2013**

Name(s) shown on return. Do not enter name and social security number if shown on other side. | **Your social security number**

Caution. The IRS compares amounts reported on your tax return with amounts shown on Schedule(s) K-1.

Part II Income or Loss From Partnerships and S Corporations

Note. If you report a loss from an at-risk activity for which **any** amount is **not** at risk, you **must** check the box in column **(e)** on line 28 and attach **Form 6198.** See instructions.

27 Are you reporting any loss not allowed in a prior year due to the at-risk, excess farm loss, or basis limitations, a prior year unallowed loss from a passive activity (if that loss was not reported on Form 8582), or unreimbursed partnership expenses? If you answered "Yes," see instructions before completing this section. ☐ **Yes** ☐ **No**

28	**(a)** Name	**(b)** Enter **P** for partnership; **S** for S corporation	**(c)** Check if foreign partnership	**(d)** Employer identification number	**(e)** Check if any amount is not at risk
A			☐		☐
B			☐		☐
C			☐		☐
D			☐		☐

	Passive Income and Loss		Nonpassive Income and Loss		
	(f) Passive loss allowed (attach **Form 8582** if required)	**(g)** Passive income from **Schedule K–1**	**(h)** Nonpassive loss from **Schedule K–1**	**(i)** Section 179 expense deduction from **Form 4562**	**(j)** Nonpassive income from **Schedule K–1**
A					
B					
C					
D					
29a Totals					
b Totals					

30	Add columns (g) and (j) of line 29a	30	
31	Add columns (f), (h), and (i) of line 29b	31	( )
32	**Total partnership and S corporation income or (loss).** Combine lines 30 and 31. Enter the result here and include in the total on line 41 below	32	

Part III Income or Loss From Estates and Trusts

33	**(a)** Name	**(b)** Employer identification number
A		
B		

	Passive Income and Loss		Nonpassive Income and Loss	
	(c) Passive deduction or loss allowed (attach **Form 8582** if required)	**(d)** Passive income from **Schedule K–1**	**(e)** Deduction or loss from **Schedule K–1**	**(f)** Other income from **Schedule K–1**
A				
B				
34a Totals				
b Totals				

35	Add columns (d) and (f) of line 34a	35	
36	Add columns (c) and (e) of line 34b	36	( )
37	**Total estate and trust income or (loss).** Combine lines 35 and 36. Enter the result here and include in the total on line 41 below	37	

Part IV Income or Loss From Real Estate Mortgage Investment Conduits (REMICs)—Residual Holder

38	**(a)** Name	**(b)** Employer identification number	**(c)** Excess inclusion from **Schedules Q,** line 2c (see instructions)	**(d)** Taxable income (net loss) from **Schedules Q,** line 1b	**(e)** Income from **Schedules Q,** line 3b

39	Combine columns (d) and (e) only. Enter the result here and include in the total on line 41 below	39	

Part V Summary

40	Net farm rental income or (loss) from **Form 4835**. Also, complete line 42 below	40	
41	**Total income or (loss).** Combine lines 26, 32, 37, 39, and 40. Enter the result here and on Form 1040, line 17, or Form 1040NR, line 18 ▶	41	
42	**Reconciliation of farming and fishing income.** Enter your **gross** farming and fishing income reported on Form 4835, line 7; Schedule K-1 (Form 1065), box 14, code B; Schedule K-1 (Form 1120S), box 17, code V; and Schedule K-1 (Form 1041), box 14, code F (see instructions)	42	
43	**Reconciliation for real estate professionals.** If you were a real estate professional (see instructions), enter the net income or (loss) you reported anywhere on Form 1040 or Form 1040NR from all rental real estate activities in which you materially participated under the passive activity loss rules	43	

Schedule E (Form 1040) 2013

SCHEDULE SE (Form 1040)

Department of the Treasury
Internal Revenue Service (99)

Self-Employment Tax

▶ **Information about Schedule SE and its separate instructions is at *www.irs.gov/schedulese.***
▶ **Attach to Form 1040 or Form 1040NR.**

OMB No. 1545-0074

2013

Attachment Sequence No. **17**

Name of person with **self-employment** income (as shown on Form 1040)	Social security number of person with **self-employment** income ▶	

Before you begin: To determine if you must file Schedule SE, see the instructions.

May I Use Short Schedule SE or Must I Use Long Schedule SE?

Note. Use this flowchart **only if** you must file Schedule SE. If unsure, see *Who Must File Schedule SE* in the instructions.

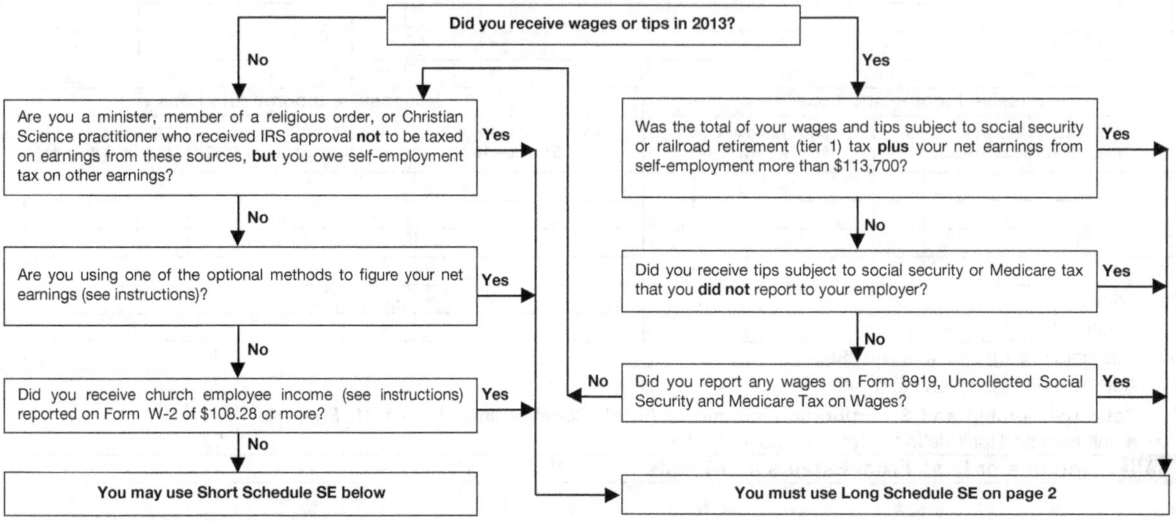

Section A—Short Schedule SE. Caution. Read above to see if you can use Short Schedule SE.

1a	Net farm profit or (loss) from Schedule F, line 34, and farm partnerships, Schedule K-1 (Form 1065), box 14, code A	**1a**	
b	If you received social security retirement or disability benefits, enter the amount of Conservation Reserve Program payments included on Schedule F, line 4b, or listed on Schedule K-1 (Form 1065), box 20, code Z	**1b**	( )
2	Net profit or (loss) from Schedule C, line 31; Schedule C-EZ, line 3; Schedule K-1 (Form 1065), box 14, code A (other than farming); and Schedule K-1 (Form 1065-B), box 9, code J1. Ministers and members of religious orders, see instructions for types of income to report on this line. See instructions for other income to report	**2**	
3	Combine lines 1a, 1b, and 2	**3**	
4	Multiply line 3 by 92.35% (.9235). If less than $400, you do not owe self-employment tax; **do not** file this schedule unless you have an amount on line 1b . . . . ▶	**4**	
	Note. If line 4 is less than $400 due to Conservation Reserve Program payments on line 1b, see instructions.		
5	**Self-employment tax.** If the amount on line 4 is: • $113,700 or less, multiply line 4 by 15.3% (.153). Enter the result here and on **Form 1040, line 56,** or **Form 1040NR, line 54** • More than $113,700, multiply line 4 by 2.9% (.029). Then, add $14,098.80 to the result. Enter the total here and on **Form 1040, line 56,** or **Form 1040NR, line 54**	**5**	
6	**Deduction for one-half of self-employment tax.** Multiply line 5 by 50% (.50). Enter the result here and on **Form 1040, line 27,** or **Form 1040NR, line 27** **6**		

For Paperwork Reduction Act Notice, see your tax return instructions. Cat. No. 11358Z **Schedule SE (Form 1040) 2013**

Name of person with **self-employment** income (as shown on Form 1040) | Social security number of person with **self-employment** income ▶

Section B—Long Schedule SE

Part I Self-Employment Tax

Note. If your only income subject to self-employment tax is **church employee income,** see instructions. Also see instructions for the definition of church employee income.

A If you are a minister, member of a religious order, or Christian Science practitioner **and** you filed Form 4361, but you had $400 or more of **other** net earnings from self-employment, check here and continue with Part I . . . . ▶ ☐

1a	Net farm profit or (loss) from Schedule F, line 34, and farm partnerships, Schedule K-1 (Form 1065), box 14, code A. **Note.** Skip lines 1a and 1b if you use the farm optional method (see instructions)	**1a**	
b	If you received social security retirement or disability benefits, enter the amount of Conservation Reserve Program payments included on Schedule F, line 4b, or listed on Schedule K-1 (Form 1065), box 20, code Z	**1b**	( )
2	Net profit or (loss) from Schedule C, line 31; Schedule C-EZ, line 3; Schedule K-1 (Form 1065), box 14, code A (other than farming); and Schedule K-1 (Form 1065-B), box 9, code J1. Ministers and members of religious orders, see instructions for types of income to report on this line. See instructions for other income to report. **Note.** Skip this line if you use the nonfarm optional method (see instructions)	**2**	
3	Combine lines 1a, 1b, and 2	**3**	
4a	If line 3 is more than zero, multiply line 3 by 92.35% (.9235). Otherwise, enter amount from line 3	**4a**	
	Note. If line 4a is less than $400 due to Conservation Reserve Program payments on line 1b, see instructions.		
b	If you elect one or both of the optional methods, enter the total of lines 15 and 17 here	**4b**	
c	Combine lines 4a and 4b. If less than $400, **stop;** you do not owe self-employment tax. **Exception.** If less than $400 and you had **church employee income,** enter -0- and continue ▶	**4c**	
5a	Enter your **church employee income** from Form W-2. See instructions for definition of church employee income . . . **5a**		
b	Multiply line 5a by 92.35% (.9235). If less than $100, enter -0-	**5b**	
6	Add lines 4c and 5b	**6**	
7	Maximum amount of combined wages and self-employment earnings subject to social security tax or the 6.2% portion of the 7.65% railroad retirement (tier 1) tax for 2013	**7**	113,700 00
8a	Total social security wages and tips (total of boxes 3 and 7 on Form(s) W-2) and railroad retirement (tier 1) compensation. If $113,700 or more, skip lines 8b through 10, and go to line 11 . . . **8a**		
b	Unreported tips subject to social security tax (from Form 4137, line 10) **8b**		
c	Wages subject to social security tax (from Form 8919, line 10) **8c**		
d	Add lines 8a, 8b, and 8c	**8d**	
9	Subtract line 8d from line 7. If zero or less, enter -0- here and on line 10 and go to line 11 . ▶	**9**	
10	Multiply the **smaller** of line 6 or line 9 by 12.4% (.124)	**10**	
11	Multiply line 6 by 2.9% (.029)	**11**	
12	**Self-employment tax.** Add lines 10 and 11. Enter here and on **Form 1040, line 56,** or **Form 1040NR, line 54**	**12**	
13	**Deduction for one-half of self-employment tax.** Multiply line 12 by 50% (.50). Enter the result here and on **Form 1040, line 27,** or **Form 1040NR, line 27** **13**		

Part II Optional Methods To Figure Net Earnings (see instructions)

Farm Optional Method. You may use this method **only** if **(a)** your gross farm income[1] was not more than $6,960, **or (b)** your net farm profits[2] were less than $5,024.

14	Maximum income for optional methods	**14**	4,640 00
15	Enter the **smaller** of: two-thirds (2/3) of gross farm income[1] (not less than zero) **or** $4,640. Also include this amount on line 4b above	**15**	

Nonfarm Optional Method. You may use this method **only** if **(a)** your net nonfarm profits[3] were less than $5,024 and also less than 72.189% of your gross nonfarm income,[4] **and (b)** you had net earnings from self-employment of at least $400 in 2 of the prior 3 years. **Caution.** You may use this method no more than five times.

16	Subtract line 15 from line 14	**16**	
17	Enter the **smaller** of: two-thirds (2/3) of gross nonfarm income[4] (not less than zero) **or** the amount on line 16. Also include this amount on line 4b above	**17**	

[1] From Sch. F, line 9, and Sch. K-1 (Form 1065), box 14, code B.

[2] From Sch. F, line 34, and Sch. K-1 (Form 1065), box 14, code A—minus the amount you would have entered on line 1b had you not used the optional method.

[3] From Sch. C, line 31; Sch. C-EZ, line 3; Sch. K-1 (Form 1065), box 14, code A; and Sch. K-1 (Form 1065-B), box 9, code J1.

[4] From Sch. C, line 7; Sch. C-EZ, line 1; Sch. K-1 (Form 1065), box 14, code C; and Sch. K-1 (Form 1065-B), box 9, code J2.

Schedule SE (Form 1040) 2013

Form **1040A** Department of the Treasury—Internal Revenue Service

U.S. Individual Income Tax Return (99) 2013

IRS Use Only—Do not write or staple in this space.

OMB No. 1545-0074

Your first name and initial	Last name	Your social security number
If a joint return, spouse's first name and initial	Last name	Spouse's social security number
Home address (number and street). If you have a P.O. box, see instructions.	Apt. no.	▲ Make sure the SSN(s) above and on line 6c are correct.
City, town or post office, state, and ZIP code. If you have a foreign address, also complete spaces below (see instructions).		**Presidential Election Campaign** Check here if you, or your spouse if filing jointly, want $3 to go to this fund. Checking a box below will not change your tax or refund. ☐ You ☐ Spouse
Foreign country name	Foreign province/state/county	Foreign postal code

Filing status

Check only one box.

1 ☐ Single
2 ☐ Married filing jointly (even if only one had income)
3 ☐ Married filing separately. Enter spouse's SSN above and full name here. ▶
4 ☐ Head of household (with qualifying person). (See instructions.) If the qualifying person is a child but not your dependent, enter this child's name here. ▶
5 ☐ Qualifying widow(er) with dependent child (see instructions)

Exemptions

6a ☐ **Yourself.** If someone can claim you as a dependent, **do not** check box 6a.
b ☐ **Spouse**

Boxes checked on 6a and 6b

c **Dependents:**

If more than six dependents, see instructions.

(1) First name Last name	(2) Dependent's social security number	(3) Dependent's relationship to you	(4) ✓ if child under age 17 qualifying for child tax credit (see instructions)
			☐
			☐
			☐
			☐
			☐
			☐

No. of children on 6c who:
- **lived with you**
- **did not live with you due to divorce or separation (see instructions)**

Dependents on 6c not entered above

d Total number of exemptions claimed.

Add numbers on lines above ▶

Income

Attach Form(s) W-2 here. Also attach Form(s) 1099-R if tax was withheld.

If you did not get a W-2, see instructions.

7	Wages, salaries, tips, etc. Attach Form(s) W-2.		7
8a	**Taxable** interest. Attach Schedule B if required.		8a
b	**Tax-exempt** interest. **Do not** include on line 8a.	8b	
9a	Ordinary dividends. Attach Schedule B if required.		9a
b	Qualified dividends (see instructions).	9b	
10	Capital gain distributions (see instructions).		10
11a	IRA distributions.	11a	**11b** Taxable amount (see instructions). 11b
12a	Pensions and annuities.	12a	**12b** Taxable amount (see instructions). 12b
13	Unemployment compensation and Alaska Permanent Fund dividends.		13
14a	Social security benefits.	14a	**14b** Taxable amount (see instructions). 14b
15	Add lines 7 through 14b (far right column). This is your **total income.** ▶		15

Adjusted gross income

16	Educator expenses (see instructions).	16	
17	IRA deduction (see instructions).	17	
18	Student loan interest deduction (see instructions).	18	
19	Tuition and fees. Attach Form 8917.	19	
20	Add lines 16 through 19. These are your **total adjustments.**		20
21	Subtract line 20 from line 15. This is your **adjusted gross income.** ▶		21

For Disclosure, Privacy Act, and Paperwork Reduction Act Notice, see separate instructions. Cat. No. 11327A Form **1040A** (2013)

Tax, credits, and payments

22 Enter the amount from line 21 (adjusted gross income). 22

23a Check if: ☐ **You** were born before January 2, 1949, ☐ Blind } **Total boxes**
☐ **Spouse** was born before January 2, 1949, ☐ Blind } **checked** ▶ 23a ☐

b If you are married filing separately and your spouse itemizes deductions, check here ▶ 23b ☐

Standard Deduction for—
• People who check any box on line 23a or 23b **or** who can be claimed as a dependent, see instructions.
• All others:
Single or Married filing separately, $6,100
Married filing jointly or Qualifying widow(er), $12,200
Head of household, $8,950

24 Enter your **standard deduction.** 24

25 Subtract line 24 from line 22. If line 24 is more than line 22, enter -0-. 25

26 **Exemptions.** Multiply $3,900 by the number on line 6d. 26

27 Subtract line 26 from line 25. If line 26 is more than line 25, enter -0-. This is your **taxable income.** ▶ 27

28 **Tax,** including any alternative minimum tax (see instructions). 28

29 Credit for child and dependent care expenses. Attach Form 2441. 29

30 Credit for the elderly or the disabled. Attach Schedule R. 30

31 Education credits from Form 8863, line 19. 31

32 Retirement savings contributions credit. Attach Form 8880. 32

33 Child tax credit. Attach Schedule 8812, if required. 33

34 Add lines 29 through 33. These are your **total credits.** 34

35 Subtract line 34 from line 28. If line 34 is more than line 28, enter -0-. This is your **total tax.** 35

36 Federal income tax withheld from Forms W-2 and 1099. 36

37 2013 estimated tax payments and amount applied from 2012 return. 37

If you have a qualifying child, attach Schedule EIC.

38a **Earned income credit (EIC).** 38a

b Nontaxable combat pay election. 38b

39 Additional child tax credit. Attach Schedule 8812. 39

40 American opportunity credit from Form 8863, line 8. 40

41 Add lines 36, 37, 38a, 39, and 40. These are your **total payments.** ▶ 41

Refund

42 If line 41 is more than line 35, subtract line 35 from line 41. This is the amount you **overpaid.** 42

Direct deposit? See instructions and fill in 43b, 43c, and 43d or Form 8888.

43a Amount of line 42 you want **refunded to you.** If Form 8888 is attached, check here ▶ ☐ 43a

▶ b Routing number ▶ c Type: ☐ Checking ☐ Savings

▶ d Account number

44 Amount of line 42 you want **applied to your 2014 estimated tax.** 44

Amount you owe

45 **Amount you owe.** Subtract line 41 from line 35. For details on how to pay, see instructions. ▶ 45

46 Estimated tax penalty (see instructions). 46

Third party designee

Do you want to allow another person to discuss this return with the IRS (see instructions)? ☐ **Yes.** Complete the following. ☐ **No**

Designee's name ▶ Phone no. ▶ Personal identification number (PIN) ▶

Sign here

Under penalties of perjury, I declare that I have examined this return and accompanying schedules and statements, and to the best of my knowledge and belief, they are true, correct, and accurately list all amounts and sources of income I received during the tax year. Declaration of preparer (other than the taxpayer) is based on all information of which the preparer has any knowledge.

Joint return? See instructions. Keep a copy for your records.

Your signature	Date	Your occupation	Daytime phone number
Spouse's signature. If a joint return, **both** must sign.	Date	Spouse's occupation	If the IRS sent you an Identity Protection PIN, enter it here (see inst.)

Paid preparer use only

Print/type preparer's name	Preparer's signature	Date	Check ▶ ☐ if self-employed	PTIN
Firm's name ▶			Firm's EIN ▶	
Firm's address ▶			Phone no.	

Form **1040A** (2013)

Department of the Treasury—Internal Revenue Service

Form **1040EZ** **Income Tax Return for Single and Joint Filers With No Dependents** (99) **2013** OMB No. 1545-0074

Your first name and initial	Last name		Your social security number
If a joint return, spouse's first name and initial	Last name		Spouse's social security number
Home address (number and street). If you have a P.O. box, see instructions.		Apt. no.	▲ Make sure the SSN(s) above are correct.
City, town or post office, state, and ZIP code. If you have a foreign address, also complete spaces below (see instructions).			**Presidential Election Campaign** Check here if you, or your spouse if filing jointly, want $3 to go to this fund. Checking a box below will not change your tax or refund. ☐ You ☐ Spouse
Foreign country name	Foreign province/state/county	Foreign postal code	

Income

Attach Form(s) W-2 here.

Enclose, but do not attach, any payment.

1	Wages, salaries, and tips. This should be shown in box 1 of your Form(s) W-2. Attach your Form(s) W-2.	1	
2	Taxable interest. If the total is over $1,500, you cannot use Form 1040EZ.	2	
3	Unemployment compensation and Alaska Permanent Fund dividends (see instructions).	3	
4	Add lines 1, 2, and 3. This is your **adjusted gross income.**	4	
5	If someone can claim you (or your spouse if a joint return) as a dependent, check the applicable box(es) below and enter the amount from the worksheet on back. ☐ **You** ☐ **Spouse** If no one can claim you (or your spouse if a joint return), enter $10,000 if **single;** $20,000 if **married filing jointly.** See back for explanation.	5	
6	Subtract line 5 from line 4. If line 5 is larger than line 4, enter -0-. This is your **taxable income.** ▶	6	

Payments, Credits, and Tax

7	Federal income tax withheld from Form(s) W-2 and 1099.	7	
8a	**Earned income credit (EIC)** (see instructions).	8a	
b	Nontaxable combat pay election. 8b		
9	Add lines 7 and 8a. These are your **total payments and credits.** ▶	9	
10	**Tax.** Use the amount on **line 6 above** to find your tax in the tax table in the instructions. Then, enter the tax from the table on this line.	10	

Refund

Have it directly deposited! See instructions and fill in 11b, 11c, and 11d or Form 8888.

11a	If line 9 is larger than line 10, subtract line 10 from line 9. This is your **refund.** If Form 8888 is attached, check here ▶ ☐	11a	
▶ b	Routing number ▶ c Type: ☐ Checking ☐ Savings		
▶ d	Account number		

Amount You Owe

12	If line 10 is larger than line 9, subtract line 9 from line 10. This is the **amount you owe.** For details on how to pay, see instructions. ▶	12	

Third Party Designee

Do you want to allow another person to discuss this return with the IRS (see instructions)? ☐ **Yes.** Complete below. ☐ **No**

Designee's name ▶ Phone no. ▶ Personal identification number (PIN) ▶

Sign Here

Joint return? See instructions.

Keep a copy for your records.

Under penalties of perjury, I declare that I have examined this return and, to the best of my knowledge and belief, it is true, correct, and accurately lists all amounts and sources of income I received during the tax year. Declaration of preparer (other than the taxpayer) is based on all information of which the preparer has any knowledge.

Your signature	Date	Your occupation	Daytime phone number
Spouse's signature. If a joint return, **both** must sign.	Date	Spouse's occupation	If the IRS sent you an Identity Protection PIN, enter it here (see inst.)

Paid Preparer Use Only

Print/Type preparer's name	Preparer's signature	Date	Check ☐ if self-employed	PTIN
Firm's name ▶		Firm's EIN ▶		
Firm's address ▶		Phone no.		

For Disclosure, Privacy Act, and Paperwork Reduction Act Notice, see instructions. Cat. No. 11329W Form **1040EZ** (2013)

Use this form if

- Your filing status is single or married filing jointly. If you are not sure about your filing status, see instructions.
- You (and your spouse if married filing jointly) were under age 65 and not blind at the end of 2013. If you were born on January 1, 1949, you are considered to be age 65 at the end of 2013.
- You do not claim any dependents. For information on dependents, see Pub. 501.
- Your taxable income (line 6) is less than $100,000.
- You do not claim any adjustments to income. For information on adjustments to income, use the TeleTax topics listed under *Adjustments to Income* at *www.irs.gov/taxtopics* (see instructions).
- The only tax credit you can claim is the earned income credit (EIC). The credit may give you a refund even if you do not owe any tax. You do not need a qualifying child to claim the EIC. For information on credits, use the TeleTax topics listed under *Tax Credits* at *www.irs.gov/taxtopics* (see instructions). If you received a Form 1098-T or paid higher education expenses, you may be eligible for a tax credit or deduction that you must claim on Form 1040A or Form 1040. For more information on tax benefits for education, see Pub. 970.
- You had only wages, salaries, tips, taxable scholarship or fellowship grants, unemployment compensation, or Alaska Permanent Fund dividends, and your taxable interest was not over $1,500. But if you earned tips, including allocated tips, that are not included in box 5 and box 7 of your Form W-2, you may not be able to use Form 1040EZ (see instructions). If you are planning to use Form 1040EZ for a child who received Alaska Permanent Fund dividends, see instructions.

Filling in your return

If you received a scholarship or fellowship grant or tax-exempt interest income, such as on municipal bonds, see the instructions before filling in the form. Also, see the instructions if you received a Form 1099-INT showing federal income tax withheld or if federal income tax was withheld from your unemployment compensation or Alaska Permanent Fund dividends.

For tips on how to avoid common mistakes, see instructions.

Remember, you must report all wages, salaries, and tips even if you do not get a Form W-2 from your employer. You must also report all your taxable interest, including interest from banks, savings and loans, credit unions, etc., even if you do not get a Form 1099-INT.

Worksheet for Line 5 — Dependents Who Checked One or Both Boxes

(keep a copy for your records)

Use this worksheet to figure the amount to enter on line 5 if someone can claim you (or your spouse if married filing jointly) as a dependent, even if that person chooses not to do so. To find out if someone can claim you as a dependent, see Pub. 501.

A. Amount, if any, from line 1 on front . . . . . . ______
+ 350.00 Enter total ▶ **A.** ______

B. Minimum standard deduction . . . . **B.** 1,000

C. Enter the **larger** of line A or line B here . . . . **C.** ______

D. Maximum standard deduction. If **single,** enter $6,100; if **married filing jointly,** enter $12,200 . **D.** ______

E. Enter the **smaller** of line C or line D here. This is your standard deduction . . . . **E.** ______

F. Exemption amount.
- If single, enter -0-.
- If married filing jointly and —
  - —both you and your spouse can be claimed as dependents, enter -0-.
  - —only one of you can be claimed as a dependent, enter $3,900.

F. ______

G. Add lines E and F. Enter the total here and on line 5 on the front . . . . **G.** ______

If you did not check any boxes on line 5, enter on line 5 the amount shown below that applies to you.
- Single, enter $10,000. This is the total of your standard deduction ($6,100) and your exemption ($3,900).
- Married filing jointly, enter $20,000. This is the total of your standard deduction ($12,200), your exemption ($3,900), and your spouse's exemption ($3,900).

Mailing Return

Mail your return by **April 15, 2014.** Mail it to the address shown on the last page of the instructions.

Form **1040EZ** (2013)

Form **1040-ES** Department of the Treasury Internal Revenue Service

2014 Estimated Tax

Payment Voucher 3 OMB No. 1545-0074

Calendar year—Due Sept. 15, 2014

File only if you are making a payment of estimated tax by check or money order. Mail this voucher with your check or money order payable to **"United States Treasury."** Write your social security number and "2014 Form 1040-ES" on your check or money order. Do not send cash. Enclose, but do not staple or attach, your payment with this voucher.

Amount of estimated tax you are paying by check or money order. | Dollars | Cents |

Print or type

Your first name and initial	Your last name	Your social security number
If joint payment, complete for spouse		
Spouse's first name and initial	Spouse's last name	Spouse's social security number
Address (number, street, and apt. no.)		
City, state, and ZIP code. (If a foreign address, enter city, also complete spaces below.)		
Foreign country name	Foreign province/county	Foreign postal code

For Privacy Act and Paperwork Reduction Act Notice, see instructions.

Tear off here

Form **1040-ES** Department of the Treasury Internal Revenue Service

2014 Estimated Tax

Payment Voucher 2 OMB No. 1545-0074

Calendar year—Due June 16, 2014

File only if you are making a payment of estimated tax by check or money order. Mail this voucher with your check or money order payable to **"United States Treasury."** Write your social security number and "2014 Form 1040-ES" on your check or money order. Do not send cash. Enclose, but do not staple or attach, your payment with this voucher.

Amount of estimated tax you are paying by check or money order. | Dollars | Cents |

Print or type

Your first name and initial	Your last name	Your social security number
If joint payment, complete for spouse		
Spouse's first name and initial	Spouse's last name	Spouse's social security number
Address (number, street, and apt. no.)		
City, state, and ZIP code. (If a foreign address, enter city, also complete spaces below.)		
Foreign country name	Foreign province/county	Foreign postal code

For Privacy Act and Paperwork Reduction Act Notice, see instructions.

Tear off here

Form **1040-ES** Department of the Treasury Internal Revenue Service

2014 Estimated Tax

Payment Voucher 1 OMB No. 1545-0074

Calendar year—Due April 15, 2014

File only if you are making a payment of estimated tax by check or money order. Mail this voucher with your check or money order payable to **"United States Treasury."** Write your social security number and "2014 Form 1040-ES" on your check or money order. Do not send cash. Enclose, but do not staple or attach, your payment with this voucher.

Amount of estimated tax you are paying by check or money order. | Dollars | Cents |

Print or type

Your first name and initial	Your last name	Your social security number
If joint payment, complete for spouse		
Spouse's first name and initial	Spouse's last name	Spouse's social security number
Address (number, street, and apt. no.)		
City, state, and ZIP code. (If a foreign address, enter city, also complete spaces below.)		
Foreign country name	Foreign province/county	Foreign postal code

For Privacy Act and Paperwork Reduction Act Notice, see instructions. **Form 1040-ES (2014)**

Form **1045**

Department of the Treasury
Internal Revenue Service

Application for Tentative Refund

► Separate instructions and additional information are available at *IRS.gov/form1045*.
► Do not attach to your income tax return. Mail in a separate envelope.
► For use by individuals, estates, or trusts.

OMB No. 1545-0098

2013

Type or print

Name(s) shown on return	**Social security or employer identification number**
Number, street, and apt. or suite no. if a P.O. box, see instructions.	**Spouse's social security number (SSN)**
City, town or post office, state, and Zip code. If a foreign address, also complete spaces below (see instructions).	Daytime phone number
Foreign country name / Foreign province/county	Foreign postal code

1 This application is filed to carry back:	**a** Net operating loss (NOL) (Sch. A, line 25, page 2) $	**b** Unused general business credit $	**c** Net section 1256 contracts loss $

2a For the calendar year 2013, or other tax year beginning , 2013, and ending , 20 — **b** Date tax return was filed

3 If this application is for an unused credit created by another carryback, enter year of first carryback ►

4 If you filed a joint return (or separate return) for some, but not all, of the tax years involved in figuring the carryback, list the years and specify whether joint (J) or separate (S) return for each ►

5 If SSN for carryback year is different from above, enter **a** SSN ► and **b** Year(s) ►

6 If you changed your accounting period, give date permission to change was granted ►

7 Have you filed a petition in Tax Court for the year(s) to which the carryback is to be applied? . . . ☐ Yes ☐ No

8 Is any part of the decrease in tax due to a loss or credit resulting from a reportable transaction required to be disclosed on Form 8886, Reportable Transaction Disclosure Statement? ☐ Yes ☐ No

9 If you are carrying back an NOL or net section 1256 contracts loss, did this cause the release of foreign tax credits or the release of other credits due to the release of the foreign tax credit (see instructions)? . . . ☐ Yes ☐ No

Computation of Decrease in Tax (see instructions)	___ preceding tax year ended ►		___ preceding tax year ended ►		___ preceding tax year ended ►	
Note: *If 1a and 1c are blank, skip lines 10 through 15.*	Before carryback	After carryback	Before carryback	After carryback	Before carryback	After carryback
10 NOL deduction after carryback (see instructions)						
11 Adjusted gross income						
12 Deductions (see instructions) . . .						
13 Subtract line 12 from line 11 . . .						
14 Exemptions (see instructions) . . .						
15 Taxable income. Line 13 minus line 14						
16 Income tax. See instructions and attach an explanation						
17 Alternative minimum tax						
18 Add lines 16 and 17						
19 General business credit (see instructions)						
20 Other credits. Identify						
21 Total credits. Add lines 19 and 20 . .						
22 Subtract line 21 from line 18 . . .						
23 Self-employment tax						
24 Other taxes						
25 Total tax. Add lines 22 through 24 . .						
26 Enter the amount from the "After carryback" column on line 25 for each year						
27 Decrease in tax. Line 25 minus line 26						
28 Overpayment of tax due to a claim of right adjustment under section 1341(b)(1) (attach computation) . . .						

Sign Here

Keep a copy of this application for your records.

Under penalties of perjury, I declare that I have examined this application and accompanying schedules and statements, and to the best of my knowledge and belief, they are true, correct, and complete.

► Your signature — Date

► Spouse's signature. If Form 1045 is filed jointly, **both** must sign. — Date

Paid Preparer Use Only				
Print/Type preparer's name	Preparer's signature	Date	Check ☐ if self-employed	PTIN
Firm's name ►			Firm's EIN ►	
Firm's address ►			Phone no.	

For Disclosure, Privacy Act, and Paperwork Reduction Act Notice, see instructions. Cat. No. 10670A Form **1045** (2013)

Schedule A—NOL (see instructions)

1	Enter the amount from your 2013 Form 1040, line 41, or Form 1040NR, line 39. Estates and trusts, enter taxable income increased by the total of the charitable deduction, income distribution deduction, and exemption amount . . .			1	
2	Nonbusiness capital losses before limitation. Enter as a positive number		2		
3	Nonbusiness capital gains (without regard to any section 1202 exclusion)		3		
4	If line 2 is more than line 3, enter the difference. Otherwise, enter -0- . .		4		
5	If line 3 is more than line 2, enter the difference. Otherwise, enter -0- . . .	5			
6	Nonbusiness deductions (see instructions) . . .		6		
7	Nonbusiness income other than capital gains (see instructions) . . .	7			
8	Add lines 5 and 7 . . .		8		
9	If line 6 is more than line 8, enter the difference. Otherwise, enter -0- . . .			9	
10	If line 8 is more than line 6, enter the difference. Otherwise, enter -0-. **But do not enter more than line 5** . . .	10			
11	Business capital losses before limitation. Enter as a positive number . .		11		
12	Business capital gains (without regard to any section 1202 exclusion) . . .	12			
13	Add lines 10 and 12 . . .		13		
14	Subtract line 13 from line 11. If zero or less, enter -0- . . .		14		
15	Add lines 4 and 14 . . .		15		
16	Enter the loss, if any, from line 16 of your 2013 Schedule D (Form 1040). (Estates and trusts, enter the loss, if any, from line 19, column (3), of Schedule D (Form 1041).) Enter as a positive number. If you do not have a loss on that line (and do not have a section 1202 exclusion), skip lines 16 through 21 and enter on line 22 the amount from line 15 . . .		16		
17	Section 1202 exclusion. Enter as a positive number . . .			17	
18	Subtract line 17 from line 16. If zero or less, enter -0- . . .		18		
19	Enter the loss, if any, from line 21 of your 2013 Schedule D (Form 1040). (Estates and trusts, enter the loss, if any, from line 20 of Schedule D (Form 1041).) Enter as a positive number . . .		19		
20	If line 18 is more than line 19, enter the difference. Otherwise, enter -0- .		20		
21	If line 19 is more than line 18, enter the difference. Otherwise, enter -0- . . .			21	
22	Subtract line 20 from line 15. If zero or less, enter -0- . . .			22	
23	Domestic production activities deduction from your 2013 Form 1040, line 35, or Form 1040NR, line 34 (or included on Form 1041, line 15a) . . .			23	
24	NOL deduction for losses from other years. Enter as a positive number . . .			24	
25	**NOL.** Combine lines 1, 9, 17, and 21 through 24. If the result is less than zero, enter it here and on page 1, line 1a. If the result is zero or more, you **do not** have an NOL . . .			25	

Form **1045** (2013)

Schedule B—NOL Carryover (see instructions)

Complete one column before going to the next column. Start with the earliest carryback year.	____ preceding tax year ended ▶		____ preceding tax year ended ▶		____ preceding tax year ended ▶	
1 **NOL deduction** (see instructions). Enter as a positive number						
2 Taxable income before 2013 NOL carryback (see instructions). Estates and trusts, increase this amount by the sum of the charitable deduction and income distribution deduction						
3 Net capital loss deduction (see instructions)						
4 Section 1202 exclusion. Enter as a positive number						
5 Domestic production activities deduction						
6 Adjustment to adjusted gross income (see instructions)						
7 Adjustment to itemized deductions (see instructions)						
8 Individuals, enter deduction for exemptions (minus any amount on Form 8914, line 6, for 2006 and 2009; line 2 for 2005 and 2008). Estates and trusts, enter exemption amount						
9 Modified taxable income. Combine lines 2 through 8. If zero or less, enter -0-						
10 **NOL carryover** (see instructions)						
Adjustment to Itemized Deductions (Individuals Only) Complete lines 11 through 38 for the carryback year(s) for which you itemized deductions **only** if line 3, 4, or 5 above is more than zero.						
11 Adjusted gross income before 2013 NOL carryback						
12 Add lines 3 through 6 above						
13 Modified adjusted gross income. Add lines 11 and 12						
14 Medical expenses from Sch. A (Form 1040), line 4 (or as previously adjusted)						
15 Medical expenses from Sch. A (Form 1040), line 1 (or as previously adjusted)						
16 Multiply line 13 by 7.5% (.075)						
17 Subtract line 16 from line 15. If zero or less, enter -0-						
18 Subtract line 17 from line 14						
19 Mortgage insurance premiums from Sch. A (Form 1040), line 13 (or as previously adjusted)						
20 Refigured mortgage insurance premiums (see instructions)						
21 Subtract line 20 from line 19						

Schedule B—NOL Carryover *(Continued)*

Complete one column before going to the next column. Start with the earliest carryback year.	____ preceding tax year ended ▶		____ preceding tax year ended ▶		____ preceding tax year ended ▶	
22 Modified adjusted gross income from line 13 on page 3 of the form . . .						
23 Enter as a positive number any NOL carryback from a year before 2013 that was deducted to figure line 11 on page 3 of the form						
24 Add lines 22 and 23						
25 Charitable contributions from Sch. A (Form 1040), line 19 (line 18 for 2003 through 2006), or Sch. A (Form 1040NR), line 5 (line 7 for 2003 through 2010), or as previously adjusted						
26 Refigured charitable contributions (see instructions)						
27 Subtract line 26 from line 25 . . .						
28 Casualty and theft losses from Form 4684, line 18 (line 23 for 2008; line 21 for 2009; line 20 for 2005, 2006, and 2010)						
29 Casualty and theft losses from Form 4684, line 16 (line 21 for 2008; line 18 for 2005, 2006, and 2010; line 19 for 2009)						
30 Multiply line 22 by 10% (.10) . . .						
31 Subtract line 30 from line 29. If zero or less, enter -0-						
32 Subtract line 31 from line 28 . . .						
33 Miscellaneous itemized deductions from Sch. A (Form 1040), line 27 (line 26 for 2003 through 2006), or Sch. A (Form 1040NR), line 13 (line 15 for 2003 through 2010), or as previously adjusted						
34 Miscellaneous itemized deductions from Sch. A (Form 1040), line 24 (line 23 for 2003 through 2006), or Sch. A (Form 1040NR), line 10 (line 12 for 2003 through 2010), or as previously adjusted						
35 Multiply line 22 by 2% (.02)						
36 Subtract line 35 from line 34. If zero or less, enter -0-						
37 Subtract line 36 from line 33 . . .						
38 Complete the worksheet in the instructions if line 22 is **more than** the applicable amount shown below (more than one-half that amount if married filing separately for that year). • $139,500 for 2003. • $142,700 for 2004. • $145,950 for 2005. • $150,500 for 2006. • $156,400 for 2007. • $159,950 for 2008. • $166,800 for 2009. Otherwise, combine lines 18, 21, 27, 32, and 37; enter the result here and on line 7 (page 3)						

Form **1045** (2013)

☐ CORRECTED (if checked)

RECIPIENT'S/LENDER'S name, street address, city or town, state or province, country, ZIP or foreign postal code, and telephone number		* **Caution:** *The amount shown may not be fully deductible by you. Limits based on the loan amount and the cost and value of the secured property may apply. Also, you may only deduct interest to the extent it was incurred by you, actually paid by you, and not reimbursed by another person.*	OMB No. 1545-0901 **2014** Form **1098**	**Mortgage Interest Statement**
RECIPIENT'S federal identification no.	PAYER'S social security number	**1** Mortgage interest received from payer(s)/borrower(s)* $		**Copy B** **For Payer/Borrower**
PAYER'S/BORROWER'S name		**2** Points paid on purchase of principal residence $		The information in boxes 1, 2, 3, and 4 is important tax information and is being furnished to the Internal Revenue Service. If you are required to file a return, a negligence penalty or other sanction may be imposed on you if the IRS determines that an underpayment of tax results because you overstated a deduction for this mortgage interest or for these points or because you did not report this refund of interest on your return.
Street address (including apt. no.)		**3** Refund of overpaid interest $		
City or town, state or province, country, and ZIP or foreign postal code		**4**		
Account number (see instructions)		**5**		

Form **1098** (keep for your records) www.irs.gov/form1098 Department of the Treasury - Internal Revenue Service

☐ CORRECTED (if checked)

DONEE'S name, street address, city or town, state or province, country, ZIP or foreign postal code, and telephone no.	**1** Date of contribution **2a** Odometer mileage	OMB No. 1545-1959 **2014** Form **1098-C**	Attachment Sequence No. **155A** **Contributions of Motor Vehicles, Boats, and Airplanes**
	2b Year / **2c** Make / **2d** Model		
DONEE'S federal identification number / DONOR'S identification number	**3** Vehicle or other identification number		
DONOR'S name	**4a** ☐ Donee certifies that vehicle was sold in arm's length transaction to unrelated party		**Copy B**
Street address (including apt. no.)	**4b** Date of sale		**For Donor**
City or town, state or province, country, and ZIP or foreign postal code	**4c** Gross proceeds from sale (see instructions) **$**		

5a ☐ Donee certifies that vehicle will not be transferred for money, other property, or services before completion of material improvements or significant intervening use

5b ☐ Donee certifies that vehicle is to be transferred to a needy individual for significantly below fair market value in furtherance of donee's charitable purpose

5c Donee certifies the following detailed description of material improvements or significant intervening use and duration of use

6a Did you provide goods or services in exchange for the vehicle? . . . . ▶ **Yes** ☐ **No** ☐

6b Value of goods and services provided in exchange for the vehicle

$

6c Describe the goods and services, if any, that were provided. If this box is checked, donee certifies that the goods and services consisted solely of intangible religious benefits . . . . ▶ ☐

7 Under the law, the donor may not claim a deduction of more than $500 for this vehicle if this box is checked . . . . . . ▶ ☐

In order to take a deduction of more than $500 for this contribution, you must attach this copy to your federal tax return.

Unless box 5a or 5b is checked, your deduction cannot exceed the amount in box 4c.

Form **1098-C** www.irs.gov/form1098c Department of the Treasury - Internal Revenue Service

☐ CORRECTED (if checked)

RECIPIENT'S/LENDER'S name, address, city or town, state or province, country, ZIP or foreign postal code, and telephone number		OMB No. 1545-1576 **2014** Form **1098-E**	**Student Loan Interest Statement**
RECIPIENT'S federal identification no.	BORROWER'S social security number	**1** Student loan interest received by lender $	**Copy B** **For Borrower**
BORROWER'S name Street address (including apt. no.) City or town, state or province, country, and ZIP or foreign postal code			This is important tax information and is being furnished to the Internal Revenue Service. If you are required to file a return, a negligence penalty or other sanction may be imposed on you if the IRS determines that an underpayment of tax results because you overstated a deduction for student loan interest.
Account number (see instructions)		**2** If checked, box 1 does **not** include loan origination fees and/or capitalized interest for loans made before September 1, 2004 . . . . ☐	

Form **1098-E** (keep for your records) www.irs.gov/form1098e Department of the Treasury - Internal Revenue Service

☐ CORRECTED

FILER'S name, street address, city or town, state or province, country, ZIP or foreign postal code, and telephone number		1 Payments received for qualified tuition and related expenses $	OMB No. 1545-1574 **2014**	**Tuition Statement**
		2 Amounts billed for qualified tuition and related expenses $	Form **1098-T**	
FILER'S federal identification no.	STUDENT'S social security number	3 If this box is checked, your educational institution has changed its reporting method for 2014 ☐		**Copy B** **For Student**
STUDENT'S name		4 Adjustments made for a prior year $	5 Scholarships or grants $	This is important tax information and is being furnished to the Internal Revenue Service.
Street address (including apt. no.)		6 Adjustments to scholarships or grants for a prior year $	7 Checked if the amount in box 1 or 2 includes amounts for an academic period beginning January - March 2015 ► ☐	
City or town, state or province, country, and ZIP or foreign postal code				
Service Provider/Acct. No. (see instr.)	8 Check if at least half-time student ☐	9 Checked if a graduate student . . . . ☐	10 Ins. contract reimb./refund $	

Form **1098-T** (keep for your records) www.irs.gov/form1098t Department of the Treasury - Internal Revenue Service

☐ CORRECTED (if checked)

LENDER'S name, street address, city or town, state or province, country, ZIP or foreign postal code, and telephone no.		OMB No. 1545-0877 **2014** Form **1099-A**	**Acquisition or Abandonment of Secured Property**
LENDER'S federal identification number / BORROWER'S identification number	**1** Date of lender's acquisition or knowledge of abandonment	**2** Balance of principal outstanding $	**Copy B** **For Borrower**
BORROWER'S name	**3**	**4** Fair market value of property $	This is important tax information and is being furnished to the Internal Revenue Service. If you are required to file a return, a negligence penalty or other sanction may be imposed on you if taxable income results from this transaction and the IRS determines that it has not been reported.
Street address (including apt. no.)	**5** If checked, the borrower was personally liable for repayment of the debt . . . . ▶ ☐		
City or town, state or province, country, and ZIP or foreign postal code	**6** Description of property		
Account number (see instructions)			

Form **1099-A** (keep for your records) www.irs.gov/form1099a Department of the Treasury - Internal Revenue Service

☐ CORRECTED (if checked)

CREDITOR'S name, street address, city or town, state or province, country, ZIP or foreign postal code, and telephone no.	1 Date of identifiable event 2 Amount of debt discharged $ 3 Interest if included in box 2 $	OMB No. 1545-1424 **2014** Form **1099-C**	**Cancellation of Debt**
CREDITOR'S federal identification number / DEBTOR'S identification number	4 Debt description		**Copy B** **For Debtor**
DEBTOR'S name Street address (including apt. no.) City or town, state or province, country, and ZIP or foreign postal code	5 If checked, the debtor was personally liable for repayment of the debt . . . . ▶ ☐		This is important tax information and is being furnished to the Internal Revenue Service. If you are required to file a return, a negligence penalty or other sanction may be imposed on you if taxable income results from this transaction and the IRS determines that it has not been reported.
Account number (see instructions)	6 Identifiable event code	7 Fair market value of property $	

Form **1099-C** (keep for your records) www.irs.gov/form1099c Department of the Treasury - Internal Revenue Service

☐ CORRECTED (if checked)

PAYER'S name, street address, city or town, state or province, country, ZIP or foreign postal code, and telephone no.	1a Total ordinary dividends $ 1b Qualified dividends $	OMB No. 1545-0110 **2014** Form **1099-DIV**	**Dividends and Distributions**
	2a Total capital gain distr. $	2b Unrecap. Sec. 1250 gain $	**Copy B** **For Recipient**
PAYER'S federal identification number / RECIPIENT'S identification number	2c Section 1202 gain $	2d Collectibles (28%) gain $	
RECIPIENT'S name	3 Nondividend distributions $	4 Federal income tax withheld $	This is important tax information and is being furnished to the Internal Revenue Service. If you are required to file a return, a negligence penalty or other sanction may be imposed on you if this income is taxable and the IRS determines that it has not been reported.
Street address (including apt. no.)		5 Investment expenses $	
City or town, state or province, country, and ZIP or foreign postal code	6 Foreign tax paid $	7 Foreign country or U.S. possession	
	8 Cash liquidation distributions $	9 Noncash liquidation distributions $	
	10 Exempt-interest dividends $	11 Specified private activity bond interest dividends $	
Account number (see instructions)	12 State / 13 State identification no.	14 State tax withheld $ $	

Form **1099-DIV** (keep for your records) www.irs.gov/form1099div Department of the Treasury - Internal Revenue Service

☐ CORRECTED (if checked)

PAYER'S name, street address, city or town, state or province, country, ZIP or foreign postal code, and telephone no.		Payer's RTN (optional)	OMB No. 1545-0112	Interest Income
		1 Interest income $	**2014** Form **1099-INT**	
		2 Early withdrawal penalty $		**Copy B** **For Recipient**
PAYER'S federal identification number	RECIPIENT'S identification number	3 Interest on U.S. Savings Bonds and Treas. obligations $		
RECIPIENT'S name		4 Federal income tax withheld $	5 Investment expenses $	This is important tax information and is being furnished to the Internal Revenue Service. If you are required to file a return, a negligence penalty or other sanction may be imposed on you if this income is taxable and the IRS determines that it has not been reported.
Street address (including apt. no.)		6 Foreign tax paid $	7 Foreign country or U.S. possession	
City or town, state or province, country, and ZIP or foreign postal code		8 Tax-exempt interest $	9 Specified private activity bond interest $	
		10 Market discount $	11 Bond premium $	
Account number (see instructions)		12 Tax-exempt bond CUSIP no.	13 State | 14 State identification no.	15 State tax withheld $ $

Form **1099-INT** (keep for your records) www.irs.gov/form1099int Department of the Treasury - Internal Revenue Service

☐ CORRECTED (if checked)

PAYER'S name, street address, city or town, state or province, country, ZIP or foreign postal code, and telephone no.	1 Rents $ 2 Royalties $	OMB No. 1545-0115 **2014** Form **1099-MISC**	**Miscellaneous Income**
	3 Other income $	4 Federal income tax withheld $	**Copy B For Recipient**
PAYER'S federal identification number / RECIPIENT'S identification number	5 Fishing boat proceeds $	6 Medical and health care payments $	
RECIPIENT'S name Street address (including apt. no.)	7 Nonemployee compensation $	8 Substitute payments in lieu of dividends or interest $	This is important tax information and is being furnished to the Internal Revenue Service. If you are required to file a return, a negligence penalty or other sanction may be imposed on you if this income is taxable and the IRS determines that it has not been reported.
City or town, state or province, country, and ZIP or foreign postal code	9 Payer made direct sales of $5,000 or more of consumer products to a buyer (recipient) for resale ▶ ☐	10 Crop insurance proceeds $	
	11	12	
Account number (see instructions)	13 Excess golden parachute payments $	14 Gross proceeds paid to an attorney $	
15a Section 409A deferrals $ / 15b Section 409A income $	16 State tax withheld $ $	17 State/Payer's state no.	18 State income $ $

Form **1099-MISC** (keep for your records) www.irs.gov/form1099misc Department of the Treasury - Internal Revenue Service

☐ CORRECTED (if checked)

PAYER'S name, street address, city or town, state or province, country, and ZIP or foreign postal code	**1** Gross distribution $ **2a** Taxable amount $	OMB No. 1545-0119 **2014** Form **1099-R**	**Distributions From Pensions, Annuities, Retirement or Profit-Sharing Plans, IRAs, Insurance Contracts, etc.**
	2b Taxable amount not determined ☐	Total distribution ☐	**Copy B** **Report this income on your federal tax return. If this form shows federal income tax withheld in box 4, attach this copy to your return.** This information is being furnished to the Internal Revenue Service.
PAYER'S federal identification number / RECIPIENT'S identification number	**3** Capital gain (included in box 2a) $	**4** Federal income tax withheld $	
RECIPIENT'S name	**5** Employee contributions /Designated Roth contributions or insurance premiums $	**6** Net unrealized appreciation in employer's securities $	
Street address (including apt. no.)	**7** Distribution code(s) — IRA/ SEP/ SIMPLE ☐	**8** Other $ %	
City or town, state or province, country, and ZIP or foreign postal code	**9a** Your percentage of total distribution %	**9b** Total employee contributions $	
10 Amount allocable to IRR within 5 years $ / **11** 1st year of desig. Roth contrib.	**12** State tax withheld $ $	**13** State/Payer's state no.	**14** State distribution $ $
Account number (see instructions)	**15** Local tax withheld $ $	**16** Name of locality	**17** Local distribution $ $

Form **1099-R** www.irs.gov/form1099r Department of the Treasury - Internal Revenue Service

Form **1116**

Department of the Treasury
Internal Revenue Service (99)

Foreign Tax Credit

(Individual, Estate, or Trust)

▶ **Attach to Form 1040, 1040NR, 1041, or 990-T.**

▶ **Information about Form 1116 and its separate instructions is at *www.irs.gov/form1116*.**

OMB No. 1545-0121

2013

Attachment
Sequence No. **19**

Name	**Identifying number** as shown on page 1 of your tax return

Use a separate Form 1116 for each category of income listed below. See **Categories of Income** in the instructions. Check only one box on each Form 1116. Report all amounts in U.S. dollars except where specified in Part II below.

a ☐ Passive category income
b ☐ General category income
c ☐ Section 901(j) income
d ☐ Certain income re-sourced by treaty
e ☐ Lump-sum distributions

f Resident of (name of country) ▶

Note: *If you paid taxes to only one foreign country or U.S. possession, use column A in Part I and line A in Part II. If you paid taxes to* ***more than one*** *foreign country or U.S. possession, use a separate column and line for each country or possession.*

Part I Taxable Income or Loss From Sources Outside the United States (for Category Checked Above)

		Foreign Country or U.S. Possession			Total
		A	B	C	(Add cols. A, B, and C.)
g	**Enter the name of the foreign country or U.S. possession** . . . . ▶				
1a	Gross income from sources within country shown above and of the type checked above (see instructions):				**1a**
b	Check if line 1a is compensation for personal services as an employee, your total compensation from all sources is $250,000 or more, and you used an alternative basis to determine its source (see instructions) . . ▶ ☐				
	Deductions and losses (*Caution:* *See instructions*):				
2	Expenses **definitely related** to the income on line 1a (attach statement)				
3	Pro rata share of other deductions **not definitely related:**				
a	Certain itemized deductions or standard deduction (see instructions)				
b	Other deductions (attach statement)				
c	Add lines 3a and 3b				
d	Gross foreign source income (see instructions) .				
e	Gross income from all sources (see instructions) .				
f	Divide line 3d by line 3e (see instructions)				
g	Multiply line 3c by line 3f				
4	Pro rata share of interest expense (see instructions):				
a	Home mortgage interest (use the Worksheet for Home Mortgage Interest in the instructions) . .				
b	Other interest expense				
5	Losses from foreign sources				
6	Add lines 2, 3g, 4a, 4b, and 5				**6**
7	Subtract line 6 from line 1a. Enter the result here and on line 15, page 2 . . . . ▶				**7**

Part II Foreign Taxes Paid or Accrued (see instructions)

Country	Credit is claimed for taxes (you must check one) (h) ☐ Paid (i) ☐ Accrued	Foreign taxes paid or accrued								
		In foreign currency				In U.S. dollars				
		Taxes withheld at source on:			**(n)** Other foreign taxes paid or accrued	Taxes withheld at source on:			**(r)** Other foreign taxes paid or accrued	**(s)** Total foreign taxes paid or accrued (add cols. (o) through (r))
	(j) Date paid or accrued	**(k)** Dividends	**(l)** Rents and royalties	**(m)** Interest		**(o)** Dividends	**(p)** Rents and royalties	**(q)** Interest		
A										
B										
C										

8 **Add lines A through C, column (s). Enter the total here and on line 9, page 2** . . . . ▶ **8**

For Paperwork Reduction Act Notice, see instructions. Cat. No. 11440U Form **1116** (2013)

Part III Figuring the Credit

9	Enter the amount from line 8. These are your total foreign taxes paid or accrued for the category of income checked above Part I . .	9	
10	Carryback or carryover (attach detailed computation)	10	
11	Add lines 9 and 10	11	
12	Reduction in foreign taxes (see instructions)	12	( )
13	Taxes reclassified under high tax kickout (see instructions) . .	13	
14	Combine lines 11, 12, and 13. This is the total amount of foreign taxes available for credit	14	
15	Enter the amount from line 7. This is your taxable income or (loss) from sources outside the United States (before adjustments) for the category of income checked above Part I (see instructions)	15	
16	Adjustments to line 15 (see instructions)	16	
17	Combine the amounts on lines 15 and 16. This is your net foreign source taxable income. (If the result is zero or less, you have no foreign tax credit for the category of income you checked above Part I. Skip lines 18 through 22. However, if you are filing more than one Form 1116, you must complete line 20.)	17	
18	**Individuals:** Enter the amount from Form 1040, line 41, or Form 1040NR, line 39. **Estates and trusts:** Enter your taxable income without the deduction for your exemption	18	
	Caution: *If you figured your tax using the lower rates on qualified dividends or capital gains, see instructions.*		
19	Divide line 17 by line 18. If line 17 is more than line 18, enter "1"	19	
20	**Individuals:** Enter the amount from Form 1040, line 44. If you are a nonresident alien, enter the amount from Form 1040NR, line 42. **Estates and trusts:** Enter the amount from Form 1041, Schedule G, line 1a, or the total of Form 990-T, lines 36 and 37	20	
	Caution: *If you are completing line 20 for separate category* **e** *(lump-sum distributions), see instructions.*		
21	Multiply line 20 by line 19 (maximum amount of credit)	21	
22	Enter the **smaller** of line 14 or line 21. If this is the only Form 1116 you are filing, skip lines 23 through 27 and enter this amount on line 28. Otherwise, complete the appropriate line in Part IV (see instructions) . . . . ▶	22	

Part IV Summary of Credits From Separate Parts III (see instructions)

23	Credit for taxes on passive category income	23	
24	Credit for taxes on general category income	24	
25	Credit for taxes on certain income re-sourced by treaty	25	
26	Credit for taxes on lump-sum distributions	26	
27	Add lines 23 through 26	27	
28	Enter the **smaller** of line 20 or line 27	28	
29	Reduction of credit for international boycott operations. See instructions for line 12	29	
30	Subtract line 29 from line 28. This is your **foreign tax credit.** Enter here and on Form 1040, line 47; Form 1040NR, line 45; Form 1041, Schedule G, line 2a; or Form 990-T, line 40a . . . . . . ▶	30	

Form **1116** (2013)

Form **2106** | **Employee Business Expenses** | OMB No. 1545-0074

Department of the Treasury
Internal Revenue Service (99)

▶ Attach to Form 1040 or Form 1040NR.
▶ Information about Form 2106 and its separate instructions is available at *www.irs.gov/form2106*.

2013
Attachment Sequence No. **129**

Your name	Occupation in which you incurred expenses	**Social security number**

Part I **Employee Business Expenses and Reimbursements**

Step 1 Enter Your Expenses		**Column A** Other Than Meals and Entertainment	**Column B** Meals and Entertainment
1 Vehicle expense from line 22 or line 29. (Rural mail carriers: See instructions.)	1		
2 Parking fees, tolls, and transportation, including train, bus, etc., that **did not** involve overnight travel or commuting to and from work	2		
3 Travel expense while away from home overnight, including lodging, airplane, car rental, etc. **Do not** include meals and entertainment	3		
4 Business expenses not included on lines 1 through 3. **Do not** include meals and entertainment	4		
5 Meals and entertainment expenses (see instructions)	5		
6 **Total expenses.** In Column A, add lines 1 through 4 and enter the result. In Column B, enter the amount from line 5	6		

Note: *If you were not reimbursed for any expenses in Step 1, skip line 7 and enter the amount from line 6 on line 8.*

Step 2 Enter Reimbursements Received From Your Employer for Expenses Listed in Step 1			
7 Enter reimbursements received from your employer that were **not** reported to you in box 1 of Form W-2. Include any reimbursements reported under code "L" in box 12 of your Form W-2 (see instructions)	7		

Step 3 Figure Expenses To Deduct on Schedule A (Form 1040 or Form 1040NR)			
8 Subtract line 7 from line 6. If zero or less, enter -0-. However, if line 7 is greater than line 6 in Column A, report the excess as income on Form 1040, line 7 (or on Form 1040NR, line 8)	8		
Note: *If* ***both columns*** *of line 8 are zero, you cannot deduct employee business expenses. Stop here and attach Form 2106 to your return.*			
9 In Column A, enter the amount from line 8. In Column B, multiply line 8 by 50% (.50). (Employees subject to Department of Transportation (DOT) hours of service limits: Multiply meal expenses incurred while away from home on business by 80% (.80) instead of 50%. For details, see instructions.)	9		

10 Add the amounts on line 9 of both columns and enter the total here. **Also, enter the total on Schedule A (Form 1040), line 21** (or on **Schedule A (Form 1040NR), line 7**). (Armed Forces reservists, qualified performing artists, fee-basis state or local government officials, and individuals with disabilities: See the instructions for special rules on where to enter the total.) ▶	10	

For Paperwork Reduction Act Notice, see your tax return instructions. Cat. No. 11700N Form **2106** (2013)

Part II Vehicle Expenses

Section A—General Information (You must complete this section if you are claiming vehicle expenses.)		**(a)** Vehicle 1	**(b)** Vehicle 2
11 Enter the date the vehicle was placed in service	11	/ /	/ /
12 Total miles the vehicle was driven during 2013	12	miles	miles
13 Business miles included on line 12	13	miles	miles
14 Percent of business use. Divide line 13 by line 12	14	%	%
15 Average daily roundtrip commuting distance	15	miles	miles
16 Commuting miles included on line 12	16	miles	miles
17 Other miles. Add lines 13 and 16 and subtract the total from line 12	17	miles	miles

18 Was your vehicle available for personal use during off-duty hours? ☐ **Yes** ☐ **No**

19 Do you (or your spouse) have another vehicle available for personal use? ☐ **Yes** ☐ **No**

20 Do you have evidence to support your deduction? ☐ **Yes** ☐ **No**

21 If "Yes," is the evidence written? ☐ **Yes** ☐ **No**

Section B—Standard Mileage Rate (See the instructions for Part II to find out whether to complete this section or Section C.)

22 Multiply line 13 by 56.5¢ (.565). Enter the result here and on line 1 . . . 22

Section C—Actual Expenses		**(a)** Vehicle 1	**(b)** Vehicle 2
23 Gasoline, oil, repairs, vehicle insurance, etc.	23		
24a Vehicle rentals	24a		
b Inclusion amount (see instructions)	24b		
c Subtract line 24b from line 24a	24c		
25 Value of employer-provided vehicle (applies only if 100% of annual lease value was included on Form W-2—see instructions)	25		
26 Add lines 23, 24c, and 25	26		
27 Multiply line 26 by the percentage on line 14	27		
28 Depreciation (see instructions)	28		
29 Add lines 27 and 28. Enter total here and on line 1	29		

Section D—Depreciation of Vehicles (Use this section only if you owned the vehicle and are completing Section C for the vehicle.)

		(a) Vehicle 1	**(b)** Vehicle 2
30 Enter cost or other basis (see instructions)	30		
31 Enter section 179 deduction and special allowance (see instructions)	31		
32 Multiply line 30 by line 14 (see instructions if you claimed the section 179 deduction or special allowance)	32		
33 Enter depreciation method and percentage (see instructions)	33		
34 Multiply line 32 by the percentage on line 33 (see instructions)	34		
35 Add lines 31 and 34	35		
36 Enter the applicable limit explained in the line 36 instructions	36		
37 Multiply line 36 by the percentage on line 14	37		
38 Enter the **smaller** of line 35 or line 37. If you skipped lines 36 and 37, enter the amount from line 35. Also enter this amount on line 28 above	38		

Form **2106** (2013)

Form **2441**

Child and Dependent Care Expenses

▶ Attach to Form 1040, Form 1040A, or Form 1040NR.

▶ Information about Form 2441 and its separate instructions is at *www.irs.gov/form2441.*

1040 / 1040A / 1040NR — 2441

OMB No. 1545-0074

2013

Attachment Sequence No. **21**

Department of the Treasury
Internal Revenue Service (99)

Name(s) shown on return | **Your social security number**

Part I **Persons or Organizations Who Provided the Care—**You **must** complete this part.
(If you have more than two care providers, see the instructions.)

1 (a) Care provider's name	(b) Address (number, street, apt. no., city, state, and ZIP code)	(c) Identifying number (SSN or EIN)	(d) Amount paid (see instructions)

Did you receive dependent care benefits?
No ▶ Complete only Part II below.
Yes ▶ Complete Part III on the back next.

Caution. If the care was provided in your home, you may owe employment taxes. If you do, you cannot file Form 1040A. For details, see the instructions for Form 1040, line 59a, or Form 1040NR, line 58a.

Part II **Credit for Child and Dependent Care Expenses**

2 Information about your **qualifying person(s).** If you have more than two qualifying persons, see the instructions.

(a) Qualifying person's name — First	Last	(b) Qualifying person's social security number	(c) **Qualified expenses** you incurred and paid in 2013 for the person listed in column (a)

3 Add the amounts in column (c) of line 2. **Do not** enter more than $3,000 for one qualifying person or $6,000 for two or more persons. If you completed Part III, enter the amount from line 31 3

4 Enter your **earned income.** See instructions 4

5 If married filing jointly, enter your spouse's earned income (if you or your spouse was a student or was disabled, see the instructions); **all others,** enter the amount from line 4 5

6 Enter the **smallest** of line 3, 4, or 5 6

7 Enter the amount from Form 1040, line 38; Form 1040A, line 22; or Form 1040NR, line 37. 7

8 Enter on line 8 the decimal amount shown below that applies to the amount on line 7

If line 7 is: Over	But not over	Decimal amount is	If line 7 is: Over	But not over	Decimal amount is
$0—	15,000	.35	$29,000—	31,000	.27
15,000—	17,000	.34	31,000—	33,000	.26
17,000—	19,000	.33	33,000—	35,000	.25
19,000—	21,000	.32	35,000—	37,000	.24
21,000—	23,000	.31	37,000—	39,000	.23
23,000—	25,000	.30	39,000—	41,000	.22
25,000—	27,000	.29	41,000—	43,000	.21
27,000—	29,000	.28	43,000—	No limit	.20

8 X .

9 Multiply line 6 by the decimal amount on line 8. If you paid 2012 expenses in 2013, see the instructions 9

10 Tax liability limit. Enter the amount from the Credit Limit Worksheet in the instructions. 10

11 **Credit for child and dependent care expenses.** Enter the **smaller** of line 9 or line 10 here and on Form 1040, line 48; Form 1040A, line 29; or Form 1040NR, line 46 11

For Paperwork Reduction Act Notice, see your tax return instructions. Cat. No. 11862M Form **2441** (2013)

Part III Dependent Care Benefits

12 Enter the total amount of **dependent care benefits** you received in 2013. Amounts you received as an employee should be shown in box 10 of your Form(s) W-2. **Do not** include amounts reported as wages in box 1 of Form(s) W-2. If you were self-employed or a partner, include amounts you received under a dependent care assistance program from your sole proprietorship or partnership		12	
13 Enter the amount, if any, you carried over from 2012 and used in 2013 during the grace period. See instructions		13	
14 Enter the amount, if any, you forfeited or carried forward to 2014. See instructions . . .		14	( )
15 Combine lines 12 through 14. See instructions		15	
16 Enter the total amount of **qualified expenses** incurred in 2013 for the care of the **qualifying person(s)** . . .	16		
17 Enter the **smaller** of line 15 or 16	17		
18 Enter your **earned income.** See instructions	18		
19 Enter the amount shown below that applies to you. • If married filing jointly, enter your spouse's earned income (if you or your spouse was a student or was disabled, see the instructions for line 5). • If married filing separately, see instructions. • All others, enter the amount from line 18.	19		
20 Enter the **smallest** of line 17, 18, or 19	20		
21 Enter $5,000 ($2,500 if married filing separately **and** you were required to enter your spouse's earned income on line 19)	21		
22 Is any amount on line 12 from your sole proprietorship or partnership? (Form 1040A filers go to line 25.) ☐ **No.** Enter -0-. ☐ **Yes.** Enter the amount here		22	
23 Subtract line 22 from line 15	23		
24 **Deductible benefits.** Enter the **smallest** of line 20, 21, or 22. Also, include this amount on the appropriate line(s) of your return. See instructions		24	
25 **Excluded benefits. Form 1040 and 1040NR filers:** If you checked "No" on line 22, enter the smaller of line 20 or 21. Otherwise, subtract line 24 from the smaller of line 20 or line 21. If zero or less, enter -0-. **Form 1040A filers:** Enter the **smaller** of line 20 or line 21 . .		25	
26 **Taxable benefits. Form 1040 and 1040NR filers:** Subtract line 25 from line 23. If zero or less, enter -0-. Also, include this amount on Form 1040, line 7, or Form 1040NR, line 8. On the dotted line next to Form 1040, line 7, or Form 1040NR, line 8, enter "DCB." **Form 1040A filers:** Subtract line 25 from line 15. Also, include this amount on Form 1040A, line 7. In the space to the left of line 7, enter "DCB"		26	

To claim the child and dependent care credit, complete lines 27 through 31 below.

27 Enter $3,000 ($6,000 if two or more qualifying persons)	27	
28 **Form 1040 and 1040NR filers:** Add lines 24 and 25. **Form 1040A filers:** Enter the amount from line 25	28	
29 Subtract line 28 from line 27. If zero or less, **stop.** You cannot take the credit. **Exception.** If you paid 2012 expenses in 2013, see the instructions for line 9	29	
30 Complete line 2 on the front of this form. **Do not** include in column (c) any benefits shown on line 28 above. Then, add the amounts in column (c) and enter the total here.	30	
31 Enter the **smaller** of line 29 or 30. Also, enter this amount on line 3 on the front of this form and complete lines 4 through 11	31	

Form **2441** (2013)

Form **3800**

Department of the Treasury
Internal Revenue Service (99)

General Business Credit

► Information about Form 3800 and its separate instructions is at *www.irs.gov/form3800.*
► You must attach all pages of Form 3800, pages 1, 2, and 3, to your tax return.

OMB No. 1545-0895

2013

Attachment Sequence No. **22**

Name(s) shown on return | **Identifying number**

Part I Current Year Credit for Credits Not Allowed Against Tentative Minimum Tax (TMT)

(See instructions and complete Part(s) III before Parts I and II)

1	General business credit from line 2 of all Parts III with box A checked			1	
2	Passive activity credits from line 2 of all Parts III with box B checked	2			
3	Enter the applicable passive activity credits allowed for 2013 (see instructions)			3	
4	Carryforward of general business credit to 2013. Enter the amount from line 2 of Part III with box C checked. See instructions for statement to attach			4	
5	Carryback of general business credit from 2014. Enter the amount from line 2 of Part III with box D checked (see instructions)			5	
6	Add lines 1, 3, 4, and 5			6	

Part II Allowable Credit

7	Regular tax before credits: • Individuals. Enter the amount from Form 1040, line 44, or Form 1040NR, line 42 • Corporations. Enter the amount from Form 1120, Schedule J, Part I, line 2; or the applicable line of your return • Estates and trusts. Enter the sum of the amounts from Form 1041, Schedule G, lines 1a and 1b; or the amount from the applicable line of your return			7	
8	Alternative minimum tax: • Individuals. Enter the amount from Form 6251, line 35 • Corporations. Enter the amount from Form 4626, line 14 • Estates and trusts. Enter the amount from Schedule I (Form 1041), line 56			8	
9	Add lines 7 and 8			9	
10a	Foreign tax credit	10a			
b	Certain allowable credits (see instructions)	10b			
c	Add lines 10a and 10b			10c	
11	**Net income tax.** Subtract line 10c from line 9. If zero, skip lines 12 through 15 and enter -0- on line 16			11	
12	**Net regular tax.** Subtract line 10c from line 7. If zero or less, enter -0-	12			
13	Enter 25% (.25) of the excess, if any, of line 12 over $25,000 (see instructions)	13			
14	Tentative minimum tax: • Individuals. Enter the amount from Form 6251, line 33 • Corporations. Enter the amount from Form 4626, line 12 • Estates and trusts. Enter the amount from Schedule I (Form 1041), line 54	14			
15	Enter the greater of line 13 or line 14			15	
16	Subtract line 15 from line 11. If zero or less, enter -0-			16	
17	Enter the **smaller** of line 6 or line 16 **C corporations:** See the line 17 instructions if there has been an ownership change, acquisition, or reorganization.			17	

For Paperwork Reduction Act Notice, see separate instructions. Cat. No. 12392F Form **3800** (2013)

Part II **Allowable Credit** *(Continued)*

Note. If you are not required to report any amounts on lines 22 or 24 below, skip lines 18 through 25 and enter -0- on line 26.

18	Multiply line 14 by 75% (.75) (see instructions)	18	
19	Enter the greater of line 13 or line 18	19	
20	Subtract line 19 from line 11. If zero or less, enter -0-	20	
21	Subtract line 17 from line 20. If zero or less, enter -0-	21	
22	Combine the amounts from line 3 of all Parts III with box A, C, or D checked	22	
23	Passive activity credit from line 3 of all Parts III with box B checked [23]		
24	Enter the applicable passive activity credit allowed for 2013 (see instructions)	24	
25	Add lines 22 and 24	25	
26	Empowerment zone and renewal community employment credit allowed. Enter the smaller of line 21 or line 25	26	
27	Subtract line 13 from line 11. If zero or less, enter -0-	27	
28	Add lines 17 and 26	28	
29	Subtract line 28 from line 27. If zero or less, enter -0-	29	
30	Enter the general business credit from line 5 of all Parts III with box A checked	30	
31	Reserved	31	
32	Passive activity credits from line 5 of all Parts III with box B checked [32]		
33	Enter the applicable passive activity credits allowed for 2013 (see instructions)	33	
34	Carryforward of business credit to 2013. Enter the amount from line 5 of Part III with box C checked and line 6 of Part III with box G checked. See instructions for statement to attach	34	
35	Carryback of business credit from 2014. Enter the amount from line 5 of Part III with box D checked (see instructions)	35	
36	Add lines 30, 33, 34, and 35	36	
37	Enter the **smaller** of line 29 or line 36	37	
38	**Credit allowed for the current year.** Add lines 28 and 37. Report the amount from line 38 (if smaller than the sum of Part I, line 6, and Part II, lines 25 and 36, see instructions) as indicated below or on the applicable line of your return: • Individuals. Form 1040, line 53, or Form 1040NR, line 50 • Corporations. Form 1120, Schedule J, Part I, line 5c • Estates and trusts. Form 1041, Schedule G, line 2b	38	

Form **3800** (2013)

Name(s) shown on return | Identifying number

Part III General Business Credits or Eligible Small Business Credits (see instructions)

Complete a separate Part III for each box checked below. (see instructions)

A ☐ General Business Credit From a Non-Passive Activity
B ☐ General Business Credit From a Passive Activity
C ☐ General Business Credit Carryforwards
D ☐ General Business Credit Carrybacks
E ☐ Reserved
F ☐ Reserved
G ☐ Eligible Small Business Credit Carryforwards
H ☐ Reserved

I If you are filing more than one Part III with box A or B checked, complete and attach first an additional Part III combining amounts from all Parts III with box A or B checked. Check here if this is the consolidated Part III . . . . . ▶ ☐

	(a) Description of credit **Note.** On any line where the credit is from more than one source, a separate Part III is needed for each pass-through entity.		(b) If claiming the credit from a pass-through entity, enter the EIN	(c) Enter the appropriate amount
1a	Investment (Form 3468, Part II only) (attach Form 3468)	1a		
b	Reserved	1b		
c	Increasing research activities (Form 6765)	1c		
d	Low-income housing (Form 8586, Part I only)	1d		
e	Disabled access (Form 8826) (see instructions for limitation)	1e		
f	Renewable electricity, refined coal, and Indian coal production (Form 8835)	1f		
g	Indian employment (Form 8845)	1g		
h	Orphan drug (Form 8820)	1h		
i	New markets (Form 8874)	1i		
j	Small employer pension plan startup costs (Form 8881) (see instructions for limitation)	1j		
k	Employer-provided child care facilities and services (Form 8882) (see instructions for limitation)	1k		
l	Biodiesel and renewable diesel fuels (attach Form 8864)	1l		
m	Low sulfur diesel fuel production (Form 8896)	1m		
n	Distilled spirits (Form 8906)	1n		
o	Nonconventional source fuel (Form 8907)	1o		
p	Energy efficient home (Form 8908)	1p		
q	Energy efficient appliance (Form 8909)	1q		
r	Alternative motor vehicle (Form 8910)	1r		
s	Alternative fuel vehicle refueling property (Form 8911)	1s		
t	Reserved	1t		
u	Mine rescue team training (Form 8923)	1u		
v	Agricultural chemicals security (Form 8931) (see instructions for limitation)	1v		
w	Employer differential wage payments (Form 8932)	1w		
x	Carbon dioxide sequestration (Form 8933)	1x		
y	Qualified plug-in electric drive motor vehicle (Form 8936)	1y		
z	Qualified plug-in electric vehicle (carryforward only)	1z		
aa	New hire retention (carryforward only)	1aa		
bb	General credits from an electing large partnership (Schedule K-1 (Form 1065-B))	1bb		
zz	Other	1zz		
2	Add lines 1a through 1zz and enter here and on the applicable line of Part I	2		
3	Enter the amount from Form 8844 here and on the applicable line of Part II	3		
4a	Investment (Form 3468, Part III) (attach Form 3468)	4a		
b	Work opportunity (Form 5884)	4b		
c	Biofuel producer (Form 6478)	4c		
d	Low-income housing (Form 8586, Part II)	4d		
e	Renewable electricity, refined coal, and Indian coal production (Form 8835)	4e		
f	Employer social security and Medicare taxes paid on certain employee tips (Form 8846)	4f		
g	Qualified railroad track maintenance (Form 8900)	4g		
h	Small employer health insurance premiums (Form 8941)	4h		
i	Reserved	4i		
j	Reserved	4j		
z	Other	4z		
5	Add lines 4a through 4z and enter here and on the applicable line of Part II	5		
6	Add lines 2, 3, and 5 and enter here and on the applicable line of Part II	6		

Form **3800** (2013)

Form **3903**

Department of the Treasury
Internal Revenue Service (99)

Moving Expenses

▶ **Information about Form 3903 and its instructions is available at *www.irs.gov/form3903*.**

▶ **Attach to Form 1040 or Form 1040NR.**

OMB No. 1545-0074

2013

Attachment Sequence No. **170**

Name(s) shown on return | **Your social security number**

Before you begin: ✓ See the **Distance Test** and **Time Test** in the instructions to find out if you can deduct your moving expenses.

✓ See **Members of the Armed Forces** in the instructions, if applicable.

1	Transportation and storage of household goods and personal effects (see instructions) . . .	1	
2	Travel (including lodging) from your old home to your new home (see instructions). **Do not** include the cost of meals	2	
3	Add lines 1 and 2	3	
4	Enter the total amount your employer paid you for the expenses listed on lines 1 and 2 that is **not** included in box 1 of your Form W-2 (wages). This amount should be shown in box 12 of your Form W-2 with code **P**	4	
5	Is line 3 **more than** line 4? ☐ **No.** You **cannot** deduct your moving expenses. If line 3 is less than line 4, subtract line 3 from line 4 and include the result on Form 1040, line 7, or Form 1040NR, line 8. ☐ **Yes.** Subtract line 4 from line 3. Enter the result here and on Form 1040, line 26, or Form 1040NR, line 26. This is your **moving expense deduction**	5	

For Paperwork Reduction Act Notice, see your tax return instructions. Cat. No. 12490K Form **3903** (2013)

☐ CORRECTED (if checked)

TRANSFEROR'S name, street address, city or town, state or province, country, and ZIP or foreign postal code		1 Date option granted 2 Date option exercised	OMB No. 1545-2129 **Form 3921** (Rev. August 2013)
TRANSFEROR'S federal identification number	EMPLOYEE'S identification number	3 Exercise price per share $	4 Fair market value per share on exercise date $
EMPLOYEE'S name		5 No. of shares transferred	
Street address (including apt. no.)		6 If other than TRANSFEROR, name, address, and EIN of corporation whose stock is being transferred	
City or town, state or province, country, and ZIP or foreign postal code			
Account number (see instructions)			

Exercise of an Incentive Stock Option Under Section 422(b)

Copy B

For Employee

This is important tax information and is being furnished to the Internal Revenue Service. If you are required to file a return, a negligence penalty or other sanction may be imposed on you if this item is required to be reported and the IRS determines that it has not been reported.

Form **3921** (Rev. August 2013) (keep for your records) www.irs.gov/form3921 Department of the Treasury - Internal Revenue Service

Form **4562**

Department of the Treasury Internal Revenue Service (99)

Depreciation and Amortization
(Including Information on Listed Property)

▶ See separate instructions. ▶ Attach to your tax return.

OMB No. 1545-0172

2013

Attachment Sequence No. **179**

Name(s) shown on return	Business or activity to which this form relates	Identifying number

Part I **Election To Expense Certain Property Under Section 179**
Note: *If you have any listed property, complete Part V before you complete Part I.*

1	Maximum amount (see instructions)	1	
2	Total cost of section 179 property placed in service (see instructions)	2	
3	Threshold cost of section 179 property before reduction in limitation (see instructions)	3	
4	Reduction in limitation. Subtract line 3 from line 2. If zero or less, enter -0-	4	
5	Dollar limitation for tax year. Subtract line 4 from line 1. If zero or less, enter -0-. If married filing separately, see instructions	5	

6	(a) Description of property	(b) Cost (business use only)	(c) Elected cost

7	Listed property. Enter the amount from line 29	7	
8	Total elected cost of section 179 property. Add amounts in column (c), lines 6 and 7	8	
9	Tentative deduction. Enter the **smaller** of line 5 or line 8	9	
10	Carryover of disallowed deduction from line 13 of your 2012 Form 4562	10	
11	Business income limitation. Enter the smaller of business income (not less than zero) or line 5 (see instructions)	11	
12	Section 179 expense deduction. Add lines 9 and 10, but do not enter more than line 11	12	
13	Carryover of disallowed deduction to 2014. Add lines 9 and 10, less line 12 ▶	13	

Note: *Do not use Part II or Part III below for listed property. Instead, use Part V.*

Part II **Special Depreciation Allowance and Other Depreciation (Do not** include listed property.) (See instructions.)

14	Special depreciation allowance for qualified property (other than listed property) placed in service during the tax year (see instructions)	14	
15	Property subject to section 168(f)(1) election	15	
16	Other depreciation (including ACRS)	16	

Part III **MACRS Depreciation (Do not** include listed property.) (See instructions.)

Section A

17	MACRS deductions for assets placed in service in tax years beginning before 2013	17	
18	If you are electing to group any assets placed in service during the tax year into one or more general asset accounts, check here ▶ ☐		

Section B—Assets Placed in Service During 2013 Tax Year Using the General Depreciation System

(a) Classification of property	(b) Month and year placed in service	(c) Basis for depreciation (business/investment use only—see instructions)	(d) Recovery period	(e) Convention	(f) Method	(g) Depreciation deduction
19a 3-year property						
b 5-year property						
c 7-year property						
d 10-year property						
e 15-year property						
f 20-year property						
g 25-year property			25 yrs.		S/L	
h Residential rental property			27.5 yrs.	MM	S/L	
			27.5 yrs.	MM	S/L	
i Nonresidential real property			39 yrs.	MM	S/L	
				MM	S/L	

Section C—Assets Placed in Service During 2013 Tax Year Using the Alternative Depreciation System

(a) Classification of property	(b)	(c)	(d)	(e)	(f)	(g)
20a Class life					S/L	
b 12-year			12 yrs.		S/L	
c 40-year			40 yrs.	MM	S/L	

Part IV **Summary** (See instructions.)

21	Listed property. Enter amount from line 28	21	
22	**Total.** Add amounts from line 12, lines 14 through 17, lines 19 and 20 in column (g), and line 21. Enter here and on the appropriate lines of your return. Partnerships and S corporations—see instructions	22	
23	For assets shown above and placed in service during the current year, enter the portion of the basis attributable to section 263A costs	23	

For Paperwork Reduction Act Notice, see separate instructions. Cat. No. 12906N Form **4562** (2013)

Part V **Listed Property** (Include automobiles, certain other vehicles, certain computers, and property used for entertainment, recreation, or amusement.)

Note: *For any vehicle for which you are using the standard mileage rate or deducting lease expense, complete* ***only*** *24a, 24b, columns (a) through (c) of Section A, all of Section B, and Section C if applicable.*

Section A—Depreciation and Other Information (Caution: *See the instructions for limits for passenger automobiles.***)**

24a Do you have evidence to support the business/investment use claimed? ☐ **Yes** ☐ **No** **24b** If "Yes," is the evidence written? ☐ **Yes** ☐ **No**

(a) Type of property (list vehicles first)	(b) Date placed in service	(c) Business/ investment use percentage	(d) Cost or other basis	(e) Basis for depreciation (business/investment use only)	(f) Recovery period	(g) Method/ Convention	(h) Depreciation deduction	(i) Elected section 179 cost
25 Special depreciation allowance for qualified listed property placed in service during the tax year and used more than 50% in a qualified business use (see instructions) .						**25**		
26 Property used more than 50% in a qualified business use:								
		%						
		%						
		%						
27 Property used 50% or less in a qualified business use:								
		%				S/L –		
		%				S/L –		
		%				S/L –		
28 Add amounts in column (h), lines 25 through 27. Enter here and on line 21, page 1 .						**28**		
29 Add amounts in column (i), line 26. Enter here and on line 7, page 1							**29**	

Section B—Information on Use of Vehicles

Complete this section for vehicles used by a sole proprietor, partner, or other "more than 5% owner," or related person. If you provided vehicles to your employees, first answer the questions in Section C to see if you meet an exception to completing this section for those vehicles.

	(a) Vehicle 1		(b) Vehicle 2		(c) Vehicle 3		(d) Vehicle 4		(e) Vehicle 5		(f) Vehicle 6	
30 Total business/investment miles driven during the year (**do not** include commuting miles) .												
31 Total commuting miles driven during the year												
32 Total other personal (noncommuting) miles driven												
33 Total miles driven during the year. Add lines 30 through 32												
	Yes	**No**	**Yes**	**No**	**Yes**	**No**	**Yes**	**No**	**Yes**	**No**	**Yes**	**No**
34 Was the vehicle available for personal use during off-duty hours?												
35 Was the vehicle used primarily by a more than 5% owner or related person? . .												
36 Is another vehicle available for personal use?												

Section C—Questions for Employers Who Provide Vehicles for Use by Their Employees

Answer these questions to determine if you meet an exception to completing Section B for vehicles used by employees who **are not** more than 5% owners or related persons (see instructions).

	Yes	**No**
37 Do you maintain a written policy statement that prohibits all personal use of vehicles, including commuting, by your employees?		
38 Do you maintain a written policy statement that prohibits personal use of vehicles, except commuting, by your employees? See the instructions for vehicles used by corporate officers, directors, or 1% or more owners . .		
39 Do you treat all use of vehicles by employees as personal use?		
40 Do you provide more than five vehicles to your employees, obtain information from your employees about the use of the vehicles, and retain the information received?		
41 Do you meet the requirements concerning qualified automobile demonstration use? (See instructions.) . . .		

Note: *If your answer to 37, 38, 39, 40, or 41 is "Yes," do not complete Section B for the covered vehicles.*

Part VI **Amortization**

(a) Description of costs	(b) Date amortization begins	(c) Amortizable amount	(d) Code section	(e) Amortization period or percentage	(f) Amortization for this year
42 Amortization of costs that begins during your 2013 tax year (see instructions):					
43 Amortization of costs that began before your 2013 tax year				**43**	
44 **Total.** Add amounts in column (f). See the instructions for where to report				**44**	

Form **4562** (2013)

Form **4684** Department of the Treasury Internal Revenue Service	**Casualties and Thefts** ▶ **Information about Form 4684 and its separate instructions is at *www.irs.gov/form4684.*** ▶ **Attach to your tax return.** ▶ **Use a separate Form 4684 for each casualty or theft.**	OMB No. 1545-0177 **2013** Attachment Sequence No. **26**

Name(s) shown on tax return | **Identifying number**

SECTION A—Personal Use Property (Use this section to report casualties and thefts of property **not** used in a trade or business or for income-producing purposes.)

1 Description of properties (show type, location, and date acquired for each property). Use a separate line for each property lost or damaged from the same casualty or theft.

Property **A** ____________________

Property **B** ____________________

Property **C** ____________________

Property **D** ____________________

		Properties A	Properties B	Properties C	Properties D
2 Cost or other basis of each property	2				
3 Insurance or other reimbursement (whether or not you filed a claim) (see instructions)	3				
Note: *If line 2 is **more** than line 3, skip line 4.*					
4 Gain from casualty or theft. If line 3 is **more** than line 2, enter the difference here and skip lines 5 through 9 for that column. See instructions if line 3 includes insurance or other reimbursement you did not claim, or you received payment for your loss in a later tax year	4				
5 Fair market value **before** casualty or theft	5				
6 Fair market value **after** casualty or theft	6				
7 Subtract line 6 from line 5	7				
8 Enter the **smaller** of line 2 or line 7	8				
9 Subtract line 3 from line 8. If zero or less, enter -0-	9				

10 Casualty or theft loss. Add the amounts on line 9 in columns A through D	10	
11 Enter the **smaller** of line 10 or $100	11	
12 Subtract line 11 from line 10	12	
Caution: *Use only one Form 4684 for lines 13 through 18.*		
13 Add the amounts on line 12 of all Forms 4684	13	
14 Add the amounts on line 4 of all Forms 4684	14	
15 • If line 14 is **more** than line 13, enter the difference here and on Schedule D. **Do not** complete the rest of this section (see instructions). • If line 14 is **less** than line 13, enter -0- here and go to line 16. • If line 14 is **equal** to line 13, enter -0- here. **Do not** complete the rest of this section.	15	
16 If line 14 is **less** than line 13, enter the difference	16	
17 Enter 10% of your adjusted gross income from Form 1040, line 38, or Form 1040NR, line 37. Estates and trusts, see instructions	17	
18 Subtract line 17 from line 16. If zero or less, enter -0-. Also enter the result on Schedule A (Form 1040), line 20, or Form 1040NR, Schedule A, line 6. Estates and trusts, enter the result on the "Other deductions" line of your tax return	18	

For Paperwork Reduction Act Notice, see instructions. Cat. No. 12997O Form **4684** (2013)

Name(s) shown on tax return. Do not enter name and identifying number if shown on other side. | **Identifying number**

SECTION B—Business and Income-Producing Property

Part I Casualty or Theft Gain or Loss (Use a separate Part I for each casualty or theft.)

19 Description of properties (show type, location, and date acquired for each property). Use a separate line for each property lost or damaged from the same casualty or theft. **See instructions if claiming a loss due to a Ponzi-type investment scheme and Section C is not completed.**

Property **A** ______

Property **B** ______

Property **C** ______

Property **D** ______

		Properties A	Properties B	Properties C	Properties D
20 Cost or adjusted basis of each property	20				
21 Insurance or other reimbursement (whether or not you filed a claim). See the instructions for line 3	21				
Note: *If line 20 is **more** than line 21, skip line 22.*					
22 Gain from casualty or theft. If line 21 is **more** than line 20, enter the difference here and on line 29 or line 34, column (c), except as provided in the instructions for line 33. Also, skip lines 23 through 27 for that column. See the instructions for line 4 if line 21 includes insurance or other reimbursement you did not claim, or you received payment for your loss in a later tax year	22				
23 Fair market value **before** casualty or theft	23				
24 Fair market value **after** casualty or theft	24				
25 Subtract line 24 from line 23	25				
26 Enter the **smaller** of line 20 or line 25	26				
Note: *If the property was totally destroyed by casualty or lost from theft, enter on line 26 the amount from line 20.*					
27 Subtract line 21 from line 26. If zero or less, enter -0-	27				

28 Casualty or theft loss. Add the amounts on line 27. Enter the total here and on line 29 **or** line 34 (see instructions) | 28 |

Part II Summary of Gains and Losses (from separate Parts I)

(a) Identify casualty or theft		(b) Losses from casualties or thefts: (i) Trade, business, rental or royalty property	(b) Losses from casualties or thefts: (ii) Income-producing and employee property	(c) Gains from casualties or thefts includible in income
Casualty or Theft of Property Held One Year or Less				
29		( )	( )	
		( )	( )	
30 Totals. Add the amounts on line 29	30	( )	( )	
31 Combine line 30, columns (b)(i) and (c). Enter the net gain or (loss) here and on Form 4797, line 14. If Form 4797 is not otherwise required, see instructions			31	
32 Enter the amount from line 30, column (b)(ii) here. Individuals, enter the amount from income-producing property on Schedule A (Form 1040), line 28, or Form 1040NR, Schedule A, line 14, and enter the amount from property used as an employee on Schedule A (Form 1040), line 23, or Form 1040NR, Schedule A, line 9. Estates and trusts, partnerships, and S corporations, see instructions			32	
Casualty or Theft of Property Held More Than One Year				
33 Casualty or theft gains from Form 4797, line 32			33	
34		( )	( )	
		( )	( )	
35 Total losses. Add amounts on line 34, columns (b)(i) and (b)(ii)	35	( )	( )	
36 Total gains. Add lines 33 and 34, column (c)			36	
37 Add amounts on line 35, columns (b)(i) and (b)(ii)			37	
38 If the loss on line 37 is **more** than the gain on line 36:				
a Combine line 35, column (b)(i) and line 36, and enter the net gain or (loss) here. Partnerships (except electing large partnerships) and S corporations, see the note below. All others, enter this amount on Form 4797, line 14. If Form 4797 is not otherwise required, see instructions			38a	
b Enter the amount from line 35, column (b)(ii) here. Individuals, enter the amount from income-producing property on Schedule A (Form 1040), line 28, or Form 1040NR, Schedule A, line 14, and enter the amount from property used as an employee on Schedule A (Form 1040), line 23, or Form 1040NR, Schedule A, line 9. Estates and trusts, enter on the "Other deductions" line of your tax return. Partnerships (except electing large partnerships) and S corporations, see the note below. Electing large partnerships, enter on Form 1065-B, Part II, line 11			38b	
39 If the loss on line 37 is **less** than or **equal** to the gain on line 36, combine lines 36 and 37 and enter here. Partnerships (except electing large partnerships), see the note below. All others, enter this amount on Form 4797, line 3			39	

Note: *Partnerships, enter the amount from line 38a, 38b, or line 39 on Form 1065, Schedule K, line 11. S corporations, enter the amount from line 38a or 38b on Form 1120S, Schedule K, line 10.*

Form **4684** (2013)

Form **4797**

Department of the Treasury
Internal Revenue Service

Sales of Business Property

(Also Involuntary Conversions and Recapture Amounts Under Sections 179 and 280F(b)(2))

► **Attach to your tax return.**

► **Information about Form 4797 and its separate instructions is at *www.irs.gov/form4797*.**

OMB No. 1545-0184

2013

Attachment Sequence No. **27**

Name(s) shown on return	**Identifying number**

1	Enter the gross proceeds from sales or exchanges reported to you for 2013 on Form(s) 1099-B or 1099-S (or substitute statement) that you are including on line 2, 10, or 20 (see instructions)	1	

Part I **Sales or Exchanges of Property Used in a Trade or Business and Involuntary Conversions From Other Than Casualty or Theft—Most Property Held More Than 1 Year** (see instructions)

2	**(a)** Description of property	**(b)** Date acquired (mo., day, yr.)	**(c)** Date sold (mo., day, yr.)	**(d)** Gross sales price	**(e)** Depreciation allowed or allowable since acquisition	**(f)** Cost or other basis, plus improvements and expense of sale	**(g) Gain or (loss)** Subtract (f) from the sum of (d) and (e)

3	Gain, if any, from Form 4684, line 39	3	
4	Section 1231 gain from installment sales from Form 6252, line 26 or 37	4	
5	Section 1231 gain or (loss) from like-kind exchanges from Form 8824	5	
6	Gain, if any, from line 32, from other than casualty or theft.	6	
7	Combine lines 2 through 6. Enter the gain or (loss) here and on the appropriate line as follows:	7	

Partnerships (except electing large partnerships) and S corporations. Report the gain or (loss) following the instructions for Form 1065, Schedule K, line 10, or Form 1120S, Schedule K, line 9. Skip lines 8, 9, 11, and 12 below.

Individuals, partners, S corporation shareholders, and all others. If line 7 is zero or a loss, enter the amount from line 7 on line 11 below and skip lines 8 and 9. If line 7 is a gain and you did not have any prior year section 1231 losses, or they were recaptured in an earlier year, enter the gain from line 7 as a long-term capital gain on the Schedule D filed with your return and skip lines 8, 9, 11, and 12 below.

8	Nonrecaptured net section 1231 losses from prior years (see instructions)	8	
9	Subtract line 8 from line 7. If zero or less, enter -0-. If line 9 is zero, enter the gain from line 7 on line 12 below. If line 9 is more than zero, enter the amount from line 8 on line 12 below and enter the gain from line 9 as a long-term capital gain on the Schedule D filed with your return (see instructions)	9	

Part II **Ordinary Gains and Losses** (see instructions)

10 Ordinary gains and losses not included on lines 11 through 16 (include property held 1 year or less):

11	Loss, if any, from line 7	11	( )
12	Gain, if any, from line 7 or amount from line 8, if applicable	12	
13	Gain, if any, from line 31	13	
14	Net gain or (loss) from Form 4684, lines 31 and 38a	14	
15	Ordinary gain from installment sales from Form 6252, line 25 or 36	15	
16	Ordinary gain or (loss) from like-kind exchanges from Form 8824.	16	
17	Combine lines 10 through 16	17	
18	For all except individual returns, enter the amount from line 17 on the appropriate line of your return and skip lines a and b below. For individual returns, complete lines a and b below:		
a	If the loss on line 11 includes a loss from Form 4684, line 35, column (b)(ii), enter that part of the loss here. Enter the part of the loss from income-producing property on Schedule A (Form 1040), line 28, and the part of the loss from property used as an employee on Schedule A (Form 1040), line 23. Identify as from "Form 4797, line 18a." See instructions . .	18a	
b	Redetermine the gain or (loss) on line 17 excluding the loss, if any, on line 18a. Enter here and on Form 1040, line 14	18b	

For Paperwork Reduction Act Notice, see separate instructions. Cat. No. 13086I Form **4797** (2013)

Part III Gain From Disposition of Property Under Sections 1245, 1250, 1252, 1254, and 1255 (see instructions)

19	(a) Description of section 1245, 1250, 1252, 1254, or 1255 property:	(b) Date acquired (mo., day, yr.)	(c) Date sold (mo., day, yr.)
A			
B			
C			
D			

	These columns relate to the properties on lines 19A through 19D. ▶		Property A	Property B	Property C	Property D
20	Gross sales price (**Note:** *See line 1 before completing.*)	20				
21	Cost or other basis plus expense of sale	21				
22	Depreciation (or depletion) allowed or allowable	22				
23	Adjusted basis. Subtract line 22 from line 21	23				
24	Total gain. Subtract line 23 from line 20	24				
25	**If section 1245 property:**					
a	Depreciation allowed or allowable from line 22	25a				
b	Enter the **smaller** of line 24 or 25a	25b				
26	**If section 1250 property:** If straight line depreciation was used, enter -0- on line 26g, except for a corporation subject to section 291.					
a	Additional depreciation after 1975 (see instructions)	26a				
b	Applicable percentage multiplied by the **smaller** of line 24 or line 26a (see instructions)	26b				
c	Subtract line 26a from line 24. If residential rental property **or** line 24 is not more than line 26a, skip lines 26d and 26e	26c				
d	Additional depreciation after 1969 and before 1976	26d				
e	Enter the **smaller** of line 26c or 26d	26e				
f	Section 291 amount (corporations only)	26f				
g	Add lines 26b, 26e, and 26f	26g				
27	**If section 1252 property:** Skip this section if you did not dispose of farmland or if this form is being completed for a partnership (other than an electing large partnership).					
a	Soil, water, and land clearing expenses	27a				
b	Line 27a multiplied by applicable percentage (see instructions)	27b				
c	Enter the **smaller** of line 24 or 27b	27c				
28	**If section 1254 property:**					
a	Intangible drilling and development costs, expenditures for development of mines and other natural deposits, mining exploration costs, and depletion (see instructions)	28a				
b	Enter the **smaller** of line 24 or 28a	28b				
29	**If section 1255 property:**					
a	Applicable percentage of payments excluded from income under section 126 (see instructions)	29a				
b	Enter the **smaller** of line 24 or 29a (see instructions)	29b				

Summary of Part III Gains. Complete property columns A through D through line 29b before going to line 30.

30	Total gains for all properties. Add property columns A through D, line 24	30	
31	Add property columns A through D, lines 25b, 26g, 27c, 28b, and 29b. Enter here and on line 13	31	
32	Subtract line 31 from line 30. Enter the portion from casualty or theft on Form 4684, line 33. Enter the portion from other than casualty or theft on Form 4797, line 6	32	

Part IV Recapture Amounts Under Sections 179 and 280F(b)(2) When Business Use Drops to 50% or Less (see instructions)

			(a) Section 179	(b) Section 280F(b)(2)
33	Section 179 expense deduction or depreciation allowable in prior years	33		
34	Recomputed depreciation (see instructions)	34		
35	Recapture amount. Subtract line 34 from line 33. See the instructions for where to report	35		

Form **4797** (2013)

Form **4868**

Department of the Treasury
Internal Revenue Service (99)

Application for Automatic Extension of Time To File U.S. Individual Income Tax Return

▶ **Information about Form 4868 and its instructions is available at *www.irs.gov/form4868*.**

OMB No. 1545-0074

2013

There are three ways to request an automatic extension of time to file a U.S. individual income tax return.

1. You can file Form 4868 and pay all or part of your estimated income tax due using the Electronic Federal Tax Payment System (EFTPS) or by using a credit or debit card.
2. You can file Form 4868 electronically by accessing IRS *e-file* using your home computer or by using a tax professional who uses *e-file.*
3. You can file a paper Form 4868.

It's Convenient, Safe, and Secure

IRS *e-file* is the IRS's electronic filing program. You can get an automatic extension of time to file your tax return by filing Form 4868 electronically. You will receive an electronic acknowledgment once you complete the transaction. Keep it with your records. Do not mail in Form 4868 if you file electronically, unless you are making a payment with a check or money order (see page 3).

Complete Form 4868 to use as a worksheet. If you think you may owe tax when you file your return, you will need to estimate your total tax liability and subtract how much you have already paid (lines 4, 5, and 6 below).

Several companies offer free e-filing of Form 4868 through the Free File program. For more details, go to IRS.gov and click on *freefile.*

Pay Electronically

You **do not** need to submit a paper Form 4868 if you file it with a payment using our electronic payment options. Your extension will be automatically processed when you pay part or all of your estimated income tax electronically. You can pay online or by phone (see page 3).

E-file Using Your Personal Computer or Through a Tax Professional

Refer to your tax software package or tax preparer for ways to file electronically. Be sure to have a copy of your 2012 tax return—you will be asked to provide information from the return for taxpayer verification. If you wish to make a payment, you can pay by electronic funds withdrawal or send your check or money order to the address shown in the middle column under *Where To File a Paper Form 4868* (see page 4).

File a Paper Form 4868

If you wish to file on paper instead of electronically, fill in the Form 4868 below and mail it to the address shown on page 4.

For information on using a private delivery service, see page 4.

Note. If you are a fiscal year taxpayer, you must file a paper Form 4868.

General Instructions

Purpose of Form

Use Form 4868 to apply for 6 more months (4 if "out of the country" (defined on page 2) and a U.S. citizen or resident) to file Form 1040, 1040A, 1040EZ, 1040NR, 1040NR-EZ, 1040-PR, or 1040-SS.

Gift and generation-skipping transfer (GST) tax return (Form 709). An extension of time to file your 2013 calendar year income tax return also extends the time to file Form 709 for 2013. However, it does not extend the time to pay any gift and GST tax you may owe for 2013. To make a payment of gift and GST tax, see Form 8892. If you do not pay the amount due by the regular due date for Form 709, you will owe interest and may also be charged penalties. If the donor died during 2013, see the instructions for Forms 709 and 8892.

Qualifying for the Extension

To get the extra time you must:

1. Properly estimate your 2013 tax liability using the information available to you,
2. Enter your total tax liability on line 4 of Form 4868, and
3. File Form 4868 by the regular due date of your return.

CAUTION *Although you are not required to make a payment of the tax you estimate as due, Form 4868 does not extend the time to pay taxes. If you do not pay the amount due by the regular due date, you will owe interest. You may also be charged penalties. For more details, see* Interest *and* Late Payment Penalty *on page 2. Any remittance you make with your application for extension will be treated as a payment of tax.*

You do not have to explain why you are asking for the extension. We will contact you only if your request is denied.

Do not file Form 4868 if you want the IRS to figure your tax or you are under a court order to file your return by the regular due date.

▼ DETACH HERE ▼

Form **4868**

Department of the Treasury
Internal Revenue Service (99)

Application for Automatic Extension of Time To File U.S. Individual Income Tax Return

For calendar year 2013, or other tax year beginning ______, 2013, ending ______, 20 ___.

OMB No. 1545-0074

2013

Part I Identification

1 Your name(s) (see instructions)

Address (see instructions)

City, town, or post office	State	ZIP Code

2 Your social security number	3 Spouse's social security number

Part II Individual Income Tax

4	Estimate of total tax liability for 2013 . .	$
5	Total 2013 payments	
6	**Balance due.** Subtract line 5 from line 4 (see instructions)	
7	Amount you are paying (see instructions).... ▶	
8	Check here if you are "out of the country" and a U.S. citizen or resident (see instructions) . . . . ▶	☐
9	Check here if you file Form 1040NR or 1040NR-EZ and did not receive wages as an employee subject to U.S. income tax withholding . . . . ▶	☐

For Privacy Act and Paperwork Reduction Act Notice, see page 4. Cat. No. 13141W Form **4868** (2013)

Form **4952**

Department of the Treasury
Internal Revenue Service (99)

Investment Interest Expense Deduction

► Information about Form 4952 and its instructions is at *www.irs.gov/form4952.*

► Attach to your tax return.

OMB No. 1545-0191

2013

Attachment
Sequence No. **51**

Name(s) shown on return	Identifying number

Part I Total Investment Interest Expense

1	Investment interest expense paid or accrued in 2013 (see instructions)	1	
2	Disallowed investment interest expense from 2012 Form 4952, line 7	2	
3	**Total investment interest expense.** Add lines 1 and 2	3	

Part II Net Investment Income

4a	Gross income from property held for investment (excluding any net gain from the disposition of property held for investment) . . .	4a			
b	Qualified dividends included on line 4a	4b			
c	Subtract line 4b from line 4a			4c	
d	Net gain from the disposition of property held for investment . .	4d			
e	Enter the **smaller** of line 4d or your net capital gain from the disposition of property held for investment (see instructions) .	4e			
f	Subtract line 4e from line 4d			4f	
g	Enter the amount from lines 4b and 4e that you elect to include in investment income (see instructions)			4g	
h	Investment income. Add lines 4c, 4f, and 4g			4h	
5	Investment expenses (see instructions)			5	
6	**Net investment income.** Subtract line 5 from line 4h. If zero or less, enter -0-			6	

Part III Investment Interest Expense Deduction

7	Disallowed investment interest expense to be carried forward to 2014. Subtract line 6 from line 3. If zero or less, enter -0-	7	
8	**Investment interest expense deduction.** Enter the **smaller** of line 3 or 6. See instructions . .	8	

For Paperwork Reduction Act Notice, see page 4. Cat. No. 13177Y Form **4952** (2013)

☐ CORRECTED (if checked)

TRUSTEE'S or ISSUER'S name, street address, city or town, state or province, country, and ZIP or foreign postal code	1 IRA contributions (other than amounts in boxes 2-4, 8-10, 13a, and 14a) $	OMB No. 1545-0747 **2014** Form **5498**	**IRA Contribution Information**
	2 Rollover contributions $		
	3 Roth IRA conversion amount $	4 Recharacterized contributions $	**Copy B**
TRUSTEE'S or ISSUER'S federal identification no. / PARTICIPANT'S social security number	5 Fair market value of account $	6 Life insurance cost included in box 1 $	**For Participant**
PARTICIPANT'S name	7 IRA ☐ SEP ☐ SIMPLE ☐ Roth IRA ☐		This information is being furnished to the Internal Revenue Service.
	8 SEP contributions $	9 SIMPLE contributions $	
Street address (including apt. no.)	10 Roth IRA contributions $	11 If checked, required minimum distribution for 2015 ☐	
	12a RMD date	12b RMD amount $	
City or town, state or province, country, and ZIP or foreign postal code	13a Postponed contribution $	13b Year / 13c Code	
	14a Repayments $	14b Code	
Account number (see instructions)	15a FMV of certain specified assets $	15b Code(s)	

Form **5498** (keep for your records) www.irs.gov/form5498 Department of the Treasury - Internal Revenue Service

Form **5695**

Department of the Treasury
Internal Revenue Service

Residential Energy Credits

▶ Information about Form 5695 and its instructions is at *www.irs.gov/form5695*.
▶ Attach to Form 1040 or Form 1040NR.

OMB No. 1545-0074

2013

Attachment Sequence No. **158**

Name(s) shown on return | **Your social security number**

Part I **Residential Energy Efficient Property Credit** (See instructions before completing this part.)

Note. *Skip lines 1 through 11 if you only have a* ***credit carryforward from 2012.***

1	Qualified solar electric property costs	1	
2	Qualified solar water heating property costs	2	
3	Qualified small wind energy property costs	3	
4	Qualified geothermal heat pump property costs	4	
5	Add lines 1 through 4	5	
6	Multiply line 5 by 30% (.30)	6	
7a	Qualified fuel cell property. Was qualified fuel cell property installed on or in connection with your main home located in the United States? (See instructions) ▶	7a	☐ Yes ☐ No
	Caution: *If you checked the "No" box, you cannot take a credit for qualified fuel cell property. Skip lines 7b through 11.*		
b	Print the complete address of the main home where you installed the fuel cell property.		
	Number and street — Unit No.		
	City, State, and ZIP code		
8	Qualified fuel cell property costs 8		
9	Multiply line 8 by 30% (.30) 9		
10	Kilowatt capacity of property on line 8 above ▶ ______ . x $1,000 10		
11	Enter the smaller of line 9 or line 10	11	
12	Credit carryforward from 2012. Enter the amount, if any, from your 2012 Form 5695, line 18 .	12	
13	Add lines 6, 11, and 12	13	
14	Limitation based on tax liability. Enter the amount from the Residential Energy Efficient Property Credit Limit Worksheet (see instructions)	14	
15	**Residential energy efficient property credit.** Enter the smaller of line 13 or line 14. Also include this amount on Form 1040, line 52, or Form 1040NR, line 49	15	
16	Credit carryforward to 2014. If line 15 is less than line 13, subtract line 15 from line 13 16		

For Paperwork Reduction Act Notice, see your tax return instructions. Cat. No. 13540P Form **5695** (2013)

Part II **Nonbusiness Energy Property Credit**

17a	Were the qualified energy efficiency improvements or residential energy property costs for your main home located in the United States? (see instructions) ▶	**17a**	☐ **Yes** ☐ **No**
	Caution: *If you checked the "No" box, you cannot claim the nonbusiness energy property credit. Do not complete Part II.*		
b	Print the complete address of the main home where you made the qualifying improvements. **Caution:** *You can only have one main home at a time.*		
	Number and street ______ Unit No. ______		
	City, State, and ZIP code ______		
c	Were any of these improvements related to the construction of this main home? ▶	**17c**	☐ **Yes** ☐ **No**
	Caution: *If you checked the "Yes" box, you can only claim the nonbusiness energy property credit for qualifying improvements that were not related to the construction of the home. Do not include expenses related to the construction of your main home, even if the improvements were made after you moved into the home.*		
18	Lifetime limitation. Enter the amount from the Lifetime Limitation Worksheet (see instructions)	**18**	
19	Qualified energy efficiency improvements (original use must begin with you and the component must reasonably be expected to last for at least 5 years; do not include labor costs) (see instructions).		
a	Insulation material or system specifically and primarily designed to reduce heat loss or gain of your home that meets the prescriptive criteria established by the 2009 IECC	**19a**	
b	Exterior doors that meet or exceed the Energy Star program requirements	**19b**	
c	Metal or asphalt roof that meets or exceeds the Energy Star program requirements and has appropriate pigmented coatings or cooling granules which are specifically and primarily designed to reduce the heat gain of your home	**19c**	
d	Exterior windows and skylights that meet or exceed the Energy Star program requirements — **19d**		
e	Maximum amount of cost on which the credit can be figured — **19e** *$2,000*		
f	If you claimed window expenses on your Form 5695 for 2006, 2007, 2009, 2010, 2011, or 2012, enter the amount from the Window Expense Worksheet (see instructions); otherwise enter -0- — **19f**		
g	Subtract line 19f from line 19e. If zero or less, enter -0- — **19g**		
h	Enter the smaller of line 19d or line 19g	**19h**	
20	Add lines 19a, 19b, 19c, and 19h	**20**	
21	Multiply line 20 by 10% (.10)	**21**	
22	Residential energy property costs (must be placed in service by you; include labor costs for onsite preparation, assembly, and original installation) (see instructions).		
a	Energy-efficient building property. Do not enter more than **$300**	**22a**	
b	Qualified natural gas, propane, or oil furnace or hot water boiler. Do not enter more than **$150**	**22b**	
c	Advanced main air circulating fan used in a natural gas, propane, or oil furnace. Do not enter more than **$50**	**22c**	
23	Add lines 22a through 22c	**23**	
24	Add lines 21 and 23	**24**	
25	Maximum credit amount. (If you jointly occupied the home, see instructions)	**25**	*$500*
26	Enter the amount, if any, from line 18	**26**	
27	Subtract line 26 from line 25. If zero or less, **stop;** you cannot take the nonbusiness energy property credit	**27**	
28	Enter the smaller of line 24 or line 27	**28**	
29	Limitation based on tax liability. Enter the amount from the Nonbusiness Energy Property Credit Limit Worksheet (see instructions)	**29**	
30	**Nonbusiness energy property credit.** Enter the smaller of line 28 or line 29. Also include this amount on Form 1040, line 52, or Form 1040NR, line 49	**30**	

Form **5695** (2013)

Form **6198**

(Rev. November 2009)
Department of the Treasury
Internal Revenue Service

At-Risk Limitations

▶ Attach to your tax return.
▶ See separate instructions.

OMB No. 1545-0712

Attachment Sequence No. **31**

Name(s) shown on return	Identifying number

Description of activity (see page 2 of the instructions)

Part I **Current Year Profit (Loss) From the Activity, Including Prior Year Nondeductible Amounts.** See page 2 of the instructions.

1	Ordinary income (loss) from the activity (see page 2 of the instructions)	1	
2	Gain (loss) from the sale or other disposition of assets used in the activity (or of your interest in the activity) that you are reporting on:		
a	Schedule D	2a	
b	Form 4797	2b	
c	Other form or schedule	2c	
3	Other income and gains from the activity, from Schedule K-1 of Form 1065, Form 1065-B, or Form 1120S, that were not included on lines 1 through 2c	3	
4	Other deductions and losses from the activity, including investment interest expense allowed from Form 4952, that were not included on lines 1 through 2c	4	( )
5	Current year profit (loss) from the activity. Combine lines 1 through 4. See page 3 of the instructions before completing the rest of this form	5	

Part II **Simplified Computation of Amount At Risk.** See page 3 of the instructions before completing this part.

6	Adjusted basis (as defined in section 1011) in the activity (or in your interest in the activity) on the first day of the tax year. **Do not** enter less than zero	6	
7	Increases for the tax year (see page 3 of the instructions)	7	
8	Add lines 6 and 7	8	
9	Decreases for the tax year (see page 4 of the instructions)	9	
10a	Subtract line 9 from line 8 ▶ 10a		
b	If line 10a is **more** than zero, enter that amount here and go to line 20 (or complete Part III). Otherwise, enter -0- and see **Pub. 925** for information on the recapture rules	10b	

Part III **Detailed Computation of Amount At Risk.** If you completed Part III of Form 6198 for the prior year, see page 4 of the instructions.

11	Investment in the activity (or in your interest in the activity) at the effective date. **Do not** enter less than zero	11	
12	Increases at effective date	12	
13	Add lines 11 and 12	13	
14	Decreases at effective date	14	
15	Amount at risk (check box that applies):		
a	☐ At effective date. Subtract line 14 from line 13. **Do not** enter less than zero.	15	
b	☐ From your prior year Form 6198, line 19b. **Do not** enter the amount from line 10b of your prior year form.		
16	Increases since (check box that applies):		
a	☐ Effective date **b** ☐ The end of your prior year	16	
17	Add lines 15 and 16	17	
18	Decreases since (check box that applies):		
a	☐ Effective date **b** ☐ The end of your prior year	18	
19a	Subtract line 18 from line 17 ▶ 19a		
b	If line 19a is **more** than zero, enter that amount here and go to line 20. Otherwise, enter -0- and see **Pub. 925** for information on the recapture rules	19b	

Part IV **Deductible Loss**

20	**Amount at risk.** Enter the **larger** of line 10b or line 19b	20	
21	**Deductible loss.** Enter the **smaller** of the line 5 loss (treated as a positive number) or line 20. See page 8 of the instructions to find out how to report any deductible loss and any carryover	21	( )

Note: *If the loss is from a passive activity, see the Instructions for* ***Form 8582,*** *Passive Activity Loss Limitations, or the Instructions for* ***Form 8810,*** *Corporate Passive Activity Loss and Credit Limitations, to find out if the loss is allowed under the passive activity rules. If only part of the loss is subject to the passive activity loss rules, report only that part on Form 8582 or Form 8810, whichever applies.*

For Paperwork Reduction Act Notice, see page 8 of the instructions. Cat. No. 50012Y Form **6198** (Rev. 11-2009)

Form **6251**

Department of the Treasury
Internal Revenue Service (99)

Alternative Minimum Tax—Individuals

▶ Information about Form 6251 and its separate instructions is at *www.irs.gov/form6251*.
▶ Attach to Form 1040 or Form 1040NR.

OMB No. 1545-0074

2013

Attachment Sequence No. **32**

Name(s) shown on Form 1040 or Form 1040NR | **Your social security number**

Part I Alternative Minimum Taxable Income (See instructions for how to complete each line.)

1	If filing Schedule A (Form 1040), enter the amount from Form 1040, line 41, and go to line 2. Otherwise, enter the amount from Form 1040, line 38, and go to line 7. (If less than zero, enter as a negative amount.)	1	
2	Medical and dental. If you or your spouse was 65 or older, enter the **smaller** of Schedule A (Form 1040), line 4, **or** 2.5% (.025) of Form 1040, line 38. If zero or less, enter -0- . . .	2	
3	Taxes from Schedule A (Form 1040), line 9 . . .	3	
4	Enter the home mortgage interest adjustment, if any, from line 6 of the worksheet in the instructions for this line	4	
5	Miscellaneous deductions from Schedule A (Form 1040), line 27. . . .	5	
6	If Form 1040, line 38, is $150,000 or less, enter -0-. Otherwise, see instructions . . .	6	( )
7	Tax refund from Form 1040, line 10 or line 21 . . .	7	( )
8	Investment interest expense (difference between regular tax and AMT). . . .	8	
9	Depletion (difference between regular tax and AMT) . . .	9	
10	Net operating loss deduction from Form 1040, line 21. Enter as a positive amount . . .	10	
11	Alternative tax net operating loss deduction . . .	11	( )
12	Interest from specified private activity bonds exempt from the regular tax . . .	12	
13	Qualified small business stock (7% of gain excluded under section 1202) . . .	13	
14	Exercise of incentive stock options (excess of AMT income over regular tax income) . . .	14	
15	Estates and trusts (amount from Schedule K-1 (Form 1041), box 12, code A) . . .	15	
16	Electing large partnerships (amount from Schedule K-1 (Form 1065-B), box 6) . . .	16	
17	Disposition of property (difference between AMT and regular tax gain or loss) . . .	17	
18	Depreciation on assets placed in service after 1986 (difference between regular tax and AMT) . . .	18	
19	Passive activities (difference between AMT and regular tax income or loss) . . .	19	
20	Loss limitations (difference between AMT and regular tax income or loss) . . .	20	
21	Circulation costs (difference between regular tax and AMT) . . .	21	
22	Long-term contracts (difference between AMT and regular tax income) . . .	22	
23	Mining costs (difference between regular tax and AMT) . . .	23	
24	Research and experimental costs (difference between regular tax and AMT) . . .	24	
25	Income from certain installment sales before January 1, 1987 . . .	25	( )
26	Intangible drilling costs preference . . .	26	
27	Other adjustments, including income-based related adjustments . . .	27	
28	**Alternative minimum taxable income.** Combine lines 1 through 27. (If married filing separately and line 28 is more than $238,550, see instructions.) . . .	28	

Part II Alternative Minimum Tax (AMT)

29 Exemption. (If you were under age 24 at the end of 2013, see instructions.)

IF your filing status is . . .	**AND line 28 is not over . . .**	**THEN enter on line 29 . . .**
Single or head of household	$115,400	$51,900
Married filing jointly or qualifying widow(er)	153,900	80,800
Married filing separately.	76,950	40,400

If line 28 is **over** the amount shown above for your filing status, see instructions. **29**

30	Subtract line 29 from line 28. If more than zero, go to line 31. If zero or less, enter -0- here and on lines 31, 33, and 35, and go to line 34 . . .	30	
31	• If you are filing Form 2555 or 2555-EZ, see instructions for the amount to enter. • If you reported capital gain distributions directly on Form 1040, line 13; you reported qualified dividends on Form 1040, line 9b; **or** you had a gain on both lines 15 and 16 of Schedule D (Form 1040) (as refigured for the AMT, if necessary), complete Part III on the back and enter the amount from line 60 here. • **All others:** If line 30 is $179,500 or less ($89,750 or less if married filing separately), multiply line 30 by 26% (.26). Otherwise, multiply line 30 by 28% (.28) and subtract $3,590 ($1,795 if married filing separately) from the result.	31	
32	Alternative minimum tax foreign tax credit (see instructions) . . .	32	
33	Tentative minimum tax. Subtract line 32 from line 31 . . .	33	
34	Tax from Form 1040, line 44 (minus any tax from Form 4972 and any foreign tax credit from Form 1040, line 47). If you used Schedule J to figure your tax, the amount from line 44 of Form 1040 must be refigured without using Schedule J (see instructions) . . .	34	
35	**AMT.** Subtract line 34 from line 33. If zero or less, enter -0-. Enter here and on Form 1040, line 45 . . .	35	

For Paperwork Reduction Act Notice, see your tax return instructions. Cat. No. 13600G Form **6251** (2013)

Part III Tax Computation Using Maximum Capital Gains Rates

Complete Part III only if you are required to do so by line 31 or by the Foreign Earned Income Tax Worksheet in the instructions.

36 Enter the amount from Form 6251, line 30. If you are filing Form 2555 or 2555-EZ, enter the amount from line 3 of the worksheet in the instructions for line 31 . . . 36

37 Enter the amount from line 6 of the Qualified Dividends and Capital Gain Tax Worksheet in the instructions for Form 1040, line 44, or the amount from line 13 of the Schedule D Tax Worksheet in the instructions for Schedule D (Form 1040), whichever applies (as refigured for the AMT, if necessary) (see instructions). If you are filing Form 2555 or 2555-EZ, see instructions for the amount to enter . . . 37

38 Enter the amount from Schedule D (Form 1040), line 19 (as refigured for the AMT, if necessary) (see instructions). If you are filing Form 2555 or 2555-EZ, see instructions for the amount to enter . . . 38

39 If you did not complete a Schedule D Tax Worksheet for the regular tax or the AMT, enter the amount from line 37. Otherwise, add lines 37 and 38, and enter the **smaller** of that result or the amount from line 10 of the Schedule D Tax Worksheet (as refigured for the AMT, if necessary). If you are filing Form 2555 or 2555-EZ, see instructions for the amount to enter . . . 39

40 Enter the **smaller** of line 36 or line 39 . . . 40

41 Subtract line 40 from line 36 . . . 41

42 If line 41 is $179,500 or less ($89,750 or less if married filing separately), multiply line 41 by 26% (.26). Otherwise, multiply line 41 by 28% (.28) and subtract $3,590 ($1,795 if married filing separately) from the result . . . ▶ 42

43 Enter:
- $72,500 if married filing jointly or qualifying widow(er),
- $36,250 if single or married filing separately, or
- $48,600 if head of household.

. . . 43

44 Enter the amount from line 7 of the Qualified Dividends and Capital Gain Tax Worksheet in the instructions for Form 1040, line 44, or the amount from line 14 of the Schedule D Tax Worksheet in the instructions for Schedule D (Form 1040), whichever applies (as figured for the regular tax). If you did not complete either worksheet for the regular tax, enter the amount from Form 1040, line 43; but do not enter less than -0- . . . 44

45 Subtract line 44 from line 43. If zero or less, enter -0- . . . 45

46 Enter the **smaller** of line 36 or line 37 . . . 46

47 Enter the **smaller** of line 45 or line 46. This amount is taxed at 0% . . . 47

48 Subtract line 47 from line 46 . . . 48

49 Enter the amount from the Line 49 Worksheet in the instructions . . . 49

50 Enter the smaller of line 48 or line 49 . . . 50

51 Multiply line 50 by 15% (.15) . . . ▶ 51

52 Add lines 47 and 50 . . . 52

If lines 52 and 36 are the same, skip lines 53 through 57 and go to line 58. Otherwise, go to line 53.

53 Subtract line 52 from line 46 . . . 53

54 Multiply line 53 by 20% (.20) . . . ▶ 54

If line 38 is zero or blank, skip lines 55 through 57 and go to line 58. Otherwise, go to line 55.

55 Add lines 41, 52, and 53 . . . 55

56 Subtract line 55 from line 36 . . . 56

57 Multiply line 56 by 25% (.25) . . . ▶ 57

58 Add lines 42, 51, 54, and 57 . . . 58

59 If line 36 is $179,500 or less ($89,750 or less if married filing separately), multiply line 36 by 26% (.26). Otherwise, multiply line 36 by 28% (.28) and subtract $3,590 ($1,795 if married filing separately) from the result . . . 59

60 Enter the **smaller** of line 58 or line 59 here and on line 31. If you are filing Form 2555 or 2555-EZ, do not enter this amount on line 31. Instead, enter it on line 4 of the worksheet in the instructions for line 31 . . 60

Form **6251** (2013)

Form **8283**

(Rev. December 2013)
Department of the Treasury
Internal Revenue Service

Noncash Charitable Contributions

▶ **Attach to your tax return if you claimed a total deduction of over $500 for all contributed property.**

▶ **Information about Form 8283 and its separate instructions is at *www.irs.gov/form8283*.**

OMB No. 1545-0908

Attachment Sequence No. **155**

Name(s) shown on your income tax return | **Identifying number**

Note. Figure the amount of your contribution deduction before completing this form. See your tax return instructions.

Section A. Donated Property of $5,000 or Less and Publicly Traded Securities—List in this section **only** items (or groups of similar items) for which you claimed a deduction of $5,000 or less. Also, list publicly traded securities even if the deduction is more than $5,000 (see instructions).

Part I **Information on Donated Property**—If you need more space, attach a statement.

1	**(a)** Name and address of the donee organization	**(b)** If donated property is a vehicle (see instructions), check the box. Also enter the vehicle identification number (unless Form 1098-C is attached)	**(c)** Description of donated property (For a vehicle, enter the year, make, model, and mileage. For securities, enter the company name and the number of shares.)
A		☐	
B		☐	
C		☐	
D		☐	
E		☐	

Note. If the amount you claimed as a deduction for an item is $500 or less, you do not have to complete columns (e), (f), and (g).

	(d) Date of the contribution	**(e)** Date acquired by donor (mo., yr.)	**(f)** How acquired by donor	**(g)** Donor's cost or adjusted basis	**(h)** Fair market value (see instructions)	**(i)** Method used to determine the fair market value
A						
B						
C						
D						
E						

Part II **Partial Interests and Restricted Use Property**—Complete lines 2a through 2e if you gave less than an entire interest in a property listed in Part I. Complete lines 3a through 3c if conditions were placed on a contribution listed in Part I; also attach the required statement (see instructions).

2a Enter the letter from Part I that identifies the property for which you gave less than an entire interest ▶ ________
If Part II applies to more than one property, attach a separate statement.

b Total amount claimed as a deduction for the property listed in Part I: **(1)** For this tax year ▶ ________
(2) For any prior tax years ▶ ________

c Name and address of each organization to which any such contribution was made in a prior year (complete only if different from the donee organization above):

Name of charitable organization (donee)

Address (number, street, and room or suite no.)

City or town, state, and ZIP code

d For tangible property, enter the place where the property is located or kept ▶ ________

e Name of any person, other than the donee organization, having actual possession of the property ▶ ________

		Yes	**No**
3a	Is there a restriction, either temporary or permanent, on the donee's right to use or dispose of the donated property?		
b	Did you give to anyone (other than the donee organization or another organization participating with the donee organization in cooperative fundraising) the right to the income from the donated property or to the possession of the property, including the right to vote donated securities, to acquire the property by purchase or otherwise, or to designate the person having such income, possession, or right to acquire?		
c	Is there a restriction limiting the donated property for a particular use?		

For Paperwork Reduction Act Notice, see separate instructions. Cat. No. 62299J Form **8283** (Rev. 12-2013)

Name(s) shown on your income tax return | **Identifying number**

Section B. Donated Property Over $5,000 (Except Publicly Traded Securities)—List in this section only items (or groups of similar items) for which you claimed a deduction of more than $5,000 per item or group (except contributions of publicly traded securities reported in Section A). An appraisal is generally required for property listed in Section B (see instructions).

Part I Information on Donated Property—To be completed by the taxpayer and/or the appraiser.

4 Check the box that describes the type of property donated:

- a ☐ Art* (contribution of $20,000 or more)
- b ☐ Qualified Conservation Contribution
- c ☐ Equipment
- d ☐ Art* (contribution of less than $20,000)
- e ☐ Other Real Estate
- f ☐ Securities
- g ☐ Collectibles**
- h ☐ Intellectual Property
- i ☐ Vehicles
- j ☐ Other

*Art includes paintings, sculptures, watercolors, prints, drawings, ceramics, antiques, decorative arts, textiles, carpets, silver, rare manuscripts, historical memorabilia, and other similar objects.

**Collectibles include coins, stamps, books, gems, jewelry, sports memorabilia, dolls, etc., but not art as defined above.

Note. In certain cases, you must attach a qualified appraisal of the property. See instructions.

5	(a) Description of donated property (if you need more space, attach a separate statement)	(b) If tangible property was donated, give a brief summary of the overall physical condition of the property at the time of the gift	(c) Appraised fair market value
A			
B			
C			
D			

	(d) Date acquired by donor (mo., yr.)	(e) How acquired by donor	(f) Donor's cost or adjusted basis	(g) For bargain sales, enter amount received	See instructions: (h) Amount claimed as a deduction	See instructions: (i) Date of contribution
A						
B						
C						
D						

Part II Taxpayer (Donor) Statement—List each item included in Part I above that the appraisal identifies as having a value of $500 or less. See instructions.

I declare that the following item(s) included in Part I above has to the best of my knowledge and belief an appraised value of not more than $500 (per item). Enter identifying letter from Part I and describe the specific item. See instructions. ▶

Signature of taxpayer (donor) ▶ Date ▶

Part III Declaration of Appraiser

I declare that I am not the donor, the donee, a party to the transaction in which the donor acquired the property, employed by, or related to any of the foregoing persons, or married to any person who is related to any of the foregoing persons. And, if regularly used by the donor, donee, or party to the transaction, I performed the majority of my appraisals during my tax year for other persons.

Also, I declare that I perform appraisals on a regular basis; and that because of my qualifications as described in the appraisal, I am qualified to make appraisals of the type of property being valued. I certify that the appraisal fees were not based on a percentage of the appraised property value. Furthermore, I understand that a false or fraudulent overstatement of the property value as described in the qualified appraisal or this Form 8283 may subject me to the penalty under section 6701(a) (aiding and abetting the understatement of tax liability). In addition, I understand that I may be subject to a penalty under section 6695A if I know, or reasonably should know, that my appraisal is to be used in connection with a return or claim for refund and a substantial or gross valuation misstatement results from my appraisal. I affirm that I have not been barred from presenting evidence or testimony by the Office of Professional Responsibility.

Sign Here Signature ▶ Title ▶ Date ▶

Business address (including room or suite no.) | **Identifying number**

City or town, state, and ZIP code

Part IV Donee Acknowledgment—To be completed by the charitable organization.

This charitable organization acknowledges that it is a qualified organization under section 170(c) and that it received the donated property as described in Section B, Part I, above on the following date ▶

Furthermore, this organization affirms that in the event it sells, exchanges, or otherwise disposes of the property described in Section B, Part I (or any portion thereof) within 3 years after the date of receipt, it will file **Form 8282,** Donee Information Return, with the IRS and give the donor a copy of that form. This acknowledgment does not represent agreement with the claimed fair market value.

Does the organization intend to use the property for an unrelated use? . . . . ▶ ☐ Yes ☐ No

Name of charitable organization (donee)	**Employer identification number**	
Address (number, street, and room or suite no.)	City or town, state, and ZIP code	
Authorized signature	Title	Date

Form **8283** (Rev. 12-2013)

Form **8582**

Department of the Treasury
Internal Revenue Service (99)

Passive Activity Loss Limitations

▶ See separate instructions.
▶ Attach to Form 1040 or Form 1041.
▶ Information about Form 8582 and its instructions is available at *www.irs.gov/form8582*.

OMB No. 1545-1008
2013
Attachment Sequence No. **88**

Name(s) shown on return	Identifying number

Part I 2013 Passive Activity Loss

Caution: *Complete Worksheets 1, 2, and 3 before completing Part I.*

Rental Real Estate Activities With Active Participation (For the definition of active participation, see **Special Allowance for Rental Real Estate Activities** in the instructions.)					
1a	Activities with net income (enter the amount from Worksheet 1, column (a))	1a			
b	Activities with net loss (enter the amount from Worksheet 1, column (b))	1b	( )		
c	Prior years unallowed losses (enter the amount from Worksheet 1, column (c))	1c	( )		
d	Combine lines 1a, 1b, and 1c			1d	
Commercial Revitalization Deductions From Rental Real Estate Activities					
2a	Commercial revitalization deductions from Worksheet 2, column (a)	2a	( )		
b	Prior year unallowed commercial revitalization deductions from Worksheet 2, column (b)	2b	( )		
c	Add lines 2a and 2b			2c	( )
All Other Passive Activities					
3a	Activities with net income (enter the amount from Worksheet 3, column (a))	3a			
b	Activities with net loss (enter the amount from Worksheet 3, column (b))	3b	( )		
c	Prior years unallowed losses (enter the amount from Worksheet 3, column (c))	3c	( )		
d	Combine lines 3a, 3b, and 3c			3d	
4	Combine lines 1d, 2c, and 3d. If this line is zero or more, stop here and include this form with your return; all losses are allowed, including any prior year unallowed losses entered on line 1c, 2b, or 3c. Report the losses on the forms and schedules normally used			4	

If line 4 is a loss and:
- Line 1d is a loss, go to Part II.
- Line 2c is a loss (and line 1d is zero or more), skip Part II and go to Part III.
- Line 3d is a loss (and lines 1d and 2c are zero or more), skip Parts II and III and go to line 15.

Caution: *If your filing status is married filing separately and you lived with your spouse at any time during the year,* **do not** *complete Part II or Part III. Instead, go to line 15.*

Part II Special Allowance for Rental Real Estate Activities With Active Participation

Note: *Enter all numbers in Part II as positive amounts. See instructions for an example.*

5	Enter the **smaller** of the loss on line 1d or the loss on line 4			5	
6	Enter $150,000. If married filing separately, see instructions	6			
7	Enter modified adjusted gross income, but not less than zero (see instructions)	7			
	Note: *If line 7 is greater than or equal to line 6, skip lines 8 and 9, enter -0- on line 10. Otherwise, go to line 8.*				
8	Subtract line 7 from line 6	8			
9	Multiply line 8 by 50% (.5). **Do not** enter more than $25,000. If married filing separately, see instructions			9	
10	Enter the **smaller** of line 5 or line 9			10	

If line 2c is a loss, go to Part III. Otherwise, go to line 15.

Part III Special Allowance for Commercial Revitalization Deductions From Rental Real Estate Activities

Note: *Enter all numbers in Part III as positive amounts. See the example for Part II in the instructions.*

11	Enter $25,000 reduced by the amount, if any, on line 10. If married filing separately, see instructions	11	
12	Enter the loss from line 4	12	
13	Reduce line 12 by the amount on line 10	13	
14	Enter the **smallest** of line 2c (treated as a positive amount), line 11, or line 13	14	

Part IV Total Losses Allowed

15	Add the income, if any, on lines 1a and 3a and enter the total	15	
16	**Total losses allowed from all passive activities for 2013.** Add lines 10, 14, and 15. See instructions to find out how to report the losses on your tax return	16	

For Paperwork Reduction Act Notice, see instructions. Cat. No. 63704F Form **8582** (2013)

Caution: *The worksheets must be filed with your tax return. Keep a copy for your records.*

Worksheet 1—For Form 8582, Lines 1a, 1b, and 1c (See instructions.)

Name of activity	Current year		Prior years	Overall gain or loss	
	(a) Net income (line 1a)	(b) Net loss (line 1b)	(c) Unallowed loss (line 1c)	(d) Gain	(e) Loss
Total. Enter on Form 8582, lines 1a, 1b, and 1c . . . . ▶					

Worksheet 2—For Form 8582, Lines 2a and 2b (See instructions.)

Name of activity	(a) Current year deductions (line 2a)	(b) Prior year unallowed deductions (line 2b)	(c) Overall loss
Total. Enter on Form 8582, lines 2a and 2b . . . . ▶			

Worksheet 3—For Form 8582, Lines 3a, 3b, and 3c (See instructions.)

Name of activity	Current year		Prior years	Overall gain or loss	
	(a) Net income (line 3a)	(b) Net loss (line 3b)	(c) Unallowed loss (line 3c)	(d) Gain	(e) Loss
Total. Enter on Form 8582, lines 3a, 3b, and 3c . . . . ▶					

Worksheet 4—Use this worksheet if an amount is shown on Form 8582, line 10 or 14 (See instructions.)

Name of activity	Form or schedule and line number to be reported on (see instructions)	(a) Loss	(b) Ratio	(c) Special allowance	(d) Subtract column (c) from column (a)
Total . . . . ▶			1.00		

Worksheet 5—Allocation of Unallowed Losses (See instructions.)

Name of activity	Form or schedule and line number to be reported on (see instructions)	(a) Loss	(b) Ratio	(c) Unallowed loss
Total . . . . ▶			1.00	

Worksheet 6—Allowed Losses (See instructions.)

Name of activity	Form or schedule and line number to be reported on (see instructions)	(a) Loss	(b) Unallowed loss	(c) Allowed loss
Total . . . . ▶				

Worksheet 7—Activities With Losses Reported on Two or More Forms or Schedules (See instructions.)

Name of activity:	(a)	(b)	(c) Ratio	(d) Unallowed loss	(e) Allowed loss
Form or schedule and line number to be reported on (see instructions): ________					
1a Net loss plus prior year unallowed loss from form or schedule . ▶					
b Net income from form or schedule . . . . ▶					
c Subtract line 1b from line 1a. If zero or less, enter -0- ▶					
Form or schedule and line number to be reported on (see instructions): ________					
1a Net loss plus prior year unallowed loss from form or schedule . ▶					
b Net income from form or schedule . . . . ▶					
c Subtract line 1b from line 1a. If zero or less, enter -0- ▶					
Form or schedule and line number to be reported on (see instructions): ________					
1a Net loss plus prior year unallowed loss from form or schedule . ▶					
b Net income from form or schedule . . . . ▶					
c Subtract line 1b from line 1a. If zero or less, enter -0- ▶					
Total . . . . ▶			1.00		

Form **8582** (2013)

Form **8606**

Department of the Treasury
Internal Revenue Service (99)

Nondeductible IRAs

▶ Information about Form 8606 and its separate instructions is at *www.irs.gov/form8606.*

▶ Attach to Form 1040, Form 1040A, or Form 1040NR.

OMB No. 1545-0074

2013

Attachment Sequence No. **48**

Name. If married, file a separate form for each spouse required to file Form 8606. See instructions.			**Your social security number**
Fill in Your Address Only If You Are Filing This Form by Itself and Not With Your Tax Return	Home address (number and street, or P.O. box if mail is not delivered to your home)		Apt. no.
	City, town or post office, state, and ZIP code. If you have a foreign address, also complete the spaces below (see instructions).		
	Foreign country name	Foreign province/state/county	Foreign postal code

Part I **Nondeductible Contributions to Traditional IRAs and Distributions From Traditional, SEP, and SIMPLE IRAs**

Complete this part only if one or more of the following apply.

- You made nondeductible contributions to a traditional IRA for 2013.
- You took distributions from a traditional, SEP, or SIMPLE IRA in 2013 **and** you made nondeductible contributions to a traditional IRA in 2013 or an earlier year. For this purpose, a distribution does not include a rollover, qualified charitable distributions, one-time distribution to fund an HSA, conversion, recharacterization, or return of certain contributions.
- You converted part, but not all, of your traditional, SEP, and SIMPLE IRAs to Roth IRAs in 2013 (excluding any portion you recharacterized) **and** you made nondeductible contributions to a traditional IRA in 2013 or an earlier year.

1	Enter your nondeductible contributions to traditional IRAs for 2013, including those made for 2013 from January 1, 2014, through April 15, 2014 (see instructions)		1
2	Enter your total basis in traditional IRAs (see instructions)		2
3	Add lines 1 and 2		3
	In 2013, did you take a distribution from traditional, SEP, or SIMPLE IRAs, or make a Roth IRA conversion? No ▶ Enter the amount from line 3 on line 14. Do not complete the rest of Part I. Yes ▶ Go to line 4.		
4	Enter those contributions included on line 1 that were made from January 1, 2014, through April 15, 2014		4
5	Subtract line 4 from line 3		5
6	Enter the value of **all** your traditional, SEP, and SIMPLE IRAs as of December 31, 2013, plus any outstanding rollovers (see instructions)	6	
7	Enter your distributions from traditional, SEP, and SIMPLE IRAs in 2013. **Do not** include rollovers, qualified charitable distributions, a one-time distribution to fund an HSA, conversions to a Roth IRA, certain returned contributions, or recharacterizations of traditional IRA contributions (see instructions)	7	
8	Enter the net amount you converted from traditional, SEP, and SIMPLE IRAs to Roth IRAs in 2013. **Do not** include amounts converted that you later recharacterized (see instructions). Also enter this amount on line 16	8	
9	Add lines 6, 7, and 8 — 9		
10	Divide line 5 by line 9. Enter the result as a decimal rounded to at least 3 places. If the result is 1.000 or more, enter "1.000"	10	× .
11	Multiply line 8 by line 10. This is the nontaxable portion of the amount you converted to Roth IRAs. Also enter this amount on line 17	11	
12	Multiply line 7 by line 10. This is the nontaxable portion of your distributions that you did not convert to a Roth IRA	12	
13	Add lines 11 and 12. This is the nontaxable portion of all your distributions		13
14	Subtract line 13 from line 3. This is **your total basis in traditional IRAs for 2013 and earlier years**		14
15	**Taxable amount.** Subtract line 12 from line 7. If more than zero, also include this amount on Form 1040, line 15b; Form 1040A, line 11b; or Form 1040NR, line 16b		15
	Note. You may be subject to an additional 10% tax on the amount on line 15 if you were under age 59½ at the time of the distribution (see instructions).		

For Privacy Act and Paperwork Reduction Act Notice, see separate instructions. Cat. No. 63966F Form **8606** (2013)

Part II 2013 Conversions From Traditional, SEP, or SIMPLE IRAs to Roth IRAs

Complete this part if you converted part or all of your traditional, SEP, and SIMPLE IRAs to a Roth IRA in 2013 (excluding any portion you recharacterized).

16	If you completed Part I, enter the amount from line 8. Otherwise, enter the net amount you converted from traditional, SEP, and SIMPLE IRAs to Roth IRAs in 2013. **Do not** include amounts you later recharacterized back to traditional, SEP, or SIMPLE IRAs in 2013 or 2014 (see instructions)	16	
17	If you completed Part I, enter the amount from line 11. Otherwise, enter your basis in the amount on line 16 (see instructions)	17	
18	**Taxable amount.** Subtract line 17 from line 16. Also include this amount on Form 1040, line 15b; Form 1040A, line 11b; or Form 1040NR, line 16b	18	

Part III Distributions From Roth IRAs

Complete this part only if you took a distribution from a Roth IRA in 2013. For this purpose, a distribution does not include a rollover, qualified charitable distributions, a one-time distribution to fund an HSA, recharacterization, or return of certain contributions (see instructions).

19	Enter your total nonqualified distributions from Roth IRAs in 2013, including any qualified first-time homebuyer distributions (see instructions)	19	
20	Qualified first-time homebuyer expenses (see instructions). **Do not** enter more than $10,000	20	
21	Subtract line 20 from line 19. If zero or less, enter -0- and skip lines 22 through 25	21	
22	Enter your basis in Roth IRA contributions (see instructions)	22	
23	Subtract line 22 from line 21. If zero or less, enter -0- and skip lines 24 and 25. If more than zero, you may be subject to an additional tax (see instructions)	23	
24	Enter your basis in conversions from traditional, SEP, and SIMPLE IRAs and rollovers from qualified retirement plans to a Roth IRA (see instructions)	24	
25	**Taxable amount.** Subtract line 24 from line 23. If more than zero, also include this amount on Form 1040, line 15b; Form 1040A, line 11b; or Form 1040NR, line 16b	25	

Sign Here Only If You Are Filing This Form by Itself and Not With Your Tax Return

Under penalties of perjury, I declare that I have examined this form, including accompanying attachments, and to the best of my knowledge and belief, it is true, correct, and complete. Declaration of preparer (other than taxpayer) is based on all information of which preparer has any knowledge.

▶ Your signature ▶ Date

Paid Preparer Use Only	Print/Type preparer's name	Preparer's signature	Date	Check ☐ if self-employed	PTIN
	Firm's name ▶			Firm's EIN ▶	
	Firm's address ▶			Phone no.	

Form **8606** (2013)

Form **8615**

Department of the Treasury
Internal Revenue Service (99)

Tax for Certain Children Who Have Unearned Income

▶ Attach only to the child's Form 1040, Form 1040A, or Form 1040NR.
▶ Information about Form 8615 and its separate instructions is at *www.irs.gov/form8615*.

OMB No. 1545-0074

2013

Attachment Sequence No. **33**

Child's name shown on return | **Child's social security number**

Before you begin: If the child, the parent, or any of the parent's other children for whom Form 8615 must be filed must use the Schedule D Tax Worksheet or has income from farming or fishing, see **Pub. 929,** Tax Rules for Children and Dependents. It explains how to figure the child's tax using the **Schedule D Tax Worksheet** or **Schedule J** (Form 1040).

A Parent's name (first, initial, and last). **Caution:** *See instructions before completing.* | **B Parent's social security number**

C Parent's filing status (check one):
☐ Single ☐ Married filing jointly ☐ Married filing separately ☐ Head of household ☐ Qualifying widow(er)

Part I Child's Net Unearned Income

1	Enter the child's unearned income (see instructions)	1	
2	If the child **did not** itemize deductions on **Schedule A** (Form 1040 or Form 1040NR), enter $2,000. Otherwise, see instructions	2	
3	Subtract line 2 from line 1. If zero or less, **stop;** do not complete the rest of this form but **do** attach it to the child's return	3	
4	Enter the child's **taxable income** from Form 1040, line 43; Form 1040A, line 27; or Form 1040NR, line 41. If the child files Form 2555 or 2555-EZ, see the instructions	4	
5	Enter the **smaller** of line 3 or line 4. If zero, **stop;** do not complete the rest of this form but **do** attach it to the child's return	5	

Part II Tentative Tax Based on the Tax Rate of the Parent

6	Enter the parent's **taxable income** from Form 1040, line 43; Form 1040A, line 27; Form 1040EZ, line 6; Form 1040NR, line 41; or Form 1040NR-EZ, line 14. If zero or less, enter -0-. If the parent files Form 2555 or 2555-EZ, see the instructions	6	
7	Enter the total, if any, from Forms 8615, line 5, of **all other** children of the parent named above. **Do not** include the amount from line 5 above	7	
8	Add lines 5, 6, and 7 (see instructions)	8	
9	Enter the tax on the amount on line 8 based on the **parent's** filing status above (see instructions). If the Qualified Dividends and Capital Gain Tax Worksheet, Schedule D Tax Worksheet, or Schedule J (Form 1040) is used to figure the tax, check here ▶ ☐	9	
10	Enter the parent's tax from Form 1040, line 44; Form 1040A, line 28, minus any alternative minimum tax; Form 1040EZ, line 10; Form 1040NR, line 42; or Form 1040NR-EZ, line 15. **Do not** include any tax from **Form 4972** or **8814** or any tax from recapture of an education credit. If the parent files Form 2555 or 2555-EZ, see the instructions. If the Qualified Dividends and Capital Gain Tax Worksheet, Schedule D Tax Worksheet, or Schedule J (Form 1040) was used to figure the tax, check here ▶ ☐	10	
11	Subtract line 10 from line 9 and enter the result. If line 7 is blank, also enter this amount on line 13 and go to **Part III**	11	
12a	Add lines 5 and 7 — 12a		
b	Divide line 5 by line 12a. Enter the result as a decimal (rounded to at least three places)	12b	× .
13	Multiply line 11 by line 12b	13	

Part III Child's Tax—If lines 4 and 5 above are the same, enter -0- on line 15 and go to line 16.

14	Subtract line 5 from line 4 — 14		
15	Enter the tax on the amount on line 14 based on the **child's** filing status (see instructions). If the Qualified Dividends and Capital Gain Tax Worksheet, Schedule D Tax Worksheet, or Schedule J (Form 1040) is used to figure the tax, check here ▶ ☐	15	
16	Add lines 13 and 15	16	
17	Enter the tax on the amount on line 4 based on the **child's** filing status (see instructions). If the Qualified Dividends and Capital Gain Tax Worksheet, Schedule D Tax Worksheet, or Schedule J (Form 1040) is used to figure the tax, check here ▶ ☐	17	
18	Enter the **larger** of line 16 or line 17 here and on the **child's** Form 1040, line 44; Form 1040A, line 28; or Form 1040NR, line 42. If the child files Form 2555 or 2555-EZ, see the instructions	18	

For Paperwork Reduction Act Notice, see your tax return instructions. Cat. No. 64113U Form **8615** (2013)

Form **8824**

Department of the Treasury
Internal Revenue Service

Like-Kind Exchanges

(and section 1043 conflict-of-interest sales)

▶ Attach to your tax return.

▶ Information about Form 8824 and its separate instructions is at *www.irs.gov/form8824*.

OMB No. 1545-1190

2013

Attachment Sequence No. **109**

Name(s) shown on tax return	**Identifying number**

Part I Information on the Like-Kind Exchange

Note: *If the property described on line 1 or line 2 is real or personal property located outside the United States, indicate the country.*

1 Description of like-kind property given up:

2 Description of like-kind property received:

3 Date like-kind property given up was originally acquired (month, day, year) . . . . . . **3** MM/DD/YYYY

4 Date you actually transferred your property to other party (month, day, year) . . . . . **4** MM/DD/YYYY

5 Date like-kind property you received was identified by written notice to another party (month, day, year). See instructions for 45-day written identification requirement . . . . **5** MM/DD/YYYY

6 Date you actually received the like-kind property from other party (month, day, year). See instructions **6** MM/DD/YYYY

7 Was the exchange of the property given up or received made with a related party, either directly or indirectly (such as through an intermediary)? See instructions. If "Yes," complete Part II. If "No," go to Part III . . . . ☐ **Yes** ☐ **No**

Part II Related Party Exchange Information

8 Name of related party	Relationship to you	Related party's identifying number
Address (no., street, and apt., room, or suite no., city or town, state, and ZIP code)		

9 During this tax year (and before the date that is 2 years after the last transfer of property that was part of the exchange), did the related party sell or dispose of any part of the like-kind property received from you (or an intermediary) in the exchange or transfer property into the exchange, directly or indirectly (such as through an intermediary), that became your replacement property? . . . . ☐ **Yes** ☐ **No**

10 During this tax year (and before the date that is 2 years after the last transfer of property that was part of the exchange), did you sell or dispose of any part of the like-kind property you received? . . . . ☐ **Yes** ☐ **No**

If both lines 9 and 10 are "No" and this is the year of the exchange, go to Part III. If both lines 9 and 10 are "No" and this is ***not*** *the year of the exchange, stop here. If either line 9 or line 10 is "Yes," complete Part III and report on this year's tax return the deferred gain or (loss) from line 24* ***unless*** *one of the exceptions on line 11 applies.*

11 If one of the exceptions below applies to the disposition, check the applicable box:

a ☐ The disposition was after the death of either of the related parties.

b ☐ The disposition was an involuntary conversion, and the threat of conversion occurred after the exchange.

c ☐ You can establish to the satisfaction of the IRS that neither the exchange nor the disposition had tax avoidance as one of its principal purposes. If this box is checked, attach an explanation (see instructions).

For Paperwork Reduction Act Notice, see the instructions. Cat. No. 12311A Form **8824** (2013)

Name(s) shown on tax return. Do not enter name and social security number if shown on other side. | **Your social security number**

Part III Realized Gain or (Loss), Recognized Gain, and Basis of Like-Kind Property Received

Caution: *If you transferred* **and** *received* **(a)** *more than one group of like-kind properties or* **(b)** *cash or other (not like-kind) property, see* **Reporting of multi-asset exchanges** *in the instructions.*

Note: *Complete lines 12 through 14* **only** *if you gave up property that was not like-kind. Otherwise, go to line 15.*

12	Fair market value (FMV) of other property given up	12	
13	Adjusted basis of other property given up	13	
14	Gain or (loss) recognized on other property given up. Subtract line 13 from line 12. Report the gain or (loss) in the same manner as if the exchange had been a sale	14	

Caution: *If the property given up was used previously or partly as a home, see* **Property used as home** *in the instructions.*

15	Cash received, FMV of other property received, plus net liabilities assumed by other party, reduced (but not below zero) by any exchange expenses you incurred (see instructions)	15	
16	FMV of like-kind property you received	16	
17	Add lines 15 and 16	17	
18	Adjusted basis of like-kind property you gave up, net amounts paid to other party, plus any exchange expenses **not** used on line 15 (see instructions)	18	
19	**Realized gain or (loss).** Subtract line 18 from line 17	19	
20	Enter the smaller of line 15 or line 19, but not less than zero	20	
21	Ordinary income under recapture rules. Enter here and on Form 4797, line 16 (see instructions)	21	
22	Subtract line 21 from line 20. If zero or less, enter -0-. If more than zero, enter here and on Schedule D or Form 4797, unless the installment method applies (see instructions)	22	
23	**Recognized gain.** Add lines 21 and 22	23	
24	Deferred gain or (loss). Subtract line 23 from line 19. If a related party exchange, see instructions	24	
25	**Basis of like-kind property received.** Subtract line 15 from the sum of lines 18 and 23	25	

Part IV Deferral of Gain From Section 1043 Conflict-of-Interest Sales

Note: *This part is to be used* **only** *by officers or employees of the executive branch of the Federal Government or judicial officers of the Federal Government (including certain spouses, minor or dependent children, and trustees as described in section 1043) for reporting nonrecognition of gain under section 1043 on the sale of property to comply with the conflict-of-interest requirements. This part can be used* **only** *if the cost of the replacement property is more than the basis of the divested property.*

26 Enter the number from the upper right corner of your certificate of divestiture. (**Do not** attach a copy of your certificate. Keep the certificate with your records.) ▶ ____

27 Description of divested property ▶ ____

28 Description of replacement property ▶ ____

29	Date divested property was sold (month, day, year)			29	MM/DD/YYYY
30	Sales price of divested property (see instructions)	30			
31	Basis of divested property	31			
32	**Realized gain.** Subtract line 31 from line 30			32	
33	Cost of replacement property purchased within 60 days after date of sale	33			
34	Subtract line 33 from line 30. If zero or less, enter -0-			34	
35	Ordinary income under recapture rules. Enter here and on Form 4797, line 10 (see instructions)			35	
36	Subtract line 35 from line 34. If zero or less, enter -0-. If more than zero, enter here and on Schedule D or Form 4797 (see instructions)			36	
37	**Deferred gain.** Subtract the sum of lines 35 and 36 from line 32			37	
38	**Basis of replacement property.** Subtract line 37 from line 33			38	

Form **8824** (2013)

Form **8829**

Department of the Treasury
Internal Revenue Service (99)

Expenses for Business Use of Your Home

► File only with Schedule C (Form 1040). Use a separate Form 8829 for each home you used for business during the year.

► Information about Form 8829 and its separate instructions is at *www.irs.gov/form8829.*

OMB No. 1545-0074
2013
Attachment Sequence No. **176**

Name(s) of proprietor(s) | Your social security number

Part I Part of Your Home Used for Business

1	Area used regularly and exclusively for business, regularly for daycare, or for storage of inventory or product samples (see instructions)	1	
2	Total area of home	2	
3	Divide line 1 by line 2. Enter the result as a percentage	3	%
	For daycare facilities not used exclusively for business, go to line 4. All others go to line 7.		
4	Multiply days used for daycare during year by hours used per day — 4 ____ hr.		
5	Total hours available for use during the year (365 days x 24 hours) (see instructions) — 5 8,760 hr.		
6	Divide line 4 by line 5. Enter the result as a decimal amount — 6 .		
7	Business percentage. For daycare facilities not used exclusively for business, multiply line 6 by line 3 (enter the result as a percentage). All others, enter the amount from line 3 ►	7	%

Part II Figure Your Allowable Deduction

8	Enter the amount from Schedule C, line 29, **plus** any gain derived from the business use of your home and shown on Schedule D or Form 4797, minus any loss from the trade or business not derived from the business use of your home and shown on Schedule D or Form 4797. See instructions	8	

See instructions for columns (a) and (b) before completing lines 9–21.

			(a) Direct expenses	(b) Indirect expenses		
9	Casualty losses (see instructions)	9				
10	Deductible mortgage interest (see instructions)	10				
11	Real estate taxes (see instructions)	11				
12	Add lines 9, 10, and 11	12				
13	Multiply line 12, column (b) by line 7			13		
14	Add line 12, column (a) and line 13				14	
15	Subtract line 14 from line 8. If zero or less, enter -0-				15	
16	Excess mortgage interest (see instructions)	16				
17	Insurance	17				
18	Rent	18				
19	Repairs and maintenance	19				
20	Utilities	20				
21	Other expenses (see instructions)	21				
22	Add lines 16 through 21	22				
23	Multiply line 22, column (b) by line 7			23		
24	Carryover of operating expenses from 2012 Form 8829, line 42			24		
25	Add line 22, column (a), line 23, and line 24				25	
26	Allowable operating expenses. Enter the **smaller** of line 15 or line 25				26	
27	Limit on excess casualty losses and depreciation. Subtract line 26 from line 15				27	
28	Excess casualty losses (see instructions)			28		
29	Depreciation of your home from line 41 below			29		
30	Carryover of excess casualty losses and depreciation from 2012 Form 8829, line 43			30		
31	Add lines 28 through 30				31	
32	Allowable excess casualty losses and depreciation. Enter the **smaller** of line 27 or line 31				32	
33	Add lines 14, 26, and 32				33	
34	Casualty loss portion, if any, from lines 14 and 32. Carry amount to **Form 4684** (see instructions)				34	
35	**Allowable expenses for business use of your home.** Subtract line 34 from line 33. Enter here and on Schedule C, line 30. If your home was used for more than one business, see instructions ►				35	

Part III Depreciation of Your Home

36	Enter the **smaller** of your home's adjusted basis or its fair market value (see instructions)	36	
37	Value of land included on line 36	37	
38	Basis of building. Subtract line 37 from line 36	38	
39	Business basis of building. Multiply line 38 by line 7	39	
40	Depreciation percentage (see instructions)	40	%
41	Depreciation allowable (see instructions). Multiply line 39 by line 40. Enter here and on line 29 above	41	

Part IV Carryover of Unallowed Expenses to 2014

42	Operating expenses. Subtract line 26 from line 25. If less than zero, enter -0-	42	
43	Excess casualty losses and depreciation. Subtract line 32 from line 31. If less than zero, enter -0-	43	

For Paperwork Reduction Act Notice, see your tax return instructions. Cat. No. 13232M Form **8829** (2013)

Form **8839**

Department of the Treasury
Internal Revenue Service (99)

Qualified Adoption Expenses

▶ Attach to Form 1040 or 1040NR.

▶ For information about Form 8839 and its separate instructions, see *www.irs.gov/form8839*.

OMB No. 1545-0074

2013

Attachment Sequence No. 38

Name(s) shown on return | Your social security number

Part I **Information About Your Eligible Child or Children**—You **must** complete this part. See instructions for details, including what to do if you need more space.

1	(a) Child's name First	Last	(b) Child's year of birth	Check if child was— (c) born **before** **1996** and disabled	(d) a child with special needs	(e) a foreign child	(f) Child's identifying number	(g) Check if adoption became final in 2013 or earlier
Child 1				☐	☐	☐		☐
Child 2				☐	☐	☐		☐
Child 3				☐	☐	☐		☐

Caution. If the child was a foreign child, see **Special rules** in the instructions for line 1, column (e) before you complete Part II or Part III. If you received **employer-provided adoption benefits,** complete Part III on the back next.

Part II **Adoption Credit**

			Child 1	Child 2	Child 3
2	Maximum adoption credit per child	2	$12,970 00	$12,970 00	$12,970 00
3	Did you file Form 8839 for a prior year for the same child? ☐ **No.** Enter -0-. ☐ **Yes.** See instructions for the amount to enter.	3			
4	Subtract line 3 from line 2 .	4			
5	**Qualified adoption expenses** (see instructions) . . . . **Caution.** Your qualified adoption expenses may not be equal to the adoption expenses you paid in 2013.	5			
6	Enter the **smaller** of line 4 or line 5	6			

7 Enter modified adjusted gross income (see instructions) . . . . . . | 7 |

8 Is line 7 more than $194,580?
☐ **No.** Skip lines 8 and 9, and enter -0- on line 10.
☐ **Yes.** Subtract $194,580 from line 7 . . . . | 8 |

9 Divide line 8 by $40,000. Enter the result as a decimal (rounded to at least three places). Do not enter more than 1.000 . . . . | 9 | × .

			Child 1	Child 2	Child 3
10	Multiply each amount on line 6 by line 9	10			
11	Subtract line 10 from line 6 .	11			

12 Add the amounts on line 11 . . . . | 12 |

13 Credit carryforward, if any, from 2012. See the 2012 to 2013 Credit Carryforward Worksheet in the instructions . . . . | 13 |

14 Add lines 12 and 13 . . . . | 14 |

15 Enter the amount from line 5 of the Credit Limit Worksheet in the instructions . . . | 15 |

16 **Adoption Credit.** Enter the smaller of line 14 or line 15 here and on Form 1040, line 53, or Form 1040NR, line 50. Check box **c** on that line and enter **"8839"** in the space next to box **c**. If line 15 is smaller than line 14, you may have a credit carryforward (see instructions) . . . . . . | 16 |

For Paperwork Reduction Act Notice, see your tax return instructions. Cat. No. 22843L Form **8839** (2013)

Part III **Employer-Provided Adoption Benefits**

			Child 1	Child 2	Child 3		
17	Maximum exclusion per child	17	$12,970 00	$12,970 00	$12,970 00		
18	Did you receive employer-provided adoption benefits for a prior year for the same child? ☐ **No.** Enter -0-. ☐ **Yes.** See instructions for the amount to enter.	18					
19	Subtract line 18 from line 17	19					
20	Employer-provided adoption benefits you received in 2013. This amount should be shown in box 12 of your 2013 Form(s) W-2 with code **T**	20					
21	Add the amounts on line 20 . . .					21	
22	Enter the **smaller** of line 19 or line 20. But if the child was a child with special needs and the adoption became final in 2013, enter the amount from line 19	22					
23	Enter modified adjusted gross income (from the worksheet in the instructions)	23					
24	Is line 23 more than $194,580? ☐ **No.** Skip lines 24 and 25, and enter -0- on line 26. ☐ **Yes.** Subtract $194,580 from line 23	24					
25	Divide line 24 by $40,000. Enter the result as a decimal (rounded to at least three places). Do not enter more than 1.000	25	× .				
26	Multiply each amount on line 22 by line 25	26					
27	**Excluded benefits.** Subtract line 26 from line 22	27					
28	Add the amounts on line 27 . . .					28	
29	**Taxable benefits.** Is line 28 more than line 21? ☐ **No.** Subtract line 28 from line 21. Also, include this amount, if more than zero, on line 7 of Form 1040 or line 8 of Form 1040NR. On the dotted line next to line 7 of Form 1040 or line 8 of Form 1040NR, enter "AB." ☐ **Yes.** Subtract line 21 from line 28. Enter the result as a negative number. Reduce the total you would enter on line 7 of Form 1040 or line 8 of Form 1040NR by the amount on Form 8839, line 29. Enter the result on line 7 of Form 1040 or line 8 of Form 1040NR. Enter "SNE" on the dotted line next to the entry line.					29	

TIP

You may be able to claim the adoption credit in Part II on the front of this form if any of the following apply.

- You paid adoption expenses in 2012, those expenses were not fully reimbursed by your employer or otherwise, and the adoption was not final by the end of 2012.
- The total adoption expenses you paid in 2013 were not fully reimbursed by your employer or otherwise, and the adoption became final in 2013 or earlier.
- You adopted a child with special needs and the adoption became final in 2013.

Form **8839** (2013)

Form **8863**

Department of the Treasury
Internal Revenue Service (99)

Education Credits
(American Opportunity and Lifetime Learning Credits)

▶ Information about Form 8863 and its separate instructions is at *www.irs.gov/form8863*.
▶ Attach to Form 1040 or Form 1040A.

OMB No. 1545-0074

2013

Attachment
Sequence No. 50

Name(s) shown on return | Your social security number

CAUTION *Complete a separate Part III on page 2 for each student for whom you are claiming either credit before you complete Parts I and II.*

Part I **Refundable American Opportunity Credit**

1	After completing Part III for each student, enter the total of all amounts from all Parts III, line 30 .		1
2	Enter: $180,000 if married filing jointly; $90,000 if single, head of household, or qualifying widow(er)	2	
3	Enter the amount from Form 1040, line 38, or Form 1040A, line 22. If you are filing Form 2555, 2555-EZ, or 4563, or you are excluding income from Puerto Rico, see Pub. 970 for the amount to enter	3	
4	Subtract line 3 from line 2. If zero or less, **stop**; you cannot take any education credit	4	
5	Enter: $20,000 if married filing jointly; $10,000 if single, head of household, or qualifying widow(er)	5	
6	If line 4 is: • Equal to or more than line 5, enter 1.000 on line 6 . . . . • Less than line 5, divide line 4 by line 5. Enter the result as a decimal (rounded to at least three places)		6 .
7	Multiply line 1 by line 6. **Caution:** If you were under age 24 at the end of the year **and** meet the conditions described in the instructions, you **cannot** take the refundable American opportunity credit; skip line 8, enter the amount from line 7 on line 9, and check this box ▶ ☐		7
8	**Refundable American opportunity credit.** Multiply line 7 by 40% (.40). Enter the amount here and on Form 1040, line 66, or Form 1040A, line 40. Then go to line 9 below.		8

Part II **Nonrefundable Education Credits**

9	Subtract line 8 from line 7. Enter here and on line 2 of the Credit Limit Worksheet (see instructions)		9
10	After completing Part III for each student, enter the total of all amounts from all Parts III, line 31. If zero, skip lines 11 through 17, enter -0- on line 18, and go to line 19		10
11	Enter the smaller of line 10 or $10,000		11
12	Multiply line 11 by 20% (.20)		12
13	Enter: $127,000 if married filing jointly; $63,000 if single, head of household, or qualifying widow(er)	13	
14	Enter the amount from Form 1040, line 38, or Form 1040A, line 22. If you are filing Form 2555, 2555-EZ, or 4563, or you are excluding income from Puerto Rico, see Pub. 970 for the amount to enter	14	
15	Subtract line 14 from line 13. If zero or less, skip lines 16 and 17, enter -0- on line 18, and go to line 19	15	
16	Enter: $20,000 if married filing jointly; $10,000 if single, head of household, or qualifying widow(er)	16	
17	If line 15 is: • Equal to or more than line 16, enter 1.000 on line 17 and go to line 18 • Less than line 16, divide line 15 by line 16. Enter the result as a decimal (rounded to at least three places)		17 .
18	Multiply line 12 by line 17. Enter here and on line 1 of the Credit Limit Worksheet (see instructions) ▶		18
19	**Nonrefundable education credits.** Enter the amount from line 7 of the Credit Limit Worksheet (see instructions) here and on Form 1040, line 49, or Form 1040A, line 31		19

For Paperwork Reduction Act Notice, see your tax return instructions. Cat. No. 25379M Form **8863** (2013)

Name(s) shown on return | Your social security number

CAUTION ***Complete Part III for each student for whom you are claiming either the American opportunity credit or lifetime learning credit. Use additional copies of Page 2 as needed for each student.***

Part III Student and Educational Institution Information
See instructions.

20 Student name (as shown on page 1 of your tax return)

21 Student social security number (as shown on page 1 of your tax return)

22 Educational institution information (see instructions)

a. Name of first educational institution	**b.** Name of second educational institution (if any)
(1) Address. Number and street (or P.O. box). City, town or post office, state, and ZIP code. If a foreign address, see instructions.	**(1)** Address. Number and street (or P.O. box). City, town or post office, state, and ZIP code. If a foreign address, see instructions.
(2) Did the student receive Form 1098-T from this institution for 2013? ☐ Yes ☐ No	**(2)** Did the student receive Form 1098-T from this institution for 2013? ☐ Yes ☐ No
(3) Did the student receive Form 1098-T from this institution for 2012 with Box 2 filled in and Box 7 checked? ☐ Yes ☐ No	**(3)** Did the student receive Form 1098-T from this institution for 2012 with Box 2 filled in and Box 7 checked? ☐ Yes ☐ No
If you checked "No" in **both (2) and (3)**, skip **(4)**.	If you checked "No" in **both (2) and (3)**, skip **(4)**.
(4) If you checked "Yes" in **(2) or (3)**, enter the institution's federal identification number (from Form 1098-T). __ __ – __ __ __ __ __ __ __	**(4)** If you checked "Yes" in **(2) or (3)**, enter the institution's federal identification number (from Form 1098-T). __ __ – __ __ __ __ __ __ __

23 Has the Hope Scholarship Credit or American opportunity credit been claimed for this student for any 4 tax years before 2013? ☐ Yes — **Stop!** Go to line 31 for this student. ☐ No — Go to line 24.

24 Was the student enrolled at least half-time for at least one academic period that began in 2013 at an eligible educational institution in a program leading towards a postsecondary degree, certificate, or other recognized postsecondary educational credential? (see instructions) ☐ Yes — Go to line 25. ☐ No — **Stop!** Go to line 31 for this student.

25 Did the student complete the first 4 years of post-secondary education before 2013? ☐ Yes — **Stop!** Go to line 31 for this student. ☐ No — Go to line 26.

26 Was the student convicted, before the end of 2013, of a felony for possession or distribution of a controlled substance? ☐ Yes — **Stop!** Go to line 31 for this student. ☐ No — See *Tip* below and complete **either** lines 27-30 **or** line 31 for this student.

TIP *When you figure your taxes, you may want to compare the American opportunity credit and lifetime learning credits, and choose the credit for each student that gives you the lower tax liability. You* ***cannot*** *take the American opportunity credit and the lifetime learning credit for the* ***same student*** *in the same year. If you complete lines 27 through 30 for this student, do not complete line 31.*

American Opportunity Credit

27	Adjusted qualified education expenses (see instructions). **Do not enter more than $4,000**	**27**	
28	Subtract $2,000 from line 27. If zero or less enter -0-	**28**	
29	Multiply line 28 by 25% (.25)	**29**	
30	If line 28 is zero, enter the amount from line 27. Otherwise, add $2,000 to the amount on line 29 and enter the result. Skip line 31. Include the total of all amounts from all Parts III, line 30 on Part I, line 1	**30**	

Lifetime Learning Credit

31	Adjusted qualified education expenses (see instructions). Include the total of all amounts from all Parts III, line 31, on Part II, line 10	**31**	

Form **8863** (2013)

Form **8880**

Department of the Treasury
Internal Revenue Service

Credit for Qualified Retirement Savings Contributions

► Attach to Form 1040, Form 1040A, or Form 1040NR.

► Information about Form 8880 and its instructions is at *www.irs.gov/form8880*.

OMB No. 1545-0074

2013

Attachment Sequence No. **54**

Name(s) shown on return | **Your social security number**

CAUTION

You **cannot** take this credit if **either** of the following applies.

- The amount on Form 1040, line 38; Form 1040A, line 22; or Form 1040NR, line 37 is more than $29,500 ($44,250 if head of household; $59,000 if married filing jointly).
- The person(s) who made the qualified contribution or elective deferral **(a)** was born after January 1, 1996, **(b)** is claimed as a dependent on someone else's 2013 tax return, or **(c)** was a **student** (see instructions).

			(a) You	(b) Your spouse
1	Traditional and Roth IRA contributions for 2013. **Do not** include rollover contributions	1		
2	Elective deferrals to a 401(k) or other qualified employer plan, voluntary employee contributions, and 501(c)(18)(D) plan contributions for 2013 (see instructions)	2		
3	Add lines 1 and 2	3		
4	Certain distributions received **after** 2010 and **before** the due date (including extensions) of your 2013 tax return (see instructions). If married filing jointly, include **both** spouses' amounts in **both** columns. See instructions for an exception	4		
5	Subtract line 4 from line 3. If zero or less, enter -0-	5		
6	In each column, enter the **smaller** of line 5 or $2,000	6		
7	Add the amounts on line 6. If zero, **stop;** you cannot take this credit			7
8	Enter the amount from Form 1040, line 38*; Form 1040A, line 22; or Form 1040NR, line 37	8		
9	Enter the applicable decimal amount shown below:			9 X.

If line 8 is—		And your filing status is—		
Over—	But not over—	Married filing jointly	Head of household	Single, Married filing separately, or Qualifying widow(er)
		Enter on line 9—		
---	$17,750	.5	.5	.5
$17,750	$19,250	.5	.5	.2
$19,250	$26,625	.5	.5	.1
$26,625	$28,875	.5	.2	.1
$28,875	$29,500	.5	.1	.1
$29,500	$35,500	.5	.1	.0
$35,500	$38,500	.2	.1	.0
$38,500	$44,250	.1	.1	.0
$44,250	$59,000	.1	.0	.0
$59,000	---	.0	.0	.0

Note: *If line 9 is zero,* ***stop;*** *you cannot take this credit.*

10	Multiply line 7 by line 9	10	
11	Limitation based on tax liability. Enter the amount from the Credit Limit Worksheet in the instructions	11	
12	**Credit for qualified retirement savings contributions.** Enter the **smaller** of line 10 or line 11 here and on Form 1040, line 50; Form 1040A, line 32; or Form 1040NR, line 47	12	

*See Pub. 590 for the amount to enter if you are filing Form 2555, 2555-EZ, or 4563 or you are excluding income from Puerto Rico.

For Paperwork Reduction Act Notice, see your tax return instructions. Cat. No. 33394D Form **8880** (2013)

Form **8903**
(Rev. December 2010)
Department of the Treasury
Internal Revenue Service

Domestic Production Activities Deduction

▶ Attach to your tax return. ▶ See separate instructions.

OMB No. 1545-1984
Attachment Sequence No. **143**

Name(s) as shown on return | **Identifying number**

Note. Do not complete column (a), unless you have oil-related production activities. Enter amounts for all activities in column (b), including oil-related production activities.

			(a) Oil-related production activities	(b) All activities
1	Domestic production gross receipts (DPGR)	1		
2	Allocable cost of goods sold. If you are using the small business simplified overall method, skip lines 2 and 3	2		
3	Enter deductions and losses allocable to DPGR (see instructions)	3		
4	If you are using the small business simplified overall method, enter the amount of cost of goods sold and other deductions or losses you ratably apportion to DPGR. All others, skip line 4	4		
5	Add lines 2 through 4	5		
6	Subtract line 5 from line 1	6		
7	Qualified production activities income from estates, trusts, and certain partnerships and S corporations (see instructions)	7		
8	Add lines 6 and 7. Estates and trusts, go to line 9, all others, skip line 9 and go to line 10	8		
9	Amount allocated to beneficiaries of the estate or trust (see instructions)	9		
10a	**Oil-related qualified production activities income.** Estates and trusts, subtract line 9, column (a), from line 8, column (a), all others, enter amount from line 8, column (a). If zero or less, enter -0- here	10a		
b	**Qualified production activities income.** Estates and trusts, subtract line 9, column (b), from line 8, column (b), all others, enter amount from line 8, column (b). If zero or less, enter -0- here, skip lines 11 through 21, and enter -0- on line 22	10b		

11	Income limitation (see instructions): • Individuals, estates, and trusts. Enter your adjusted gross income figured without the domestic production activities deduction • All others. Enter your taxable income figured without the domestic production activities deduction (tax-exempt organizations, see instructions)	11	
12	Enter the smaller of line 10b or line 11. If zero or less, enter -0- here, skip lines 13 through 21, and enter -0- on line 22	12	
13	Enter 9% of line 12	13	
14a	Enter the smaller of line 10a or line 12 | 14a |		
b	Reduction for oil-related qualified production activities income. Multiply line 14a by 3%	14b	
15	Subtract line 14b from line 13	15	
16	Form W-2 wages (see instructions)	16	
17	Form W-2 wages from estates, trusts, and certain partnerships and S corporations (see instructions)	17	
18	Add lines 16 and 17. Estates and trusts, go to line 19, all others, skip line 19 and go to line 20	18	
19	Amount allocated to beneficiaries of the estate or trust (see instructions)	19	
20	Estates and trusts, subtract line 19 from line 18, all others, enter amount from line 18	20	
21	Form W-2 wage limitation. Enter 50% of line 20	21	
22	Enter the smaller of line 15 or line 21	22	
23	Domestic production activities deduction from cooperatives. Enter deduction from Form 1099-PATR, box 6	23	
24	Expanded affiliated group allocation (see instructions)	24	
25	**Domestic production activities deduction.** Combine lines 22 through 24 and enter the result here and on Form 1040, line 35; Form 1120, line 25; or the applicable line of your return	25	

For Paperwork Reduction Act Notice, see separate instructions. Cat. No. 37712F Form **8903** (Rev. 12-2010)

Form **8949**

Department of the Treasury
Internal Revenue Service

Sales and Other Dispositions of Capital Assets

▶ Information about Form 8949 and its separate instructions is at *www.irs.gov/form8949*.

▶ File with your Schedule D to list your transactions for lines 1b, 2, 3, 8b, 9, and 10 of Schedule D.

OMB No. 1545-0074

2013

Attachment Sequence No. **12A**

Name(s) shown on return	**Social security number or taxpayer identification number**

Most brokers issue their own substitute statement instead of using Form 1099-B. They also may provide basis information (usually your cost) to you on the statement even if it is not reported to the IRS. Before you check Box A, B, or C below, determine whether you received any statement(s) and, if so, the transactions for which basis was reported to the IRS. Brokers are required to report basis to the IRS for most stock you bought in 2011 or later.

Part I **Short-Term.** Transactions involving capital assets you held one year or less are short term. For long-term transactions, see page 2.

Note. You may aggregate all short-term transactions reported on Form(s) 1099-B showing basis was reported to the IRS and for which no adjustments or codes are required. Enter the total directly on Schedule D, line 1a; you are not required to report these transactions on Form 8949 (see instructions).

You *must* check Box A, B, *or* C below. Check only one box. If more than one box applies for your short-term transactions, complete a separate Form 8949, page 1, for each applicable box. If you have more short-term transactions than will fit on this page for one or more of the boxes, complete as many forms with the same box checked as you need.

☐ **(A)** Short-term transactions reported on Form(s) 1099-B showing basis was reported to the IRS (see **Note** above)

☐ **(B)** Short-term transactions reported on Form(s) 1099-B showing basis was **not** reported to the IRS

☐ **(C)** Short-term transactions not reported to you on Form 1099-B

1 (a) Description of property (Example: 100 sh. XYZ Co.)	(b) Date acquired (Mo., day, yr.)	(c) Date sold or disposed (Mo., day, yr.)	(d) Proceeds (sales price) (see instructions)	(e) Cost or other basis. See the **Note** below and see *Column (e)* in the separate instructions	**Adjustment, if any, to gain or loss.** If you enter an amount in column (g), enter a code in column (f). **See the separate instructions.** (f) Code(s) from instructions	(g) Amount of adjustment	(h) **Gain or (loss).** Subtract column (e) from column (d) and combine the result with column (g)
2 Totals. Add the amounts in columns (d), (e), (g), and (h) (subtract negative amounts). Enter each total here and include on your Schedule D, **line 1b** (if **Box A** above is checked), **line 2** (if **Box B** above is checked), or **line 3** (if **Box C** above is checked) ▶							

Note. If you checked Box A above but the basis reported to the IRS was incorrect, enter in column (e) the basis as reported to the IRS, and enter an adjustment in column (g) to correct the basis. See *Column (g)* in the separate instructions for how to figure the amount of the adjustment.

For Paperwork Reduction Act Notice, see your tax return instructions. Cat. No. 37768Z Form **8949** (2013)

Name(s) shown on return. (Name and SSN or taxpayer identification no. not required if shown on other side.)	**Social security number or taxpayer identification number**

Most brokers issue their own substitute statement instead of using Form 1099-B. They also may provide basis information (usually your cost) to you on the statement even if it is not reported to the IRS. Before you check Box D, E, or F below, determine whether you received any statement(s) and, if so, the transactions for which basis was reported to the IRS. Brokers are required to report basis to the IRS for most stock you bought in 2011 or later.

Part II **Long-Term.** Transactions involving capital assets you held more than one year are long term. For short-term transactions, see page 1.

Note. You may aggregate all long-term transactions reported on Form(s) 1099-B showing basis was reported to the IRS and for which no adjustments or codes are required. Enter the total directly on Schedule D, line 8a; you are not required to report these transactions on Form 8949 (see instructions).

You *must* check Box D, E, *or* F below. Check only one box. If more than one box applies for your long-term transactions, complete a separate Form 8949, page 2, for each applicable box. If you have more long-term transactions than will fit on this page for one or more of the boxes, complete as many forms with the same box checked as you need.

☐ **(D)** Long-term transactions reported on Form(s) 1099-B showing basis was reported to the IRS (see **Note** above)
☐ **(E)** Long-term transactions reported on Form(s) 1099-B showing basis was **not** reported to the IRS
☐ **(F)** Long-term transactions not reported to you on Form 1099-B

1 (a) Description of property (Example: 100 sh. XYZ Co.)	(b) Date acquired (Mo., day, yr.)	(c) Date sold or disposed (Mo., day, yr.)	(d) Proceeds (sales price) (see instructions)	(e) Cost or other basis. See the **Note** below and see *Column (e)* in the separate instructions	**Adjustment, if any, to gain or loss.** If you enter an amount in column (g), enter a code in column (f). **See the separate instructions.** (f) Code(s) from instructions	(g) Amount of adjustment	(h) **Gain or (loss).** Subtract column (e) from column (d) and combine the result with column (g)
2 Totals. Add the amounts in columns (d), (e), (g), and (h) (subtract negative amounts). Enter each total here and include on your Schedule D, **line 8b** (if **Box D** above is checked), **line 9** (if **Box E** above is checked), or **line 10** (if **Box F** above is checked) ▶							

Note. If you checked Box D above but the basis reported to the IRS was incorrect, enter in column (e) the basis as reported to the IRS, and enter an adjustment in column (g) to correct the basis. See *Column (g)* in the separate instructions for how to figure the amount of the adjustment.

Form **8949** (2013)

Form **SS-8** (Rev. August 2011) Department of the Treasury Internal Revenue Service	**Determination of Worker Status for Purposes of Federal Employment Taxes and Income Tax Withholding**	OMB. No. 1545-0004 **For IRS Use Only: Case Number:** **Earliest Receipt Date:**

Name of firm (or person) for whom the worker performed services		Worker's name	
Firm's mailing address (include street address, apt. or suite no., city, state, and ZIP code)		Worker's mailing address (include street address, apt. or suite no., city, state, and ZIP code)	
Trade name	Firm's email address	Worker's daytime telephone number	Worker's email address
Firm's fax number	Firm's website	Worker's alternate telephone number	Worker's fax number
Firm's telephone number (include area code)	Firm's employer identification number	Worker's social security number	Worker's employer identification number (if any)

Note. If the worker is paid for these services by a firm other than the one listed on this form, enter the name, address, and employer identification number of the payer. ▶

Disclosure of Information

The information provided on Form SS-8 may be disclosed to the firm, worker, or payer named above to assist the IRS in the determination process. For example, if you are a worker, we may disclose the information you provide on Form SS-8 to the firm or payer named above. The information can only be disclosed to assist with the determination process. If you provide incomplete information, we may not be able to process your request. See *Privacy Act and Paperwork Reduction Act Notice* on page 6 for more information. **If you do not want this information disclosed to other parties, do not file Form SS-8.**

Parts I–V. All filers of Form SS-8 must complete all questions in Parts I–IV. Part V must be completed if the worker provides a service directly to customers or is a salesperson. If you cannot answer a question, enter "Unknown" or "Does not apply." If you need more space for a question, attach another sheet with the part and question number clearly identified. Write your firm's name (or workers' name) and employer identification number (or social security number) at the top of each additional sheet attached to this form.

Part I General Information

1 This form is being completed by: ☐ Firm ☐ Worker; for services performed ________ (beginning date) to ________ (ending date).

2 Explain your reason(s) for filing this form (for example, you received a bill from the IRS, you believe you erroneously received a Form 1099 or Form W-2, you are unable to get worker's compensation benefits, or you were audited or are being audited by the IRS).

3 Total number of workers who performed or are performing the same or similar services: ________.

4 How did the worker obtain the job? ☐ Application ☐ Bid ☐ Employment Agency ☐ Other (specify)

5 **Attach copies of all supporting documentation (for example, contracts, invoices, memos, Forms W-2 or Forms 1099-MISC issued or received, IRS closing agreements or IRS rulings).** In addition, please inform us of any current or past litigation concerning the worker's status. If no income reporting forms (Form 1099-MISC or W-2) were furnished to the worker, enter the amount of income earned for the year(s) at issue $ ________.

If both Form W-2 and Form 1099-MISC were issued or received, explain why.

6 Describe the firm's business.

For Privacy Act and Paperwork Reduction Act Notice, see page 6. Cat. No. 16106T Form **SS-8** (Rev. 8-2011)

Part I General Information (continued)

7 If the worker received pay from more than one entity because of an event such as the sale, merger, acquisition, or reorganization of the firm for whom the services are performed, provide the following: Name of the firm's previous owner:

Previous owner's taxpayer identification number: Change was a: ☐ Sale ☐ Merger ☐ Acquisition ☐ Reorganization

☐ Other (specify)

Description of above change:

Date of change (MM/DD/YY):

8 Describe the work done by the worker and provide the worker's job title.

9 Explain why you believe the worker is an employee or an independent contractor.

10 Did the worker perform services for the firm in any capacity before providing the services that are the subject of this determination request?

☐ **Yes** ☐ **No** ☐ **N/A**

If "Yes," what were the dates of the prior service?

If "Yes," explain the differences, if any, between the current and prior service.

11 If the work is done under a written agreement between the firm and the worker, attach a copy (preferably signed by both parties). Describe the terms and conditions of the work arrangement.

Part II Behavioral Control (Provide names and titles of specific individuals, if applicable.)

1 What specific training and/or instruction is the worker given by the firm?

2 How does the worker receive work assignments?

3 Who determines the methods by which the assignments are performed?

4 Who is the worker required to contact if problems or complaints arise and who is responsible for their resolution?

5 What types of reports are required from the worker? Attach examples.

6 Describe the worker's daily routine such as his or her schedule or hours.

7 At what location(s) does the worker perform services (for example, firm's premises, own shop or office, home, customer's location)? Indicate the appropriate percentage of time the worker spends in each location, if more than one.

8 Describe any meetings the worker is required to attend and any penalties for not attending (for example, sales meetings, monthly meetings, staff meetings).

9 Is the worker required to provide the services personally? . . . . . ☐ **Yes** ☐ **No**

10 If substitutes or helpers are needed, who hires them?

11 If the worker hires the substitutes or helpers, is approval required? . . . . . ☐ **Yes** ☐ **No**

If "Yes," by whom?

12 Who pays the substitutes or helpers?

13 Is the worker reimbursed if the worker pays the substitutes or helpers? . . . . . ☐ **Yes** ☐ **No**

If "Yes," by whom?

Part III Financial Control (Provide names and titles of specific individuals, if applicable.)

1 List the supplies, equipment, materials, and property provided by each party:
The firm:
The worker:
Other party:

2 Does the worker lease equipment, space, or a facility? ☐ Yes ☐ No
If "Yes," what are the terms of the lease? (Attach a copy or explanatory statement.)

3 What expenses are incurred by the worker in the performance of services for the firm?

4 Specify which, if any, expenses are reimbursed by:
The firm:
Other party:

5 Type of pay the worker receives: ☐ Salary ☐ Commission ☐ Hourly Wage ☐ Piece Work ☐ Lump Sum ☐ Other (specify)
If type of pay is commission, and the firm guarantees a minimum amount of pay, specify amount. $

6 Is the worker allowed a drawing account for advances? ☐ Yes ☐ No
If "Yes," how often?
Specify any restrictions.

7 Whom does the customer pay? ☐ Firm ☐ Worker
If worker, does the worker pay the total amount to the firm? ☐ Yes ☐ No If "No," explain.

8 Does the firm carry workers' compensation insurance on the worker? ☐ Yes ☐ No

9 What economic loss or financial risk, if any, can the worker incur beyond the normal loss of salary (for example, loss or damage of equipment, material)?

10 Does the worker establish the level of payment for the services provided or the products sold? ☐ Yes ☐ No
If "No," who does?

Part IV Relationship of the Worker and Firm

1 Please check the benefits available to the worker: ☐ Paid vacations ☐ Sick pay ☐ Paid holidays ☐ Personal days ☐ Pensions ☐ Insurance benefits ☐ Bonuses ☐ Other (specify)

2 Can the relationship be terminated by either party without incurring liability or penalty? ☐ Yes ☐ No
If "No," explain your answer.

3 Did the worker perform similar services for others during the time period entered in Part I, line 1? ☐ Yes ☐ No
If "Yes," is the worker required to get approval from the firm? ☐ Yes ☐ No

4 Describe any agreements prohibiting competition between the worker and the firm while the worker is performing services or during any later period. Attach any available documentation.

5 Is the worker a member of a union? ☐ Yes ☐ No

6 What type of advertising, if any, does the worker do (for example, a business listing in a directory or business cards)? Provide copies, if applicable.

7 If the worker assembles or processes a product at home, who provides the materials and instructions or pattern?

8 What does the worker do with the finished product (for example, return it to the firm, provide it to another party, or sell it)?

9 How does the firm represent the worker to its customers (for example, employee, partner, representative, or contractor), and under whose business name does the worker perform these services?

10 If the worker no longer performs services for the firm, how did the relationship end (for example, worker quit or was fired, job completed, contract ended, firm or worker went out of business)?

Form SS-8 (Rev. 8-2011)

Part V **For Service Providers or Salespersons.** Complete this part if the worker provided a service directly to customers or is a salesperson.

1 What are the worker's responsibilities in soliciting new customers? ____________

2 Who provides the worker with leads to prospective customers? ____________

3 Describe any reporting requirements pertaining to the leads. ____________

4 What terms and conditions of sale, if any, are required by the firm? ____________

5 Are orders submitted to and subject to approval by the firm? . . . ☐ Yes ☐ No

6 Who determines the worker's territory? ____________

7 Did the worker pay for the privilege of serving customers on the route or in the territory? . . . ☐ Yes ☐ No

If "Yes," whom did the worker pay? ____________

If "Yes," how much did the worker pay? . . . $ ____________

8 Where does the worker sell the product (for example, in a home, retail establishment)? ____________

9 List the product and/or services distributed by the worker (for example, meat, vegetables, fruit, bakery products, beverages, or laundry or dry cleaning services). If more than one type of product and/or service is distributed, specify the principal one. ____________

10 Does the worker sell life insurance full time? . . . ☐ Yes ☐ No

11 Does the worker sell other types of insurance for the firm? . . . ☐ Yes ☐ No

If "Yes," enter the percentage of the worker's total working time spent in selling other types of insurance . . . ______ %

12 If the worker solicits orders from wholesalers, retailers, contractors, or operators of hotels, restaurants, or other similar establishments, enter the percentage of the worker's time spent in the solicitation . . . ______ %

13 Is the merchandise purchased by the customers for resale or use in their business operations? . . . ☐ Yes ☐ No

Describe the merchandise and state whether it is equipment installed on the customers' premises. ____________

Sign Here

Under penalties of perjury, I declare that I have examined this request, including accompanying documents, and to the best of my knowledge and belief, the facts presented are true, correct, and complete.

► ____________ Title ► ____________ Date ► ____________

Type or print name below signature.

Form **SS-8** (Rev. 8-2011)

General Instructions

Section references are to the Internal Revenue Code unless otherwise noted.

Purpose

Firms and workers file Form SS-8 to request a determination of the status of a worker for purposes of federal employment taxes and income tax withholding.

A Form SS-8 determination may be requested only in order to resolve federal tax matters. If Form SS-8 is submitted for a tax year for which the statute of limitations on the tax return has expired, a determination letter will not be issued. The statute of limitations expires 3 years from the due date of the tax return or the date filed, whichever is later.

The IRS does not issue a determination letter for proposed transactions or on hypothetical situations. We may, however, issue an information letter when it is considered appropriate.

Definition

Firm. For the purposes of this form, the term "firm" means any individual, business enterprise, organization, state, or other entity for which a worker has performed services. The firm may or may not have paid the worker directly for these services.

CAUTION *If the firm was not responsible for payment for services, be sure to enter the name, address, and employer identification number of the payer on the first page of Form SS-8, below the identifying information for the firm and the worker.*

The Form SS-8 Determination Process

The IRS will acknowledge the receipt of your Form SS-8. Because there are usually two (or more) parties who could be affected by a determination of employment status, the IRS attempts to get information from all parties involved by sending those parties blank Forms SS-8 for completion. Some or all of the information provided on this Form SS-8 may be shared with the other parties listed on page 1. The case will be assigned to a technician who will review the facts, apply the law, and render a decision. The technician may ask for additional information from the requestor, from other involved parties, or from third parties that could help clarify the work relationship before rendering a decision. The IRS will generally issue a formal determination to the firm or payer (if that is a different entity), and will send a copy to the worker. A determination letter applies only to a worker (or a class of workers) requesting it, and the decision is binding on the IRS. In certain cases, a formal determination will not be issued. Instead, an information letter may be issued. Although an information letter is advisory only and is not binding on the IRS, it may be used to assist the worker to fulfill his or her federal tax obligations.

Neither the Form SS-8 determination process nor the review of any records in connection with the determination constitutes an examination (audit) of any federal tax return. If the periods under consideration have previously been examined, the Form SS-8 determination process will not constitute a reexamination under IRS reopening procedures. Because this is not an examination of any federal tax return, the appeal rights available in connection with an examination do not apply to a Form SS-8 determination. However, if you disagree with a determination or you have additional information concerning the work relationship that you believe was not previously considered, you may request that the determining office reconsider the determination.

Completing Form SS-8

Answer all questions as completely as possible. Attach additional sheets if you need more space. Provide information for **all** years the worker provided services for the firm. Determinations are based on the entire relationship between the firm and the worker. Also indicate if there were any significant changes in the work relationship over the service term.

Additional copies of this form may be obtained on IRS.gov or by calling 1-800-TAX-FORM (1-800-829-3676).

Fee

There is no fee for requesting a Form SS-8 determination letter.

Signature

Form SS-8 must be signed and dated by the taxpayer. A stamped signature will not be accepted.

The person who signs for a corporation must be an officer of the corporation who has personal knowledge of the facts. If the corporation is a member of an affiliated group filing a consolidated return, it must be signed by an officer of the common parent of the group.

The person signing for a trust, partnership, or limited liability company must be, respectively, a trustee, general partner, or member-manager who has personal knowledge of the facts.

Where To File

Send the completed and signed Form SS-8 to the address below for the firm's location. Faxed, photocopied, or electronic versions of Form SS-8 are not acceptable for the initial request for the Form SS-8 determination. However, only for cases involving federal agencies, send Form SS-8 to the Internal Revenue Service, Attn: CC:CORP:T:C, Ben Franklin Station, P.O. Box 7604, Washington, DC 20044. **Do not submit Form SS-8 with your tax return as that will delay processing time.**

Firm's location:	Send to:
Alaska, Arizona, Arkansas, California, Colorado, Hawaii, Idaho, Illinois, Iowa, Kansas, Minnesota, Missouri, Montana, Nebraska, Nevada, New Mexico, North Dakota, Oklahoma, Oregon, South Dakota, Texas, Utah, Washington, Wisconsin, Wyoming, American Samoa, Guam, Puerto Rico, U.S. Virgin Islands	Internal Revenue Service Form SS-8 Determinations P.O. Box 630 Stop 631 Holtsville, NY 11742-0630
Alabama, Connecticut, Delaware, District of Columbia, Florida, Georgia, Indiana, Kentucky, Louisiana, Maine, Maryland, Massachusetts, Michigan, Mississippi, New Hampshire, New Jersey, New York, North Carolina, Ohio, Pennsylvania, Rhode Island, South Carolina, Tennessee, Vermont, Virginia, West Virginia, all other locations not listed	Internal Revenue Service Form SS-8 Determinations 40 Lakemont Road Newport, VT 05855-1555

Instructions for Workers

If you are requesting a determination for more than one firm, complete a separate Form SS-8 for each firm.

CAUTION *Form SS-8 is not a claim for refund of social security and Medicare taxes or federal income tax withholding.*

If the IRS determines that you are an employee, you are responsible for filing an amended return for any corrections related to this decision. A determination that a worker is an employee does not necessarily reduce any current or prior tax liability. For more information, call 1-800-829-1040.

Time for filing a claim for refund. Generally, you must file your claim for a credit or refund within 3 years from the date your original return was filed or within 2 years from the date the tax was paid, whichever is later.

Filing Form SS-8 does not prevent the expiration of the time in which a claim for a refund must be filed. If you are concerned about a refund, and the statute of limitations for filing a claim for refund for the year(s) at issue has not yet expired, you should file Form 1040X, Amended U.S. Individual Income Tax Return, to protect your statute of limitations. File a separate Form 1040X for each year.

On the Form 1040X you file, do not complete lines 1 through 22 on the form. Write "Protective Claim" at the top of the form, sign and date it. In addition, enter the following statement in Part III: "Filed Form SS-8 with the Internal Revenue Service Office in (Holtsville, NY; Newport, VT; or Washington, DC; as appropriate). By filing this protective claim, I reserve the right to file a claim for any refund that may be due after a determination of my employment tax status has been completed."

Filing Form SS-8 does not alter the requirement to timely file an income tax return. Do not delay filing your tax return in anticipation of an answer to your Form SS-8 request. In addition, if applicable, do not delay in responding to a request for payment while waiting for a determination of your worker status.

Instructions for Firms

If a **worker** has requested a determination of his or her status while working for you, you will receive a request from the IRS to complete a Form SS-8. In cases of this type, the IRS usually gives each party an opportunity to present a statement of the facts because any decision will affect the employment tax status of the parties. Failure to respond to this request will not prevent the IRS from issuing a determination letter based on the information he or she has made available so that the worker may fulfill his or her federal tax obligations. However, the information that you provide is extremely valuable in determining the status of the worker.

If you are requesting a determination for a particular class of worker, complete the form for one individual who is representative of the class of workers whose status is in question. If you want a written determination for more than one class of workers, complete a separate Form SS-8 for one worker from each class whose status is typical of that class. A written determination for any worker will apply to other workers of the same class if the facts are not materially different for these workers. Please provide a list of names and addresses of all workers potentially affected by this determination.

If you have a reasonable basis for not treating a worker as an employee, you may be relieved from having to pay employment taxes for that worker under section 530 of the 1978 Revenue Act. However, this relief provision cannot be considered in conjunction with a Form SS-8 determination because the determination does not constitute an examination of any tax return. For more information regarding section 530 of the 1978 Revenue Act and to determine if you qualify for relief under this section, visit IRS.gov.

Privacy Act and Paperwork Reduction Act Notice. We ask for the information on Form SS-8 to carry out the Internal Revenue laws of the United States. This information will be used to determine the employment status of the worker(s) described on the form. Subtitle C, Employment Taxes, of the Internal Revenue Code imposes employment taxes on wages, including income tax withholding. Sections 3121(d), 3306(a), and 3401(c) and (d) and the related regulations define employee and employer for purposes of employment taxes imposed under Subtitle C. Section 6001 authorizes the IRS to request information needed to determine if a worker(s) or firm is subject to these taxes. Section 6109 requires you to provide your taxpayer identification number. Neither workers nor firms are required to request a status determination, but if you choose to do so, you must provide the information requested on this form. Failure to provide the requested information may prevent us from making a status determination. If any worker or the firm has requested a status determination and you are being asked to provide information for use in that determination, you are not required to provide the requested information. However, failure to provide such information will prevent the IRS from considering it in making the status determination. Providing false or fraudulent information may subject you to penalties. Generally, tax returns and return information are confidential, as required by section 6103. However, section 6103 allows or requires the IRS to disclose or give the information shown on your tax return to others as described in the Code. Routine uses of this information include providing it to the Department of Justice for use in civil and criminal litigation, to the Social Security Administration for the administration of social security programs, and to cities, states, the District of Columbia, and U.S. commonwealths and possessions for the administration of their tax laws. We also may disclose this information to other countries under a tax treaty, to federal and state agencies to enforce federal nontax criminal laws, or to federal law enforcement and intelligence agencies to combat terrorism. We may provide this information to the affected worker(s), the firm, or payer as part of the status determination process.

You are not required to provide the information requested on a form that is subject to the Paperwork Reduction Act unless the form displays a valid OMB control number. Books or records relating to a form or its instructions must be retained as long as their contents may become material in the administration of any Internal Revenue law.

The time needed to complete and file this Form SS-8 will vary depending on individual circumstances. The estimated average time is: Recordkeeping, 23 hrs., 55 min.; Learning about the law or the form, 1 hr., 48 min.; Preparing the form, 5 hrs., 03 min.; and Sending the form to the IRS, 48 min. If you have comments concerning the accuracy of these time estimates or suggestions for making this form simpler, we would be happy to hear from you. You can write to the Internal Revenue Service, Tax Products Coordinating Committee, SE:W:CAR:MP:T:M:S, 1111 Constitution Ave. NW, IR-6526, Washington, DC 20224. Do not send the tax form to this address. Instead, see *Where To File* on page 5.

Form SSA-1099, Social Security Benefit Statement 2013

Every person who received social security benefits will receive a Form SSA-1099. If you receive benefits on more than one social security record, you may get more than one Form SSA-1099. IRS Notice 703 will be enclosed with this form. It contains a worksheet to help you figure if any of your benefits are taxable. Do not mail Notice 703 to either the IRS or the SSA.

Box 1—Name

The name shown in this box refers to the person for whom the social security benefits shown on the statement were paid. If you received benefits for yourself, your name will be shown.

Box 2—Beneficiary's Social Security Number

This is the U.S. social security number, if known, of the person named in box 1.

TIP *In all your correspondence with the SSA, be sure to use the claim number shown in box 8.*

Box 3—Benefits Paid in 2013

The figure shown in this box is the total benefits paid in 2013 to you (the person named in box 1). This figure may not agree with the amounts you actually received because adjustments may have been made to your benefits before you received them. An asterisk (*) after the figure shown in this box means that it includes benefits received in 2013 for one or more earlier years.

Description of Amount in Box 3

This part of the form describes the items included in the amount shown in box 3. It lists the benefits paid and any adjustments made. Only the adjustments that apply to you will be shown. If no adjustments were made to the benefits paid, the word "none" will be shown.

Paid by check or direct deposit. This is the amount you actually received or that was deposited directly into your account in a financial institution in 2013.

Additions. The following adjustment items may have been deducted from your benefits in 2013. If amounts appear on your Form SSA-1099 next to these items, they will be added to the amount shown in "Paid by check or direct deposit."

FORM SSA-1099 – SOCIAL SECURITY BENEFIT STATEMENT

2013 • PART OF YOUR SOCIAL SECURITY BENEFITS SHOWN IN BOX 5 MAY BE TAXABLE INCOME.
• SEE THE REVERSE FOR MORE INFORMATION.

Box 1. Name		Box 2. Beneficiary's Social Security Number
Box 3. Benefits Paid in 2013	Box 4. Benefits Repaid to SSA in 2013	Box 5. Net Benefits for 2013 *(Box 3 minus Box 4)*

DESCRIPTION OF AMOUNT IN BOX 3	**DESCRIPTION OF AMOUNT IN BOX 4**
	Box 6. Voluntary Federal Income Tax Withheld
	Box 7. Address
	Box 8. Claim Number *(Use this number if you need to contact SSA.)*

SAMPLE

Form **SSA-1099-SM** (1-2014) **DO NOT RETURN THIS FORM TO SSA OR IRS**

	a Employee's social security number	OMB No. 1545-0008	Safe, accurate, FAST! Use e-file — Visit the IRS website at *www.irs.gov/efile*
b Employer identification number (EIN)		1 Wages, tips, other compensation	2 Federal income tax withheld
c Employer's name, address, and ZIP code		3 Social security wages	4 Social security tax withheld
		5 Medicare wages and tips	6 Medicare tax withheld
		7 Social security tips	8 Allocated tips
d Control number		9	10 Dependent care benefits
e Employee's first name and initial Last name Suff.		11 Nonqualified plans	12a See instructions for box 12 Code
		13 Statutory employee ☐ Retirement plan ☐ Third-party sick pay ☐	12b Code
		14 Other	12c Code
f Employee's address and ZIP code			12d Code

15 State Employer's state ID number	16 State wages, tips, etc.	17 State income tax	18 Local wages, tips, etc.	19 Local income tax	20 Locality name

Form **W-2** **Wage and Tax Statement** **2014**

Department of the Treasury—Internal Revenue Service

Copy B—To Be Filed With Employee's FEDERAL Tax Return.
This information is being furnished to the Internal Revenue Service.

☐ CORRECTED (if checked)

PAYER'S name, street address, city or town, province or state, country, and ZIP or foreign postal code	1 Gross winnings $	2 Date won	OMB No. 1545-0238 **2014** **Form W-2G** **Certain Gambling Winnings**
	3 Type of wager	**4 Federal income tax withheld** $	
	5 Transaction	6 Race	
	7 Winnings from identical wagers $	8 Cashier	
PAYER'S federal identification number	PAYER'S telephone number	9 Winner's taxpayer identification no.	10 Window	This information is being furnished to the Internal Revenue Service
WINNER'S name	11 First I.D.	12 Second I.D.	
Street address (including apt. no.)	13 State/Payer's state identification no.	14 State winnings $	**Copy B** **Report this income on your federal tax return. If this form shows federal income tax withheld in box 4, attach this copy to your return.**
City or town, province or state, country, and ZIP or foreign postal code	15 State income tax withheld $	16 Local winnings $	
	17 Local income tax withheld $	18 Name of locality	

Under penalties of perjury, I declare that, to the best of my knowledge and belief, the name, address, and taxpayer identification number that I have furnished correctly identify me as the recipient of this payment and any payments from identical wagers, and that no other person is entitled to any part of these payments.

Signature ▶ **Date ▶**

Form **W-2G** www.irs.gov/w2g Department of the Treasury - Internal Revenue Service

Form W-4 (2014)

Purpose. Complete Form W-4 so that your employer can withhold the correct federal income tax from your pay. Consider completing a new Form W-4 each year and when your personal or financial situation changes.

Exemption from withholding. If you are exempt, complete **only** lines 1, 2, 3, 4, and 7 and sign the form to validate it. Your exemption for 2014 expires February 17, 2015. See Pub. 505, Tax Withholding and Estimated Tax.

Note. If another person can claim you as a dependent on his or her tax return, you cannot claim exemption from withholding if your income exceeds $1,000 and includes more than $350 of unearned income (for example, interest and dividends).

Exceptions. An employee may be able to claim exemption from withholding even if the employee is a dependent, if the employee:

- Is age 65 or older,
- Is blind, or
- Will claim adjustments to income; tax credits; or itemized deductions, on his or her tax return.

The exceptions do not apply to supplemental wages greater than $1,000,000.

Basic instructions. If you are not exempt, complete the **Personal Allowances Worksheet** below. The worksheets on page 2 further adjust your withholding allowances based on itemized deductions, certain credits, adjustments to income, or two-earners/multiple jobs situations.

Complete all worksheets that apply. However, you may claim fewer (or zero) allowances. For regular wages, withholding must be based on allowances you claimed and may not be a flat amount or percentage of wages.

Head of household. Generally, you can claim head of household filing status on your tax return only if you are unmarried and pay more than 50% of the costs of keeping up a home for yourself and your dependent(s) or other qualifying individuals. See Pub. 501, Exemptions, Standard Deduction, and Filing Information, for information.

Tax credits. You can take projected tax credits into account in figuring your allowable number of withholding allowances. Credits for child or dependent care expenses and the child tax credit may be claimed using the **Personal Allowances Worksheet** below. See Pub. 505 for information on converting your other credits into withholding allowances.

Nonwage income. If you have a large amount of nonwage income, such as interest or dividends, consider making estimated tax payments using Form 1040-ES, Estimated Tax for Individuals. Otherwise, you may owe additional tax. If you have pension or annuity iincome, see Pub. 505 to find out if you should adjust your withholding on Form W-4 or W-4P.

Two earners or multiple jobs. If you have a working spouse or more than one job, figure the total number of allowances you are entitled to claim on all jobs using worksheets from only one Form W-4. Your withholding usually will be most accurate when all allowances are claimed on the Form W-4 for the highest paying job and zero allowances are claimed on the others. See Pub. 505 for details.

Nonresident alien. If you are a nonresident alien, see Notice 1392, Supplemental Form W-4 Instructions for Nonresident Aliens, before completing this form.

Check your withholding. After your Form W-4 takes effect, use Pub. 505 to see how the amount you are having withheld compares to your projected total tax for 2014. See Pub. 505, especially if your earnings exceed $130,000 (Single) or $180,000 (Married).

Future developments. Information about any future developments affecting Form W-4 (such as legislation enacted after we release it) will be posted at *www.irs.gov/w4.*

Personal Allowances Worksheet (Keep for your records.)

A Enter "1" for **yourself** if no one else can claim you as a dependent . . . . . **A** ______

B Enter "1" if:
- You are single and have only one job; or
- You are married, have only one job, and your spouse does not work; or
- Your wages from a second job or your spouse's wages (or the total of both) are $1,500 or less.

. . . **B** ______

C Enter "1" for your **spouse.** But, you may choose to enter "-0-" if you are married and have either a working spouse or more than one job. (Entering "-0-" may help you avoid having too little tax withheld.) . . . . . **C** ______

D Enter number of **dependents** (other than your spouse or yourself) you will claim on your tax return . . . . **D** ______

E Enter "1" if you will file as **head of household** on your tax return (see conditions under **Head of household** above) . . **E** ______

F Enter "1" if you have at least $2,000 of **child or dependent care expenses** for which you plan to claim a credit . . . **F** ______
(**Note.** Do **not** include child support payments. See Pub. 503, Child and Dependent Care Expenses, for details.)

G **Child Tax Credit** (including additional child tax credit). See Pub. 972, Child Tax Credit, for more information.
- If your total income will be less than $65,000 ($95,000 if married), enter "2" for each eligible child; then **less** "1" if you have three to six eligible children or **less** "2" if you have seven or more eligible children.
- If your total income will be between $65,000 and $84,000 ($95,000 and $119,000 if married), enter "1" for each eligible child . . . **G** ______

H Add lines A through G and enter total here. (**Note.** This may be different from the number of exemptions you claim on your tax return.) ▶ **H** ______

For accuracy, **complete all worksheets that apply.**
- If you plan to **itemize** or **claim adjustments to income** and want to reduce your withholding, see the **Deductions and Adjustments Worksheet** on page 2.
- If you are **single and have more than one job** or are **married and you and your spouse both work** and the combined earnings from all jobs exceed $50,000 ($20,000 if married), see the **Two-Earners/Multiple Jobs Worksheet** on page 2 to avoid having too little tax withheld.
- If **neither** of the above situations applies, **stop here** and enter the number from line H on line 5 of Form W-4 below.

--- **Separate here and give Form W-4 to your employer. Keep the top part for your records.** ---

Form **W-4**
Department of the Treasury
Internal Revenue Service

Employee's Withholding Allowance Certificate

▶ **Whether you are entitled to claim a certain number of allowances or exemption from withholding is subject to review by the IRS. Your employer may be required to send a copy of this form to the IRS.**

OMB No. 1545-0074
2014

1 Your first name and middle initial	Last name	2 **Your social security number**
Home address (number and street or rural route)	3 ☐ Single ☐ Married ☐ Married, but withhold at higher Single rate. **Note.** If married, but legally separated, or spouse is a nonresident alien, check the "Single" box.	
City or town, state, and ZIP code	4 **If your last name differs from that shown on your social security card, check here. You must call 1-800-772-1213 for a replacement card.** ▶ ☐	

5 Total number of allowances you are claiming (from line **H** above **or** from the applicable worksheet on page 2) **5** ______

6 Additional amount, if any, you want withheld from each paycheck . . . . . **6** $ ______

7 I claim exemption from withholding for 2014, and I certify that I meet **both** of the following conditions for exemption.
- Last year I had a right to a refund of **all** federal income tax withheld because I had **no** tax liability, **and**
- This year I expect a refund of **all** federal income tax withheld because I expect to have **no** tax liability.

If you meet both conditions, write "Exempt" here . . . . . ▶ **7** ______

Under penalties of perjury, I declare that I have examined this certificate and, to the best of my knowledge and belief, it is true, correct, and complete.

Employee's signature
(This form is not valid unless you sign it.) ▶ **Date** ▶

8 Employer's name and address (Employer: Complete lines 8 and 10 only if sending to the IRS.)	9 Office code (optional)	10 Employer identification number (EIN)

For Privacy Act and Paperwork Reduction Act Notice, see page 2. Cat. No. 10220Q Form **W-4** (2014)

Deductions and Adjustments Worksheet

Note. Use this worksheet *only* if you plan to itemize deductions or claim certain credits or adjustments to income.

1 Enter an estimate of your 2014 itemized deductions. These include qualifying home mortgage interest, charitable contributions, state and local taxes, medical expenses in excess of 10% (7.5% if either you or your spouse was born before January 2, 1950) of your income, and miscellaneous deductions. For 2014, you may have to reduce your itemized deductions if your income is over $305,050 and you are married filing jointly or are a qualifying widow(er); $279,650 if you are head of household; $254,200 if you are single and not head of household or a qualifying widow(er); or $152,525 if you are married filing separately. See Pub. 505 for details . . . . **1** $ ______

2 Enter: { $12,400 if married filing jointly or qualifying widow(er) / $9,100 if head of household / $6,200 if single or married filing separately } . . . . **2** $ ______

3 **Subtract** line 2 from line 1. If zero or less, enter "-0-" . . . . **3** $ ______

4 Enter an estimate of your 2014 adjustments to income and any additional standard deduction (see Pub. 505) **4** $ ______

5 **Add** lines 3 and 4 and enter the total. (Include any amount for credits from the *Converting Credits to Withholding Allowances for 2014 Form W-4* worksheet in Pub. 505.) . . . . **5** $ ______

6 Enter an estimate of your 2014 nonwage income (such as dividends or interest) . . . . **6** $ ______

7 **Subtract** line 6 from line 5. If zero or less, enter "-0-" . . . . **7** $ ______

8 **Divide** the amount on line 7 by $3,950 and enter the result here. Drop any fraction . . . . **8** ______

9 Enter the number from the **Personal Allowances Worksheet,** line H, page 1 . . . . **9** ______

10 **Add** lines 8 and 9 and enter the total here. If you plan to use the **Two-Earners/Multiple Jobs Worksheet,** also enter this total on line 1 below. Otherwise, **stop here** and enter this total on Form W-4, line 5, page 1 **10** ______

Two-Earners/Multiple Jobs Worksheet (See *Two earners or multiple jobs* on page 1.)

Note. Use this worksheet *only* if the instructions under line H on page 1 direct you here.

1 Enter the number from line H, page 1 (or from line 10 above if you used the **Deductions and Adjustments Worksheet**) **1** ______

2 Find the number in **Table 1** below that applies to the **LOWEST** paying job and enter it here. **However,** if you are married filing jointly and wages from the highest paying job are $65,000 or less, do not enter more than "3" . . . . **2** ______

3 If line 1 is **more than or equal to** line 2, subtract line 2 from line 1. Enter the result here (if zero, enter "-0-") and on Form W-4, line 5, page 1. **Do not** use the rest of this worksheet . . . . **3** ______

Note. If line 1 is **less than** line 2, enter "-0-" on Form W-4, line 5, page 1. Complete lines 4 through 9 below to figure the additional withholding amount necessary to avoid a year-end tax bill.

4 Enter the number from line 2 of this worksheet . . . . **4** ______

5 Enter the number from line 1 of this worksheet . . . . **5** ______

6 **Subtract** line 5 from line 4 . . . . **6** ______

7 Find the amount in **Table 2** below that applies to the **HIGHEST** paying job and enter it here . . . . **7** $ ______

8 **Multiply** line 7 by line 6 and enter the result here. This is the additional annual withholding needed . . **8** $ ______

9 Divide line 8 by the number of pay periods remaining in 2014. For example, divide by 25 if you are paid every two weeks and you complete this form on a date in January when there are 25 pay periods remaining in 2014. Enter the result here and on Form W-4, line 6, page 1. This is the additional amount to be withheld from each paycheck **9** $ ______

Table 1

Married Filing Jointly		All Others	
If wages from **LOWEST** paying job are—	Enter on line 2 above	If wages from **LOWEST** paying job are—	Enter on line 2 above
$0 - $6,000	0	$0 - $6,000	0
6,001 - 13,000	1	6,001 - 16,000	1
13,001 - 24,000	2	16,001 - 25,000	2
24,001 - 26,000	3	25,001 - 34,000	3
26,001 - 33,000	4	34,001 - 43,000	4
33,001 - 43,000	5	43,001 - 70,000	5
43,001 - 49,000	6	70,001 - 85,000	6
49,001 - 60,000	7	85,001 - 110,000	7
60,001 - 75,000	8	110,001 - 125,000	8
75,001 - 80,000	9	125,001 - 140,000	9
80,001 - 100,000	10	140,001 and over	10
100,001 - 115,000	11		
115,001 - 130,000	12		
130,001 - 140,000	13		
140,001 - 150,000	14		
150,001 and over	15		

Table 2

Married Filing Jointly		All Others	
If wages from **HIGHEST** paying job are—	Enter on line 7 above	If wages from **HIGHEST** paying job are—	Enter on line 7 above
$0 - $74,000	$590	$0 - $37,000	$590
74,001 - 130,000	990	37,001 - 80,000	990
130,001 - 200,000	1,110	80,001 - 175,000	1,110
200,001 - 355,000	1,300	175,001 - 385,000	1,300
355,001 - 400,000	1,380	385,001 and over	1,560
400,001 and over	1,560		

Privacy Act and Paperwork Reduction Act Notice. We ask for the information on this form to carry out the Internal Revenue laws of the United States. Internal Revenue Code sections 3402(f)(2) and 6109 and their regulations require you to provide this information; your employer uses it to determine your federal income tax withholding. Failure to provide a properly completed form will result in your being treated as a single person who claims no withholding allowances; providing fraudulent information may subject you to penalties. Routine uses of this information include giving it to the Department of Justice for civil and criminal litigation; to cities, states, the District of Columbia, and U.S. commonwealths and possessions for use in administering their tax laws; and to the Department of Health and Human Services for use in the National Directory of New Hires. We may also disclose this information to other countries under a tax treaty, to federal and state agencies to enforce federal nontax criminal laws, or to federal law enforcement and intelligence agencies to combat terrorism.

You are not required to provide the information requested on a form that is subject to the Paperwork Reduction Act unless the form displays a valid OMB control number. Books or records relating to a form or its instructions must be retained as long as their contents may become material in the administration of any Internal Revenue law. Generally, tax returns and return information are confidential, as required by Code section 6103.

The average time and expenses required to complete and file this form will vary depending on individual circumstances. For estimated averages, see the instructions for your income tax return.

If you have suggestions for making this form simpler, we would be happy to hear from you. See the instructions for your income tax return.

U.S. DEPARTMENT OF THE TREASURY

INTERNAL REVENUE SERVICE

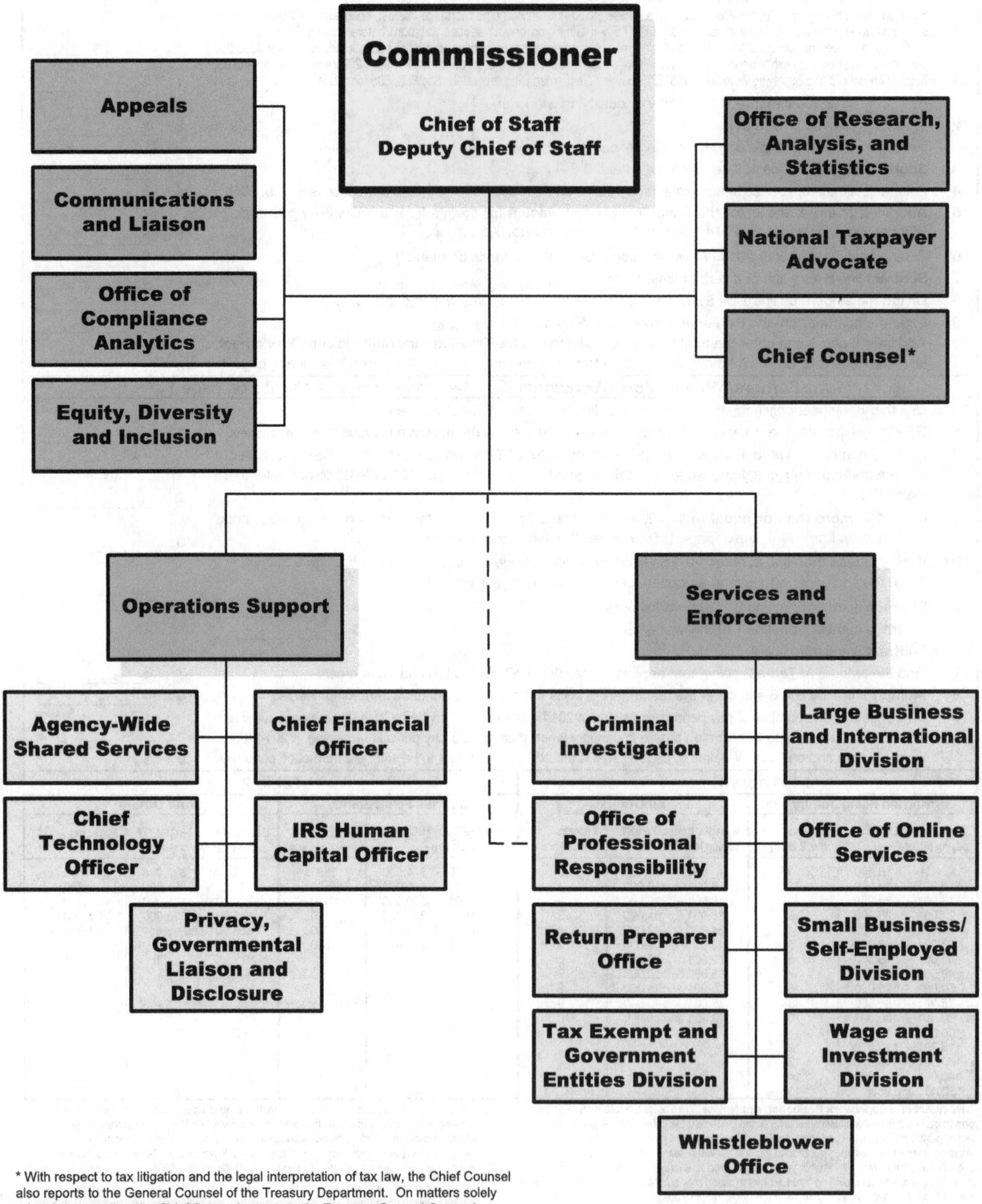

* With respect to tax litigation and the legal interpretation of tax law, the Chief Counsel also reports to the General Counsel of the Treasury Department. On matters solely related to tax policy, the Chief Counsel reports to the Treasury General Counsel.

Department of the Treasury
Internal Revenue Service

Publication 15-B
Cat. No. 29744N

Employer's Tax Guide to Fringe Benefits

For use in **2014**

Get forms and other Information faster and easier by Internet at IRS.gov

Dec 04, 2013

Contents

Future Developments

For the latest information about developments related to Publication 15-B, such as legislation enacted after it was published, go to *www.irs.gov/pub15b*.

What's New

Cents-per-mile rule. The business mileage rate for 2014 is 56 cents per mile. You may use this rate to reimburse an employee for business use of a personal vehicle, and under certain conditions, you may use the rate under the cents-per-mile rule to value the personal use of a vehicle you provide to an employee. See Cents-Per-Mile Rule in section 3.

Qualified parking exclusion and commuter transportation benefit. For 2014, the monthly exclusion for qualified parking is $250 and the monthly exclusion for commuter highway vehicle transportation and transit passes is $130. See Qualified Transportation Benefits in section 2.

Same-sex Marriage For federal tax purposes, individuals of the same sex are considered married if they were lawfully married in a state (or foreign country) whose laws authorize the marriage of two individuals of the same sex, even if the state (or foreign country) in which they now live does not recognize same-sex marriage. For more information, see Revenue Ruling 2013-17, 2013-38 I.R.B. 201, available at *www.irs.gov/irb/2013-38_IRB/ar07.html*. Notice 2013-61 provides special administrative procedures for employers to make claims for refund or adjustments of overpayments of social security and Medicare taxes with respect to certain same-sex spouse benefits before expiration of the period of limitations. Notice 2013-61, 2013-44 I.R.B. 432, is available at *www.irs.gov/irb/2013-44_IRB/ar10.html*.

Recent changes to certain rules for cafeteria plans. Notice 2013-71, 2013-47 I.R.B. 532, available at *www.irs.gov/irb/2013-47_IRB/ar10.html*, discusses recent changes to the "use-or-lose" rule for health flexible spending arrangements (FSAs) and clarifies the transitional rule for 2013-2014 non-calendar year salary reduction elections. See Notice 2013-71 for details on these changes.

Reminders

$2,500 limit on a health flexible spending arrangement (FSA). For plan years beginning after December 31, 2012, a cafeteria plan may not allow an employee to request salary reduction contributions for a health FSA in excess of $2,500. For plan years beginning after December 31, 2013, the limit is unchanged at $2,500. For more information, see *Cafeteria Plans* in section 1.

Additional Medicare Tax withholding. In addition to withholding Medicare tax at 1.45%, you must withhold a 0.9% Additional Medicare Tax from wages you pay to an employee in excess of $200,000 in a calendar year. You are required to begin withholding Additional Medicare Tax in the pay period in which you pay wages in excess of $200,000 to an employee and continue to withhold it each pay period until the end of the calendar year. Additional Medicare Tax is only imposed on the employee. There is no employer share of Additional Medicare Tax. All wages that are subject to Medicare tax are subject to Additional Medicare Tax withholding if paid in excess of the $200,000 withholding threshold. Unless otherwise noted, references to Medicare tax include Additional Medicare Tax.

For more information on what wages are subject to Medicare tax, see Table 2-1, later, and the chart, *Special Rules for Various Types of Services and Payments*, in section 15 of Publication 15, (Circular E), Employer's Tax Guide. For more information on Additional Medicare Tax, visit IRS.gov and enter "Additional Medicare Tax" in the search box.

Photographs of missing children. The IRS is a proud partner with the National Center for Missing and Exploited Children. Photographs of missing children selected by the Center may appear in this publication on pages that would otherwise be blank. You can help bring these children home by looking at the photographs and calling 1-800-THE-LOST (1-800-843-5678) if you recognize a child.

Introduction

This publication supplements Publication 15 (Circular E), Employer's Tax Guide, and Publication 15-A, Employer's Supplemental Tax Guide. It contains information for employers on the employment tax treatment of fringe benefits.

Comments and suggestions. We welcome your comments about this publication and your suggestions for future editions.

You can write to us at the following address:

Internal Revenue Service
Tax Forms and Publications Division
1111 Constitution Ave. NW, IR-6526
Washington, DC 20224

We respond to many letters by telephone. Therefore, it would be helpful if you would include your daytime phone number, including the area code, in your correspondence.

You can also send us comments from *www.irs.gov/formspubs*. Click on *More Information* and then click on *Comment on Tax Forms and Publications.*

Although we cannot respond individually to each comment received, we do appreciate your feedback and will consider your comments as we revise our tax products.

1. Fringe Benefit Overview

A fringe benefit is a form of pay for the performance of services. For example, you provide an employee with a fringe benefit when you allow the employee to use a business vehicle to commute to and from work.

Performance of services. A person who performs services for you does not have to be your employee. A person may perform services for you as an independent contractor, partner, or director. Also, for fringe benefit purposes, treat a person who agrees not to perform services (such as under a covenant not to compete) as performing services.

Provider of benefit. You are the provider of a fringe benefit if it is provided for services performed for you. You are considered the provider of a fringe benefit even if a third party, such as your client or customer, provides the benefit to your employee for services the employee performs for you. For example, if, in exchange for goods or services, your customer provides day care services as a fringe benefit to your employees for services they provide for you as their employer, then you are the provider of this fringe benefit even though the customer is actually providing the day care.

Recipient of benefit. The person who performs services for you is considered the recipient of a fringe benefit provided for those services. That person may be considered the recipient even if the benefit is provided to someone who did not perform services for you. For example, your employee may be the recipient of a fringe benefit you provide to a member of the employee's family.

Are Fringe Benefits Taxable?

Any fringe benefit you provide is taxable and must be included in the recipient's pay unless the law specifically excludes it. Section 2 discusses the exclusions that apply to certain fringe benefits. Any benefit not excluded under the rules discussed in section 2 is taxable.

Including taxable benefits in pay. You must include in a recipient's pay the amount by which the value of a fringe benefit is more than the sum of the following amounts.

- Any amount the law excludes from pay.
- Any amount the recipient paid for the benefit.

The rules used to determine the value of a fringe benefit are discussed in section 3.

If the recipient of a taxable fringe benefit is your employee, the benefit is subject to employment taxes and must be reported on Form W-2, Wage and Tax Statement. However, you can use special rules to withhold, deposit, and report the employment taxes. These rules are discussed in section 4.

If the recipient of a taxable fringe benefit is not your employee, the benefit is not subject to employment taxes. However, you may have to report the benefit on one of the following information returns.

If the recipient receives the benefit as:	Use:
An independent contractor	Form 1099-MISC, Miscellaneous Income
A partner	Schedule K-1 (Form 1065), Partner's Share of Income, Deductions, Credits, etc.

For more information, see the instructions for the forms listed above.

Cafeteria Plans

A cafeteria plan, including a flexible spending arrangement, is a written plan that allows your employees to choose between receiving cash or taxable benefits instead of certain qualified benefits for which the law provides an exclusion from wages. If an employee chooses to receive a qualified benefit under the plan, the fact that the employee could have received cash or a taxable benefit instead will not make the qualified benefit taxable.

Generally, a cafeteria plan does not include any plan that offers a benefit that defers pay. However, a cafeteria plan can include a qualified 401(k) plan as a benefit. Also, certain life insurance plans maintained by educational institutions can be offered as a benefit even though they defer pay.

Qualified benefits. A cafeteria plan can include the following benefits discussed in section 2.

- Accident and health benefits (but not Archer medical savings accounts (Archer MSAs) or long-term care insurance).
- Adoption assistance.
- Dependent care assistance.
- Group-term life insurance coverage (including costs that cannot be excluded from wages).
- Health savings accounts (HSAs). Distributions from an HSA may be used to pay eligible long-term care insurance premiums or qualified long-term care services.

Benefits not allowed. A cafeteria plan **cannot** include the following benefits discussed in section 2.

- Archer MSAs. See *Accident and Health Benefits* in section 2.
- Athletic facilities.
- *De minimis* (minimal) benefits.
- Educational assistance.
- Employee discounts.
- Employer-provided cell phones.
- Lodging on your business premises.
- Meals.
- Moving expense reimbursements.
- No-additional-cost services.
- Transportation (commuting) benefits.
- Tuition reduction.
- Working condition benefits.

It also cannot include scholarships or fellowships (discussed in Publication 970, Tax Benefits for Education).

$2,500 limit on a health flexible spending arrangement (FSA). For plan years beginning after December 31, 2012, a cafeteria plan may not allow an employee to request salary reduction contributions for a health FSA in excess of $2,500. For plan years beginning after December 31, 2013, the limit is unchanged at $2,500.

A cafeteria plan offering a health FSA must be amended to specify the $2,500 limit (or any lower limit set by the employer). While cafeteria plans generally must be amended on a prospective basis, an amendment that is adopted on or before December 31, 2014, may be made effective retroactively, provided that in operation the cafeteria plan meets the limit for plan years beginning after December 31, 2012. A cafeteria plan that does not limit health FSA contributions to the dollar limit is not a cafeteria plan and all benefits offered under the plan are includible in the employee's gross income.

For more information, see Notice 2012-40, 2012-26 I.R.B. 1046, available at *www.irs.gov/irb/2012-26_IRB/ar09.html*.

Employee. For these plans, treat the following individuals as employees.

- A current common-law employee. See section 2 in Publication 15 (Circular E) for more information.
- A full-time life insurance agent who is a current statutory employee.
- A leased employee who has provided services to you on a substantially full-time basis for at least a year if the services are performed under your primary direction or control.

Exception for S corporation shareholders. Do not treat a 2% shareholder of an S corporation as an employee of the corporation for this purpose. A 2% shareholder for this purpose is someone who directly or indirectly owns (at any time during the year) more than 2% of the corporation's stock or stock with more than 2% of the voting power. Treat a 2% shareholder as you would a partner in a partnership for fringe benefit purposes, but do not treat the benefit as a reduction in distributions to the 2% shareholder.

Plans that favor highly compensated employees. If your plan favors highly compensated employees as to eligibility to participate, contributions, or benefits, you must include in their wages the value of taxable benefits they could have selected. A plan you maintain under a collective bargaining agreement does not favor highly compensated employees.

A highly compensated employee for this purpose is any of the following employees.

1. An officer.
2. A shareholder who owns more than 5% of the voting power or value of all classes of the employer's stock.
3. An employee who is highly compensated based on the facts and circumstances.
4. A spouse or dependent of a person described in (1), (2), or (3).

Plans that favor key employees. If your plan favors key employees, you must include in their wages the value of taxable benefits they could have selected. A plan favors key employees if more than 25% of the total of the nontaxable benefits you provide for all employees under the plan go to key employees. However, a plan you maintain under a collective bargaining agreement does not favor key employees.

A key employee during 2014 is generally an employee who is either of the following.

1. An officer having annual pay of more than $170,000.
2. An employee who for 2014 is either of the following.
   a. A 5% owner of your business.
   b. A 1% owner of your business whose annual pay was more than $150,000.

Simple Cafeteria Plans

Eligible employers meeting contribution requirements and eligibility and participation requirements can establish a simple cafeteria plan. Simple cafeteria plans are treated as meeting the nondiscrimination requirements of a cafeteria plan and certain benefits under a cafeteria plan.

Eligible employer. You are an eligible employer if you employ an average of 100 or fewer employees during either of the 2 preceding years. If your business was not in existence throughout the preceding year, you are eligible if you reasonably expect to employ an average of 100 or fewer employees in the current year. If you establish a simple cafeteria plan in a year that you employ an average of 100 or fewer employees, you are considered an eligible employer for any subsequent year as long as you do not employ an average of 200 or more employees in a subsequent year.

Eligibility and participation requirements. These requirements are met if all employees who had at least 1,000 hours of service for the preceding plan year are eligible to participate and each employee eligible to participate in the plan may elect any benefit available under the plan. You may elect to exclude from the plan employees who:

1. Are under age 21 before the close of the plan year,
2. Have less than 1 year of service with you as of any day during the plan year,
3. Are covered under a collective bargaining agreement, or
4. Are nonresident aliens working outside the United States whose income did not come from a U.S. source.

Contribution requirements. You must make a contribution to provide qualified benefits on behalf of each qualified employee in an amount equal to:

1. A uniform percentage (not less than 2%) of the employee's compensation for the plan year, or
2. An amount which is at least 6% of the employee's compensation for the plan year or twice the amount of

the salary reduction contributions of each qualified employee, whichever is less.

If the contribution requirements are met using option (2), the rate of contribution to any salary reduction contribution of a highly compensated or key employee can not be greater than the rate of contribution to any other employee.

More information. For more information about cafeteria plans, see section 125 of the Internal Revenue Code and its regulations.

2. Fringe Benefit Exclusion Rules

This section discusses the exclusion rules that apply to fringe benefits. These rules exclude all or part of the value of certain benefits from the recipient's pay.

The excluded benefits are not subject to federal income tax withholding. Also, in most cases, they are not subject to social security, Medicare, or federal unemployment (FUTA) tax and are not reported on Form W-2.

This section discusses the exclusion rules for the following fringe benefits.

- Accident and health benefits.
- Achievement awards.
- Adoption assistance.
- Athletic facilities.
- *De minimis* (minimal) benefits.
- Dependent care assistance.
- Educational assistance.
- Employee discounts.
- Employee stock options.
- Employer-provided cell phones.
- Group-term life insurance coverage.
- Health savings accounts (HSAs).
- Lodging on your business premises.
- Meals.
- Moving expense reimbursements.
- No-additional-cost services.
- Retirement planning services.
- Transportation (commuting) benefits.
- Tuition reduction.
- Working condition benefits.

See Table 2-1, later, for an overview of the employment tax treatment of these benefits.

Accident and Health Benefits

This exclusion applies to contributions you make to an accident or health plan for an employee, including the following.

- Contributions to the cost of accident or health insurance including qualified long-term care insurance.
- Contributions to a separate trust or fund that directly or through insurance provides accident or health benefits.
- Contributions to Archer MSAs or health savings accounts (discussed in Publication 969, Health Savings Accounts and Other Tax-Favored Health Plans).

This exclusion also applies to payments you directly or indirectly make to an employee under an accident or health plan for employees that are either of the following.

- Payments or reimbursements of medical expenses.
- Payments for specific injuries or illnesses (such as the loss of the use of an arm or leg). The payments must be figured without regard to any period of absence from work.

Accident or health plan. This is an arrangement that provides benefits for your employees, their spouses, their dependents, and their children (under age 27) in the event of personal injury or sickness. The plan may be insured or noninsured and does not need to be in writing.

Employee. For this exclusion, treat the following individuals as employees.

- A current common-law employee.
- A full-time life insurance agent who is a current statutory employee.
- A retired employee.
- A former employee you maintain coverage for based on the employment relationship.
- A widow or widower of an individual who died while an employee.
- A widow or widower of a retired employee.
- For the exclusion of contributions to an accident or health plan, a leased employee who has provided services to you on a substantially full-time basis for at least a year if the services are performed under your primary direction or control.

Special rule for certain government plans. For certain government accident and health plans, payments to a deceased plan participant's beneficiary may qualify for the exclusion from gross income if the other requirements for exclusion are met. See section 105(j) for details.

Table 2-1. Special Rules for Various Types of Fringe Benefits
(For more information, see the full discussion in this section.)

Type of Fringe Benefit	Treatment Under Employment Taxes: Income Tax Withholding	Social Security and Medicare (including Additional Medicare Tax when wages are paid in excess of $200,000)	Federal Unemployment (FUTA)
Accident and health benefits	Exempt[1,2], except for long-term care benefits provided through a flexible spending or similar arrangement.	Exempt, except for certain payments to S corporation employees who are 2% shareholders.	Exempt
Achievement awards	Exempt[1] up to $1,600 for qualified plan awards ($400 for nonqualified awards).		
Adoption assistance	Exempt[1,3]	Taxable	Taxable
Athletic facilities	Exempt if substantially all use during the calendar year is by employees, their spouses, and their dependent children and the facility is operated by the employer on premises owned or leased by the employer.		
De minimis (minimal) benefits	Exempt	Exempt	Exempt
Dependent care assistance	Exempt[3] up to certain limits, $5,000 ($2,500 for married employee filing separate return).		
Educational assistance	Exempt up to $5,250 of benefits each year. (See Educational Assistance, later in this section.)		
Employee discounts	Exempt[3] up to certain limits. (See Employee Discounts, later in this section.)		
Employee stock options	See Employee Stock Options, later in this section.		
Employer-provided cell phones	Exempt if provided primarily for noncompensatory business purposes.		
Group-term life insurance coverage	Exempt	Exempt[1,4,7] up to cost of $50,000 of coverage. (Special rules apply to former employees.)	Exempt
Health savings accounts (HSAs)	Exempt for qualified individuals up to the HSA contribution limits. (See Health Savings Accounts, later in this section.)		
Lodging on your business premises	Exempt[1] if furnished for your convenience as a condition of employment.		
Meals	Exempt if furnished on your business premises for your convenience.		
	Exempt if *de minimis*.		
Moving expense reimbursements	Exempt[1] if expenses would be deductible if the employee had paid them.		
No-additional-cost services	Exempt[3]	Exempt[3]	Exempt[3]
Retirement planning services	Exempt[5]	Exempt[5]	Exempt[5]
Transportation (commuting) benefits	Exempt[1] up to certain limits if for rides in a commuter highway vehicle and/or transit passes ($130), qualified parking ($250), or qualified bicycle commuting reimbursement[6] ($20). (See Transportation (Commuting) Benefits, later in this section.)		
	Exempt if *de minimis*.		
Tuition reduction	Exempt[3] if for undergraduate education (or graduate education if the employee performs teaching or research activities).		
Working condition benefits	Exempt	Exempt	Exempt

[1] Exemption does not apply to S corporation employees who are 2% shareholders.
[2] Exemption does not apply to certain highly compensated employees under a self-insured plan that favors those employees.
[3] Exemption does not apply to certain highly compensated employees under a program that favors those employees.
[4] Exemption does not apply to certain key employees under a plan that favors those employees.
[5] Exemption does not apply to services for tax preparation, accounting, legal, or brokerage services.
[6] If the employee receives a qualified bicycle commuting reimbursement in a qualified bicycle commuting month, the employee cannot receive commuter highway vehicle, transit pass, or qualified parking benefits in that same month.
[7] You must include in your employee's wages the cost of group-term life insurance beyond $50,000 worth of coverage, reduced by the amount the employee paid toward the insurance. Report it as wages in boxes 1, 3, and 5 of the employee's Form W-2. Also, show it in box 12 with code "C." The amount is subject to social security and Medicare taxes, and you may, at your option, withhold federal income tax.

Exception for S corporation shareholders. Do not treat a 2% shareholder of an S corporation as an employee of the corporation for this purpose. A 2% shareholder is someone who directly or indirectly owns (at any time during the year) more than 2% of the corporation's stock or stock with more than 2% of the voting power. Treat a 2% shareholder as you would a partner in a partnership for fringe benefit purposes, but do not treat the benefit as a reduction in distributions to the 2% shareholder.

Exclusion from wages. You can generally exclude the value of accident or health benefits you provide to an employee from the employee's wages.

Exception for certain long-term care benefits. You cannot exclude contributions to the cost of long-term care insurance from an employee's wages subject to federal income tax withholding if the coverage is provided through a flexible spending or similar arrangement. This is a benefit program that reimburses specified expenses up to a maximum amount that is reasonably available to the employee and is less than five times the total cost of the insurance. However, you can exclude these contributions from the employee's wages subject to social security, Medicare, and federal unemployment (FUTA) taxes.

S corporation shareholders. Because you cannot treat a 2% shareholder of an S corporation as an employee for this exclusion, you must include the value of accident or health benefits you provide to the employee in the employee's wages subject to federal income tax withholding. However, you can exclude the value of these benefits (other than payments for specific injuries or illnesses) from the employee's wages subject to social security, Medicare, and FUTA taxes.

Exception for highly compensated employees. If your plan is a self-insured medical reimbursement plan that favors highly compensated employees, you must include all or part of the amounts you pay to these employees in their wages subject to federal income tax withholding. However, you can exclude these amounts (other than payments for specific injuries or illnesses) from the employee's wages subject to social security, Medicare, and FUTA taxes.

A self-insured plan is a plan that reimburses your employees for medical expenses not covered by an accident or health insurance policy.

A highly compensated employee for this exception is any of the following individuals.

- One of the five highest paid officers.
- An employee who owns (directly or indirectly) more than 10% in value of the employer's stock.
- An employee who is among the highest paid 25% of all employees (other than those who can be excluded from the plan).

For more information on this exception, see section 105(h) of the Internal Revenue Code and its regulations.

COBRA premiums. The exclusion for accident and health benefits applies to amounts you pay to maintain medical coverage for a current or former employee under the Combined Omnibus Budget Reconciliation Act of 1986 (COBRA). The exclusion applies regardless of the length of employment, whether you directly pay the premiums or reimburse the former employee for premiums paid, and whether the employee's separation is permanent or temporary.

Achievement Awards

This exclusion applies to the value of any tangible personal property you give to an employee as an award for either length of service or safety achievement. The exclusion does not apply to awards of cash, cash equivalents, gift certificates, or other intangible property such as vacations, meals, lodging, tickets to theater or sporting events, stocks, bonds, and other securities. The award must meet the requirements for employee achievement awards discussed in chapter 2 of Publication 535, Business Expenses.

Employee. For this exclusion, treat the following individuals as employees.

- A current employee.
- A former common-law employee you maintain coverage for in consideration of or based on an agreement relating to prior service as an employee.
- A leased employee who has provided services to you on a substantially full-time basis for at least a year if the services are performed under your primary direction or control.

Exception for S corporation shareholders. Do not treat a 2% shareholder of an S corporation as an employee of the corporation for this purpose. A 2% shareholder is someone who directly or indirectly owns (at any time during the year) more than 2% of the corporation's stock or stock with more than 2% of the voting power. Treat a 2% shareholder as you would a partner in a partnership for fringe benefit purposes, but do not treat the benefit as a reduction in distributions to the 2% shareholder.

Exclusion from wages. You can generally exclude the value of achievement awards you give to an employee from the employee's wages if their cost is not more than the amount you can deduct as a business expense for the year. The excludable annual amount is $1,600 ($400 for awards that are not "qualified plan awards"). See chapter 2 of Publication 535 for more information about the limit on deductions for employee achievement awards.

CAUTION *To determine for 2014 whether an achievement award is a "qualified plan award" under the deduction rules described in Publication 535, treat any employee who received more than $115,000 in pay for 2013 as a highly compensated employee.*

If the cost of awards given to an employee is more than your allowable deduction, include in the employee's wages the larger of the following amounts.

- The part of the cost that is more than your allowable deduction (up to the value of the awards).
- The amount by which the value of the awards exceeds your allowable deduction.

Exclude the remaining value of the awards from the employee's wages.

Adoption Assistance

An adoption assistance program is a separate written plan of an employer that meets all of the following requirements.

1. It benefits employees who qualify under rules set up by you, which do not favor highly compensated employees or their dependents. To determine whether your plan meets this test, do not consider employees excluded from your plan who are covered by a collective bargaining agreement, if there is evidence that adoption assistance was a subject of good-faith bargaining.
2. It does not pay more than 5% of its payments during the year for shareholders or owners (or their spouses or dependents). A shareholder or owner is someone who owns (on any day of the year) more than 5% of the stock or of the capital or profits interest of your business.
3. You give reasonable notice of the plan to eligible employees.

4. Employees provide reasonable substantiation that payments or reimbursements are for qualifying expenses.

For this exclusion, a highly compensated employee for 2014 is an employee who meets either of the following tests.

1. The employee was a 5% owner at any time during the year or the preceding year.
2. The employee received more than $115,000 in pay for the preceding year.

You can choose to ignore test (2) if the employee was not also in the top 20% of employees when ranked by pay for the preceding year.

You must exclude all payments or reimbursements you make under an adoption assistance program for an employee's qualified adoption expenses from the employee's wages subject to federal income tax withholding. However, you cannot exclude these payments from wages subject to social security, Medicare, and federal unemployment (FUTA) taxes. For more information, see the Instructions for Form 8839, Qualified Adoption Expenses.

You must report all qualifying adoption expenses you paid or reimbursed under your adoption assistance program for each employee for the year in box 12 of the employee's Form W-2. Use code "T" to identify this amount.

Exception for S corporation shareholders. For this exclusion, do not treat a 2% shareholder of an S corporation as an employee of the corporation. A 2% shareholder is someone who directly or indirectly owns (at any time during the year) more than 2% of the corporation's stock or stock with more than 2% of the voting power. Treat a 2% shareholder as you would a partner in a partnership for fringe benefit purposes, including using the benefit as a reduction in distributions to the 2% shareholder.

Athletic Facilities

You can exclude the value of an employee's use of an on-premises gym or other athletic facility you operate from an employee's wages if substantially all use of the facility during the calendar year is by your employees, their spouses, and their dependent children. For this purpose, an employee's dependent child is a child or stepchild who is the employee's dependent or who, if both parents are deceased, has not attained the age of 25.

On-premises facility. The athletic facility must be located on premises you own or lease. It does not have to be located on your business premises. However, the exclusion does not apply to an athletic facility for residential use, such as athletic facilities that are part of a resort.

Employee. For this exclusion, treat the following individuals as employees.

- A current employee.
- A former employee who retired or left on disability.
- A widow or widower of an individual who died while an employee.
- A widow or widower of a former employee who retired or left on disability.
- A leased employee who has provided services to you on a substantially full-time basis for at least a year if the services are performed under your primary direction or control.
- A partner who performs services for a partnership.

De Minimis (Minimal) Benefits

You can exclude the value of a *de minimis* benefit you provide to an employee from the employee's wages. A *de minimis* benefit is any property or service you provide to an employee that has so little value (taking into account how frequently you provide similar benefits to your employees) that accounting for it would be unreasonable or administratively impracticable. Cash and cash equivalent fringe benefits (for example, use of gift card, charge card, or credit card), no matter how little, are never excludable as a *de minimis* benefit, except for occasional meal money or transportation fare.

Examples of *de minimis* benefits include the following.

- Personal use of an employer-provided cell phone provided primarily for noncompensatory business purposes. See Employer-Provided Cell Phones, later in this section, for details.
- Occasional personal use of a company copying machine if you sufficiently control its use so that at least 85% of its use is for business purposes.
- Holiday gifts, other than cash, with a low fair market value.
- Group-term life insurance payable on the death of an employee's spouse or dependent if the face amount is not more than $2,000.
- Meals. See Meals, later in this section, for details.
- Occasional parties or picnics for employees and their guests.
- Occasional tickets for theater or sporting events.
- Transportation fare. See Transportation (Commuting) Benefits, later in this section, for details.

Employee. For this exclusion, treat any recipient of a *de minimis* benefit as an employee.

Dependent Care Assistance

This exclusion applies to household and dependent care services you directly or indirectly pay for or provide to an employee under a dependent care assistance program that covers only your employees. The services must be for a qualifying person's care and must be provided to allow the employee to work. These requirements are basically the same as the tests the employee would have to meet to claim the dependent care credit if the employee paid for the services. For more information, see *Qualifying Person Test* and *Work-Related Expense Test* in Publication 503, Child and Dependent Care Expenses.

Employee. For this exclusion, treat the following individuals as employees.

- A current employee.
- A leased employee who has provided services to you on a substantially full-time basis for at least a year if the services are performed under your primary direction or control.
- Yourself (if you are a sole proprietor).
- A partner who performs services for a partnership.

Exclusion from wages. You can exclude the value of benefits you provide to an employee under a dependent care assistance program from the employee's wages if you reasonably believe that the employee can exclude the benefits from gross income.

An employee can generally exclude from gross income up to $5,000 of benefits received under a dependent care assistance program each year. This limit is reduced to $2,500 for married employees filing separate returns.

However, the exclusion cannot be more than the smaller of the earned income of either the employee or employee's spouse. Special rules apply to determine the earned income of a spouse who is either a student or not able to care for himself or herself. For more information on the earned income limit, see Publication 503.

Exception for highly compensated employees. You cannot exclude dependent care assistance from the wages of a highly compensated employee unless the benefits provided under the program do not favor highly compensated employees and the program meets the requirements described in section 129(d) of the Internal Revenue Code.

For this exclusion, a highly compensated employee for 2014 is an employee who meets either of the following tests.

1. The employee was a 5% owner at any time during the year or the preceding year.
2. The employee received more than $115,000 in pay for the preceding year.

You can choose to ignore test (2) if the employee was not also in the top 20% of employees when ranked by pay for the preceding year.

Form W-2. Report the value of all dependent care assistance you provide to an employee under a dependent care assistance program in box 10 of the employee's Form W-2. Include any amounts you cannot exclude from the employee's wages in boxes 1, 3, and 5. Report both the nontaxable portion of assistance (up to $5,000) and any assistance above the amount that is non-taxable to the employee.

Example. Company A provides a dependent care assistance flexible spending arrangement to its employees through a cafeteria plan. In addition, it provides occasional on-site dependent care to its employees at no cost. Emily, an employee of company A, had $4,500 deducted from her pay for the dependent care flexible spending arrangement. In addition, Emily used the on-site dependent care several times. The fair market value of the on-site care was $700. Emily's Form W-2 should report $5,200 of dependent care assistance in box 10 ($4,500 flexible spending arrangement plus $700 on-site dependent care). Boxes 1, 3, and 5 should include $200 (the amount in excess of the nontaxable assistance), and applicable taxes should be withheld on that amount.

Educational Assistance

This exclusion applies to educational assistance you provide to employees under an educational assistance program. The exclusion also applies to graduate level courses.

Educational assistance means amounts you pay or incur for your employees' education expenses. These expenses generally include the cost of books, equipment, fees, supplies, and tuition. However, these expenses do not include the cost of a course or other education involving sports, games, or hobbies, unless the education:

- Has a reasonable relationship to your business, or
- Is required as part of a degree program.

Education expenses do not include the cost of tools or supplies (other than textbooks) your employee is allowed to keep at the end of the course. Nor do they include the cost of lodging, meals, or transportation.

Educational assistance program. An educational assistance program is a separate written plan that provides educational assistance only to your employees. The program qualifies only if all of the following tests are met.

- The program benefits employees who qualify under rules set up by you that do not favor highly compensated employees. To determine whether your program meets this test, do not consider employees excluded from your program who are covered by a collective bargaining agreement if there is evidence that educational assistance was a subject of good-faith bargaining.
- The program does not provide more than 5% of its benefits during the year for shareholders or owners. A shareholder or owner is someone who owns (on any day of the year) more than 5% of the stock or of the capital or profits interest of your business.
- The program does not allow employees to choose to receive cash or other benefits that must be included in gross income instead of educational assistance.
- You give reasonable notice of the program to eligible employees.

Your program can cover former employees if their employment is the reason for the coverage.

For this exclusion, a highly compensated employee for 2014 is an employee who meets either of the following tests.

1. The employee was a 5% owner at any time during the year or the preceding year.
2. The employee received more than $115,000 in pay for the preceding year.

You can choose to ignore test (2) if the employee was not also in the top 20% of employees when ranked by pay for the preceding year.

Employee. For this exclusion, treat the following individuals as employees.

- A current employee.
- A former employee who retired, left on disability, or was laid off.
- A leased employee who has provided services to you on a substantially full-time basis for at least a year if the services are performed under your primary direction or control.
- Yourself (if you are a sole proprietor).
- A partner who performs services for a partnership.

Exclusion from wages. You can exclude up to $5,250 of educational assistance you provide to an employee under an educational assistance program from the employee's wages each year.

Assistance over $5,250. If you do not have an educational assistance plan, or you provide an employee with assistance exceeding $5,250, you must include the value of these benefits as wages, unless the benefits are working condition benefits. Working condition benefits may be excluded from wages. Property or a service provided is a working condition benefit to the extent that if the employee paid for it, the amount paid would have been deductible as a business or depreciation expense. See Working Condition Benefits, later, in this section.

Employee Discounts

This exclusion applies to a price reduction you give an employee on property or services you offer to customers in the ordinary course of the line of business in which the employee performs substantial services. However, it does not apply to discounts on real property or discounts on personal property of a kind commonly held for investment (such as stocks or bonds).

Employee. For this exclusion, treat the following individuals as employees.

- A current employee.
- A former employee who retired or left on disability.
- A widow or widower of an individual who died while an employee.
- A widow or widower of an employee who retired or left on disability.
- A leased employee who has provided services to you on a substantially full-time basis for at least a year if the services are performed under your primary direction or control.
- A partner who performs services for a partnership.

Exclusion from wages. You can generally exclude the value of an employee discount you provide an employee from the employee's wages, up to the following limits.

- For a discount on services, 20% of the price you charge nonemployee customers for the service.
- For a discount on merchandise or other property, your gross profit percentage times the price you charge nonemployee customers for the property.

Determine your gross profit percentage in the line of business based on all property you offer to customers (including employee customers) and your experience during the tax year immediately before the tax year in which the discount is available. To figure your gross profit percentage, subtract the total cost of the property from the total sales price of the property and divide the result by the total sales price of the property.

Exception for highly compensated employees. You cannot exclude from the wages of a highly compensated employee any part of the value of a discount that is not available on the same terms to one of the following groups.

- All of your employees.
- A group of employees defined under a reasonable classification you set up that does not favor highly compensated employees.

For this exclusion, a highly compensated employee for 2014 is an employee who meets either of the following tests.

1. The employee was a 5% owner at any time during the year or the preceding year.
2. The employee received more than $115,000 in pay for the preceding year.

You can choose to ignore test (2) if the employee was not also in the top 20% of employees when ranked by pay for the preceding year.

Employee Stock Options

There are three kinds of stock options—incentive stock options, employee stock purchase plan options, and nonstatutory (nonqualified) stock options.

Wages for social security, Medicare, and federal unemployment (FUTA) taxes do not include remuneration resulting from the exercise, after October 22, 2004, of an incentive stock option or under an employee stock purchase plan option, or from any disposition of stock acquired by exercising such an option. The IRS will not apply these taxes to an exercise before October 23, 2004, of an incentive stock option or an employee stock purchase plan option or to a disposition of stock acquired by such exercise.

Additionally, federal income tax withholding is not required on the income resulting from a disqualifying disposition of stock acquired by the exercise after October 22, 2004, of an incentive stock option or under an employee stock purchase plan option, or on income equal to the discount portion of stock acquired by the exercise, after October 22, 2004, of an employee stock purchase plan option resulting from any disposition of the stock. The IRS will not apply federal income tax withholding upon the disposition of stock acquired by the exercise, before October 23, 2004, of an incentive stock option or an employee stock purchase plan option. However, the employer must report as income in box 1 of Form W-2, (a) the discount portion of stock acquired by the exercise of an employee stock purchase plan option upon disposition of the stock, and (b) the spread (between the exercise price and the fair market value of the stock at the time of exercise) upon a disqualifying disposition of stock acquired by the exercise of an incentive stock option or an employee stock purchase plan option.

An employer must report the excess of the fair market value of stock received upon exercise of a nonstatutory stock option over the amount paid for the stock option on Form W-2 in boxes 1, 3 (up to the social security wage base), 5, and in box 12 using the code "V." See Regulations section 1.83-7.

An employee who transfers his or her interest in nonstatutory stock options to the employee's former spouse incident to a divorce is not required to include an amount in gross income upon the transfer. The former spouse, rather than the employee, is required to include an amount in gross income when the former spouse exercises the stock options. See Revenue Ruling 2002-22 and Revenue Ruling 2004-60 for details. You can find Revenue Ruling 2002-22 on page 849 of Internal Revenue Bulletin 2002-19 at *www.irs.gov/pub/irs-irbs/irb02-19.pdf*. See Revenue Ruling 2004-60, 2004-24 I.R.B. 1051, available at *www.irs.gov/irb/2004-24_IRB/ar13.html*.

For more information about employee stock options, see sections 421, 422, and 423 of the Internal Revenue Code and their related regulations.

Employer-Provided Cell Phones

The value of an employer-provided cell phone, provided primarily for noncompensatory business reasons, is excludable from an employee's income as a working condition fringe benefit. Personal use of an employer-provided cell phone, provided primarily for noncompensatory business reasons, is excludable from an employee's income as a *de minimis* fringe benefit. For the rules relating to these types of benefits, see De Minimis *(Minimal) Benefits*, earlier in this section, and *Working Condition Benefits*, later in this section.

Noncompensatory business purposes. You provide a cell phone primarily for noncompensatory business purposes if there are substantial business reasons for providing the cell phone. Examples of substantial business reasons include the employer's:

- Need to contact the employee at all times for work-related emergencies,
- Requirement that the employee be available to speak with clients at times when the employee is away from the office, and
- Need to speak with clients located in other time zones at times outside the employee's normal workday.

Cell phones provided to promote goodwill, boost morale, or attract prospective employees. You cannot exclude from an employee's wages the value of a cell phone provided to promote goodwill of an employee, to attract a prospective employee, or as a means of providing additional compensation to an employee.

Additional information. For additional information on the tax treatment of employer-provided cell phones, see Notice 2011-72, 2011-38 I.R.B. 407, available at *www.irs.gov/irb/2011-38_IRB/ar07.html*.

Group-Term Life Insurance Coverage

This exclusion applies to life insurance coverage that meets all the following conditions.

- It provides a general death benefit that is not included in income.
- You provide it to a group of employees. See *The 10-employee rule*, later.
- It provides an amount of insurance to each employee based on a formula that prevents individual selection. This formula must use factors such as the employee's age, years of service, pay, or position.
- You provide it under a policy you directly or indirectly carry. Even if you do not pay any of the policy's cost, you are considered to carry it if you arrange for payment of its cost by your employees and charge at least one employee less than, and at least one other employee more than, the cost of his or her insurance. Determine the cost of the insurance, for this purpose, as explained under *Coverage over the limit*, later.

Group-term life insurance does not include the following insurance.

- Insurance that does not provide general death benefits, such as travel insurance or a policy providing only accidental death benefits.
- Life insurance on the life of your employee's spouse or dependent. However, you may be able to exclude the cost of this insurance from the employee's wages as a *de minimis* benefit. See De Minimis *(Minimal) Benefits*, earlier in this section.

- Insurance provided under a policy that provides a permanent benefit (an economic value that extends beyond 1 policy year, such as paid-up or cash surrender value), unless certain requirements are met. See Regulations section 1.79-1 for details.

Employee. For this exclusion, treat the following individuals as employees.

1. A current common-law employee.
2. A full-time life insurance agent who is a current statutory employee.
3. An individual who was formerly your employee under (1) or (2).
4. A leased employee who has provided services to you on a substantially full-time basis for at least a year if the services are performed under your primary direction and control.

Exception for S corporation shareholders. Do not treat a 2% shareholder of an S corporation as an employee of the corporation for this purpose. A 2% shareholder is someone who directly or indirectly owns (at any time during the year) more than 2% of the corporation's stock or stock with more than 2% of the voting power. Treat a 2% shareholder as you would a partner in a partnership for fringe benefit purposes, but do not treat the benefit as a reduction in distributions to the 2% shareholder.

The 10-employee rule. Generally, life insurance is not group-term life insurance unless you provide it to at least 10 full-time employees at some time during the year.

For this rule, count employees who choose not to receive the insurance unless, to receive it, they must contribute to the cost of benefits other than the group-term life insurance. For example, count an employee who could receive insurance by paying part of the cost, even if that employee chooses not to receive it. However, do not count an employee who must pay part or all of the cost of permanent benefits to get insurance, unless that employee chooses to receive it. A permanent benefit is an economic value extending beyond one policy year (for example, a paid-up or cash-surrender value) that is provided under a life insurance policy.

Exceptions. Even if you do not meet the 10-employee rule, two exceptions allow you to treat insurance as group-term life insurance.

Under the first exception, you do not have to meet the 10-employee rule if all the following conditions are met.

1. If evidence that the employee is insurable is required, it is limited to a medical questionnaire (completed by the employee) that does not require a physical.
2. You provide the insurance to all your full-time employees or, if the insurer requires the evidence mentioned in (1), to all full-time employees who provide evidence the insurer accepts.
3. You figure the coverage based on either a uniform percentage of pay or the insurer's coverage brackets that meet certain requirements. See Regulations section 1.79-1 for details.

Under the second exception, you do not have to meet the 10-employee rule if all the following conditions are met.

- You provide the insurance under a common plan covering your employees and the employees of at least one other employer who is not related to you.
- The insurance is restricted to, but mandatory for, all your employees who belong to, or are represented by, an organization (such as a union) that carries on substantial activities besides obtaining insurance.
- Evidence of whether an employee is insurable does not affect an employee's eligibility for insurance or the amount of insurance that employee gets.

To apply either exception, do not consider employees who were denied insurance for any of the following reasons.

- They were 65 or older.
- They customarily work 20 hours or less a week or 5 months or less in a calendar year.
- They have not been employed for the waiting period given in the policy. This waiting period cannot be more than 6 months.

Exclusion from wages. You can generally exclude the cost of up to $50,000 of group-term life insurance from the wages of an insured employee. You can exclude the same amount from the employee's wages when figuring social security and Medicare taxes. In addition, you do not have to withhold federal income tax or pay FUTA tax on any group-term life insurance you provide to an employee.

Coverage over the limit. You must include in your employee's wages the cost of group-term life insurance beyond $50,000 worth of coverage, reduced by the amount the employee paid toward the insurance. Report it as wages in boxes 1, 3, and 5 of the employee's Form W-2. Also, show it in box 12 with code "C." The amount is subject to social security and Medicare taxes, and you may, at your option, withhold federal income tax.

Figure the monthly cost of the insurance to include in the employee's wages by multiplying the number of thousands of dollars of all insurance coverage over $50,000 (figured to the nearest $100) by the cost shown in Table 2-2. For all coverage provided within the calendar year, use the employee's age on the last day of the employee's tax year. You must prorate the cost from the table if less than a full month of coverage is involved.

Table 2-2. Cost Per $1,000 of Protection For 1 Month

Age	Cost
Under 25	$ .05
25 through 29	.06
30 through 34	.08
35 through 39	.09
40 through 44	.10
45 through 49	.15
50 through 54	.23
55 through 59	.43
60 through 64	.66
65 through 69	1.27
70 and older	2.06

You figure the total cost to include in the employee's wages by multiplying the monthly cost by the number of full months' coverage at that cost.

Example. Tom's employer provides him with group-term life insurance coverage of $200,000. Tom is 45 years old, is not a key employee, and pays $100 per year toward the cost of the insurance. Tom's employer must include $170 in his wages. The $200,000 of insurance coverage is reduced by $50,000. The yearly cost of $150,000 of coverage is $270 ($.15 x 150 x 12), and is reduced by the $100 Tom pays for the insurance. The employer includes $170 in boxes 1, 3, and 5 of Tom's Form W-2. The employer also enters $170 in box 12 with code "C."

Coverage for dependents. Group-term life insurance coverage paid by the employer for the spouse or dependents of an employee may be excludable from income as a *de minimis* fringe benefit if the face amount is not more than $2,000. If the face amount is greater than $2,000, the entire cost of the dependent coverage must be included in income unless the amount over $2,000 is purchased with employee contributions on an after-tax basis. The cost of the insurance is determined by using Table 2-2.

Former employees. When group-term life insurance over $50,000 is provided to an employee (including retirees) after his or her termination, the employee share of social security and Medicare taxes on that period of coverage is paid by the former employee with his or her tax return and is not collected by the employer. You are not required to collect those taxes. Use the table above to determine the amount of social security and Medicare taxes owed by the former employee for coverage provided after separation from service. Report those uncollected amounts separately in box 12 of Form W-2 using codes "M" and "N." See the General Instructions for Forms W-2 and W-3 and the Instructions for Form 941.

Exception for key employees. Generally, if your group-term life insurance plan favors key employees as to participation or benefits, you must include the entire cost of the insurance in your key employees' wages. This exception generally does not apply to church plans. When figuring social security and Medicare taxes, you must also include the entire cost in the employees' wages. Include the cost in boxes 1, 3, and 5 of Form W-2. However, you do not have to withhold federal income tax or pay FUTA tax on the cost of any group-term life insurance you provide to an employee.

For this purpose, the cost of the insurance is the greater of the following amounts.

- The premiums you pay for the employee's insurance. See Regulations section 1.79-4T(Q&A 6) for more information.
- The cost you figure using Table 2-2.

For this exclusion, a key employee during 2014 is an employee or former employee who is one of the following individuals. See section 416(i) of the Internal Revenue Code for more information.

1. An officer having annual pay of more than $170,000.
2. An individual who for 2014 was either of the following.
   a. A 5% owner of your business.
   b. A 1% owner of your business whose annual pay was more than $150,000.

A former employee who was a key employee upon retirement or separation from service is also a key employee.

Your plan does not favor key employees as to participation if at least one of the following is true.

- It benefits at least 70% of your employees.
- At least 85% of the participating employees are not key employees.
- It benefits employees who qualify under a set of rules you set up that do not favor key employees.

Your plan meets this participation test if it is part of a cafeteria plan (discussed in section 1) and it meets the participation test for those plans.

When applying this test, do not consider employees who:

- Have not completed 3 years of service,
- Are part-time or seasonal,
- Are nonresident aliens who receive no U.S. source earned income from you, or
- Are not included in the plan but are in a unit of employees covered by a collective bargaining agreement, if the benefits provided under the plan were the subject of good-faith bargaining between you and employee representatives.

Your plan does not favor key employees as to benefits if all benefits available to participating key employees are also available to all other participating employees. Your plan does not favor key employees just because the amount of insurance you provide to your employees is uniformly related to their pay.

S corporation shareholders. Because you cannot treat a 2% shareholder of an S corporation as an employee for this exclusion, you must include the cost of all group-term life insurance coverage you provide the 2%

shareholder in his or her wages. When figuring social security and Medicare taxes, you must also include the cost of this coverage in the 2% shareholder's wages. Include the cost in boxes 1, 3, and 5 of Form W-2. However, you do not have to withhold federal income tax or pay federal unemployment tax on the cost of any group-term life insurance coverage you provide to the 2% shareholder.

Health Savings Accounts

A Health Savings Account (HSA) is an account owned by a qualified individual who is generally your employee or former employee. Any contributions that you make to an HSA become the employee's property and cannot be withdrawn by you. Contributions to the account are used to pay current or future medical expenses of the account owner, his or her spouse, and any qualified dependent. The medical expenses must not be reimbursable by insurance or other sources and their payment from HSA funds (distribution) will not give rise to a medical expense deduction on the individual's federal income tax return. For more information about HSAs, visit the Department of Treasury's website at www.treasury.gov and enter "HSA" in the search box.

Eligibility. A qualified individual must be covered by a High Deductible Health Plan (HDHP) and not be covered by other health insurance except for permitted insurance listed under section 223(c)(3) or insurance for accidents, disability, dental care, vision care, or long-term care. For calendar year 2014, a qualifying HDHP must have a deductible of at least $1,250 for self-only coverage or $2,500 for family coverage and must limit annual out-of-pocket expenses of the beneficiary to $6,350 for self-only coverage and $12,700 for family coverage.

There are no income limits that restrict an individual's eligibility to contribute to an HSA nor is there a requirement that the account owner have earned income to make a contribution.

Exceptions. An individual is not a qualified individual if he or she can be claimed as a dependent on another person's tax return. Also, an employee's participation in a health flexible spending arrangement (FSA) or health reimbursement arrangement (HRA) generally disqualifies the individual (and employer) from making contributions to his or her HSA. However, an individual may qualify to participate in an HSA if he or she is participating in only a limited-purpose FSA or HRA or a post-deductible FSA. For more information, see *Other employee health plans* in Publication 969.

Employer contributions. Up to specified dollar limits, cash contributions to the HSA of a qualified individual (determined monthly) are exempt from federal income tax withholding, social security tax, Medicare tax, and FUTA tax. For 2014, you can contribute up to $3,300 for self-only coverage or $6,550 for family coverage to a qualified individual's HSA.

The contribution amounts listed above are increased by $1,000 for a qualified individual who is age 55 or older at any time during the year. For two qualified individuals who are married to each other and who each are age 55 or older at any time during the year, each spouse's contribution limit is increased by $1,000 provided each spouse has a separate HSA. No contributions can be made to an individual's HSA after he or she becomes enrolled in Medicare Part A or Part B.

Nondiscrimination rules. Your contribution amount to an employee's HSA must be comparable for all employees who have comparable coverage during the same period. Otherwise, there will be an excise tax equal to 35% of the amount you contributed to all employees' HSAs.

For guidance on employer comparable contributions to HSAs under section 4980G in instances where an employee has not established an HSA by December 31 and in instances where an employer accelerates contributions for the calendar year for employees who have incurred qualified medical expenses, see Regulations section 54.4980G-4.

Exception. The Tax Relief and Health Care Act of 2006 allows employers to make larger HSA contributions for a nonhighly compensated employee than for a highly compensated employee. A highly compensated employee for 2014 is an employee who meets either of the following tests.

1. The employee was a 5% owner at any time during the year or the preceding year.
2. The employee received more than $115,000 in pay for the preceding year.

You can choose to ignore test (2) if the employee was not also in the top 20% of employees when ranked by pay for the preceding year.

Partnerships and S corporations. Partners and 2% shareholders of an S corporation are not eligible for salary reduction (pre-tax) contributions to an HSA. Employer contributions to the HSA of a bona fide partner or 2% shareholder are treated as distributions or guaranteed payments as determined by the facts and circumstances.

Cafeteria plans. You may contribute to an employee's HSA using a cafeteria plan and your contributions are not subject to the statutory comparability rules. However, cafeteria plan nondiscrimination rules still apply. For example, contributions under a cafeteria plan to employee HSAs cannot be greater for higher-paid employees than they are for lower-paid employees. Contributions that favor lower-paid employees are not prohibited.

Reporting requirements. You must report your contributions to an employee's HSA in box 12 of Form W-2 using code "W." The trustee or custodian of the HSA, generally a bank or insurance company, reports distributions from the HSA using Form 1099-SA, Distributions From an HSA, Archer MSA, or Medicare Advantage MSA.

Lodging on Your Business Premises

You can exclude the value of lodging you furnish to an employee from the employee's wages if it meets the following tests.

- It is furnished on your business premises.
- It is furnished for your convenience.
- The employee must accept it as a condition of employment.

Different tests may apply to lodging furnished by educational institutions. See section 119(d) of the Internal Revenue Code for details.

The exclusion does not apply if you allow your employee to choose to receive additional pay instead of lodging.

On your business premises. For this exclusion, your business premises is generally your employee's place of work. For special rules that apply to lodging furnished in a camp located in a foreign country, see section 119(c) of the Internal Revenue Code and its regulations.

For your convenience. Whether or not you furnish lodging for your convenience as an employer depends on all the facts and circumstances. You furnish the lodging to your employee for your convenience if you do this for a substantial business reason other than to provide the employee with additional pay. This is true even if a law or an employment contract provides that the lodging is furnished as pay. However, a written statement that the lodging is furnished for your convenience is not sufficient.

Condition of employment. Lodging meets this test if you require your employees to accept the lodging because they need to live on your business premises to be able to properly perform their duties. Examples include employees who must be available at all times and employees who could not perform their required duties without being furnished the lodging.

It does not matter whether you must furnish the lodging as pay under the terms of an employment contract or a law fixing the terms of employment.

Example. A hospital gives Joan, an employee of the hospital, the choice of living at the hospital free of charge or living elsewhere and receiving a cash allowance in addition to her regular salary. If Joan chooses to live at the hospital, the hospital cannot exclude the value of the lodging from her wages because she is not required to live at the hospital to properly perform the duties of her employment.

S corporation shareholders. For this exclusion, do not treat a 2% shareholder of an S corporation as an employee of the corporation. A 2% shareholder is someone who directly or indirectly owns (at any time during the year) more than 2% of the corporation's stock or stock with more than 2% of the voting power. Treat a 2% shareholder as you would a partner in a partnership for fringe benefit purposes, but do not treat the benefit as a reduction in distributions to the 2% shareholder.

Meals

This section discusses the exclusion rules that apply to *de minimis* meals and meals on your business premises.

De Minimis Meals

You can exclude any occasional meal or meal money you provide to an employee if it has so little value (taking into account how frequently you provide meals to your employees) that accounting for it would be unreasonable or administratively impracticable. The exclusion applies, for example, to the following items.

- Coffee, doughnuts, or soft drinks.
- Occasional meals or meal money provided to enable an employee to work overtime. However, the exclusion does not apply to meal money figured on the basis of hours worked.
- Occasional parties or picnics for employees and their guests.

This exclusion also applies to meals you provide at an employer-operated eating facility for employees if the annual revenue from the facility equals or exceeds the direct costs of the facility. For this purpose, your revenue from providing a meal is considered equal to the facility's direct operating costs to provide that meal if its value can be excluded from an employee's wages as explained under Meals on Your Business Premises, later.

TIP *If food or beverages you furnish to employees qualify as a* de minimis *benefit, you can deduct their full cost. The 50% limit on deductions for the cost of meals does not apply. The deduction limit on meals is discussed in chapter 2 of Publication 535.*

Employee. For this exclusion, treat any recipient of a *de minimis* meal as an employee.

Employer-operated eating facility for employees. An employer-operated eating facility for employees is an eating facility that meets all the following conditions.

- You own or lease the facility.
- You operate the facility. You are considered to operate the eating facility if you have a contract with another to operate it.
- The facility is on or near your business premises.
- You provide meals (food, drinks, and related services) at the facility during, or immediately before or after, the employee's workday.

Exclusion from wages. You can generally exclude the value of *de minimis* meals you provide to an employee from the employee's wages.

Exception for highly compensated employees. You cannot exclude from the wages of a highly compensated employee the value of a meal provided at an employer-operated eating facility that is not available on the same terms to one of the following groups.

- All of your employees.
- A group of employees defined under a reasonable classification you set up that does not favor highly compensated employees.

For this exclusion, a highly compensated employee for 2014 is an employee who meets either of the following tests.

1. The employee was a 5% owner at any time during the year or the preceding year.
2. The employee received more than $115,000 in pay for the preceding year.

You can choose to ignore test (2) if the employee was not also in the top 20% of employees when ranked by pay for the preceding year.

Meals on Your Business Premises

You can exclude the value of meals you furnish to an employee from the employee's wages if they meet the following tests.

- They are furnished on your business premises.
- They are furnished for your convenience.

This exclusion does not apply if you allow your employee to choose to receive additional pay instead of meals.

On your business premises. Generally, for this exclusion, the employee's place of work is your business premises.

For your convenience. Whether you furnish meals for your convenience as an employer depends on all the facts and circumstances. You furnish the meals to your employee for your convenience if you do this for a substantial business reason other than to provide the employee with additional pay. This is true even if a law or an employment contract provides that the meals are furnished as pay. However, a written statement that the meals are furnished for your convenience is not sufficient.

Meals excluded for all employees if excluded for more than half. If more than half of your employees who are furnished meals on your business premises are furnished the meals for your convenience, you can treat all meals you furnish to employees on your business premises as furnished for your convenience.

Food service employees. Meals you furnish to a restaurant or other food service employee during, or immediately before or after, the employee's working hours are furnished for your convenience. For example, if a waitress works through the breakfast and lunch periods, you can exclude from her wages the value of the breakfast and lunch you furnish in your restaurant for each day she works.

Example. You operate a restaurant business. You furnish your employee, Carol, who is a waitress working 7:00 a.m. to 4:00 p.m., two meals during each workday. You encourage but do not require Carol to have her breakfast on the business premises before starting work. She must have her lunch on the premises. Since Carol is a food service employee and works during the normal breakfast and lunch periods, you can exclude from her wages the value of her breakfast and lunch.

If you also allow Carol to have meals on your business premises without charge on her days off, you cannot exclude the value of those meals from her wages.

Employees available for emergency calls. Meals you furnish during working hours so an employee will be available for emergency calls during the meal period are furnished for your convenience. You must be able to show these emergency calls have occurred or can reasonably be expected to occur.

Example. A hospital maintains a cafeteria on its premises where all of its 230 employees may get meals at no charge during their working hours. The hospital must have 120 of its employees available for emergencies. Each of these 120 employees is, at times, called upon to perform services during the meal period. Although the hospital does not require these employees to remain on the premises, they rarely leave the hospital during their meal period. Since the hospital furnishes meals on its premises to its employees so that more than half of them are available for emergency calls during meal periods, the hospital can exclude the value of these meals from the wages of all of its employees.

Short meal periods. Meals you furnish during working hours are furnished for your convenience if the nature of your business restricts an employee to a short meal period (such as 30 or 45 minutes) and the employee cannot be expected to eat elsewhere in such a short time. For example, meals can qualify for this treatment if your peak work-load occurs during the normal lunch hour. However, they do not qualify if the reason for the short meal period is to allow the employee to leave earlier in the day.

Example. Frank is a bank teller who works from 9 a.m. to 5 p.m. The bank furnishes his lunch without charge in a cafeteria the bank maintains on its premises. The bank furnishes these meals to Frank to limit his lunch period to 30 minutes, since the bank's peak workload occurs during the normal lunch period. If Frank got his lunch elsewhere, it would take him much longer than 30 minutes and the bank strictly enforces the time limit. The bank can exclude the value of these meals from Frank's wages.

Proper meals not otherwise available. Meals you furnish during working hours are furnished for your convenience if the employee could not otherwise eat proper meals within a reasonable period of time. For example, meals can qualify for this treatment if there are insufficient eating facilities near the place of employment.

Meals after work hours. Meals you furnish to an employee immediately after working hours are furnished for your convenience if you would have furnished them during working hours for a substantial nonpay business reason but, because of the work duties, they were not eaten during working hours.

Meals you furnish to promote goodwill, boost morale, or attract prospective employees. Meals you furnish to promote goodwill, boost morale, or attract prospective employees are not considered furnished for your convenience. However, you may be able to exclude their value as discussed under De Minimis *Meals*, earlier.

Meals furnished on nonworkdays or with lodging. You generally cannot exclude from an employee's wages the value of meals you furnish on a day when the employee is not working. However, you can exclude these meals if they are furnished with lodging that is excluded from the employee's wages as discussed under *Lodging on Your Business Premises*, earlier in this section.

Meals with a charge. The fact that you charge for the meals and that your employees may accept or decline the meals is not taken into account in determining whether or not meals are furnished for your convenience.

S corporation shareholder-employee. For this exclusion, do not treat a 2% shareholder of an S corporation as an employee of the corporation. A 2% shareholder is someone who directly or indirectly owns (at any time during the year) more than 2% of the corporation's stock or stock with more than 2% of the voting power. Treat a 2% shareholder as you would a partner in a partnership for fringe benefit purposes, but do not treat the benefit as a reduction in distributions to the 2% shareholder.

Moving Expense Reimbursements

This exclusion applies to any amount you directly or indirectly give to an employee, (including services furnished in kind) as payment for, or reimbursement of, moving expenses. You must make the reimbursement under rules similar to those described in chapter 11 of Publication 535 for reimbursement of expenses for travel, meals, and entertainment under accountable plans.

The exclusion applies only to reimbursement of moving expenses that the employee could deduct if he or she had paid or incurred them without reimbursement. However, it does not apply if the employee actually deducted the expenses in a previous year.

Deductible moving expenses. Deductible moving expenses include only the reasonable expenses of:

- Moving household goods and personal effects from the former home to the new home, and
- Traveling (including lodging) from the former home to the new home.

Deductible moving expenses do not include any expenses for meals and must meet both the distance test and the time test. The distance test is met if the new job location is at least 50 miles farther from the employee's old home than the old job location was. The time test is met if the employee works at least 39 weeks during the first 12 months after arriving in the general area of the new job location.

For more information on deductible moving expenses, see Publication 521, Moving Expenses.

Employee. For this exclusion, treat the following individuals as employees.

- A current employee.
- A leased employee who has provided services to you on a substantially full-time basis for at least a year if the services are performed under your primary direction or control.

Exception for S corporation shareholders. Do not treat a 2% shareholder of an S corporation as an employee of the corporation for this purpose. A 2% shareholder is someone who directly or indirectly owns (at any time during the year) more than 2% of the corporation's stock or stock with more than 2% of the voting power. Treat a 2% shareholder as you would a partner in a partnership for fringe benefit purposes, but do not treat the benefit as a reduction in distributions to the 2% shareholder.

Exclusion from wages. Generally, you can exclude qualifying moving expense reimbursement you provide to an employee from the employee's wages. If you paid the reimbursement directly to the employee, report the amount in box 12 of Form W-2 with the code "P." Do not report payments to a third party for the employee's moving expenses or the value of moving services you provided in kind.

No-Additional-Cost Services

This exclusion applies to a service you provide to an employee if it does not cause you to incur any substantial additional costs. The service must be offered to customers in the ordinary course of the line of business in which the employee performs substantial services.

Generally, no-additional-cost services are excess capacity services, such as airline, bus, or train tickets; hotel rooms; or telephone services provided free or at a reduced price to employees working in those lines of business.

Substantial additional costs. To determine whether you incur substantial additional costs to provide a service to an employee, count any lost revenue as a cost. Do not reduce the costs you incur by any amount the employee pays for the service. You are considered to incur substantial additional costs if you or your employees spend a substantial amount of time in providing the service, even if the time spent would otherwise be idle or if the services are provided outside normal business hours.

Reciprocal agreements. A no-additional-cost service provided to your employee by an unrelated employer may qualify as a no-additional-cost service if all the following tests are met.

- The service is the same type of service generally provided to customers in both the line of business in which the employee works and the line of business in which the service is provided.
- You and the employer providing the service have a written reciprocal agreement under which a group of employees of each employer, all of whom perform substantial services in the same line of business, may receive no-additional-cost services from the other employer.
- Neither you nor the other employer incurs any substantial additional cost either in providing the service or because of the written agreement.

Employee. For this exclusion, treat the following individuals as employees.

1. A current employee.
2. A former employee who retired or left on disability.
3. A widow or widower of an individual who died while an employee.
4. A widow or widower of a former employee who retired or left on disability.
5. A leased employee who has provided services to you on a substantially full-time basis for at least a year if the services are performed under your primary direction or control.
6. A partner who performs services for a partnership.

Treat services you provide to the spouse or dependent child of an employee as provided to the employee. For this fringe benefit, dependent child means any son, stepson, daughter, or stepdaughter who is a dependent of the employee, or both of whose parents have died and who has not reached age 25. Treat a child of divorced parents as a dependent of both parents.

Treat any use of air transportation by the parent of an employee as use by the employee. This rule does not apply to use by the parent of a person considered an employee because of item (3) or (4) above.

Exclusion from wages. You can generally exclude the value of a no-additional-cost service you provide to an employee from the employee's wages.

Exception for highly compensated employees. You cannot exclude from the wages of a highly compensated employee the value of a no-additional-cost service that is not available on the same terms to one of the following groups.

- All of your employees.
- A group of employees defined under a reasonable classification you set up that does not favor highly compensated employees.

For this exclusion, a highly compensated employee for 2014 is an employee who meets either of the following tests.

1. The employee was a 5% owner at any time during the year or the preceding year.
2. The employee received more than $115,000 in pay for the preceding year.

You can choose to ignore test (2) if the employee was not also in the top 20% of employees when ranked by pay for the preceding year.

Retirement Planning Services

You may exclude from an employee's wages the value of any retirement planning advice or information you provide to your employee or his or her spouse if you maintain a qualified retirement plan as defined in section 219(g)(5) of the Internal Revenue Code. In addition to employer plan advice and information, the services provided may include general advice and information on retirement. However, the exclusion does not apply to services for tax preparation, accounting, legal, or brokerage services. You cannot exclude from the wages of a highly compensated employee retirement planning services that are not available on the same terms to each member of a group of employees normally provided education and information about the employer's qualified retirement plan.

Transportation (Commuting) Benefits

This section discusses exclusion rules that apply to benefits you provide to your employees for their personal transportation, such as commuting to and from work. These rules apply to the following transportation benefits.

- *De minimis* transportation benefits.
- Qualified transportation benefits.

Special rules that apply to demonstrator cars and qualified nonpersonal use vehicles are discussed under Working Condition Benefits, later in this section.

De Minimis Transportation Benefits

You can exclude the value of any *de minimis* transportation benefit you provide to an employee from the employee's wages. A *de minimis* transportation benefit is any local transportation benefit you provide to an employee if it has so little value (taking into account how frequently you provide transportation to your employees) that accounting for it would be unreasonable or administratively impracticable. For example, it applies to occasional transportation fare you give an employee because the employee is working overtime if the benefit is reasonable and is not based on hours worked.

Employee. For this exclusion, treat any recipient of a *de minimis* transportation benefit as an employee.

Qualified Transportation Benefits

This exclusion applies to the following benefits.

- A ride in a commuter highway vehicle between the employee's home and work place.
- A transit pass.
- Qualified parking.
- Qualified bicycle commuting reimbursement.

The exclusion applies whether you provide only one or a combination of these benefits to your employees.

Qualified transportation benefits can be provided directly by you or through a bona fide reimbursement arrangement. However, cash reimbursements for transit passes qualify only if a voucher or a similar item that the employee can exchange only for a transit pass is not readily available for direct distribution by you to your employee. A voucher is readily available for direct distribution only if an employee can obtain it from a voucher provider that does not impose fare media charges or other restrictions that effectively prevent the employer from obtaining vouchers. See Regulations section 1.132-9(b)(Q&A 16–19) for more information.

Generally, you can exclude qualified transportation fringe benefits from an employee's wages even if you provide them in place of pay. However, qualified bicycle commuting reimbursements cannot be excluded if the reimbursements are provided in place of pay. For information about providing qualified transportation fringe benefits under a compensation reduction agreement, see Regulations section 1.132-9(b)(Q&A 11–15).

Commuter highway vehicle. A commuter highway vehicle is any highway vehicle that seats at least 6 adults (not including the driver). In addition, you must reasonably expect that at least 80% of the vehicle mileage will be for transporting employees between their homes and work place with employees occupying at least one-half the vehicle's seats (not including the driver's).

Transit pass. A transit pass is any pass, token, farecard, voucher, or similar item entitling a person to ride, free of charge or at a reduced rate, on one of the following.

- On mass transit.
- In a vehicle that seats at least 6 adults (not including the driver) if a person in the business of transporting persons for pay or hire operates it.

Mass transit may be publicly or privately operated and includes bus, rail, or ferry. For guidance on the use of smart cards and debit cards to provide qualified transportation fringes, see Revenue Ruling 2006-57, 2006-47 I.R.B. 911, available at *www.irs.gov/irb/2006-47_IRB/ar05.html* and Notice 2010-94, 2010-52 I.R.B. 927, available at *www.irs.gov/irb/2010-52_IRB/ar18.html*.

Qualified parking. Qualified parking is parking you provide to your employees on or near your business premises. It includes parking on or near the location from which your employees commute to work using mass transit, commuter highway vehicles, or carpools. It does not include parking at or near your employee's home.

Qualified bicycle commuting reimbursement. For any calendar year, the exclusion for qualified bicycle commuting reimbursement includes any employer reimbursement during the 15-month period beginning with the first day of the calendar year for reasonable expenses incurred by the employee during the calendar year.

Reasonable expenses include:

- The purchase of a bicycle, and
- Bicycle improvements, repair, and storage.

These are considered reasonable expenses as long as the bicycle is regularly used for travel between the employee's residence and place of employment.

Employee. For this exclusion, treat the following individuals as employees.

- A current employee.
- A leased employee who has provided services to you on a substantially full-time basis for at least a year if the services are performed under your primary direction or control.

A self-employed individual is not an employee for qualified transportation benefit purposes.

Exception for S corporation shareholders. Do not treat a 2% shareholder of an S corporation as an employee of the corporation for this purpose. A 2% shareholder is someone who directly or indirectly owns (at any time during the year) more than 2% of the corporation's stock or stock with more than 2% of the voting power. Treat a 2% shareholder as you would a partner in a partnership for fringe benefit purposes, but do not treat the benefit as a reduction in distributions to the 2% shareholder.

Relation to other fringe benefits. You cannot exclude a qualified transportation benefit you provide to an employee under the *de minimis* or working condition benefit rules. However, if you provide a local transportation benefit other than by transit pass or commuter highway vehicle, or to a person other than an employee, you may be able to exclude all or part of the benefit under other fringe benefit rules (*de minimis*, working condition, etc.).

Exclusion from wages. You can generally exclude the value of transportation benefits that you provide to an employee during 2014 from the employee's wages up to the following limits.

- $130 per month for combined commuter highway vehicle transportation and transit passes.
- $250 per month for qualified parking.

- For a calendar year, $20 multiplied by the number of qualified bicycle commuting months during that year for qualified bicycle commuting reimbursement of expenses incurred during the year.

Qualified bicycle commuting month. For any employee, a qualified bicycle commuting month is any month the employee:

1. Regularly uses the bicycle for a substantial portion of the travel between the employee's residence and place of employment and
2. Does not receive:
   a. Transportation in a commuter highway vehicle,
   b. Any transit pass, or
   c. Qualified parking benefits.

Benefits more than the limit. If the value of a benefit for any month is more than its limit, include in the employee's wages the amount over the limit minus any amount the employee paid for the benefit. You cannot exclude the excess from the employee's wages as a *de minimis* transportation benefit.

More information. For more information on qualified transportation benefits, including van pools, and how to determine the value of parking, see Regulations section 1.132-9.

Tuition Reduction

An educational organization can exclude the value of a qualified tuition reduction it provides to an employee from the employee's wages.

A tuition reduction for undergraduate education generally qualifies for this exclusion if it is for the education of one of the following individuals.

1. A current employee.
2. A former employee who retired or left on disability.
3. A widow or widower of an individual who died while an employee.
4. A widow or widower of a former employee who retired or left on disability.
5. A dependent child or spouse of any individual listed in (1) through (4) above.

A tuition reduction for graduate education qualifies for this exclusion only if it is for the education of a graduate student who performs teaching or research activities for the educational organization.

For more information on this exclusion, see Publication 970.

Working Condition Benefits

This exclusion applies to property and services you provide to an employee so that the employee can perform his or her job. It applies to the extent the employee could deduct the cost of the property or services as a business expense or depreciation expense if he or she had paid for it. The employee must meet any substantiation requirements that apply to the deduction. Examples of working condition benefits include an employee's use of a company car for business, an employer-provided cell phone provided primarily for noncompensatory business purposes, and job-related education provided to an employee.

This exclusion also applies to a cash payment you provide for an employee's expenses for a specific or prearranged business activity for which a deduction is otherwise allowable to the employee. You must require the employee to verify that the payment is actually used for those expenses and to return any unused part of the payment.

For information on deductible employee business expenses, see *Unreimbursed Employee Expenses* in Publication 529, Miscellaneous Deductions.

The exclusion does not apply to the following items.

- A service or property provided under a flexible spending account in which you agree to provide the employee, over a time period, a certain level of unspecified noncash benefits with a predetermined cash value.
- A physical examination program you provide, even if mandatory.
- Any item to the extent the employee could deduct its cost as an expense for a trade or business other than your trade or business.

Employee. For this exclusion, treat the following individuals as employees.

- A current employee.
- A partner who performs services for a partnership.
- A director of your company.
- An independent contractor who performs services for you.

Vehicle allocation rules. If you provide a car for an employee's use, the amount you can exclude as a working condition benefit is the amount that would be allowable as a deductible business expense if the employee paid for its use. If the employee uses the car for both business and personal use, the value of the working condition benefit is the part determined to be for business use of the vehicle. See *Business use of your car* under *Personal versus Business Expenses* in chapter 1 of Publication 535. Also, see the special rules for certain demonstrator cars and qualified nonpersonal use vehicles discussed later.

However, instead of excluding the value of the working condition benefit, you can include the entire annual lease value of the car in the employee's wages. The employee can then claim any deductible business expense for the car as an itemized deduction on his or her personal income tax return. This option is available only if you use the lease value rule (discussed in section 3) to value the benefit.

Demonstrator cars. Generally, all of the use of a demonstrator car by your full-time auto salesperson qualifies as a working condition benefit if the use is primarily to facilitate the services the salesperson provides for you and there are substantial restrictions on personal use. For more information and the definition of "full-time auto salesperson," see Regulations section 1.132-5(o). For optional, simplified methods used to determine if full, partial, or no exclusion of income to the employee for personal use of a demonstrator car applies, see Revenue Procedure 2001-56. You can find Revenue Procedure 2001-56 on page 590 of Internal Revenue Bulletin 2001-51 at www.irs.gov/pub/irs-irbs/irb01-51.pdf.

Qualified nonpersonal use vehicles. All of an employee's use of a qualified nonpersonal use vehicle is a working condition benefit. A qualified nonpersonal use vehicle is any vehicle the employee is not likely to use more than minimally for personal purposes because of its design. Qualified nonpersonal use vehicles generally include all of the following vehicles.

- Clearly marked, through painted insignia or words, police, fire, and public safety vehicles.
- Unmarked vehicles used by law enforcement officers if the use is officially authorized.
- An ambulance or hearse used for its specific purpose.
- Any vehicle designed to carry cargo with a loaded gross vehicle weight over 14,000 pounds.
- Delivery trucks with seating for the driver only, or the driver plus a folding jump seat.
- A passenger bus with a capacity of at least 20 passengers used for its specific purpose.
- School buses.
- Tractors and other special-purpose farm vehicles.
- Bucket trucks, cement mixers, combines, cranes and derricks, dump trucks (including garbage trucks), flatbed trucks, forklifts, qualified moving vans, qualified specialized utility repair trucks, and refrigerated trucks.

See Regulations section 1.274-5(k) for the definition of qualified moving van and qualified specialized utility repair truck.

Pickup trucks. A pickup truck with a loaded gross vehicle weight of 14,000 pounds or less is a qualified nonpersonal use vehicle if it has been specially modified so it is not likely to be used more than minimally for personal purposes. For example, a pickup truck qualifies if it is clearly marked with permanently affixed decals, special painting, or other advertising associated with your trade, business, or function and meets either of the following requirements.

1. It is equipped with at least one of the following items.
   a. A hydraulic lift gate.
   b. Permanent tanks or drums.
   c. Permanent side boards or panels that materially raise the level of the sides of the truck bed.
   d. Other heavy equipment (such as an electric generator, welder, boom, or crane used to tow automobiles and other vehicles).
2. It is used primarily to transport a particular type of load (other than over the public highways) in a construction, manufacturing, processing, farming, mining, drilling, timbering, or other similar operation for which it was specially designed or significantly modified.

Vans. A van with a loaded gross vehicle weight of 14,000 pounds or less is a qualified nonpersonal use vehicle if it has been specially modified so it is not likely to be used more than minimally for personal purposes. For example, a van qualifies if it is clearly marked with permanently affixed decals, special painting, or other advertising associated with your trade, business, or function and has a seat for the driver only (or the driver and one other person) and either of the following items.

- Permanent shelving that fills most of the cargo area.
- An open cargo area and the van always carries merchandise, material, or equipment used in your trade, business, or function.

Education. Certain job-related education you provide to an employee may qualify for exclusion as a working condition benefit. To qualify, the education must meet the same requirements that would apply for determining whether the employee could deduct the expenses had the employee paid the expenses. Degree programs as a whole do not necessarily qualify as a working condition benefit. Each course in the program must be evaluated individually for qualification as a working condition benefit. The education must meet at least one of the following tests.

- The education is required by the employer or by law for the employee to keep his or her present salary, status, or job. The required education must serve a bona fide business purpose of the employer.
- The education maintains or improves skills needed in the job.

However, even if the education meets one or both of the above tests, it is not qualifying education if it:

- Is needed to meet the minimum educational requirements of the employee's present trade or business, or
- Is part of a program of study that will qualify the employee for a new trade or business.

Outplacement services. An employee's use of outplacement services qualifies as a working condition benefit if you provide the services to the employee on the basis of need, you get a substantial business benefit from the services distinct from the benefit you would get from the payment of additional wages, and the employee is seeking employment in the same trade or business of the employer. Substantial business benefits include promoting a positive business image, maintaining employee morale, and avoiding wrongful termination suits.

Outplacement services do not qualify as a working condition benefit if the employee can choose to receive cash or taxable benefits in place of the services. If you maintain a severance plan and permit employees to get outplacement services with reduced severance pay, include in the employee's wages the difference between the unreduced severance and the reduced severance payments.

Exclusion from wages. You can generally exclude the value of a working condition benefit you provide to an employee from the employee's wages.

Exception for independent contractors. You cannot exclude the value of parking (unless *de minimis*), transit passes (if their monthly value exceeds $130 per month), or the use of consumer goods you provide in a product testing program from the compensation you pay to an independent contractor who performs services for you.

Exception for company directors. You cannot exclude the value of the use of consumer goods you provide in a product testing program from the compensation you pay to a director.

3. Fringe Benefit Valuation Rules

This section discusses the rules you must use to determine the value of a fringe benefit you provide to an employee. You must determine the value of any benefit you cannot exclude under the rules in section 2 or for which the amount you can exclude is limited. See Including taxable benefits in pay in section 1.

In most cases, you must use the general valuation rule to value a fringe benefit. However, you may be able to use a special valuation rule to determine the value of certain benefits.

This section does not discuss the special valuation rule used to value meals provided at an employer-operated eating facility for employees. For that rule, see Regulations section 1.61-21(j). This section also does not discuss the special valuation rules used to value the use of aircraft. For those rules, see Regulations sections 1.61-21(g) and (h). The fringe benefit valuation formulas are published in the Internal Revenue Bulletin as Revenue Rulings twice during the year. The formula applicable for the first half of the year is usually available at the end of March. The formula applicable for the second half of the year is usually available at the end of September.

General Valuation Rule

You must use the general valuation rule to determine the value of most fringe benefits. Under this rule, the value of a fringe benefit is its fair market value.

Fair market value. The fair market value (FMV) of a fringe benefit is the amount an employee would have to pay a third party in an arm's-length transaction to buy or lease the benefit. Determine this amount on the basis of all the facts and circumstances.

Neither the amount the employee considers to be the value of the fringe benefit nor the cost you incur to provide the benefit determines its FMV.

Employer-provided vehicles. In general, the FMV of an employer-provided vehicle is the amount the employee would have to pay a third party to lease the same or similar vehicle on the same or comparable terms in the geographic area where the employee uses the vehicle. A comparable lease term would be the amount of time the vehicle is available for the employee's use, such as a 1-year period.

Do not determine the FMV by multiplying a cents-per-mile rate times the number of miles driven unless the employee can prove the vehicle could have been leased on a cents-per-mile basis.

Cents-Per-Mile Rule

Under this rule, you determine the value of a vehicle you provide to an employee for personal use by multiplying the standard mileage rate by the total miles the employee drives the vehicle for personal purposes. Personal use is any use of the vehicle other than use in your trade or business. This amount must be included in the employee's wages or reimbursed by the employee. For 2014, the standard mileage rate is 56 cents per mile.

You can use the cents-per-mile rule if either of the following requirements is met.

- You reasonably expect the vehicle to be regularly used in your trade or business throughout the calendar year (or for a shorter period during which you own or lease it).
- The vehicle meets the mileage test.

CAUTION ***Maximum automobile value.*** *You cannot use the cents-per-mile rule for an automobile (any four-wheeled vehicle, such as a car, pickup truck, or van) if its value when you first make it available to any employee for personal use is more than an amount determined by the IRS as the maximum automobile value for the year. For example, you cannot use the cents-per-mile rule for an automobile that you first made available to an employee in 2013 if its value at that time exceeded $16,000 for a passenger automobile or $17,000 for a truck or van. The maximum automobile value for 2014 will be published in a notice in the Internal Revenue Bulletin early in 2014. If you and the employee own or lease the automobile together, see Regulations section 1.61-21(e)(1)(iii)(B).*

Vehicle. For the cents-per-mile rule, a vehicle is any motorized wheeled vehicle, including an automobile, manufactured primarily for use on public streets, roads, and highways.

Regular use in your trade or business. A vehicle is regularly used in your trade or business if at least one of the following conditions is met.

- At least 50% of the vehicle's total annual mileage is for your trade or business.
- You sponsor a commuting pool that generally uses the vehicle each workday to drive at least three employees to and from work.
- The vehicle is regularly used in your trade or business on the basis of all of the facts and circumstances. Infrequent business use of the vehicle, such as for occasional trips to the airport or between your multiple business premises, is not regular use of the vehicle in your trade or business.

Mileage test. A vehicle meets the mileage test for a calendar year if both of the following requirements are met.

- The vehicle is actually driven at least 10,000 miles during the year. If you own or lease the vehicle only part of the year, reduce the 10,000 mile requirement proportionately.
- The vehicle is used during the year primarily by employees. Consider the vehicle used primarily by employees if they use it consistently for commuting. Do not treat the use of the vehicle by another individual whose use would be taxed to the employee as use by the employee.

For example, if only one employee uses a vehicle during the calendar year and that employee drives the vehicle at least 10,000 miles in that year, the vehicle meets the mileage test even if all miles driven by the employee are personal.

Consistency requirements. If you use the cents-per-mile rule, the following requirements apply.

- You must begin using the cents-per-mile rule on the first day you make the vehicle available to any employee for personal use. However, if you use the commuting rule (discussed later) when you first make the vehicle available to any employee for personal use, you can change to the cents-per-mile rule on the first day for which you do not use the commuting rule.
- You must use the cents-per-mile rule for all later years in which you make the vehicle available to any employee and the vehicle qualifies, except that you can use the commuting rule for any year during which use of the vehicle qualifies under the commuting rules. However, if the vehicle does not qualify for the cents-per-mile rule during a later year, you can use for that year and thereafter any other rule for which the vehicle then qualifies.
- You must continue to use the cents-per-mile rule if you provide a replacement vehicle to the employee (and the vehicle qualifies for the use of this rule) and your primary reason for the replacement is to reduce federal taxes.

Items included in cents-per-mile rate. The cents-per-mile rate includes the value of maintenance and insurance for the vehicle. Do not reduce the rate by the value of any service included in the rate that you did not provide. You can take into account the services actually provided for the vehicle by using the General Valuation Rule, earlier.

For miles driven in the United States, its territories and possessions, Canada, and Mexico, the cents-per-mile rate includes the value of fuel you provide. If you do not provide fuel, you can reduce the rate by no more than 5.5 cents.

For special rules that apply to fuel you provide for miles driven outside the United States, Canada, and Mexico, see Regulations section 1.61-21(e)(3)(ii)(B).

The value of any other service you provide for a vehicle is not included in the cents-per-mile rate. Use the general valuation rule to value these services.

Commuting Rule

Under this rule, you determine the value of a vehicle you provide to an employee for commuting use by multiplying each one-way commute (that is, from home to work or from work to home) by $1.50. If more than one employee commutes in the vehicle, this value applies to each employee. This amount must be included in the employee's wages or reimbursed by the employee.

You can use the commuting rule if all the following requirements are met.

- You provide the vehicle to an employee for use in your trade or business and, for bona fide noncompensatory business reasons, you require the employee to commute in the vehicle. You will be treated as if you had met this requirement if the vehicle is generally used each workday to carry at least three employees to and from work in an employer sponsored commuting pool.
- You establish a written policy under which you do not allow the employee to use the vehicle for personal purposes other than for commuting or *de minimis* personal use (such as a stop for a personal errand on the way between a business delivery and the employee's home). Personal use of a vehicle is all use that is not for your trade or business.
- The employee does not use the vehicle for personal purposes other than commuting and *de minimis* personal use.
- If this vehicle is an automobile (any four-wheeled vehicle, such as a car, pickup truck, or van), the employee who uses it for commuting is not a control employee. See Control employee, later.

Vehicle. For this rule, a vehicle is any motorized wheeled vehicle, including an automobile manufactured primarily for use on public streets, roads, and highways.

Control employee. A control employee of a nongovernment employer for 2014 is generally any of the following employees.

- A board or shareholder-appointed, confirmed, or elected officer whose pay is $105,000 or more.
- A director.
- An employee whose pay is $210,000 or more.
- An employee who owns a 1% or more equity, capital, or profits interest in your business.

A control employee for a government employer for 2014 is either of the following.

- A government employee whose compensation is equal to or exceeds Federal Government Executive Level V. See the Office of Personnel Management website at www.opm.gov/policy-data-oversight/pay-leave/salaries-wages/ for 2014 compensation information.
- An elected official.

Highly compensated employee alternative. Instead of using the preceding definition, you can choose to define a control employee as any highly compensated employee. A highly compensated employee for 2014 is an employee who meets either of the following tests.

1. The employee was a 5% owner at any time during the year or the preceding year.
2. The employee received more than $115,000 in pay for the preceding year.

You can choose to ignore test (2) if the employee was not also in the top 20% of employees when ranked by pay for the preceding year.

Lease Value Rule

Under this rule, you determine the value of an automobile you provide to an employee by using its annual lease value. For an automobile provided only part of the year, use either its prorated annual lease value or its daily lease value.

If the automobile is used by the employee in your business, you generally reduce the lease value by the amount that is excluded from the employee's wages as a working condition benefit. In order to do this, the employee must account to the employer for the business use. This is done by substantiating the usage (mileage, for example), the time and place of the travel, and the business purpose of the travel. Written records made at the time of each business use are the best evidence. Any use of a company-provided vehicle that is not substantiated as business use is included in income. The working condition benefit is the amount that would be an allowable business expense deduction for the employee if the employee paid for the use of the vehicle. However, you can choose to include the entire lease value in the employee's wages. See Vehicle allocation rules, under *Working Condition Benefit* in section 2.

Automobile. For this rule, an automobile is any four-wheeled vehicle (such as a car, pickup truck, or van) manufactured primarily for use on public streets, roads, and highways.

Consistency requirements. If you use the lease value rule, the following requirements apply.

1. You must begin using this rule on the first day you make the automobile available to any employee for personal use. However, the following exceptions apply.
   a. If you use the commuting rule (discussed earlier in this section) when you first make the automobile available to any employee for personal use, you can change to the lease value rule on the first day for which you do not use the commuting rule.
   b. If you use the cents-per-mile rule (discussed earlier in this section) when you first make the automobile available to any employee for personal use, you can change to the lease value rule on the first day on which the automobile no longer qualifies for the cents-per-mile rule.
2. You must use this rule for all later years in which you make the automobile available to any employee, except that you can use the commuting rule for any year during which use of the automobile qualifies.
3. You must continue to use this rule if you provide a replacement automobile to the employee and your primary reason for the replacement is to reduce federal taxes.

Annual Lease Value

Generally, you figure the annual lease value of an automobile as follows.

1. Determine the fair market value (FMV) of the automobile on the first date it is available to any employee for personal use.
2. Using *Table 3-1. Annual Lease Value Table*, read down column (1) until you come to the dollar range within which the FMV of the automobile falls. Then read across to column (2) to find the annual lease value.
3. Multiply the annual lease value by the percentage of personal miles out of total miles driven by the employee.

Table 3-1. Annual Lease Value Table

(1) Automobile FMV	(2) Annual Lease
$0 to 999	$ 600
1,000 to 1,999	850
2,000 to 2,999	1,100
3,000 to 3,999	1,350
4,000 to 4,999	1,600
5,000 to 5,999	1,850
6,000 to 6,999	2,100
7,000 to 7,999	2,350
8,000 to 8,999	2,600
9,000 to 9,999	2,850
10,000 to 10,999	3,100
11,000 to 11,999	3,350
12,000 to 12,999	3,600
13,000 to 13,999	3,850
14,000 to 14,999	4,100
15,000 to 15,999	4,350
16,000 to 16,999	4,600
17,000 to 17,999	4,850
18,000 to 18,999	5,100
19,000 to 19,999	5,350
20,000 to 20,999	5,600
21,000 to 21,999	5,850
22,000 to 22,999	6,100
23,000 to 23,999	6,350
24,000 to 24,999	6,600
25,000 to 25,999	6,850
26,000 to 27,999	7,250
28,000 to 29,999	7,750
30,000 to 31,999	8,250
32,000 to 33,999	8,750
34,000 to 35,999	9,250
36,000 to 37,999	9,750
38,000 to 39,999	10,250
40,000 to 41,999	10,750
42,000 to 43,999	11,250
44,000 to 45,999	11,750
46,000 to 47,999	12,250
48,000 to 49,999	12,750
50,000 to 51,999	13,250
52,000 to 53,999	13,750
54,000 to 55,999	14,250
56,000 to 57,999	14,750
58,000 to 59,999	15,250

For automobiles with a FMV of more than $59,999, the annual lease value equals (.25 × the FMV of the automobile) + $500.

FMV. The FMV of an automobile is the amount a person would pay to buy it from a third party in an arm's-length transaction in the area in which the automobile is bought or leased. That amount includes all purchase expenses, such as sales tax and title fees.

If you have 20 or more automobiles, see Regulations section 1.61-21(d)(5)(v). If you and the employee own or lease the automobile together, see Regulations section 1.61-21(d)(2)(ii).

You do not have to include the value of a telephone or any specialized equipment added to, or carried in, the automobile if the equipment is necessary for your business. However, include the value of specialized equipment if the employee to whom the automobile is available uses the specialized equipment in a trade or business other than yours.

Neither the amount the employee considers to be the value of the benefit nor your cost for either buying or leasing the automobile determines its FMV. However, see *Safe-harbor value*, next.

Safe-harbor value. You may be able to use a safe-harbor value as the FMV.

For an automobile you bought at arm's length, the safe-harbor value is your cost, including sales tax, title, and other purchase expenses. You cannot have been the manufacturer of the automobile.

For an automobile you lease, you can use any of the following as the safe-harbor value.

- The manufacturer's invoice price (including options) plus 4%.
- The manufacturer's suggested retail price minus 8% (including sales tax, title, and other expenses of purchase).
- The retail value of the automobile reported by a nationally recognized pricing source if that retail value is reasonable for the automobile.

Items included in annual lease value table. Each annual lease value in the table includes the value of maintenance and insurance for the automobile. Do not reduce the annual lease value by the value of any of these services that you did not provide. For example, do not reduce the annual lease value by the value of a maintenance service contract or insurance you did not provide. You can take into account the services actually provided for the automobile by using the general valuation rule discussed earlier.

Items not included. The annual lease value does not include the value of fuel you provide to an employee for personal use, regardless of whether you provide it, reimburse its cost, or have it charged to you. You must include the value of the fuel separately in the employee's wages. You can value fuel you provided at FMV or at 5.5 cents per mile for all miles driven by the employee. However, you cannot value at 5.5 cents per mile fuel you provide for miles driven outside the United States (including its possessions and territories), Canada, and Mexico.

If you reimburse an employee for the cost of fuel, or have it charged to you, you generally value the fuel at the amount you reimburse, or the amount charged to you if it was bought at arm's length.

If you have 20 or more automobiles, see Regulations section 1.61-21(d)(3)(ii)(D).

If you provide any service other than maintenance and insurance for an automobile, you must add the FMV of that service to the annual lease value of the automobile to figure the value of the benefit.

4-year lease term. The annual lease values in the table are based on a 4-year lease term. These values will generally stay the same for the period that begins with the first date you use this rule for the automobile and ends on December 31 of the fourth full calendar year following that date.

Figure the annual lease value for each later 4-year period by determining the FMV of the automobile on January 1 of the first year of the later 4-year period and selecting the amount in column (2) of the table that corresponds to the appropriate dollar range in column (1).

Using the special accounting rule. If you use the special accounting rule for fringe benefits discussed in section 4, you can figure the annual lease value for each later 4-year period at the beginning of the special accounting period that starts immediately before the January 1 date described in the previous paragraph.

For example, assume that you use the special accounting rule and that, beginning on November 1, 2013, the special accounting period is November 1 to October 31. You elected to use the lease value rule as of January 1, 2014. You can refigure the annual lease value on November 1, 2017, rather than on January 1, 2018.

Transferring an automobile from one employee to another. Unless the primary purpose of the transfer is to reduce federal taxes, you can refigure the annual lease value based on the FMV of the automobile on January 1 of the calendar year of transfer.

However, if you use the special accounting rule for fringe benefits discussed in section 4, you can refigure the annual lease value (based on the FMV of the automobile) at the beginning of the special accounting period in which the transfer occurs.

Prorated Annual Lease Value

If you provide an automobile to an employee for a continuous period of 30 or more days but less than an entire calendar year, you can prorate the annual lease value. Figure the prorated annual lease value by multiplying the annual lease value by a fraction, using the number of days of availability as the numerator and 365 as the denominator.

If you provide an automobile continuously for at least 30 days, but the period covers 2 calendar years (or 2 special accounting periods if you are using the special accounting rule for fringe benefits discussed in section 4), you can use the prorated annual lease value or the daily lease value.

If you have 20 or more automobiles, see Regulations section 1.61-21(d)(6).

If an automobile is unavailable to the employee because of his or her personal reasons (for example, if the employee is on vacation), you cannot take into account the periods of unavailability when you use a prorated annual lease value.

CAUTION *You cannot use a prorated annual lease value if the reduction of federal tax is the main reason the automobile is unavailable.*

Daily Lease Value

If you provide an automobile to an employee for a continuous period of less than 30 days, use the daily lease value to figure its value. Figure the daily lease value by multiplying the annual lease value by a fraction, using four times the number of days of availability as the numerator and 365 as the denominator.

However, you can apply a prorated annual lease value for a period of continuous availability of less than 30 days by treating the automobile as if it had been available for 30 days. Use a prorated annual lease value if it would result in a lower valuation than applying the daily lease value to the shorter period of availability.

Unsafe Conditions Commuting Rule

Under this rule, the value of commuting transportation you provide to a qualified employee solely because of unsafe conditions is $1.50 for a one-way commute (that is, from home to work or from work to home). This amount must be included in the employee's wages or reimbursed by the employee.

You can use the unsafe conditions commuting rule for qualified employees if all of the following requirements are met.

- The employee would ordinarily walk or use public transportation for commuting.
- You have a written policy under which you do not provide the transportation for personal purposes other than commuting because of unsafe conditions.
- The employee does not use the transportation for personal purposes other than commuting because of unsafe conditions.

These requirements must be met on a trip-by-trip basis.

Commuting transportation. This is transportation to or from work using any motorized wheeled vehicle (including an automobile) manufactured for use on public streets, roads, and highways. You or the employee must buy the transportation from a party that is not related to you. If the employee buys it, you must reimburse the employee for its cost (for example, cab fare) under a bona fide reimbursement arrangement.

Qualified employee. A qualified employee for 2014 is one who:

- Performs services during the year;
- Is paid on an hourly basis;
- Is not claimed under section 213(a)(1) of the Fair Labor Standards Act (FLSA) of 1938 (as amended) to be exempt from the minimum wage and maximum hour provisions;
- Is within a classification for which you actually pay, or have specified in writing that you will pay, overtime pay of at least one and one-half times the regular rate provided in section 207 of FLSA; and

• Received pay of not more than $115,000 during 2013.

However, an employee is not considered a qualified employee if you do not comply with the recordkeeping requirements concerning the employee's wages, hours, and other conditions and practices of employment under section 211(c) of FLSA and the related regulations.

Unsafe conditions. Unsafe conditions exist if, under the facts and circumstances, a reasonable person would consider it unsafe for the employee to walk or use public transportation at the time of day the employee must commute. One factor indicating whether it is unsafe is the history of crime in the geographic area surrounding the employee's workplace or home at the time of day the employee commutes.

4. Rules for Withholding, Depositing, and Reporting

Use the following guidelines for withholding, depositing, and reporting taxable noncash fringe benefits. For additional information on how to withhold on fringe benefits, see section 5 in Publication 15 (Circular E).

Valuation of fringe benefits. Generally, you must determine the value of noncash fringe benefits no later than January 31 of the next year. Before January 31, you may reasonably estimate the value of the fringe benefits for purposes of withholding and depositing on time.

Choice of period for withholding, depositing, and reporting. For employment tax and withholding purposes, you can treat noncash fringe benefits (including personal use of employer-provided highway motor vehicles) as paid on a pay period, quarter, semiannual, annual, or other basis. But the benefits must be treated as paid no less frequently than annually. You do not have to choose the same period for all employees. You can withhold more frequently for some employees than for others.

You can change the period as often as you like as long as you treat all of the benefits provided in a calendar year as paid no later than December 31 of the calendar year.

You can also treat the value of a single fringe benefit as paid on one or more dates in the same calendar year, even if the employee receives the entire benefit at one time. For example, if your employee receives a fringe benefit valued at $1,000 in one pay period during 2014, you can treat it as made in four payments of $250, each in a different pay period of 2014. You do not have to notify the IRS of the use of the periods discussed above.

Transfer of property. The above choice for reporting and withholding does not apply to a cash fringe benefit or a fringe benefit that is a transfer of tangible or intangible personal property of a kind normally held for investment or a transfer of real property. For these kinds of fringe benefits, you must use the actual date the property was transferred to the employee.

Withholding and depositing taxes. You can add the value of fringe benefits to regular wages for a payroll period and figure income tax withholding on the total. Or you can withhold federal income tax on the value of fringe benefits at the flat 25% rate that applies to supplemental wages. See section 7 in Publication 15 (Circular E) for the flat rate (39.6%) when supplemental wage payments to an individual exceed $1 million during the year.

You must withhold the applicable income, social security, and Medicare taxes on the date or dates you chose to treat the benefits as paid. Deposit the amounts withheld as discussed in section 11 of Publication 15 (Circular E).

Additional Medicare Tax withholding. In addition to withholding Medicare tax at 1.45%, you must withhold a 0.9% Additional Medicare Tax from wages you pay to an employee in excess of $200,000 in a calendar year. You are required to begin withholding Additional Medicare Tax in the pay period in which you pay wages in excess of $200,000 to an employee and continue to withhold it each pay period until the end of the calendar year. Additional Medicare Tax is only imposed on the employee. There is no employer share of Additional Medicare Tax. All wages that are subject to Medicare tax are subject to Additional Medicare Tax withholding if paid in excess of the $200,000 withholding threshold.

For more information on what wages are subject to Medicare tax, see Table 2-1, earlier, and the chart, *Special Rules for Various Types of Services and Payments*, in section 15 of Publication 15, (Circular E). For more information on Additional Medicare Tax, visit IRS.gov and enter "Additional Medicare Tax" in the search box.

Amount of deposit. To estimate the amount of income tax withholding and employment taxes and to deposit them on time, make a reasonable estimate of the value of the fringe benefits provided on the date or dates you chose to treat the benefits as paid. Determine the estimated deposit by figuring the amount you would have had to deposit if you had paid cash wages equal to the estimated value of the fringe benefits and withheld taxes from those cash wages. Even if you do not know which employee will receive the fringe benefit on the date the deposit is due, you should follow this procedure.

If you underestimate the value of the fringe benefits and deposit less than the amount you would have had to deposit if the applicable taxes had been withheld, you may be subject to a penalty.

If you overestimate the value of the fringe benefit and overdeposit, you can either claim a refund or have the overpayment applied to your next Form 941, Employer's QUARTERLY Federal Tax Return. See the Instructions for Form 941.

If you paid the required amount of taxes but withheld a lesser amount from the employee, you can recover from the employee the social security, Medicare, or income taxes you deposited on the employee's behalf and included on the employee's Form W-2. However, you must recover the income taxes before April 1 of the following year.

Paying your employee's share of social security and Medicare taxes. If you choose to pay your employee's social security and Medicare taxes on taxable fringe benefits without deducting them from his or her pay, you must include the amount of the payments in the employee's income. Also, if your employee leaves your employment and you have unpaid and uncollected taxes for noncash benefits, you are still liable for those taxes. You must add the uncollected employee share of social security and Medicare tax to the employee's wages. Follow the procedure discussed under *Employee's Portion of Taxes Paid by Employer* in section 7 of Publication 15-A. Do not use withheld federal income tax to pay the social security and Medicare tax.

Special accounting rule. You can treat the value of taxable noncash benefits as paid on a pay period, quarterly, semi-annually, annually, or on another basis, provided that the benefits are treated as paid no less frequently than annually. You can treat the value of taxable noncash fringe benefits provided during the last two months of the calendar year, or any shorter period within the last two months, as paid in the next year. Thus, the value of taxable noncash benefits actually provided in the last two months of 2013 could be treated as provided in 2014 together with the value of benefits provided in the first 10 months of 2014. This does not mean that all benefits treated as paid during the last two months of a calendar year can be deferred until the next year. Only the value of benefits actually provided during the last two months of the calendar year can be treated as paid in the next calendar year.

Limitation. The special accounting rule cannot be used, however, for a fringe benefit that is a transfer of tangible or intangible personal property of a kind normally held for investment or a transfer of real property.

Conformity rules. Use of the special accounting rule is optional. You can use the rule for some fringe benefits but not others. The period of use need not be the same for each fringe benefit. However, if you use the rule for a particular fringe benefit, you must use it for all employees who receive that benefit.

If you use the special accounting rule, your employee also must use it for the same period you use it. But your employee cannot use the special accounting rule unless you do.

You do not have to notify the IRS if you use the special accounting rule. You may also, for appropriate reasons, change the period for which you use the rule without notifying the IRS. But you must report the income and deposit the withheld taxes as required for the changed period.

Special rules for highway motor vehicles. If an employee uses the employer's vehicle for personal purposes, the value of that use must be determined by the employer and included in the employee's wages. The value of the personal use must be based on fair market value or determined by using one of the following three special valuation rules previously discussed in section 3.

- The lease value rule.
- The cents-per-mile rule.
- The commuting rule (for commuting use only).

Election not to withhold income tax. You can choose not to withhold income tax on the value of an employee's personal use of a highway motor vehicle you provided. You do not have to make this choice for all employees. You can withhold income tax from the wages of some employees but not others. You must, however, withhold the applicable social security and Medicare taxes on such benefits.

You can choose not to withhold income tax on an employee's personal use of a highway motor vehicle by:

- Notifying the employee as described below that you choose not to withhold, and
- Including the value of the benefits in boxes 1, 3, 5, and 14 on a timely furnished Form W-2. For use of a separate statement in lieu of using box 14, see the General Instructions for Forms W-2 and W-3.

The notice must be in writing and must be provided to the employee by January 31 of the election year or within 30 days after a vehicle is first provided to the employee, whichever is later. This notice must be provided in a manner reasonably expected to come to the attention of the affected employee. For example, the notice may be mailed to the employee, included with a paycheck, or posted where the employee could reasonably be expected to see it. You can also change your election not to withhold at any time by notifying the employee in the same manner.

Amount to report on Forms 941 (or Form 944) and W-2. The actual value of fringe benefits provided during a calendar year (or other period as explained under Special accounting rule, earlier in this section) must be determined by January 31 of the following year. You must report the actual value on Forms 941 (or Form 944) and W-2. If you choose, you can use a separate Form W-2 for fringe benefits and any other benefit information.

Include the value of the fringe benefit in box 1 of Form W-2. Also include it in boxes 3 and 5, if applicable. You may show the total value of the fringe benefits provided in the calendar year or other period in box 14 of Form W-2. However, if you provided your employee with the use of a highway motor vehicle and included 100% of its annual lease value in the employee's income, you must also report it separately in box 14 or provide it in a separate statement to the employee so that the employee can compute the value of any business use of the vehicle.

If you use the special accounting rule, you must notify the affected employees of the period in which you used it. You must give this notice at or near the date you give the Form W-2, but not earlier than with the employee's last paycheck of the calendar year.

How To Get Tax Help

Whether it's help with a tax issue or a need for a free publication or form, get the help you need the way you want it:

online, use a smart phone, call or walk in to an IRS office or volunteer site near you.

Internet. IRS.gov and **IRS2Go** are ready when you are—24 hours a day, 7 days a week to.

- Download the free IRS2Go app from the iTunes app store or from Google Play. Use it to watch the IRS YouTube channel, get IRS news as soon as it's released to the public, subscribe to filing season updates or daily tax tips, and follow the IRS Twitter news feed, @IRSnews, to get the latest federal tax news, including information about tax law changes and important IRS programs.
- Use *Tax Trails*, one of the Tax Topics on IRS.gov which contain general individual and business tax information or by searching the *IRS Tax Map*, which includes an **international subject index**. You can use the **IRS Tax Map**, to search publications and instructions by topic or keyword. The IRS Tax Map integrates forms and publications into one research tool and provides single-point access to tax law information by subject. When the user searches the IRS Tax Map, they will be provided with links to related content in existing IRS publications, forms and instructions, questions and answers, and Tax Topics.
- Visit *Understanding Your IRS Notice or Letter* to get answers to questions about a notice or letter you received from the IRS.
- Make a payment using one of several safe and convenient electronic payment options available on IRS.gov. Select the Payment tab on the front page of IRS.gov for more information.
- Request an **Electronic Filing PIN** by going to IRS.gov and entering *Electronic Filing PIN* in the search box.
- Download forms, instructions and publications, including accessible versions for people with disabilities.
- Locate the nearest **Taxpayer Assistance Center (TAC)** using the *Office Locator* tool on IRS.gov, or choose the *Contact Us* option on the IRS2Go app and search *Local Offices*. An employee can answer questions about your tax account or help you set up a payment plan. Before you visit, check the *Office Locator* on IRS.gov, or *Local Offices* under Contact Us on IRS2Go to confirm the address, phone number, days and hours of operation, and the services provided. If you have a special need, such as a disability, you can request an appointment. Call the local number listed in the Office Locator, or look in the phone book under United States Government, Internal Revenue Service.
- Apply for an **Employer Identification Number (EIN).** Go to IRS.gov and enter *Apply for an EIN* in the search box.
- Read the Internal Revenue Code, regulations, or other official guidance.
- Read Internal Revenue Bulletins.
- Sign up to receive local and national tax news and more by email. Just click on "subscriptions" above the search box on IRS.gov and choose from a variety of options.

Phone. You can call the IRS, or you can carry it in your pocket with the IRS2Go app on your smart phone or tablet. Download the free IRS2Go app from the iTunes app store or from Google Play.

- Call 1-800-TAX-FORM (1-800-829-3676) to order current-year forms, instructions, publications, and prior-year forms and instructions (limited to 5 years). You should receive your order within 10 business days.
- Call **TeleTax**, 1-800-829-4477 to listen to pre-recorded messages covering general and business tax information.
- Call the IRS Business and Specialty Tax Line with your employment tax questions at 1-800-829-4933.
- Call using TDD/TTY equipment, 1-800-829-4059 to ask tax questions or order forms and publications. The TDD/TTY telephone number is for people who are deaf, hard of hearing, or have a speech disability. These individuals can also contact the IRS through relay services such as the *Federal Relay Service*.

Walk-in. You can find a selection of forms, publications and services — in-person.

- Products. You can walk in to some post offices, libraries, and IRS offices to pick up certain forms, instructions, and publications. Some IRS offices, libraries, and city and county government offices have a collection of products available to photocopy from reproducible proofs.
- Services. You can walk in to your local TAC for face-to-face tax help. An employee can answer questions about your tax account or help you set up a payment plan. Before visiting, use the *Office Locator* tool on IRS.gov, or choose the *Contact Us* option on the IRS2Go app and search *Local Offices* for days and hours of operation, and services provided.

Mail. You can send your order for forms, instructions, and publications to the address below. You should receive a response within 10 business days after your request is received.

Internal Revenue Service
1201 N. Mitsubishi Motorway
Bloomington, IL 61705-6613

The Taxpayer Advocate Service Is Here to Help You. **The Taxpayer Advocate Service (TAS)** is your voice at the IRS. Our job is to ensure that every taxpayer is treated fairly and that you know and understand your rights.

What can TAS do for you? We can offer you free help with IRS problems that you can't resolve on your own. We know this process can be confusing, but the worst thing you can do is nothing at all! TAS can help if you can't resolve your tax problem and:

- Your problem is causing financial difficulties for you, your family, or your business.
- You face (or your business is facing) an immediate threat of adverse action.
- You've tried repeatedly to contact the IRS but no one has responded, or the IRS hasn't responded by the date promised.

If you qualify for our help, you'll be assigned to one advocate who'll be with you at every turn and will do everything possible to resolve your problem. Here's why we can help:

- TAS is an independent organization within the IRS.
- Our advocates know how to work with the IRS.
- Our services are free and tailored to meet your needs.
- We have offices in every state, the District of Columbia, and Puerto Rico.

How can you reach us? If you think TAS can help you, call your local advocate, whose number is in your local directory and at Taxpayer Advocate, or call us toll-free at 1-877-777-4778.

How else does TAS help taxpayers?

TAS also works to resolve large-scale, systemic problems that affect many taxpayers. If you know of one of these broad issues, please report it to us through our Systemic Advocacy Management System.

Index

To help us develop a more useful index, please let us know if you have ideas for index entries. See "Comments and Suggestions" in the "Introduction" for the ways you can reach us.

This list identifies the codes used on Schedule K-1 for all partners and provides summarized reporting information for partners who file Form 1040. For detailed reporting and filing information, see the separate Partner's Instructions for Schedule K-1 and the instructions for your income tax return.

1. Ordinary business income (loss). Determine whether the income (loss) is passive or nonpassive and enter on your return as follows.

	Report on
Passive loss	See the Partner's Instructions
Passive income	Schedule E, line 28, column (g)
Nonpassive loss	Schedule E, line 28, column (h)
Nonpassive income	Schedule E, line 28, column (j)
2. Net rental real estate income (loss)	See the Partner's Instructions
3. Other net rental income (loss)	
Net income	Schedule E, line 28, column (g)
Net loss	See the Partner's Instructions
4. Guaranteed payments	Schedule E, line 28, column (j)
5. Interest income	Form 1040, line 8a
6a. Ordinary dividends	Form 1040, line 9a
6b. Qualified dividends	Form 1040, line 9b
7. Royalties	Schedule E, line 4
8. Net short-term capital gain (loss)	Schedule D, line 5
9a. Net long-term capital gain (loss)	Schedule D, line 12
9b. Collectibles (28%) gain (loss)	28% Rate Gain Worksheet, line 4 (Schedule D instructions)
9c. Unrecaptured section 1250 gain	See the Partner's Instructions
10. Net section 1231 gain (loss)	See the Partner's Instructions
11. Other income (loss)	
Code	
A Other portfolio income (loss)	See the Partner's Instructions
B Involuntary conversions	See the Partner's Instructions
C Sec. 1256 contracts & straddles	Form 6781, line 1
D Mining exploration costs recapture	See Pub. 535
E Cancellation of debt	Form 1040, line 21 or Form 982
F Other income (loss)	See the Partner's Instructions
12. Section 179 deduction	See the Partner's Instructions
13. Other deductions	
A Cash contributions (50%)	} See the Partner's Instructions (A–G)
B Cash contributions (30%)	
C Noncash contributions (50%)	
D Noncash contributions (30%)	
E Capital gain property to a 50% organization (30%)	
F Capital gain property (20%)	
G Contributions (100%)	
H Investment interest expense	Form 4952, line 1
I Deductions—royalty income	Schedule E, line 19
J Section 59(e)(2) expenditures	See the Partner's Instructions
K Deductions—portfolio (2% floor)	Schedule A, line 23
L Deductions—portfolio (other)	Schedule A, line 28
M Amounts paid for medical insurance	Schedule A, line 1 or Form 1040, line 29
N Educational assistance benefits	See the Partner's Instructions
O Dependent care benefits	Form 2441, line 12
P Preproductive period expenses	See the Partner's Instructions
Q Commercial revitalization deduction from rental real estate activities	See Form 8582 instructions
R Pensions and IRAs	See the Partner's Instructions
S Reforestation expense deduction	See the Partner's Instructions
T Domestic production activities information	See Form 8903 instructions
U Qualified production activities income	Form 8903, line 7b
V Employer's Form W-2 wages	Form 8903, line 17
W Other deductions	See the Partner's Instructions
14. Self-employment earnings (loss)	

Note. *If you have a section 179 deduction or any partner-level deductions, see the Partner's Instructions before completing Schedule SE.*

A Net earnings (loss) from self-employment	Schedule SE, Section A or B
B Gross farming or fishing income	See the Partner's Instructions
C Gross non-farm income	See the Partner's Instructions
15. Credits	
A Low-income housing credit (section 42(j)(5)) from pre-2008 buildings	} See the Partner's Instructions (A–F)
B Low-income housing credit (other) from pre-2008 buildings	
C Low-income housing credit (section 42(j)(5)) from post-2007 buildings	
D Low-income housing credit (other) from post-2007 buildings	
E Qualified rehabilitation expenditures (rental real estate)	
F Other rental real estate credits	
G Other rental credits	
H Undistributed capital gains credit	Form 1040, line 71; check box a
I Biofuel producer credit	} See the Partner's Instructions (I–K)
J Work opportunity credit	
K Disabled access credit	

Code	*Report on*
L Empowerment zone employment credit	} See the Partner's Instructions (L–P)
M Credit for increasing research activities	
N Credit for employer social security and Medicare taxes	
O Backup withholding	
P Other credits	
16. Foreign transactions	
A Name of country or U.S. possession	} Form 1116, Part I (A–C)
B Gross income from all sources	
C Gross income sourced at partner level	
Foreign gross income sourced at partnership level	
D Passive category	} Form 1116, Part I (D–F)
E General category	
F Other	
Deductions allocated and apportioned at partner level	
G Interest expense	Form 1116, Part I
H Other	Form 1116, Part I
Deductions allocated and apportioned at partnership level to foreign source income	
I Passive category	} Form 1116, Part I (I–K)
J General category	
K Other	
Other information	
L Total foreign taxes paid	Form 1116, Part II
M Total foreign taxes accrued	Form 1116, Part II
N Reduction in taxes available for credit	Form 1116, line 12
O Foreign trading gross receipts	Form 8873
P Extraterritorial income exclusion	Form 8873
Q Other foreign transactions	See the Partner's Instructions
17. Alternative minimum tax (AMT) items	
A Post-1986 depreciation adjustment	} See the Partner's Instructions and the Instructions for Form 6251 (A–F)
B Adjusted gain or loss	
C Depletion (other than oil & gas)	
D Oil, gas, & geothermal—gross income	
E Oil, gas, & geothermal—deductions	
F Other AMT items	
18. Tax-exempt income and nondeductible expenses	
A Tax-exempt interest income	Form 1040, line 8b
B Other tax-exempt income	See the Partner's Instructions
C Nondeductible expenses	See the Partner's Instructions
19. Distributions	
A Cash and marketable securities	} See the Partner's Instructions (A–C)
B Distribution subject to section 737	
C Other property	
20. Other information	
A Investment income	Form 4952, line 4a
B Investment expenses	Form 4952, line 5
C Fuel tax credit information	Form 4136
D Qualified rehabilitation expenditures (other than rental real estate)	See the Partner's Instructions
E Basis of energy property	See the Partner's Instructions
F Recapture of low-income housing credit (section 42(j)(5))	Form 8611, line 8
G Recapture of low-income housing credit (other)	Form 8611, line 8
H Recapture of investment credit	See Form 4255
I Recapture of other credits	See the Partner's Instructions
J Look-back interest—completed long-term contracts	See Form 8697
K Look-back interest—income forecast method	See Form 8866
L Dispositions of property with section 179 deductions	} See the Partner's Instructions (L–Z)
M Recapture of section 179 deduction	
N Interest expense for corporate partners	
O Section 453(l)(3) information	
P Section 453A(c) information	
Q Section 1260(b) information	
R Interest allocable to production expenditures	
S CCF nonqualified withdrawals	
T Depletion information—oil and gas	
U Amortization of reforestation costs	
V Unrelated business taxable income	
W Precontribution gain (loss)	
X Section 108(i) information	
Y Net investment income	
Z Other information	

Table A-1. **3-, 5-, 7-, 10-, 15-, and 20-Year Property Half-Year Convention**

Year	Depreciation rate for recovery period					
	3-year	**5-year**	**7-year**	**10-year**	**15-year**	**20-year**
1	33.33%	20.00%	14.29%	10.00%	5.00%	3.750%
2	44.45	32.00	24.49	18.00	9.50	7.219
3	14.81	19.20	17.49	14.40	8.55	6.677
4	7.41	11.52	12.49	11.52	7.70	6.177
5		11.52	8.93	9.22	6.93	5.713
6		5.76	8.92	7.37	6.23	5.285
7			8.93	6.55	5.90	4.888
8			4.46	6.55	5.90	4.522
9				6.56	5.91	4.462
10				6.55	5.90	4.461
11				3.28	5.91	4.462
12					5.90	4.461
13					5.91	4.462
14					5.90	4.461
15					5.91	4.462
16					2.95	4.461
17						4.462
18						4.461
19						4.462
20						4.461
21						2.231

Table A-2. **3-, 5-, 7-, 10-, 15-, and 20-Year Property Mid-Quarter Convention Placed in Service in First Quarter**

Year	Depreciation rate for recovery period					
	3-year	**5-year**	**7-year**	**10-year**	**15-year**	**20-year**
1	58.33%	35.00%	25.00%	17.50%	8.75%	6.563%
2	27.78	26.00	21.43	16.50	9.13	7.000
3	12.35	15.60	15.31	13.20	8.21	6.482
4	1.54	11.01	10.93	10.56	7.39	5.996
5		11.01	8.75	8.45	6.65	5.546
6		1.38	8.74	6.76	5.99	5.130
7			8.75	6.55	5.90	4.746
8			1.09	6.55	5.91	4.459
9				6.56	5.90	4.459
10				6.55	5.91	4.459
11				0.82	5.90	4.459
12					5.91	4.460
13					5.90	4.459
14					5.91	4.460
15					5.90	4.459
16					0.74	4.460
17						4.459
18						4.460
19						4.459
20						4.460
21						0.565

Table A-3. **3-, 5-, 7-, 10-, 15-, and 20-Year Property Mid-Quarter Convention Placed in Service in Second Quarter**

Year	Depreciation rate for recovery period					
	3-year	5-year	7-year	10-year	15-year	20-year
1	41.67%	25.00%	17.85%	12.50%	6.25%	4.688%
2	38.89	30.00	23.47	17.50	9.38	7.148
3	14.14	18.00	16.76	14.00	8.44	6.612
4	5.30	11.37	11.97	11.20	7.59	6.116
5		11.37	8.87	8.96	6.83	5.658
6		4.26	8.87	7.17	6.15	5.233
7			8.87	6.55	5.91	4.841
8			3.34	6.55	5.90	4.478
9				6.56	5.91	4.463
10				6.55	5.90	4.463
11				2.46	5.91	4.463
12					5.90	4.463
13					5.91	4.463
14					5.90	4.463
15					5.91	4.462
16					2.21	4.463
17						4.462
18						4.463
19						4.462
20						4.463
21						1.673

Table A-4. **3-, 5-, 7-, 10-, 15-, and 20-Year Property Mid-Quarter Convention Placed in Service in Third Quarter**

Year	Depreciation rate for recovery period					
	3-year	5-year	7-year	10-year	15-year	20-year
1	25.00%	15.00%	10.71%	7.50%	3.75%	2.813%
2	50.00	34.00	25.51	18.50	9.63	7.289
3	16.67	20.40	18.22	14.80	8.66	6.742
4	8.33	12.24	13.02	11.84	7.80	6.237
5		11.30	9.30	9.47	7.02	5.769
6		7.06	8.85	7.58	6.31	5.336
7			8.86	6.55	5.90	4.936
8			5.53	6.55	5.90	4.566
9				6.56	5.91	4.460
10				6.55	5.90	4.460
11				4.10	5.91	4.460
12					5.90	4.460
13					5.91	4.461
14					5.90	4.460
15					5.91	4.461
16					3.69	4.460
17						4.461
18						4.460
19						4.461
20						4.460
21						2.788

Table A-5. **3-, 5-, 7-, 10-, 15-, and 20-Year Property Mid-Quarter Convention Placed in Service in Fourth Quarter**

Year	Depreciation rate for recovery period					
	3-year	5-year	7-year	10-year	15-year	20-year
1	8.33%	5.00%	3.57%	2.50%	1.25%	0.938%
2	61.11	38.00	27.55	19.50	9.88	7.430
3	20.37	22.80	19.68	15.60	8.89	6.872
4	10.19	13.68	14.06	12.48	8.00	6.357
5		10.94	10.04	9.98	7.20	5.880
6		9.58	8.73	7.99	6.48	5.439
7			8.73	6.55	5.90	5.031
8			7.64	6.55	5.90	4.654
9				6.56	5.90	4.458
10				6.55	5.91	4.458
11				5.74	5.90	4.458
12					5.91	4.458
13					5.90	4.458
14					5.91	4.458
15					5.90	4.458
16					5.17	4.458
17						4.458
18						4.459
19						4.458
20						4.459
21						3.901

Table A-6. **Residential Rental Property Mid-Month Convention Straight Line—27.5 Years**

Year	Month property placed in service											
	1	2	3	4	5	6	7	8	9	10	11	12
1	3.485%	3.182%	2.879%	2.576%	2.273%	1.970%	1.667%	1.364%	1.061%	0.758%	0.455%	0.152%
2–9	3.636	3.636	3.636	3.636	3.636	3.636	3.636	3.636	3.636	3.636	3.636	3.636
10	3.637	3.637	3.637	3.637	3.637	3.637	3.636	3.636	3.636	3.636	3.636	3.636
11	3.636	3.636	3.636	3.636	3.636	3.636	3.637	3.637	3.637	3.637	3.637	3.637
12	3.637	3.637	3.637	3.637	3.637	3.637	3.636	3.636	3.636	3.636	3.636	3.636
13	3.636	3.636	3.636	3.636	3.636	3.636	3.637	3.637	3.637	3.637	3.637	3.637
14	3.637	3.637	3.637	3.637	3.637	3.637	3.636	3.636	3.636	3.636	3.636	3.636
15	3.636	3.636	3.636	3.636	3.636	3.636	3.637	3.637	3.637	3.637	3.637	3.637
16	3.637	3.637	3.637	3.637	3.637	3.637	3.636	3.636	3.636	3.636	3.636	3.636
17	3.636	3.636	3.636	3.636	3.636	3.636	3.637	3.637	3.637	3.637	3.637	3.637
18	3.637	3.637	3.637	3.637	3.637	3.637	3.636	3.636	3.636	3.636	3.636	3.636
19	3.636	3.636	3.636	3.636	3.636	3.636	3.637	3.637	3.637	3.637	3.637	3.637
20	3.637	3.637	3.637	3.637	3.637	3.637	3.636	3.636	3.636	3.636	3.636	3.636
21	3.636	3.636	3.636	3.636	3.636	3.636	3.637	3.637	3.637	3.637	3.637	3.637
22	3.637	3.637	3.637	3.637	3.637	3.637	3.636	3.636	3.636	3.636	3.636	3.636
23	3.636	3.636	3.636	3.636	3.636	3.636	3.637	3.637	3.637	3.637	3.637	3.637
24	3.637	3.637	3.637	3.637	3.637	3.637	3.636	3.636	3.636	3.636	3.636	3.636
25	3.636	3.636	3.636	3.636	3.636	3.636	3.637	3.637	3.637	3.637	3.637	3.637
26	3.637	3.637	3.637	3.637	3.637	3.637	3.636	3.636	3.636	3.636	3.636	3.636
27	3.636	3.636	3.636	3.636	3.636	3.636	3.637	3.637	3.637	3.637	3.637	3.637
28	1.97	2.273	2.576	2.879	3.182	3.485	3.636	3.636	3.636	3.636	3.636	3.636
29							0.152	0.455	0.758	1.061	1.364	1.667

Table A-7. **Nonresidential Real Property Mid-Month Convention Straight Line—31.5 Years**

Year	Month property placed in service											
	1	2	3	4	5	6	7	8	9	10	11	12
1	3.042%	2.778%	2.513%	2.249%	1.984%	1.720%	1.455%	1.190%	0.926%	0.661%	0.397%	0.132%
2–7	3.175	3.175	3.175	3.175	3.175	3.175	3.175	3.175	3.175	3.175	3.175	3.175
8	3.175	3.174	3.175	3.174	3.175	3.174	3.175	3.175	3.175	3.175	3.175	3.175
9	3.174	3.175	3.174	3.175	3.174	3.175	3.174	3.175	3.174	3.175	3.174	3.175
10	3.175	3.174	3.175	3.174	3.175	3.174	3.175	3.174	3.175	3.174	3.175	3.174
11	3.174	3.175	3.174	3.175	3.174	3.175	3.174	3.175	3.174	3.175	3.174	3.175
12	3.175	3.174	3.175	3.174	3.175	3.174	3.175	3.174	3.175	3.174	3.175	3.174
13	3.174	3.175	3.174	3.175	3.174	3.175	3.174	3.175	3.174	3.175	3.174	3.175
14	3.175	3.174	3.175	3.174	3.175	3.174	3.175	3.174	3.175	3.174	3.175	3.174
15	3.174	3.175	3.174	3.175	3.174	3.175	3.174	3.175	3.174	3.175	3.174	3.175
16	3.175	3.174	3.175	3.174	3.175	3.174	3.175	3.174	3.175	3.174	3.175	3.174
17	3.174	3.175	3.174	3.175	3.174	3.175	3.174	3.175	3.174	3.175	3.174	3.175
18	3.175	3.174	3.175	3.174	3.175	3.174	3.175	3.174	3.175	3.174	3.175	3.174
19	3.174	3.175	3.174	3.175	3.174	3.175	3.174	3.175	3.174	3.175	3.174	3.175
20	3.175	3.174	3.175	3.174	3.175	3.174	3.175	3.174	3.175	3.174	3.175	3.174
21	3.174	3.175	3.174	3.175	3.174	3.175	3.174	3.175	3.174	3.175	3.174	3.175
22	3.175	3.174	3.175	3.174	3.175	3.174	3.175	3.174	3.175	3.174	3.175	3.174
23	3.174	3.175	3.174	3.175	3.174	3.175	3.174	3.175	3.174	3.175	3.174	3.175
24	3.175	3.174	3.175	3.174	3.175	3.174	3.175	3.174	3.175	3.174	3.175	3.174
25	3.174	3.175	3.174	3.175	3.174	3.175	3.174	3.175	3.174	3.175	3.174	3.175
26	3.175	3.174	3.175	3.174	3.175	3.174	3.175	3.174	3.175	3.174	3.175	3.174
27	3.174	3.175	3.174	3.175	3.174	3.175	3.174	3.175	3.174	3.175	3.174	3.175
28	3.175	3.174	3.175	3.174	3.175	3.174	3.175	3.174	3.175	3.174	3.175	3.174
29	3.174	3.175	3.174	3.175	3.174	3.175	3.174	3.175	3.174	3.175	3.174	3.175
30	3.175	3.174	3.175	3.174	3.175	3.174	3.175	3.174	3.175	3.174	3.175	3.174
31	3.174	3.175	3.174	3.175	3.174	3.175	3.174	3.175	3.174	3.175	3.174	3.175
32	1.720	1.984	2.249	2.513	2.778	3.042	3.175	3.174	3.175	3.174	3.175	3.174
33							0.132	0.397	0.661	0.926	1.190	1.455

Table A-7a. **Nonresidential Real Property Mid-Month Convention Straight Line—39 Years**

Year	Month property placed in service											
	1	2	3	4	5	6	7	8	9	10	11	12
1	2.461%	2.247%	2.033%	1.819%	1.605%	1.391%	1.177%	0.963%	0.749%	0.535%	0.321%	0.107%
2–39	2.564	2.564	2.564	2.564	2.564	2.564	2.564	2.564	2.564	2.564	2.564	2.564
40	0.107	0.321	0.535	0.749	0.963	1.177	1.391	1.605	1.819	2.033	2.247	2.461